24122

9427

D1514785

THE NORTH COUNTRY

The Regions of Britain

THE
NORTH
COUNTRY

G. BERNARD WOOD

Robert Hale & Company, Publishers
London

© G. Bernard Wood 1973
First published in Great Britain 1973

ISBN 0 7091 3628 5

Robert Hale & Company
63 Old Brompton Road
London SW7

PRINTED IN GREAT BRITAIN BY
EBENEZER BAYLIS AND SON LIMITED
THE TRINITY PRESS, WORCESTER, AND LONDON

Contents

	Acknowledgements	12
	Introduction	13
1	Stage Setting	19
2	The Sleepers Awake	44
3	On the Map	60
4	Matins and Vespers	70
5	Sermons in Stones	87
6	On Guard	109
7	Ancestral Homes	123
8	In Community: Amongst the Towns	137
9	In Community: Amongst the Villages	161
10	History in Little	180
11	Romance of Industry	192
12	Town and Country Craftsmanship	209
13	At Leisure Through the Centuries	225
14	Believe It or Not	238
15	In Gay Mood	254
16	By Right of Birth	274
17	Some of Our Guests	292
18	Preservation and Peril	309
	A Short Bibliography	314
	Index	315

Maps

	pages
The North Country	10–11
Cumberland and Westmorland	16–17
Yorkshire	20–21
County Durham	26–27
Lancashire	34–35
Northumberland	38–39

Illustrations

facing page

Sunset over the Solway Firth   24

Looking south-west into Upper Wharfedale from the   *between pages*
    summit of Horse House Pass, North Yorkshire   *24 and 25*

facing page

The Ruskin Monument on Friar's Crag, Derwentwater   25

The sands of Morecambe Bay at Arnside, Westmorland   32

Lagoons bordering the tidal road to Sunderland Point,
    Lancashire   32

The limestone clint pavement on top of Malham Cove, West
    Yorkshire   33

Buttertubs Pass between Wensleydale and Swaledale   33

Arnside, Morecambe Bay   48

Wainwath Falls near Keld, Upper Swaledale   49

Hadrian's Wall near Housesteads   64

A Roman aqueduct exposed at Corbridge, Northumberland   65

A wild boar emblem of the 20th Roman Legion, found at
    Corbridge   80

A playing-card map from a set made in 1676 by Robert Morden   80

Fountains Abbey, Yorkshire: looking north-east into the
    presbytery   81

Roche Abbey near Maltby, South Yorkshire   96

Norman masonry at Lindisfarne Priory, Holy Island, Northum-
    berland   96

St Cuthbert's Cross in Durham Cathedral Library   97

7

8 ILLUSTRATIONS

facing page

Trinity design on medieval misericord in Cartmel Priory
Church, Lancashire 97

Beverley Minster, East Yorkshire: nineteenth-century choir
screen by J. E. Elwell 112

St Anthony's Chapel, Cartmel Fell: the Burblethwaite Hall pew
and the seventeenth-century three-decker pulpit 113

St Mary's, Whitby: a Norman church remodelled by local shipwrights in the seventeenth and eighteenth centuries 120

Liverpool: part of the university precinct, looking *between pages*
towards the city centre and the river and flanked by 120 *and* 121
the two cathedrals

facing page

Locomotion No. 1 carved on a pew-end at Stockton-on-Tees
parish church to mark the Centenary of the Stockton and
Darlington Railway 121

The Vicar's Pele within the churchyard at Corbridge 121

Ford Castle, Northumberland 128

Warkworth Castle, Northumberland 129

The Tudor Courtyard at Skipton Castle, West Yorkshire 144

Topiary work in the grounds of Levens Hall, Westmorland 145

Bell Scott's painting of Grace Darling's rescue of the survivors
of the *Forfarshire*, in the Central Hall at Wallington, Northumberland 160

Mulgrave Castle near Whitby, North Yorkshire 161

Wilberforce House, Kingston-upon-Hull: the Wilberforce eagle
emblem in plasterwork 161

Evening in Scarborough Harbour 176

Headpiece of Berwick-upon-Tweed's Civic Mace 177

Ripon's Charter Horn of A.D. 886 and silver badges representing
past Wakemen 177

Richmond's Seal of Two Pieces given by Charles II 177

Leeds Corn Exchange: detail of the nineteenth-century steel
dome 192

Chetham's Hospital schoolboys with Manchester Cathedral
behind them 193

A modernized spinning gallery at Troutbeck, Westmorland 208

Robin Hood's Bay, North Yorkshire 209

Pendle Hill from Downham Village, Lancashire 209

The Carillon Tower on the Civic Centre, Newcastle-upon-
Tyne 224

Rushbearers portrayed on a hotel sign at Grasmere 225

facing page

One of Lady Waterford's Biblical paintings in Ford School, Northumberland   225

The waterfront at Staithes, North Yorkshire   240

York Castle Museum: early twentieth-century garage and cycle shop   241

Kirkstall Abbey House Museum, Leeds: an eighteenth-century creamware cistern   241

Sir George Cayley's sketch of the ornithopter he invented   248

Whale's teeth 'scrimshawed' by Hull whalers   248

between pages

Tarn Hows, near Coniston, Lakeland   248 *and* 249

facing page

Scale-model of the "Salamanca", made in 1812 by Matthew Murray for the Middleton Colliery Railway   249

Memorial to Samuel Marsden, pioneer of the Australian wool industry, at Farsley, near Bradford   249

A Durham hand-made quilt with rose, feather and shell motifs   256

Part of the Doom window at All Saints' Church, York   256

Thomas E. Whittaker and his gnome signboard   257

An oak kist made by Mr Whittaker   257

Rope-making at Hawes, Wensleydale   272

Mould for charms against witches   272

A Yorkshire witch cross of rowan wood, to protect its owner against the 'evil eye'   272

St Wilfrid's understudy ready for Ripon's annual August Fair   273

F. W. Elwell's painting of 'elevenses' at the Beverley Arms Hotel   288

The Captain Cook Monument at Whitby   289

Storrs Hall Hotel, Windermere: the causeway where black boys were once smuggled ashore   304

Bowland, near Slaidburn, West Yorkshire   304

The Wishing Rocks, Brimham, Nidderdale   305

PICTURE CREDITS

With the exception of the pictures of the Solway Firth (by courtesy of the City Librarian, Carlisle), the Liverpool panorama (by courtesy of the University of Liverpool) and the Newcastle Civic Centre (by courtesy of G. Kenyon, City Architect), all photographs were taken by the author.

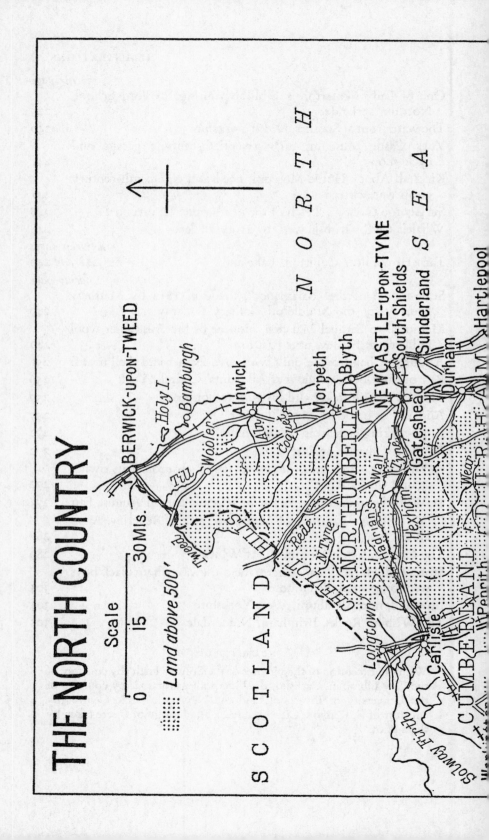

THE NORTH COUNTRY

Scale

0   15   30 Mls.

::::: Land above 500'

SCOTLAND

NORTH SEA

BERWICK-UPON-TWEED

Holy I.

Bamburgh

Alnwick

Wooler

Till

Tweed

Aln

Coquet

Morpeth

Blyth

NEWCASTLE-UPON-TYNE

South Shields

Gateshead

Sunderland

Durham

Hartlepool

CHEVIOT HILLS

Reed

N.Tyne

NORTHUMBERLAND

Hadrian's Wall

Hexham

Tyne

Wear

CUMBERLAND

Carlisle

Longtown

Penrith

Solway Firth

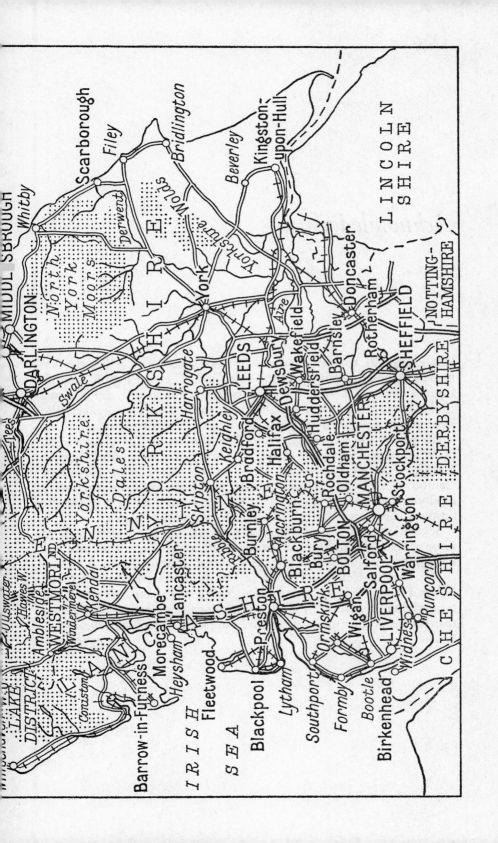

Acknowledgements

It is impossible to name everybody who, directly or indirectly, has made some useful contribution to this book. They are legion, ranging from owners of various country houses, church authorities, town clerks, librarians and museum curators, to innumerable persons who have supplied personal or family anecdotes of amusing vintage.

For permission to quote from the late Sir Charles Trevelyan's book on Wallington, Northumberland, and for her own valuable comments, I am particularly grateful to his daughter, Mrs Pauline Dower of Cambo. Mrs Eleanor Winthrop Young has been similarly generous in kindly allowing me to quote a few passages from the works of her late husband, Geoffrey Winthrop Young, mountaineer and poet.

Several other books consulted are named in the appropriate section; some of these would have been quite unobtainable but for the zeal and unflagging co-operation of my good friend, Edward Kelly, A.L.A.

Mrs Audrey Kelly and Mrs Marjorie Branston also deserve praise for their timely help — during a long period of the author's illness—in transcribing his difficult MSS and completing the typescript. For her own share in the production of the book I cannot thank my wife enough.

G.B.W.

Introduction

"Speak of the North!"

After thus opening one of her poems, Charlotte Brontë takes up her own challenge and evokes a pattern of radiant joy as she portrays that part of the North she knew best:

> A lonely moor
> Silent and dark and trackless swells,
> The waves of some wild streamlet pour
> Hurriedly through its ferny dells. . . .
>
> And far away a mountain zone,
> A cold, white waste of snow drifts lies,
> And one star, large and soft and lone,
> Silently lights the unclouded skies.

It is the Haworth countryside she is trying to epitomise, that heathery region in the lea of the Yorkshire Pennines which still seems part of the elemental nature of things. It can be bleak and forbidding. It can also cheer, as it so often cheered Emily Brontë as she fled from the chores and anxieties of their father's parsonage and took

> A little and lone green lane,
> That opened on a common wide;
> A distant, dreamy, dim blue chain
> Of mountains circling every side. . . .

But to others the North has meant something very different. To Laurence Sterne it meant the "golden valley of Coxwold" which furnished his table at Shandy Hall with venison, wild fowl, strawberries and cream; with chickens, rabbits and trout in plenty. Thomas

Bewick, the engraver, revelled in his own corner of the North, where he could "admire the dangling woodbine and roses" and commiserate with that part of mankind which knew so little of "the serenity and the stillness of . . . summer mornings in the country", that is, the *Tyneside* country.

And so one could go on, seeing the North through various eyes. George Hudson, early in the nineteenth century, beheld little but railways and yet more railways, most of them converging profitably upon his adopted York. Other visionaries were the industrialists intent upon coal, iron, steel and (much more recently) potash and North Sea gas.

Then, in a different category altogether, came the geologists, fascinated by unfolding patterns of mountain and magnesian limestone, tough sinewy gritstone, chalk, and the hard, dolorous bands of Whin Sill, each creating its peculiar type of scenery, and shaping events as diverse as prehistoric man living a troglodite existence amongst the limestone hills, and the building of Hadrian's Wall across the cresting whinstone crags of Northumberland.

Archaeologists delve below the surface of this vast terrain and disclose many a forgotten drama, even the signs of a murder committed some 1,800 years ago, or of medieval monks hiding some of their treasures before Henry VIII pounced on the abbeys.

Other facets of the North are revealed by the historians. Through the mists of time—and the dusty aroma of ancient documents—they view the area as a battleground of various forces and ideologies, also as a seed-bed of Christianity and of many kinds of social reform. The Pilgrimage of Grace and the Rising in the North stemmed from the marshland and the summery meadows of this same tract of country.

Many voices are therefore needed to speak, adequately, of the North. This book is intended as a kind of sounding board for some of them. We shall hear shepherds as well as soldiers, poets and bards as well as the gentry who often gave them patronage; pioneers in various spheres,—seamen, navigators; craftsmen creating beauty in some tiny spot amongst the hills; writers and artists struggling towards an eloquence that shall move thousands; and, not least, ordinary men and women who have for so long supplied the warp and woof of North Country life against a background of some of Britain's finest scenery.

Even amongst North Countrymen themselves, however, there are different notions as to who may qualify for inclusion. A Northumbrian worthy once had the temerity to tell me, a Yorkshireman by birth and almost life-long domicile, that I was not of the true breed, but was a Midlander! Nobody living south of the Tyne or, by concession, the Tees, would satisfy him. And yet, to a Londoner, the 'wild north' began—so it was long averred—soon after one ventured beyond Hertfordshire!

It is generally agreed, however, that the North constitutes that area of country which narrows towards the Scottish Border from a line drawn between the Humber and the Mersey; in short, the six counties of Yorkshire, Durham, Northumberland, Cumberland, Westmorland and Lancashire. As Cheshire has one foot in Wales and another in the Midlands, its people cannot be accorded the honours that accrue to real Northerners. A pity, perhaps, because Cheshire (like Derbyshire, Nottinghamshire and Lincolnshire) peeps repeatedly over our southern borderline and often scatters grains of history that help to ripen our own pastures.

If only to placate Liverpudlians and Mancunians, therefore, Cheshire's northern fringe will be given an occasional nod of recognition in the following pages. For precedent, one need only cite that intrusive element from the far north with which the good folk of Carlisle and Berwick-upon-Tweed had to battle against for centuries, up there amongst the peat mosses and the heathery burns that gave Sir Walter Scott so much to rhapsodise about in his stirring romances. After all, boundaries are man-made, though Nature may play a large part in their shaping, as we shall see to our pleasure.

The scheme of this book is so arranged that some subjects will be mentioned lightly in one context and more fully in another. In this way the fascinating interplay of life and history in the northern area is, I hope, agreeably emphasized.

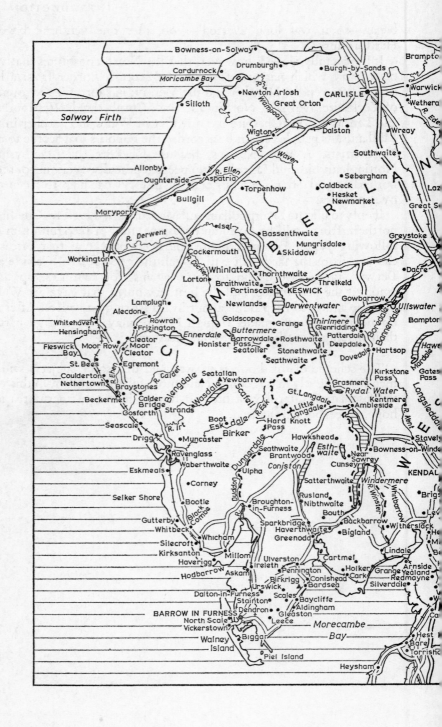

swald
•Melmerby
gwathby
•Skirwith

•Milburn
•Temple Sowerby

L A N D

R

ings•
urn

•Murton
•Appleby

O

•Maulds
Meaburn
Crosby
Ravensworth

•Great Ormside
•Brough
Great Musgrave

R. Eden

Crosby Garrett•

•Kirkby Stephen

•Tebay

Swaledale

•Lambrigg

R. Rawthey

•Sedbergh

Wensleydale

•Killington
utton

R. Lune

•Kirby Lonsdale

Ribblesdale

rs

To all those who in past and present times have in any way enriched, or helped to preserve, our great North Country heritage

I

Stage Setting

WHEN Dame Nature raised a roof over Northern England in the form of the Pennine Range, she gave the country a rich endowment that was not appreciated as such until comparatively modern times. For long ages people feared this mountain range as the abode of demons, and even as late as the eighteenth century a Northumbrian clergyman, 'exiled' in the Elsdon parish, could write with horror of the Cheviot Hills that later inspired Sir Walter Scott and now provide the northernmost reach of the Pennine Way.

As applied to this range—which starts north of Derby and continues to within sight of the Scottish Border—the name 'Pennine' is even newer than the belated appreciation of the magnificent country through which it shoulders its knobbly way. And the use of that name was born of fraud.

Little over a century ago two pioneer geologists, W. D. Conybeare and William Phillips, proposed that this hitherto un-named mountain chain be called 'Penine' [sic], basing their idea upon a Latin pamphlet purporting to be a picture of Britain in Roman times and 'discovered' in 1747 by one Charles Bertram. The pamphlet stated that Britain was "divided into two equal parts by a chain of mountains called [that is, by the Romans] Penine Alps which . . . extend toward the north in a continued series of 50 miles". Bertram had attributed the pamphlet

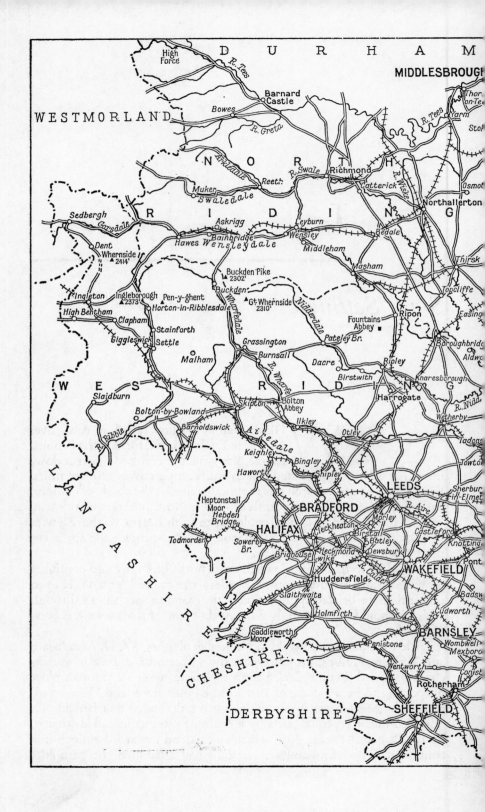

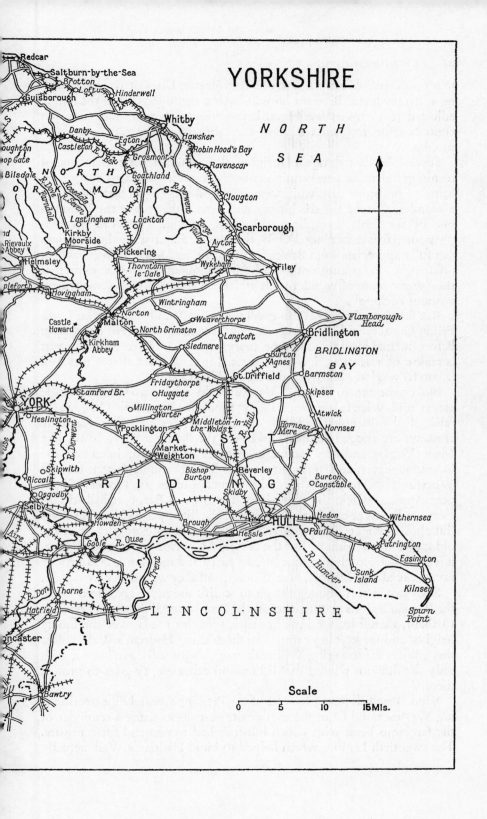

to a fourteenth-century monk of Westminster. Later, it was proved to be a literary hoax, Bertram himself having compiled it; but the name, adjusted to Pennine, was nevertheless adopted for the range, which continues for 100 miles beyond the estimate of Bertram's mythical monk.

Several kinds of rock contribute their characteristic elements of scenic grandeur to the Pennine country. Limestone scarps and caves. 'caps' of millstone grit, whinstone crags and ridges—all have provided a wonderful arena for the history and legend that make the Pennines one of the most rewarding regions of Britain. They can produce phenomenal weather, too. Only those acquainted with the Pennines can fully appreciate John Ruskin's comment, in *Modern Painters*, when, referring to the strength of a Yorkshire mountain breeze, he expressed the "vague sense of wonder with which I watched Ingleborough stand without rocking".

But for sheer fury what can excel the Helm Wind that rises on Cross Fell in Cumberland! A spring-time phenomenon, it sweeps everything before it, making the otherwise peaceful Vale of Eden into one vast corridor of relentless, icy-cold blasts. Little wonder that Cross Fell (2,930 ft) was long known and feared as Fiend's Fell.

No doubt the mythical Giant Rumbald who was wont to stride across mid-Wharfedale from Ilkley Moor to Almscliffe Crag was a relic of the 'Pennine host of demons'. Stories of other fearsome creatures are encountered up and down the Pennine Way. Some, like Giant Yordas and the mountain witches of Craven, inhabited the limestone caves and potholes around Ingleborough (2,373 ft) and Whernside (2,414 ft), while within such gullies as Trollers Ghyll, near Appletreewick, the ghost-hound known as Barguest had its lair. Fairy traditions abound too. Sometimes the 'little people' lived in caves (Elbolton Cave at Thorpe, near Grassington, is an example) or in the old lead-mine workings. But the fairies of Cheviot were bolder. Once, it is said, their ravishing music lured a party of stag-hunters into a rocky ravine called the Henhole, near Wooler, and they were never seen again.

Such stories were quite enough to scarify the more credulous when the Roman legions ventured across the Pennines. All the greater honour to them, therefore, for building such splendid roads over the lonely heights, and for keeping camps like those along Hadrian's Wall, where this follows the towering Whin Sill crags, continually garrisoned, with only the dubious powers of Mithras and other empty gods to protect them.

Wild Boar Fell (2,324 ft), one of the Pennine sentinel hills overlooking Westmorland from the south-east, bears in its name a reminder of the ferocious beast with which hill-folk had to contend for centuries. The twentieth Legion, which helped to build Hadrian's Wall, actually used a running boar as its emblem. The animal persisted in England until the Middle Ages; Wild Boar Fell is one of several places in the North where the last of its kind is said to have been slain.

The roof of England is no longer the forbidding place it used to be. Every weekend young zealots in anoraks and nailed boots turn out to explore this or that section of the 'great divide'—and the tales and traditions that once awed our ancestors are readily becoming the stock-in-trade for the wayfaring raconteur.

For the late C. E. Montague this lofty area held a kind of rhapsody.

A range of mountain [he wrote]* may not be the Alps, and yet have a career. And the Pennine has done its big things. The way that its strata are bent and worn has shaped the industrial history of England. A kind of life that is not precisely lived anywhere else made the Brontës just what they were. On Pennine heights there stick out the raw ends of forces that help to set us all our work and to map out our lives. As you walk over Dead Head Moss, at the top of the ridge, on a wet day of south-westerly wind, you leave behind a steep, drenched western slant on which the wind has dropped most of its takings of water from the Atlantic. The cause of the different work and life of Yorkshire and Lancashire pours itself in at the doors of your senses; you see it in breaking clouds, hear it in the lowered voices of moorland streams, and feel it in the slackening drip of raindrops from a soaked cap to your nose.

The Pennines that divide east from west also unite. They have been breached by passes that bind the whole area together, like the veins of a leaf.

There is no finer way of getting to know the Pennine country than by storming these high-level routes, either by car (where feasible) or on foot. Some are fairly close together, like Buttertubs and Oxnop in the North Riding. Others may be miles apart. The rhythm they provide— up hill, down dale and over yet another sinuous pass, edged maybe with limestone spurs haunted by raven or kestrel—is only part of their timeless appeal.

Let us traverse a few of these passes.

Not long ago the Youth Hostels Association acquired a new hostel for the convenience of those who wish to explore the southern region of the Pennine Way. Situated high on the moors to the west of Marsden, the hostel embodies the curiously-named Hades Farm. The Standedge Pass into Lancashire looms ahead. Hades Farm is sufficiently elevated, at 1,050 feet, to be ranked as one of the coldest spots in the North.

A few miles farther south, the Isle of Skye route winds over Saddle-worth Moor (1,616 ft) to almost the same destination, and as one peers still deeper into the grey, bleak distances, the television mast on the summit of Holme Moss (1,725 ft) marks an age-old track which

* In *The Right Place* (Chatto & Windus, 1924.)

precipitates motorists into Derbyshire near the notorious Devil's Elbow.
A second place named Hades, 2 miles east of Holme Moss, seems to
confirm the sinister reputation of these parts; but the other Hades,
above Marsden, is encouragingly offset by a farm on the lower,
warmer slopes, called Elysium—a reversal of normal expectations!

Other passes penetrate these wild uplands. My own favourite is one
that climbs out of Ripponden with steady determination and descends
ultimately to Littleborough, having crossed the Pennine watershed at
1,269 feet. This is the Blackstone Edge route which exasperated Daniel
Defoe when—travelling in the opposite direction—he left Lancashire
for the Halifax countryside on his celebrated Tour Through Great
Britain (1727). One has to trudge on foot along that lonely, switchback
road to savour his comments: "We thought now we were come into
a Christian country again, and that our Difficulties were over; but we
soon found ourselves mistaken in the Matter: for we had not gone
fifty yards . . . but we found the Way began to ascend again, and soon
after to go up very steep, till in about half a Mile we found we had
another Mountain to ascend, in our apprehension as bad as the first. . . ."

Others before Defoe had doubtless groaned over the same "Difficulties", for a Roman road careers over much of the same grand, though
inhospitable terrain. Parts of the Roman road can be seen about half
a mile south of the present highway, near the pass summit. I had the
world seemingly to myself when that Roman causeway once lured me
amongst the peaty quags, with only them and the spiked grasses for
company. At length my feet struck the track which the legions had
used; a gritstone track worn hollow at the sides by chariot wheels.
Where the causeway dips downhill for a few yards, a central groove
becomes a pronounced trough. Most archaeologists agree that the
trough was probably formed by the use of a pole or faggot brake
applied to the front or rear of baggage wagons and chariots as they took
the decline.

One day in May 1957 I was to see these grand solitudes *thronged* with
people. Wakefield Corporation's new reservoir, Baitings, was to be
opened nearby and I had been invited to join the civic party. Opposite
the beautifully-sited reservoir a large dining marquee stood in readiness
for us; some Roman contingent, I thought while munching my meat
salad, might well have bivouaced thereabouts long ago. But why were
so many police stationed up there that day? Not only traffic-control
men, but hordes of top-rank officers? The evening newspaper gave me
the answer when I returned to Wakefield. Early that morning, it
transpired, an anonymous telephone call had come through, indicating
that the new dam was about to be blown up! A hoax, evidently, for
the swarming police found neither explosives nor suspicious characters
in this ancient mountain ambush.

Sunset over the Solway Firth

Looking south-west into Upper Wharfedale from the summit of Horse House
Pass, North Yorkshire

The Ruskin Monument on Friar's Crag, Derwentwater

The Trough of Bowland is another fine pass which Yorkshire shares with Lancashire. From the Yorkshire side it begins near Dunsop Bridge and is soon enclosed, as in a vice, between Hareden Fell and Staple Oak Fell, with other steep nabs and brows contributing an almost tangible pressure from both flanks. The contours reach up to 1,100 feet before the pressure is gradually relaxed.

Impressive at all seasons, the Trough is no longer gated, as formerly. I never go that way without visualizing the Lancashire Witches, sulky and desperate, as they were led through the pass to their trial at Lancaster, some 300 years ago. But up there the real witchery is of Nature's own making, with hills of heather and tough bracken folding across each other, utterly unmindful of the road trying to wriggle a course for itself through the slightest of defiles.

From Settle, a few miles north of the Bowland country, several passes insinuate amongst the limestone scars and fells. Particularly attractive for walkers is one that begins as Stockdale Lane, on the east of the market town, and then winds as an exalted bridle path through virgin spaces perforated with jagged outcrops, until a steep descent beside Pikedaw Hill takes one within easy striding distance of the wonderful limestone pavement above Malham Cove. Malham village lies 240 feet below. Cattle drovers, lead miners, pedlars once knew these high places, and feared them, too, lest the Brown Man of the Moors or some boggart should suddenly materialize.

The various passes that serve Malham may be on a lesser scale than some others, yet who could resist the elemental appeal of such accompanying natural features as the Dry Valley, which curves back from the Cove summit; Malham Tarn, trapped like a faery patch of blue at an altitude of 1,229 feet; or Gordale Scar? The agile can climb Gordale's waterfall gorge to join the ancient green road, Mastiles Lane, which eventually drops down beside Kilnsey Crag in Upper Wharfedale. One day I stepped aside from Mastiles Lane to see Calf Hole Cave in which some of Prince Charlie's disillusioned Highlanders are said to have sheltered on their way home after the 1745 debacle. It is perhaps easier to visualize the monks of Fountains Abbey and Bolton Priory panting their way up by this route from Wharfedale to visit their granges at Malham.

A plan to turn Mastiles Lane into a motoring road has fortunately come to naught, so far, yet the roads that already thread through some of our northern passes can be the very quintessence of solitude. From Stainforth in Ribblesdale, for example, a track beginning as Goat Lane and continuing upwards as Silverdale Road, runs at length along the southern flank of Penyghent (2,231 ft) and then descends through Hesleden Ghyll to Littondale. This is an enchanting ride; I have often loitered beside the little waterfalls that bound beneath the road, near

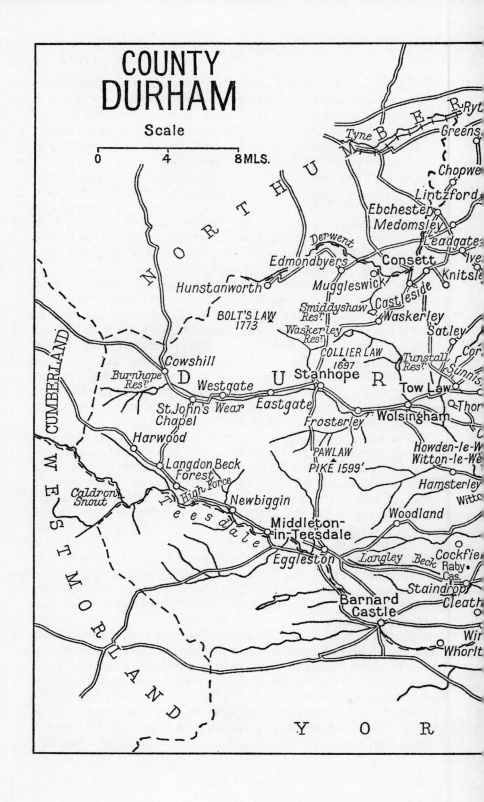

COUNTY DURHAM

Scale

0   4   8 MLS.

NORTHU...

Tyne   B   E   R.   Ryt...

Greens...

Chopwe...

Lintzford...

Ebchester

Medomsley

Leadgate

Derwent

Edmondbyers   Consett   Ive...

Hunstanworth   Muggleswick   Knitsle...

Castleside

BOLT'S LAW   Smiddyshaw   Waskerley   Satley
1773   Res.^r

Waskerley   Cor...
Res.^r

COLLIER LAW   Tunstall   Sunnis...
1697   Res.^r

Cowshill   D   U   Stanhope   R   Tow Law   Thor...

Burnhope   Westgate
Res.^r   Eastgate   Wolsingham

St. John's   Wear
Chapel   Frosterley   Howden-le-W...
Witton-le-We...

Harwood   PAWLAW   Hamsterley
PIKE 1599'   Witto...

Langdon Beck
Forest   High Force   Woodland

Caldron   Newbiggin
Snout   Teesdale   Middleton-   Cockfie...
in-Teesdale   Langley   Beck   Raby
Eggleston   Cas.

Staindrop...
Cleath...

Barnard
Castle   Wir...
Whorl...

CUMBERLAND

W E S T M O R L A N D   Y O R   O R

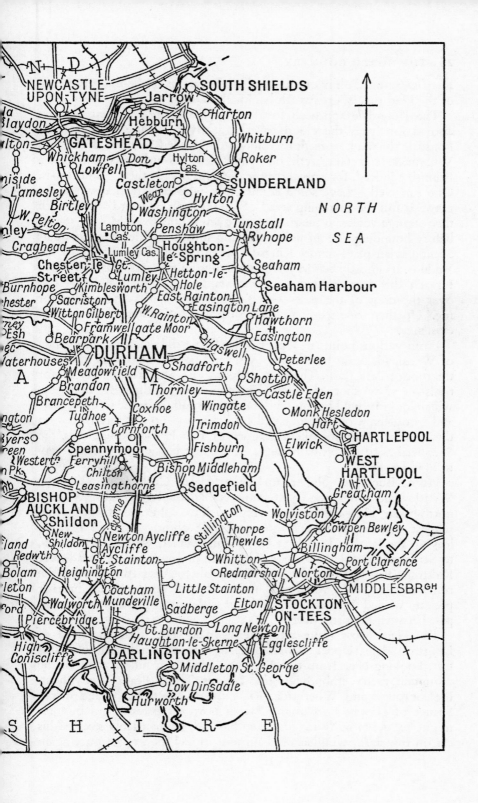

the pass summit, oblivious to anything but an overwhelming Presence of the kind that Wordsworth habitually sensed.

The Kingsdale approach to Dent, in Yorkshire's farthest west, is also as lonely as the clouds overhead. After leaving Thornton-in-Lonsdale the road proceeds for a few miles beside Kingsdale Beck, with Whernside and Gragareth on either flank as primitive guardians. Primitive indeed, for only a couple of farms invade these gaunt slopes. One can well believe some countryfolk who declare that when the moon is full the marching tread of Vikings can be heard, along with their strange voices, as the road twists over White Shaw Moss (1,583 ft) before bounding like an untamed thing into Dentdale. Because of its Scandinavian place-names Kingsdale is often called the Valley of the Vikings. Its ghostly echoes have never rung in my ears, alas, but when I reach the deep, sunless grotto containing Lockingarth Falls—just over the crest of the pass—Grieg's mountain spirits come alive for me. Up there one seems to have surprised something from another existence.

From various points in Upper Wharfedale the neighbouring valley of Wensleydale can be reached by several passes. Kettlewell nestles at the foot of Park Rash. The first, daunting rise—hazard of early motor trials—is now short-circuited, but the main undulating highway, which looks its wild best in winter snows, is still the route to Coverdale and Middleham once frequented by kings and nobles and armies on the march. Over the silent leagues of this Horse House Pass the Shepherd Lord led his halberdiers on the first part of their weary way to Flodden Field.

From Buckden, higher up Wharfedale, Cray Gill takes the Wensleydale-bound road past innumerable small waterfalls. When a north-easter blows these are whipped into columns of spray that suggest dancing sprites. About one mile ahead the road divides, leaving the left-hand track to trot its unmetalled way, as Stake Pass, to Semerwater and Bainbridge. The main highway forges ahead over Kidstones Pass and then through Bishopdale to Aysgarth. This was the route usually taken when the Archbishop of York and his brother prelates wished to hunt deer. Today it is the most popular and easiest pass between the sister dales.

The Fleet Moss route into Wensleydale starts near the head of Langstrothdale (Upper Wharfedale) and reaches a height of 1,934 feet. Looking back from this point one gets a stupendous view of the mountain arena embodying the famous Three Peaks—Penyghent, Ingleborough and Whernside. Kit Calvert, cheese-factor and dairy-farmer of Hawes, once told me that however pressing his business might be, down in Wharfedale and beyond, he invariably stopped his car on this stark, wind-scoured summit to feel the impact once again of such a breath-taking panorama. How I should love to plant a few harassed city-dwellers on the top of Fleet Moss!

Facing north, from the same vantage point. one looks down to the green pastures of Wensleydale. Immediately beyond Hawes and Bainbridge and Askrigg, however, there are yet more hills, culminating in Great Shunnor Fell (2,340 ft), Lovely Seat (2,213 ft), Abbotside Common (1,900 ft) and Askrigg Common (1,800 ft). The Bainbridge horn-blowing custom (see page 270) was originally established to guide benighted wayfarers safely down from these neighbouring passes and fells.

One breach in that mountain phalanx is the Oxnop Pass from Askrigg into Swaledale. Just beyond the watershed this pass is bordered by huge limestone scars with fluted columns that suggest the outer rampart of some hidden stronghold.

Equally exhilarating is the Buttertubs Pass, linking Hawes in Wensleydale with Thwaite in Swaledale. Sixty years ago the author of *Highways and Byways in Yorkshire* wrote rather disparagingly of this pass: "I am told that it is a very ancient byway; and that may be true, for it is certainly decrepit, and is not likely to be restored to health by any such desultory sprinklings of sharp-pointed stones as I found strewn upon its surface," and so on. Even so, an accompanying sketch illustrates the wild beauty of the scene by resorting to considerable fancy; it exaggerates the escarpments, chasms and waterfalls which characterise the pass near the summit.

That was a great pity, I always think, for Buttertubs needs no artistic licence to proclaim its attractions. Moreover, since *Highways and Byways* was published, this mountain pass—like so many others in the Pennine and Lakeland areas—has been resurfaced and made fit for motoring.

Yet Buttertubs will never be completely tamed. Something of its romance grips one on peering down the actual buttertubs, which are vertical fissures, or incipient potholes, in the gleaming limestone. In bygone times, thieves were reputed to find them convenient dumps for the itinerant pedlars they had first robbed up here. Some folk said they were bottomless; in fact, Mouths of Hell. But I once talked with a dalesman who, as a boy, routed all such superstition after being lowered by rope down several of these eerie chasms. The average depth was some 50–60 feet. At the bottom he found—not human skeletons—but several alternate layers of snow and leaves; a wonderful record of successive seasons. Even in high summer the sun never penetrates to the lowest depths, so the winter's snow remains, being covered each autumn by leaves from the rowan bushes that beautify the upper ledges.

A curious incident once happened to a couple, friends of mine, who had pulled up beside this fantastic group of potholes. Thinking his wife was stepping too close to the jagged rim of one buttertub, the man grabbed her arm and accidentally dislodged her handbag. Down into the dark hole it fell, complete with driving licence, ignition keys, money, etc. Undaunted by the buttertubs' evil reputation, my friend sought the aid of a passing motorist, fetched a ladder from neighbouring Thwaite, and soon emerged from the 'bottomless pit'—grinning and triumphant—with his wife's bag, and a rare tale to tell.

If one tackles the Buttertubs Pass in winter, as my wife and I have done, the reason for the roadside posts placed at intervals over the unfenced summit becomes apparent. They are meant to guide shepherds and others through the snowdrifts.

Some of the higher Lakeland passes are accessible only to walkers. These include Esk Hause (2,490 ft), Rossett Ghyll (2,000 ft), Sty Head (1,600 ft) and Scarf Gap (1,400 ft). In my younger days I trudged over most of them; they gave me a nostalgia for mountain solitudes and many a thrill, as when a mist suddenly descended on Sty Head and cut me off from my companions. For that half hour I felt utterly alone. I could hear my friends' voices from beyond the well-known tarn in the crutch of the pass, but they might have emanated from so many disembodied spirits. When the mist finally scattered, like wraiths suddenly called away to bewilder other trampers, I found I had been heading blindly for Wasdale, far below to the west.

My motoring friends often recount tales of their own 'pass' experiences, either here in Lakeland or in the Pennines. We all have our favourite routes, as an angler will have his favourite lake or stream. Wrynose and Hardknott Passes take six or seven majestic miles of untamed country to link the Coniston area with the Cumberland coast near Ravenglass. It echoes something from Man's primordial past. Although I glory in this switchback route, I still contend that the finest Lakeland passes are those afforded by the 'Buttermere round', as it is called in the Keswick district.

The 'Buttermere round' is one of the most superb car-runs in Britain, yet I know several motorists who will never attempt the Honister section because of the steep, winding gradients. But provided the car is in good condition and a reliable person takes the wheel, there is nothing to fear. My wife and I went over Honister Pass a few summers ago after several days' torrential rain, which left the approach roads awash for miles. This really enhanced our pleasure, for it meant that the enclosing slopes were creamed with scores of fresh cascades. They spouted around us in every direction and filled the air with new descants.

After enjoying the views from the summit—backwards into Borrowdale, our route from Keswick, and forward to Red Pike and

High Stile—we kept in low gear for the long, serpentine descent to Buttermere. From the shores of this beautiful lake, Honister Pass— presided over by the majestic and well-nigh vertical Honister Crag— looks almost impregnable. Little wonder that British tribesfolk hereabouts considered the Buttermere valley inviolate. To Lakelanders 'in the know' it was the Secret Valley.

Two other road passes lead from the Secret Valley to the outer world. Buttermere or Newlands Hause links Buttermere village with Portin- scale, near Keswick; then, a few miles north, beyond the rather ethereal Crummock Water, Whinlatter Pass sweeps through some extensive larch plantations before dropping to Braithwaite for Keswick.

In the pages ahead much of a different nature will be said about our mountain areas, also about the moors and dales that spread from them like flowing draperies of varying hues and texture.

But an anticipatory word seems necessary at this point. Walking across the moors often results in one's boots filling uncomfortably with small lumps of peat. To our forefathers, however, peat was a godsend. It gave them fuel and horse-litter. Some of our oldest tracks are the peat-ways used by those who cut peat on the moors and took it down by wagon or sled to the nearest farms or villages. Many farms still have a peat-house (now put to other uses) where the fuel was stacked. Chequers Inn, above Osmotherley, and Saltersgate Inn on the Pickering Moors, kept peat fires burning continuously for many years. In Lancashire, Chat Moss and Barton Moss are, or were, vast peat mosses where elk antlers have been found embedded below the surface, also the much-prized bog oak which re-appears in many an old homestead as heirloom furniture. In one old house near York time is ticked away, very appropriately, by a 'grandmother' clock fashioned from bog oak that must have been 'imprisoned' for untold ages.

Yet peat mosses can be treacherous. Although sphagnum, bog myrtle and gay tufts of cotton grass may seductively clothe the surface, the whole area can *move*, with alarming results. On the night of 16th December, 1771, for example, Solway Moss broke free. Heavy rains "kept the moss in motion until about 500 acres were covered" with the water-laden peat, and thirty-five families were left destitute.

From the Haworth moors came another tale of woe. On 2nd Sep- tember 1824, Crow Hill—actuated by pent-up waters—began to slide towards the Ponden Valley. A boy sent to lead the cattle to safety said that the oncoming tide looked like "a dark semi-liquid mass which rolled over and over, more like thick treacle than water ...". It carried along "stones, trees, heather, gorse and dead sheep". To the Reverend Patrick Brontë, over at Haworth, the Bog Slide was a dire warning from Heaven. A sermon which he preached on the subject a few days afterwards was later published as a kind of tract. Emily Brontë must have had the event in mind when, years afterwards, she laid the scene of *Wuthering Heights* on this same peaty moorland. Her Penistone Crag is Ponden Kirk, the gritstone crag which lay directly in the path of that slow, sticky bog-lava.

The North Country streams and valleys provide a theme song of their own. They include the glorious Yorkshire Dales and the valleys that carry the Northumbrian Wansbeck and Coquet through acres quite as enchanting as the upper reaches of the Wear, in County Durham. The Tyne and the Wear leave the central watershed as sparkling rills among mossy boulders, and end by launching stately vessels that sail the world's oceans with merchandise. The Eden makes its first gurgling overtures in Hell Ghyll, on Abbotside Common, and then tosses through Kirkby Stephen, Appleby and Carlisle as a running accompaniment to innumerable historic happenings.

Every one of our rivers and streams has its own story to tell. Throughout his adult life a friend of mine has specialised on Wensleydale's River Ure. He spends all his holidays at some point in its career, which starts on Abbotside Common (where it soon parts company with the Eden) and goes on for over forty delightful miles. The photographic biography he has compiled shows all its moods and caprices, from infancy onwards. Every village it nurtures and some of the people who live in them, also have their place in this unique commentary.

This book of mine attempts to portray on a much wider canvas what the Ure and other rivers see and know of castles, abbeys and farms; of market towns and solitary places; of men striving for a gallant cause, and others shaping art, music and literature to an inspiration born of their surroundings.

The canvas is so very wide, however, that here and there little cameos must suffice to suggest certain aspects of the living scene.

Here is what I once wrote, for example, in praise of Derwentwater. It was designed to bring the Lake District to particular focus.

Derwentwater—fed by the River Derwent after its Borrowdale infancy—is part of my very life, so often have I been drawn back to its enchanting shores. I can look back nostalgically to the 1920s, when a horse-drawn wagonette would take one round the lake and put one on the Derwent track to Borrowdale and Great Gable; to youthful picnics on St Herbert's Island; and to many a quiet saunter around its wooded margins, as the years went by.

The lake is only three miles long and at most one mile wide, yet its impact on local affairs has been, and still is, considerable. On all sides the lake reflects mountains which Coleridge saw as "giants' tents"— noble peaks like Skiddaw, lesser heights such as Castle Crag, also the

(*top*) The sands of Morecambe Bay at Arnside, Westmorland. (*bottom*) Lagoons bordering the tidal road to Sunderland Point, Lancashire

The limestone clint pavement on top of Malham Cove, West Yorkshire

Buttertubs Pass between Wensleydale and Swaledale

shapely Catbells and Causey Pike which have given so many 'Lakers' their first climbing legs.

The lake reflects history, too. One story concerns Lord's Island, opposite Walla Crag. Here, among the trees now surrounded every spring by a golden carpet of daffodils, lived the Derwentwater family. In an attempt to rescue her husband—imprisoned for his part in the 1715 Jacobite rebellion—Lady Derwentwater left their island redoubt and climbed Walla Crag *en route* for Carlisle. Legend says that the family jewels with which she schemed to secure his pardon, or effect a bribe, somehow slipped from her grasp and fell into the lake, where they still await a finder!

Derwentwater is only a quarter as deep as Windermere (which boasts 237 feet) and the different islands seem to be moored in place by invisible chains. One exception is the so-called Floating Island, near Lodore. This comes and goes at the caprice of marsh gases, which surface the coagulated mass of vegetation for a season or two and then gradually disperse, to the complete bewilderment of strangers.

At one time, visitors would flock to see this phenomenon. It was as great an attraction as the gunfire that reverberated across the lake. One gun was kept at Lodore Hotel for this 'romantic' purpose, and others were disposed strategically on Derwent Island. Mock battles and echoes were part of the Picturesque cult, and meant far more to eighteenth-century tourists than vast sheets of water bordered by "horrid mountains".

Derwent Island, the nearest island to the Keswick boat-landings, was long regarded as a private kingdom. Its least romantic name was Pocklington's Island, after the strange individual who fired some of those resounding volleys down the lake, and who—amongst other peccadillos—had the famous Castlerigg Druid Circle, above Keswick, reproduced on his own lawn.

Except where this lawn dips to the water's edge, the island is effectively curtained off with trees, lying "like a dark hand upon the water", as Hugh Walpole puts it when describing one of Pocklington's firework displays in *Judith Paris*.

An air of mystery still clings to the place, as it did when William Wordsworth recommended the island as a suitable home for Henry Marshall, son of an old flax-manufacturing friend from Leeds (see pages 201-5).

Henry and his wife succeeded Pocklington and soon gave new meaning to the island's alternative name, Paradise Island. Their house can be glimpsed on the west side. Astronomy, bird-watching, and Mrs Marshall's cultivated garden increased the amenities for the family and the few intimates privileged to ferry over from Keswick.

Even today this 7-acre island remains virtually unknown. Some day

3

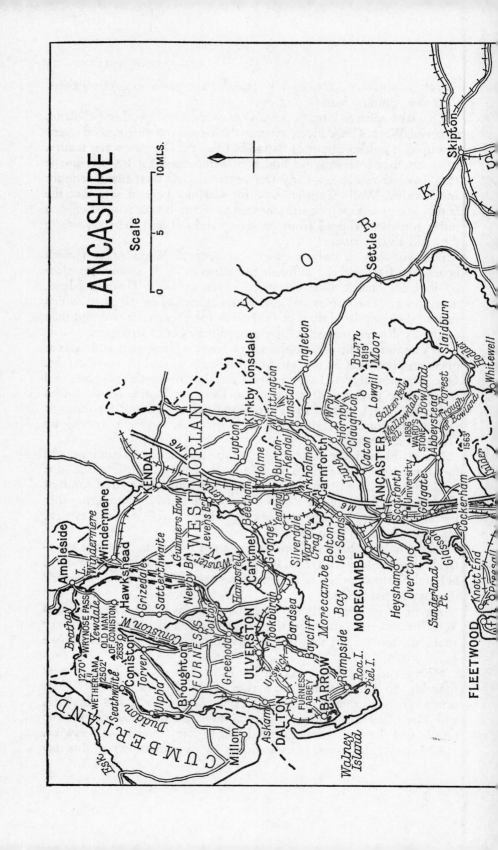

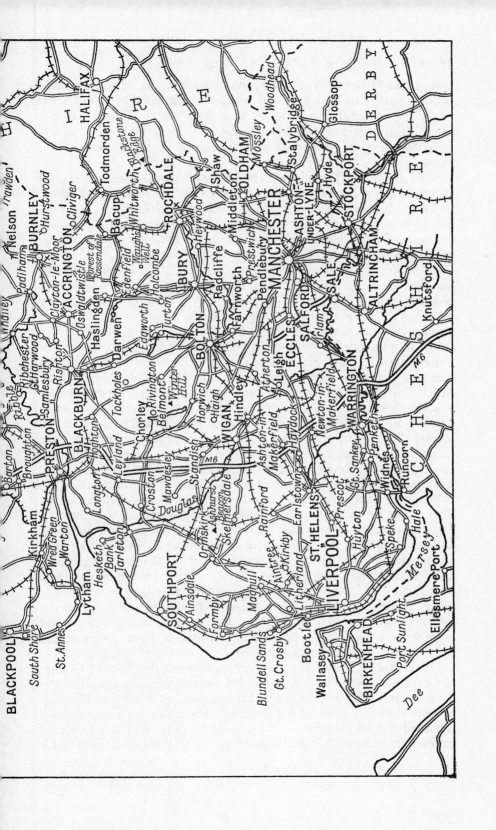

perhaps the National Trust, who now own the island, may allow small boating parties to land here and wander about like Crusoes. That is what my youthful friends and I had done on St Herbert's Island, though this retreat on the western side of the lake had remained un-inhabited, save by wild creatures, since the time of St Herbert, 1,300 years ago.

Wild creatures! The lakeside abounds with them. There are several heronries along the shore. Mallard nest in the tall reeds near Lodore, and black-headed gulls perch like watchful water-bailiffs on the moor-ing posts of the various jetties. Foxes lurk in the surrounding woods, and otters forage unhindered. Some otters had left their imprint on the muddy Isthmus when I once called to see Herbert Birkett.

From him I learned as much about local wild life as about the motor launches which his firm operate on the lake. The *May Queen* and other boats ply to and fro, as their predecessors have done for over seventy years. Deep below their keels, I was told, the rare vendace thrives—a small silvery fish which the monks of old found very palatable.

On another day I made the acquaintance of Dick Gill. Having just retired from ferrying generations of people between Portinscale and Keswick, he was in reminiscent mood. . . . His grandfather, Richard Mitchell, had also run the ferry here, and one of his frequent visitors was the Reverend H. D. Rawnsley, lately appointed to Crosthwaite Church, Keswick. An 'off-comer', Rawnsley delighted to get Mitchell talking about the neighbourhood and its magnificent scenery. The little clergyman was insatiable. The reason became clear, later, when Rawnsley joined forces with Miss Octavia Hill and Sir Robert Hunter, who between them founded the National Trust. That was in 1895.

National Trust property around Derwentwater now includes Castle Crag; some land adjoining Grange Bridge, beneath which the sparkling Derwent swirls towards the lake; Manesty Park nearby; the four larger lake islands; the Isthmus and Crow Park; Calf Close Bay; and several cottages and farms. It is significant that the very first piece of Lake District property acquired by the Trust (in 1902) embraces Brandlehow Woods near the Nichol End foreshore where those timely conversations took place between Rawnsley and Mitchell the ferryman. In 1922 Friars Crag, near the Keswick boat-landings, was bought by an appreciative public and given to the Trust as a memorial to Rawnsley, who had earlier become a canon of Carlisle Cathedral.

Of this rocky, tree-capped promontory where the friars of Grange were accustomed to land, John Ruskin—another great nature lover— once wrote: "The first thing that I remember . . . was being taken by my nurse to the brow of Friars Crag." Ruskin's own memorial, an inscribed slab of Borrowdale slate, is set up here, within a tangle of exposed tree roots. Canon Rawnsley, the Nichol End ferryman's "li'le parson from Crosthwaite", has his memorial slab nearby. They make a well-matched pair. Thanks to such devoted characters, the spell of Derwentwater remains, and the National Trust has taken firm root, here and all over Britain.

Mountains, moorland, dale and lake. And then, for good measure, two fascinating coastlines. All are needed to set our northern stage for its interminable pageant of history.

The eastern seaboard stretches from Berwick-upon-Tweed to the bird sanctuary on Spurn Point; the western, from Solway Firth and its peat waths to the wide, tumultuous Mersey.

When Swinburne wrote "Land beloved, where naught of legend's dream outshines the truth . . ." he was thinking of the entire county of Northumberland, with its seventy-odd miles of Roman Wall; its many silver-streamed valleys; its rolling moors flanked on the west by the brooding Cheviots; of fortressed towns and villages lichened with age; of the eloquent silences of its remoter parts—also of its "lordly strand", which, though studded with rock-girt castles gleaming above quiet little communities, yet belongs by ancient right to the razorbill, the guillemot, the cormorant, and St Cuthbert's prime favourite, the eider duck.

At Craster you see one of the old Border peles. From here a fine cliff-top walk leads direct into history at Dunstanborough Castle, whose foundations seem to spring from the very rock bases of its sea-pounded promontory. It is a lonely spot. While standing on the seaward edge of the ruins, a pair of fulmar petrel might swoop up from your feet, as it were, and then fly screeching from the strange phenomenon they have just beheld! It is eerie, too. The vertical chasm of Rumbling Churn gives a glimpse of the foaming waters far below, while the winds howl and moan through every crevice. But it is beautiful also; beautiful and sad as vanished glory usually is.

After Embleton and Beadnell Bays have been skirted, Sea Houses comes into view, and for about the first time, the Farne Islands too. It is at lovely Bamburgh, three miles ahead, however, that the full appeal of the Farnes may be felt—and responded to, perhaps, if an obliging boatman can be found hereabouts. Despite the wildness of the seascape and the rugged nature of the coastline, you are now on the verge of holy ground. Much of Britain's story as a Christian country sprang from the largest and nearest of that jagged island group, the Farne itself, and also from Lindisfarne a few miles farther north. St Aidan, who brought the Christian gospel to the folk of Lindisfarne, occasionally retired to Farne for meditation; his successor, St Cuthbert, did likewise.

Lindisfarne, or Holy Island as it is called today, is reached from Beal,

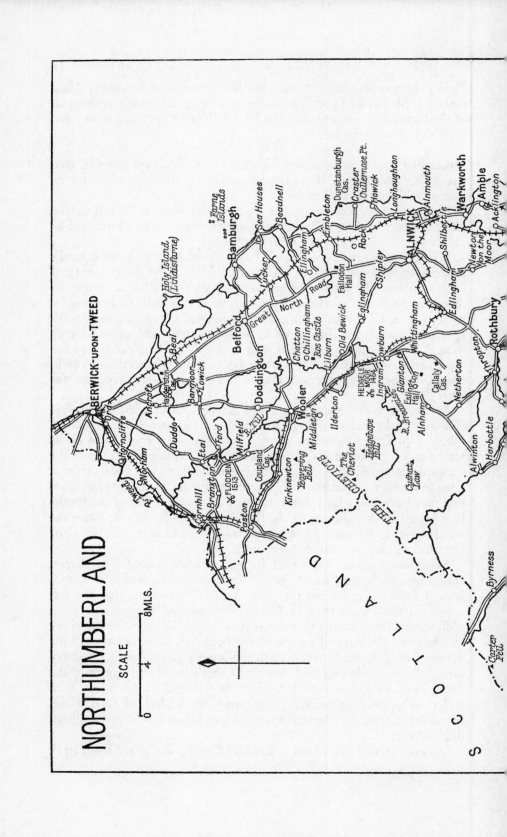

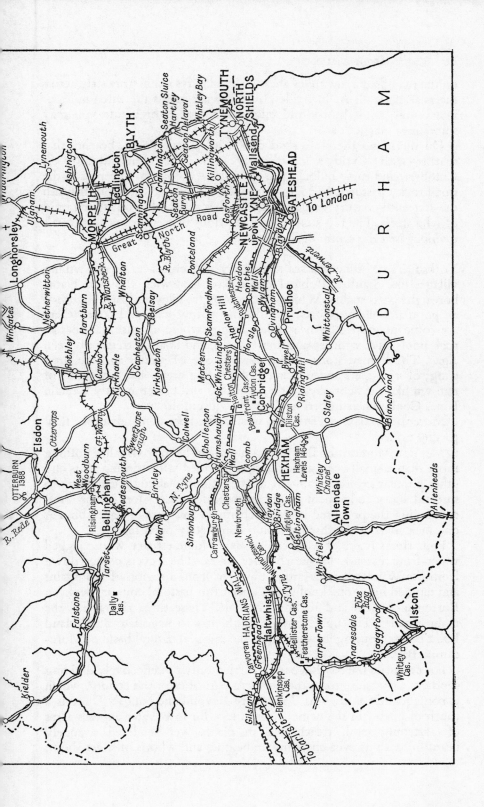

on the mainland a few miles ahead. The island is a thin grey strip across the near horizon. At low tide you can walk across the three miles of intervening sands by the old pilgrims' route; at high tide you may sometimes take a boat.

On the island there are sand dunes, jolly little coves, beaches that sparkle with 'Cuddy's beads'—tiny grey pebbles named after St Cuthbert, and turfy hillocks prinked with sea flowers. Sheep crop the small rocky pastures, and Highland cattle glower at you from beneath the sixteenth-century castle which perches, fairy-like, on its pyramid of whinstone. The red-stone Norman priory that enshrines Cuthbert's memory is at the centre of things . . . .

Yorkshire's coastline is a sea symphony that embraces quaint fishing villages like Staithes, Robin Hood's Bay, Runswick Bay and Flamborough; ports such as Whitby, Scarborough, Filey and Bridlington—all popular holiday resorts; and dozens of tiny bays and coves (there are some magical ones near Filey Brigg) where all care vanishes in rock pools alive with sea anemones, crabs, and floating tresses of green algae. The human story of this coast is one of pirates and the press gang; of smugglers and wreckers; of whaling crews and navigators of renown like the Scoresbys (father and son) and pre-eminently Captain James Cook. Their imperishable story will unfold later.

Morecambe Bay, over on the west coast, here demands more than passing notice.

Mention Morecambe Bay to a stranger and he may visualize nothing more than a small coastal indentation, studded with bathing tents and other popular seaside paraphernalia. One thing that could cause him to suspend hasty judgement is the oft-repeated discussion in the Press concerning the proposed barrage scheme in this part of Lancashire. A one-inch map of the district would completely open his eyes.

Four rivers make of Morecambe Bay a huge estuary whose jagged water-front extends for nearly fifty miles. The Leven comes down from the Windermere country; the Kent from a region of mountains and tangled limestone knolls; the Keer from pastoral country between Burton-in-Kendal and Kirkby Lonsdale. These three rivers feed the main estuary. The Lune, farther south, has to negotiate Sunderland Point before pouring its waters into the mighty, natural basin of Morecambe Bay.

For centuries the bay has been a barrier, only too effectively dividing southern Lancashire from the northern part of the same county, which is consequently known as 'Lancashire Beyond the Sands'. There is a touch of poetry in the name; realism too, for low water exposes acres of glistening sand, treacherous in places, yet rendered strangely beautiful with its ever-changing arabesques and whorls of silver sheen, beloved by myriads of waders and sea birds. Since very early times travellers have crossed these sands, on foot or on horseback. Guides were provided at one period by the monks of Cartmel, Conishead and Furness on the northern shore. Later, the crossing to or from Kents Bank near Cartmel could be undertaken by coach. Turner painted a fine study of one such coach party coming ashore at Hest Bank, near Morecambe. By braving the hazards, the passengers had saved themselves the long, circuitous journey far inland. An exciting if tragic literature has grown up around this peculiar bay traffic.

The Sunderland Point region provides a dramatic foretaste of Morecambe Bay and its shifting channels. The Point is reached from Overton, near Lancaster, by a tidal road. This is completely covered at high tide, but as the water drops again, some metal rails begin to emerge, giving the curious impression of a submarine surfacing. They are handrails that flank particularly vulnerable parts of the road. Gradually, the road 'shakes' off its incubus of water, and little bird-haunted lagoons form alongside an astonishing variety of terraces and amphitheatres sculptured in gleaming mud and sand. It is difficult to realise that the small village beyond, which becomes an island twice every twenty-four hours, was at one time the chief port for Lancaster.

As viewed from Morecambe promenade, five miles north of Sunderland Point, the Lakeland hills are as tantalising as a mirage. A clear day will reveal them, grand and alluring, on the northern skyline, like a vision of Olympus. But for that intervening watery waste, one could reach the nearest of them, by car, in half an hour. Yet they often seem quite unattainable, a paradise from which one is barred.

Nevertheless, the roads that skirt Morecambe Bay, though long, tortuous and partly inland, have the merit of linking together several attractive villages. Silverdale is one of them. Approaching it over Warton Crag, one first sees far over the estuary, whose shallow waters are streaked and coloured like a bird's wing. White Creek, on the shore below, strikes a bizarre note with its strange back eddies and odd little continents of fluted sandbars.

Silverdale itself is attractively poised between this creek and a knobbly array of limestone outcrops. Beyond these crags, only a couple of miles inland, are the three Yealand villages, centring upon a charming though simple Quaker meeting house, dated 1692, and its early eighteenth-century school. The loveliness of the surroundings did not shield the old-time Quakers here from persecution, yet it was said of one of them, a farmer, that 'one could feel his strength in the still spirit that kept him'.

There is a witchery about those limestone knolls. Footpaths and lanes wind temptingly among them in all directions, but eventually one drops down to Silverdale again, or to its near neighbour, Arnside.

Nobody would ever guess that Arnside was once a busy port. Indeed, this is where the county of Westmorland pushes Lancashire aside to make a brief seaboard of its own. In this elegant spot the houses step upwards from the gently curving waterfront, giving their fortunate owners magnificent views across the Kent estuary and beyond.

This hairpin-shaped seafront—which once gave the head of the Clifford family the right to preen himself as Hereditary Admiral for the Coasts of Westmorland—enjoys its frolic with the neighbouring county for six or seven miles, round the inner bend of the Kent estuary, and then Lancashire resumes control, near Lindale on the north bank.

Only at Levens Bridge, fifteen miles north-east of Morecambe, can one begin to round the awkward corner, or succession of corners, created by what Wordsworth called "this majestic barrier". Travellers by train have a slight advantage, for the Furness Railway spans the narrow part of the estuary at Arnside and then makes another leap over the Leven Sands, between Cark and Ulverston. It is a fascinating route, but how much one gains by sticking to the more natural, if devious, ways and byways! R. L. Stevenson's dictum, "to travel hopefully is a better thing than to arrive", has a special application hereabouts.

The old market town of Cartmel is the chief key to this northern shore. Smaller than many a village, it has a priory dating back to Norman times, where the prior organised his guide service over the sands. About the year 1501 a man called Edmondson held the office of "Carter upon Kent Sands" under the said prior. The guide's house has long been established down by the waterside, at Kents Bank, but Cartmel preserves some interesting milestones which coach passengers of a later day would consult, perhaps with growing apprehension. One large square stone informed them that Lancaster meant a fifteen-mile journey over the Kent Sands, and Ulverston (in the opposite direction) seven miles over the Leven Sands. Let us hope there was nobody around just then with scarifying tales of coaches that had been overturned on the way or engulfed in quicksand. Perhaps passengers would be somewhat mollified on seeing the guide press ahead with his 'brogs', bundles of broom or furze which he would strew here and there to indicate safe fording places, for the river channels are quixotic.

The Leven Sands were considered even more perilous than the wider Kent Sands. A small island roughly halfway across the Leven estuary looks insignificant, but it was here that the Prior of Conishead, near Ulverston, arranged that prayers should constantly be offered for pilgrims and wayfarers who were 'taking their chance'.

Until recently, Conishead Priory, practically rebuilt, was a convalescent home for Durham miners. There was a special aptness about this. Once, after passing its lovely grounds on my way through the Furness

peninsula, Morecambe Bay's final embracing arm, I was in the mood
to recreate for myself a scene from long ago. . . .

I looked across the sands and 'saw' a group of monks approaching. It
was the so-called Congregation of St Cuthbert, chanting their offices
as they struggled along and carrying between them—a coffin. This
contained the relics of their beloved leader. The place where they
stepped ashore and rested their precious burden is thought to have
been Aldingham. There were to be many other resting places in
northern parts before the last bourne was reached, at Durham, and a
worthy cathedral built to accommodate Cuthbert's shrine. But here at
quiet Aldingham a fine little church dedicated to Cuthbert stands
within its own sea-wall, to which the waters of Morecambe Bay creep
up and sometimes batter in a sort of wild cadenza.

We are now ready to ring up the curtain for a fuller performance of
North Country life and lore from early times onward.

2

The Sleepers Awake

. . . on Tuesday I opened a barrow near Chollerton [near Hadrian's Wall]. Found two bodies, one in an urn, sadly broken and decayed, with a central cist, in which were the very trifling remains of [another] body. Nothing had been buried with any of these bodies. The snow was six inch deep on the Ground, and a high wind, so you may imagine that the work was done under difficulties. The cist was examined by candle-light, and the scene was a very picturesque one, the workmen standing round in the partial light, some fine old bushes waving above us, and myself on my knees, with a candle held in front of me, discussing the mouldering remains. . . .

A picturesque scene indeed, though few archaeological digs are conducted under the macabre conditions described by this un-named excavator in December 1847. Often there is much toil for little reward. One needs to be both dedicated and skilled to extract much romance from old bones and broken potsherds. And yet the romance is there, as testified by so many archaeological finds and the story behind them. It is as though, by means of pick and spade, our forebears are sufficiently awakened from age-old slumbers to reveal something of their own ways of life, or even some tragic episode.

In 1958, while the present by-pass was being made near Catterick in North Yorkshire, road-makers and archaeologists unearthed many remains of the Roman fort, Cataractonium. A Roman altar came to light, remains of several buildings, and part of the fort's west wall. And then, tragedy: a skeleton with a knife still embedded in the ribs, lay on top of that wall. Not a Roman knife, but a Saxon one, suggesting some private vendetta or death in a battle known to have been fought around here in A.D. 600, long after the Romans had departed from Britain.

In 1734, while gathering firewood along the banks of the Tyne, near Corbridge, a blacksmith's daughter saw something that glistened amongst the loose soil. Pulling it out she found herself handling something like a tea-tray, though crusted with dirt. It proved to be a silver lanx, or dish, decorated with repoussé figures of Diana, Minerva, Juno, Vesta and Apollo in mythological postures. Perhaps it had once graced the Roman Commandant's luxurious table at Corstopitum, which spread its outpost of civilisation nearby, with centrally-heated houses, granaries and a public fountain. The lord of the manor claimed the treasure, but a replica in the museum on the site excites as much admiration as though it were the original, ready to be laden with sweetmeats for some Roman banquet.

There must be a special thrill in discovering some ancient treasure by pure chance. Several of us would like to have been with a certain postman, one day in 1915, when he was delivering letters to a remote farm at Carvoran, on the Roman Wall. An old 'bucket' sticking from the ground aroused his interest. In this area anything of the kind, however trifling it may seem, merits inspection. That postman would probably have trodden over other parts of the wall on his regular rounds, and have heard of John Clayton and later archaeologists who had uncovered so much history hereabouts. So the 'bucket' was worth a second glance. It turned out to be a bronze corn-measure of Roman workmanship, and in perfect condition. From the inscriptions around its circumference the name of an emperor had evidently been erased, but the titles still appended make it clear that Domitian (A.D. 81-96) was the man. One small object found by an observant postman had shown how, after Domitian's death, the senate in far-off Rome sought to expunge all memory of him—the fate of many hated emperors.

One of the first deliberate treasure seekers along the wall was King John, he who is supposed to have lost his own treasure in the Wash. He concentrated on Corstopitum (Corbridge), mistaking it for a kind of Pompeii overcome by some dread visitation. His only reward was the sight of a few strangely marked stones. No good at all for the depleted royal coffers!

Hadrian's Wall had to wait a long time for true appraisal, not only as a source of archaeological treasure, but as one of the finest Roman survivals in Europe.

Even so, with some people, a general haziness still seems to exist regarding the character and scenic appeal of the wall. You have only to mention this remarkable feature of northern England, and many people, even well travelled ones, will listen politely for a moment, and then change the subject. It is so much safer, more companionable, to talk about some well-known resort in Devon, say, or Switzerland.

And yet those who have seen some spectacular part of the wall are rarely satisfied until they see yet more. They may feel an urge to go on from one camp to the next; to go untiringly from grand stretches of the rampart as it strides for miles over ridge and towering crag, down to boulder-strewn defiles, there to ferret amongst the bracken and heather for remnants of a mile-castle, say, or of a well in which some legionary might have cast an offering to placate some strange god; and even then to go on, for the wall is a tantalizing mistress, always withholding more than is readily given. No sooner have you pieced together one part of the fascinating story, than some fresh thing rivets attention.

Throughout its length of approximately 73 miles, the wall exercises this irresistible lure in spite, perhaps because of, many gaps in the old fortification—gaps caused by stones having been removed by the cartload at various times since the Romans departed. Lanercost Priory (twelfth century) was built from Roman stones, perhaps even from the masonry of Petriana, one of the now 'missing' stations on the wall. Thirlwall Castle (fourteenth century), Denton Hall, Sewingshields Farm and many other buildings *en route* all testify to a similar origin. St Wilfrid used Corstopitum as a quarry when he built Hexham Priory about A.D. 674, and when, over 1,000 years later, General Wade tried to get his guns across to Carlisle to intercept Prince Charlie—and failed—the Government ordered a military road to be made over this territory. Practically the whole of the wall from Newcastle to Sewingshields was dismantled and used for its foundations! "Formerly", wrote Collingwood Bruce, "the facing stones were often seen protruding through the macadam, but are now hidden by the bitumenised surface."

More recently, local farmers have followed ancient precedent by taking some of the conveniently shaped stones to repair field-walls and outbuildings, while large-scale quarrying operations beside the wall near Greenhead have threatened and partially destroyed particularly fine stretches of what is, after all, a unique historic monument.

Though the wall itself and the magnificent country of which it has for eighteen centuries formed an almost integral part, has thus been open to considerable pillaging, several of the most important forts and camps associated with the wall have already been rescued from modern despoilers, though somewhat belatedly. Borcovicium has been protected by the National Trust since 1930, Cilurnum has long been in enlightened private ownership, while Corstopitum is controlled by the Ministry of Public Building and Works.

Actually the wall is a generic term, for it embraces several features. First, the stone rampart itself which is generally 7 feet 6 inches thick and of varying heights—originally it may have stood 15 feet or more from ground level. Then, slightly to the north is the ditch—except where precipitous crags such as those carrying the wall between Sewingshields and Peel Crag made this unnecessary; while to the south stretches the vallum, another ditch-like construction which acted as a kind of boundary beyond which, perhaps, Britons trading with the Romans were not allowed to pass.

Add to these features several forts, each garrisoned by 500 to 1,000 men, with a series of mile-castles (separated by Roman miles, that is, about 1,600 yards to the mile) for the convenience of soldiers on sentry duty, and a number of turrets where sentries would give warning of danger by fire or smoke signals, and you have a picture of the elaborate system which the Emperor Hadrian and his commandants devised to check the raiding Picts. A dedicatory tablet discovered in 1936 indicates how long it took to build the wall—only four years (A.D. 122-6), though some of the forts were extended later.

Three Roman legions were engaged on the task—the Second from Caerlon-on-Usk, the Sixth from York, and the Twentieth—the famous 'Valeria Victrix' which had the running boar as its emblem—from Chester. Though several British tribes helped to build certain sections of the wall—which, after all, was designed to keep out their own hereditary enemies from Caledonia—there must have been many clashes between Roman and Briton.

'Wall fever' will make some enthusiasts go on to explore the western and eastern limits of the fortification, where comparatively little that is visible now remains. There is more to be seen as you work inland from either coast, but for sheer concentrated romance take the section between Peel Crag and Sewingshields. Here a thousand unwritten stories of love and jealousy, of malice, sport and adventure, and of stern military duty, have been enacted against a background of stark grandeur. For the Roman builders took advantage, hereabouts, of the massive, wave-like ridge of basaltic rock known as the Great Whin Sill, much of which rises almost vertically from the shimmering waters of Crag Lough and Broomlee Lough. They set their wall and forts along its very crest.

"Confronting the North with mailed breast", as one writer put it, the whinstone ridge must have seemed vastly inhospitable, bleak and barren compared with the sunny climes of Italy, France and Spain.

Some of the natural gaps in the whinstone ridge have eloquent names: Busy Gap, Scots Gap, Cat Stairs etc., that conjure up many a vivid picture of sharp, fierce skirmishes between the Roman garrison and raiding parties. Milking Gap, however, marks a former village which the occupants had to evacuate when the Romans came imperiously on the scene.

A few of the gaps were to be used by moss-troopers right down to the seventeenth century; indeed, these raiders of later days turned Borcovicium (Housesteads) into their den, and even built themselves a pele tower on the site! The evil reputation which clung to the place in consequence had the curious effect of preserving the fort from complete destruction by those who coveted stone for building purposes!

The soldiers and their families are not difficult to recall, for excavations have laid bare their granaries and baths, shops, inns and a military way still showing clearly the grooves worn by their chariot wheels. A rather touching sight, nowadays, is the small artificial cave at Housesteads once devoted to the worship of Mithras, the sun god. Women were barred from this cult, so one gets a picture of their menfolk lining up for a session in the dark hollow, where a stone relief at one end showed the god rising from the rock, with signs of the Zodiac circling all about him. There was a space around the central figure so that it could be outlined by strong light theatrically managed from the rear.

Drama here took many forms. Listen to the late Dr G. M. Trevelyan describe the result of a dig here in the 1920s: "It was a great moment when the spade revealed the secret of a Third Century tragedy by exposing a skeleton with a knife in its ribs, buried under the floor of a house. Murder will out, even after sixteen centuries. We also found the apparatus of a coiner of false money. They must have been a lively lot at Borcovicium in the brave days of old."

The wild scenery of the wall in the neighbourhood of Housesteads and Sewingshields has given place, near Chesters and Chollerford, to a lovely stretch of parkland laved by the swirling waters of the north Tyne. The wall itself is here buried beneath the turnpike road, and of the bridge that carried it over the river only the abutments remain. Yet Chesters (Cilurnum) evokes the Roman *persona* in graphic manner with its Praetorium, barracks, commandant's house, and the regimental bath-house furnished with an *apodyterium*, or lounge, where the spare Asturians (from Spain) who garrisoned the fort gossiped in their time and gambled after enjoying what approximated to a Turkish bath.

Various temple remains at this and other forts reveal, imaginatively, numbers of folk worshipping at strange shrines, including some devoted to the Three Mother Goddesses. At Carrawburgh there was a sacred well (cleaned out in 1876) whose presiding genius or nymph could be placated by suitable invocations, by tiny votive offerings like coins or trinkets dropped hopefully into the water, or a small stone

Arnside, Morecambe Bay

Wainwath Falls, near Keld, Upper Swaledale

altar dedicated to this popular goddess, Coventina, to win private or family advantages. Christianity had practically no footing along the wall. The mighty Romans worshipped myths and fantasies.

The museum at Corstopitum helps to fill out a composite picture of this important Roman town, which was partly a civil settlement and partly a supply depot for the eastern range of Hadrian's Wall. You can walk amongst the remains of their vast forum, their shops, and a range of workshops which sufficiently indicate that this highly civilised place had its potters, blacksmiths and other kinds of craftsmen.

One of the most amusing finds, here, is a clay mould for making statuettes of a Romano-British god who wears knee-length tunic, shield, helmet—and a woebegone expression. He also carries a crooked club or walking stick. When it was found over half a century ago, its concert-hall likeness to Harry Lauder ensured a new currency for this ancient deity!

It is odd to think of all this show of imperial pomp and power serving as background for Roman children. Yet they were certainly here with their strange little toys, and who can doubt that bits of their mothers' broken jewellery—found here in plenty—would re-appear in their games as they played hide and seek amongst the buildings or splashed each other by the fountain?

What new things await discovery in this prolific area?—especially at Vindolanda, 2 miles south of Housesteads, which is even now being excavated under the direction of Robin Birley. In 1937 Eric Birley had revealed the magnificent headquarters building of this fourth-century fort, and the two gateways; but the Second World War and later commitments prevented further digging on this promising site, where a Roman milestone still spells out its message and a bath-house long known to local folk as the Fairies' Kitchen seems to invite reconstruction.

In 1969 Mrs Daphne Archibald of Tarset, near Hexham, bought the farm on which Vindolanda is situated and gave it to a trust, chaired by Professor Eric Birley, so that the entire *vicus*, or civilian self-governing village adjoining the fort, could be thoroughly excavated and at length shown to the public. Robin Birley, "born and brought up in the shadow of the fort", was evidently nurtured in anticipation with copious draughts of Hodgson, Clayton, Bruce, Collingwood and others. The discovery of Coventina's Well, and of that murdered person hidden in the back room of an inn at Housesteads, were also part of his Romanised education, making a fitting prelude to work now opening out at Vindolanda.

Domestic life in the *vicus* is slowly taking shape again. Life was made tolerable for the garrison at the fort by the presence nearby of their women and children, also by a community of farmers, craftsmen and

4

merchants. A *mansio*, or inn for the accommodation of minor officials while making their tours of the frontier, is the explanation of a fifteen-roomed courtyard house, which has its own bathing facilities. Perhaps those officials acted also as news-carriers? Certainly, the families here would have plenty to talk about and enjoyed small refinements introduced by the merchants.

A gold ring mounted with a chalcedony cameo representing Medusa was found in the *mansio*. Its loss, some 1,600 years ago, must have caused a great stir in the community. Another gold ring, bearing a cornelian intaglio inscribed *Anima Mea* seems to have slipped beneath some flooring, about the same time. "This ring", says Robin Birley, "is the sole evidence so far of Christianity at Vindolanda in the fourth century. The phrase *Anima Mea* is Christian, meaning *My Soul*, and suggests that the female owner of the ring belonged to the new faith." It also suggests certain difficulties in human relationships here, for, according to the large variety of inscriptions, on altars, tombstones, silver plaques etc, the gods chiefly in favour ranged from Jupiter, "best and greatest", Fortuna and Mars, to Vulcan and the Mother Goddesses.

Wooden hair-combs and bone hairpins, bronze brooches and jet rings, a gold ear-ring and a child's sandal; through all these and much else the people of Vindolanda are speaking again, as it were, in a language that all can understand. And nobody could miss the import of a betrothal medallion, fashioned in jet long ago for some Roman maiden who could look out, as we can also, from this elevated village and see, in one turn of the head, Hadrian's fortification as it sweeps over the countryside from Sewingshields Crag to the Nine Nicks of Thirlwall. Somewhere across that vast landscape, as the girl would scan it, her lover might be hurrying to keep tryst. One side of the medallion shows a pair of clasped hands; on the other a couple exchange a kiss. It would be ungallant to eavesdrop further.

For anybody whom the Roman sceptre has touched with imaginative zeal, the North Country offers almost boundless scope. At Bowness, beyond Carlisle, the westernmost fort of Hadrian's Wall looked over the Solway from a cliff some 50 feet high. The site is a thrilling one, for nearby is the Stonewath or ford which allows such an easy, low-water passage to and from Scotland that one can still sympathise with the Roman garrison who had to keep it under constant vigilance. Little remains of the actual fort, but a villager of much later times acquired one of the inscribed altars for his own use. On this altar Jupiter's protection had been invoked on behalf of the Emperors Gallus and Volusianus. Jupiter now has the responsible oversight of that villager's stable!

Moving farther down the Cumberland coast, once lined with Roman forts and watch towers, one comes to Ravenglass, where the Roman bath building now known as Walls Castle almost alone speaks of the vanished station, though Roman masonry in many a later house still faces towards the sea where the triremes put into harbour.

From a chain of signal stations set up along the Yorkshire coast, at Huntcliff, Goldsborough, Ravenscar, Scarborough and Filey, the Romans flashed beacon warnings along the adjacent coast and inland to such fortresses as that at Malton, whenever raiders approached from the North Sea. By this time, however, Roman rule in Britain was on the decline. The Scarborough signal station, later enclosed by the Norman castle, spreads along the bold oolitic cliff that separates the town's two wide bays, and commands a magnificent view of this deeply indented coastline, with Filey Brigg nearby and Flamborough Head, not unlike a stranded whale, farther south in the sea haze.

Of Britain's Roman towns, York (Eboracum) ranks highest with Chester and Bath. Petilius Cerialis, Governor of Britain, established the first legionary fortress at Eboracum in A.D. 71. It began as a comparatively simple affair of wooden palisading on a mound, but within about fifty years stone replaced the palisading. By the beginning of the fourth century the city had a fine range of buildings of which the chief survival is the so-called Multangular Tower, now enclosed by the lovely grounds of St Mary's Abbey.

Fragments of Roman masonry can still be detected in certain sections of the city wall, but apart from the fine collection of Roman antiquities in the Yorkshire Museum (which should certainly be seen), one has to be content with walking along such streets as Petergate and Stonegate to get something of the authentic thrill, for they overlay Roman thoroughfares that centred upon the Praetorium, where the Minster now stands. Current excavation work at the Minster has already revealed parts of the second century Praetorium and its hypocaust, the usual Roman heating method. Eventually, visitors will be able to see these discoveries, below the present floor level, and muse on the transitoriness of a way of life that must have seemed impregnable and permanent when the Emperor Severus was here and, later, when Constantine was crowned as Caesar (A.D. 306) in this same colonial town, roughly two-thirds of the way between London and the Roman Wall.

About forty years ago I used to share an intimate memory of Eboracum with a York sculptor (now dead). It was a cavity beneath Bootham Bar in which were exposed a few courses of the original Roman city wall. Steps led down to the small cavity, which was so dark that my sculptor friend invited me to change my photographic plates down there whenever I wanted, using the low wall as a table. When he, or perhaps his father, first excavated this corner of their building yard, three wooden stakes were found in the wall foundations, along with a lot of oyster shells. The stakes had presumably been cut from oak grown in the Forest of Galtres, which for centuries reached to the very walls of York, on that side. The oyster shells? Remains of a delicacy which the Romans loved.

And so one could go through northern England in quest of Roman life and lore. Aldborough, 17 miles north-west of York, was the Isurium known to wealthy Romans as a place where they could relax, find sport in the stadium, and share the luxury of handsome villas, each centrally heated, 'carpeted' with mosaic pavements, and served, perhaps, by negro pages. Two such pavements, now housed in wooden huts can be seen in the yard of the present inn, opposite the village green. Other features, including the inevitable baths, have been located in the grounds of Aldborough Manor.

These grounds also embrace part of the red sandstone wall built around Isurium. Grass-covered, the wall is now the centrepiece of a characteristically straight alley, dotted with Roman altars and querns found nearby. When I was there, daffodils, tulips and primroses added their charm, beneath a canopy of beeches and yews. It was a rare pleasure to saunter in such surroundings, in the cool of a spring day, knowing a little of the life that had been lived thereabouts many springs ago—a life spelt out for us now in rings and brooches, lamps and hairpins, scent bottles and oyster spoons, ivory counters and dice, and much else preserved in the village museum.

At Ribchester, lying in an attractive corner of Ribblesdale, most of the evidence of Roman craftsmanship, industry, military prowess and so on, is confined to the museum, but a local inn, the 'White Bull', has apparently taken unto itself some of the bygone grandeur. The four thick pillars supporting the porch once supported the fort's temple to Minerva.

Whalley Church nearby makes room for a little Roman handiwork amongst all its later treasures, while the altar at Tunstall Church now embodies another altar, which the Romans dedicated to Hygeia, goddess of health, and Aesculapius, god of medicine. Charlotte and Emily Brontë must have seen this curiosity when they came over to worship with the other girls from Cowan Bridge School.

The Lake District also felt the Roman impact. Some of their roads can be followed over the fells, but to be able to enjoy lunch beside a double Roman fort, Galava, at Ambleside, is something rather special. The whole of Windermere, all 10 miles of it, from north to south, stretches before you. What a magnificent view for the garrison! Camden had reported that this was the "carcase of a large city". Later folk have called it Borrans Field. To archaeologists it is a 'double-decker' fort, the lower one dating from the first century A.D. and the one on top from the Hadrianic period. According to a large collection of acorn-shaped leaden sling-bullets found there, a unit of slingers must have operated from this commanding spot.

Many other bygone ages have become vocal again in recent years. An Iron Age barrow on Malham Moor, in the Yorkshire Pennines, yielded a pipe made from the tibia (shin-bone) of a sheep. It naturally conjures up a little idyll in which some hill shepherd plays tunes to amuse himself while watching his flock. The pipe has three finger-holes. Leeds City Museum has a recording of this instrument—the earliest known of its kind—being played. At an exhibition held in connection with a recent Leeds Musical Festival, this small pipe, first fingered 2,000 years or so ago, took its place beside such other rarities as an ivory harp from ancient Egypt; a kissar fringed with part of a lion's mane, from East Africa; and a sheng, or bamboo pipe mouth-organ from China. This unique orchestration was enhanced by a set of Northumberland pipes (*circa* 1650) and a violin made by L. P. Balmforth of Leeds, whose son organised the exhibition.

The limestone hills and caves around Malham and Settle have proved abundantly rewarding to archaeologists. The entrance to Victoria Cave—discovered on Queen Victoria's Coronation Day in 1838—opens like a gigantic yawn in the broad face of King's Scar, between Settle and Malham. On my last visit some wild goats stood on the rock ledges and sagely wagged their beards at me. Thick, oozy mud made penetration of its chambers and passages somewhat tricky that day. Yet the mud is deceptive. It has hidden a fine stalagmite floor 2 feet thick, some fossilized clay with ancient water-marks rippling the surface, several 'cave pearls' and much else.

When Kirkdale Cave, near Pickering, was excavated by Dr Buckland in 1819 his finds proved that extinct animals, whose remains were continually being dug up in Britain, had indeed *lived* in this country "and were not borne into their resting places by a deluge, nor, as was suggested, imported by Romans for war or sport". Professor W. Boyd Dawkins found it necessary to repeat these words when describing the first yield of Victoria Cave, excavated some twenty years later.

The cave had been the setting for many age-old dramas. Hyenas had evidently made the place their den, dragging inside carcasses of hippopotamus, woolly rhinoceros and other beasts found in the neighbouring Ribble valley. Later, after a drastic climatic change, the cave became a bears' den. Aeons passed, and then man appeared on the scene, leaving evidence of his fishing activities in the form of a harpoon cleverly shaped with *reverse* barbs. About 4 inches long and cut from deer horn, the harpoon is probably of the Azilian period (pre-Neolithic). The mere that provided the fishing nearby has long been drained.

As time moved on, the cave floor was piled yet higher with debris, which, of course, covered the earlier occupation relics. The early-British wearer of a certain bronze brooch, shaped like a dragon and coloured with enamels, would have no notion of her animal predecessors in the cave!

Roman pottery and coins record a yet later chapter in the cave's remarkable palimpsest. And what a thrilling story it is! The coins are of two distinct periods, the earliest being of the reign of Emperor Trojanus (A.D. 98–117), while the latest carry the impress of Constans (A.D. 337–53). These two periods coincide roughly with a couple of insurrections by wild hill-men of the Ilkley and Skipton area, in the second and fourth centuries respectively. The tribesmen sacked forts and villas, forcing many families to take refuge in the caves of Craven. The coins, pottery and trinkets are eloquent of that twice-repeated evacuation. The human tenants of Victoria Cave round about this time left sufficient litter for their daily menu to be reconstructed. They feasted mainly on the flesh of shorthorn cattle (*bos longifrons*), with occasional mutton cutlets provided by the goat (*capra aegagrus*), or pork obtained from a domestic breed of pig. In addition there was venison of the roe deer and stag, also wild duck, grouse and two kinds of domestic fowl. Meat fit for a king!

And so the centuries passed, making of Victoria Cave and others in the district a time-chart for archaeologists like McKenny Hughes and Boyd Dawkins to decipher. They were followed this century by Tot Lord of Settle and his fellow members of the Pig Yard Club, a noted caving fraternity. In the club's museum at Town Head, Settle, much of the above-mentioned evidence is displayed as just one part of the history of this neighbourhood.

As we have already seen, the finds are sometimes accidental. It was Michael Horner's dog, for example, that first pushed its inquisitive nose into Victoria Cave, the entrance in 1838 being almost entirely blocked by debris. But it was a workman's pick that located the treasure chest of the Viking army, in 1840. After heavy storms the River Ribble had burst its banks at Cuerdale, near Preston, and men had been sent to repair the damage.

For centuries, tales had been told locally, from father to son, about some treasure that lay hidden nearby—fabulous treasure buried hastily as the Vikings forded the river while fleeing from their enemies. The story of the subsequent battle between Viking and Saxon hereabouts would lose nothing in the telling, down the years, but as the treasure never showed up, the whole story became a legend. For Lancashire children brought up on stirring tales of King Arthur and St George and the Dragon, it would make a pleasant change as they sat by the fire on winter nights. . . .

And then, 900 years later, the 'mythical' treasure chest materialized. That workman's pick had hit against something hard. It was a wooden chest, lined with lead, and crammed full of silver coins (about 700 in number), silver ingots and jewellery. Most of the coins had evidently been issued by the Viking kings of Northumbria and many of them were minted at York. Others, nearly 1,000 of them, bore the stamp of Alfred the Great. Before the find was officially reported, however, much of the jewellery was snapped up and went into private hands. The coins are in excellent condition and can now be seen in the museums at Preston and Liverpool.

Much more recently (1970) a treasure of a different kind set the same neighbourhood agog. Elk antlers have been found before, in the peat beds of Chat and Barton Mosses. But the new find is the *complete skeleton* of an elk, with a bone barb thrust into its ribs. First noticed in part beneath their garage by a Poulton couple, it has now been disinterred from its ancient bedding of peat, which suggests that the stricken beast foundered at last in a marsh or lake.

As a species, the elk had probably become extinct in Britain by the ninth century A.D., but that barb—which could be of the Mesolithic period—and another found near the hind hooves of the Poulton elk, relegates the drama of the hunt leading to its death to perhaps 10,000 years ago.

It was not chance, but dogged determination that has led to some equally exciting, though very different discoveries, within the precincts of Kirkstall Abbey, near Leeds. When Dr David Owen became director of Leeds City Museums about twenty years ago, he was assured that the ruins of this Cistercian house, founded in A.D. 1152, had been thoroughly excavated in earlier years and could afford no further scope for archaeological digs. But 'they' were mistaken. In 1950 Dr Owen and his team began to probe afresh and the digs have continued ever since. One year amateur frogmen helped the diggers by scouring the bed of the Aire, which flows past the abbey, for any discarded pottery and metalwork which the monks might have thrown into the water. Another time, a dowser's help was enlisted.

A complete record of their discoveries might be tedious to anybody not versed in archaeology, but the veriest tyro must be impressed by the remains of the monks' iron furnace, or bloomery, in the cloisters. It was here that the first monks of Kirkstall—or the iron smelters who prepared the way—fashioned materials for making tools, door-nails, water-taps, and even clasps for the monastery's precious books. The small forge is believed to be the progenitor of Kirkstall Forge, a well-known engineering firm which sends its products all over the world.

The Butler family of Kirkstall Forge have documentary evidence showing that a monastic forge existed here in the thirteenth century. The Kirkstall excavations push back the date another 100 years or so.

A monastic bath has also been revealed, and a sufficient number of encaustic tiles to reconstruct in part what must have been a colourful centrepiece for the floor of the refectory. Roman artisans could have designed nothing finer, of their kind. It is somehow comforting to know that the austere life of the Kirkstall fraternity was to some extent mitigated by such splendid decorative work as they silently partook of their fish, meat and vegetable stews.

The full story of the Kirkstall excavations so far, is told in a set of annual reports published by the (Leeds) Thoresby Society.

Meaux Abbey, near Beverley, has left practically nothing of itself save a number of similar tiles. A great pity, especially as the man who chose the site in 1150 (he was a monk from Fountains) had declared, "Here shall be the hall of the Eternal King, the vineyard of Heaven and the Gate of Life."

As a boy, G. K. Beaulah of Hull had unique opportunities for going over this 'vineyard of Heaven', his father having acquired the surrounding farm. With an improvised raft the boy explored the traditional tunnel (as any boy would) and then went carefully over the old floor area of the church, unearthing literally thousands of tiles. One clause of the Cistercian rule stated that "there shall be no superfluity and curiosity in sculptures, pictures, *pavements* [my italics] and the like in our abbeys". Even so, the monks of Meaux (pronounced Muce) had their little pleasantries. One tile design shows what appears to be a hound eating from a plate. Two white doves, perched back to back, are an amusing reference, perhaps, to the Holy Spirit, while the fleur-de-lys—emblem of the Blessed Virgin Mary—provides a choice motif repeated many times.

Somebody has written that "the brick mosaics favoured by the Yorkshire monasteries may be looked upon as the earliest decorative pavements, on a large scale, after Roman times". Before G. K. Beaulah started his youthful hobby, however, many of the tiles from Meaux were carted away to mend neighbouring roads. A selection of the best surviving tiles later decorated the walls of Mr Beaulah's house at Wawne, near the site of the abbey. I believe they have since gone to enrich the medieval collection at Hull Museum.

It seems fitting that this chapter should end with a brief account of some antiquities that needed no discovery, as they stand on the ground surface. They are nevertheless objects of wonder.

Long Meg and her Daughters are a group of standing stones high above Salkeld in Cumberland. William Wordsworth's reaction on beholding this strange assembly is worth quoting:

A Weight of awe not easy to be borne
Fell suddenly upon my spirit, cast
From the dread bosom of the unknown past,
When first I saw that sisterhood forlorn.

And then, addressing Long Meg herself, the poet cries: "Speak, Giant Mother . . .", but all he heard were his own fancies.

Meg stands some 60 feet away from most of her 'daughters', as if in contemplation; that is, if one can ascribe any sort of credence to the tale that they are all witches, turned to stone by a travelling saint who surprised them in one of their godless dances! According to another curious story, a magician cast a spell upon them so that nobody, then or since, can count them correctly. Camden gave the number as 77. Hutchinson, a Lakeland historian, said 72. Arthur Mee makes the family circle 67 strong, while Dr Pevsner declares for 59. The spell certainly seems to have been effective! If, as yet another legend avers, the 'daughters' were really Meg's numerous lovers, some of them seem to have gradually dwindled away with time, their wooing unwanted.

Long Meg, robed in red freestone, is a towering though rather bent figure of some 18 feet height and 15 feet girth—a formidable mistress! Her daughters, or lovers, are mostly about 10 feet high. Altogether, an impressive gathering, within an arena of 360 feet diameter. And there they stand, as mute as Stonehenge and as puzzling to antiquaries, with nothing but legend and conjecture to animate the strange conclave with life and purpose.

Legend and superstition are apt to thrive when men are faced with such conundrums. For untold centuries three huge menhirs have stood in a line on open land (now encroached upon by houses) near Borough-bridge, in West Yorkshire. But nobody knows why. Until about 300 years ago there was a fourth stone in this mysterious arrangement, but somebody with no sense of history (except for the treasure supposedly buried beneath) removed it. Later, perhaps in disgust at the absence of treasure, the uprooted stone was used for making a bridge nearby.

In recent years one archaeologist has suggested that the stones might have been set up, originally, to indicate a neighbouring ford over the River Ure. But why such enormous sign-posts? They vary in height from 16 to 22 feet and are fluted towards the top. In the absence of any satisfying theory as to their former significance, Yorkshireman will continue to call them the Devil's Arrows, even though the accompanying story has long been treated as a bit of folklore to amuse the children. The story relates how the Devil, after his priestly disguise had been discovered at an assembly of Druids, climbed Howe Hill and flung four stone 'arrows' in an attempt to destroy ancient Aldborough. His anger must have interfered with his marksmanship, for the arrows fell harmlessly between Aldborough and Boroughbridge.

The Devil's Arrows are as secretive as the tall menhir that rears itself within the churchyard at Rudston on the Wolds. Shall we ever know who erected them, and for what purpose? Shall we ever break into their long sleep?

No finer stage setting for prehistoric scenes in Britain could be desired than the glorious moors and hills which, from west and east, press down upon Wooler in Northumberland. They are still patterned with the remains of villages and other contemporary features. Pioneer work in deciphering these features was done earlier this century by William Brand of Wooler, whom I once joined in his activities.

We located moot hills and the tracks leading to them, but I was chiefly impressed with the guide stones and 'rock maps' on Weetwood Moor, which attains a height of 500 feet. The guide stones are rudely-carved pieces of gritstone, deeply inscribed with grooves that corresponded almost exactly with the direction of ancient moorland tracks. One such stone is raised on a mound—a device, perhaps, meant to attract attention to the stone and prevent its obliteration by snow.

When Mr Brand first noticed this stone he followed its 'directions' and found that in most cases he was led to ancient camp sites marked as such on Ordnance Survey maps. One groove pointed in a westerly direction, where the natural lift of the moor put a limit to what could be seen from the guidestone. He kept closely to the direction indicated, however, and soon after passing over the crest of the moor found that he had arrived at a large stone circle not recorded on any Ordnance Survey map.

On the outer edge of this circle a 'foreign' stone points to a Hill of Laws, or moot hill, not far away, on which other antiquaries had worked for some years. This part of Weetwood Moor is known as Whitsun Bank; until about seventy years ago an annual fair of some antiquity—where cattle and sheep were sold, and games and festivities were shared by all comers—was held on this outlandish spot. Was this usage an 'echo' from the times when the ancient tribesfolk who lived on the moor held their moots here?

The suggestion is certainly speculative, but little if any doubt can exist regarding the significance of numerous 'rock sculptures' which abound on Weetwood Moor and neighbouring Dod Law. Proof that these are nothing less than maps, inscribed upon the horizontal surfaces of rock outcrops by the ancients, whoever they were, is readily forthcoming because almost every relevant feature can be traced with their aid.

Camp sites are shown by concentric circles, the number of rings varying according to the size or importance of a camp. Lines of communication appear as deeply-scored markings which connect the various map symbols. It was extremely interesting to read some of those maps, after the passing of untold ages. They were not made to scale, but they do lead direct to 'village' after 'village', whose remains —in the form of earthen ramparts, etc.—sometimes had to be sought amongst the bracken and heather.

Some of the maps are provincial in scope. A good example occurs near the guidestone already mentioned. It gives a survey of the ancient province of Weetwood, the camps, or hill-villages shown on the map being traceable even now at Weetwood, Fowberry, Trickly, Highcairn etc.

Other maps—like some of ours today—are simply local, giving greater detail but covering a smaller area. Provincial or local, however, these rock-maps would be of great use to the clansmen of remote centuries, enabling them to move quickly from camp to camp within any particular province.

But how shall we picture those remote peoples? Were they Bronze Age folk? Did they wear animal skins, paint their bodies with woad, and fish from coracles? Their rock-maps can offer no answer. With Wordsworth we can only feel "a weight of awe" from the "unknown past".

3

On the Map

> I am told there are people who do not care for maps, and
> I find it hard to believe.
>
> R. L. Stevenson.

I have loved maps and map-lore all my life. First came the fictitious charts as found, for example, in Stevenson's own *Treasure Island*; then, tantalising reports of a long-lost donkey-skin chart of Knaresborough Castle which was supposed to show its underground passages and the place where some of Charles I's regalia remains hidden; and eventually, such curiosities as the famous thirteenth-century Mappa Mundi in Hereford Cathedral.

Furthermore, near my boyhood home in West Yorkshire the hill-top hamlet of Dunningley had long been known to me as the reputed birthplace of Christopher Saxton. When the British Museum began to sell replicas of his beautiful Elizabethan maps, some years ago, I gleefully climbed up to the hamlet once again, but nobody there had ever heard of Saxton or his remarkable atlas. I felt rather crestfallen, on Saxton's behalf!

Then, one day during the last war, I read about a wonderful collection of maps and road-books, compiled over many years by the late Dr Harold Whitaker of Lightcliffe, near Halifax. Unable to resist such a lure, I soon found myself (by appointment) in a charming

Georgian villa, where one large room had become a cartographer's universe. All the map-makers I had ever heard of, and many more, were enshrined there. One by one they emerged at Dr Whitaker's bidding, but I was specially delighted when down from their shelf came several editions of Christopher Saxton's *Atlas of the Counties of England and Wales*. Queen Elizabeth I dominates the coloured frontispiece; on either side of her, surveyors and cartographers are busily at work with their curious instruments, while, above, cherubs prepare to drop laurel leaves on those who have so richly deserved them.

The maps themselves are a continual pleasure. Even though Saxton employed scientific methods that have earned him the title, 'Father of English Cartography', he still resorted to picturesque illustrations born of romance and fancy. His seas are particularly rewarding; they are patrolled by magnificent galleons like those that were to face the Spanish Armada, also by spouting whales and fabulous monsters.

One thing that intrigued me just as much was to find the forgetful hamlet of Saxton's youth marked on one Yorkshire map with bold, proud lettering which seems to claim for tiny Dunningley an importance denied to some local *towns*! Dunningley, through which one can walk in three minutes, is even shown on his general map of England and Wales (1584). There's loyalty for you!

Yet it is a fine tribute to Saxton that for the next 150 years most English county maps by other men were based on his atlas. Certain cartographers frequently passed off his surveys as their own. While Dr Whitaker showed me some of these 'borrowings', and their originals in Saxton's own work, I tried to visualize this redoubtable Yorkshireman. . . .

Little is known about him, personally, but a placart, or patent, mentioned in the Privy Council Register for 1575 was not actually issued until 1577, perhaps because Elizabeth's scruples had meanwhile to be overcome, for Saxton was a Catholic. The placart directs that the Justices of each district to be mapped "shalbe aiding and assisting unto him to see him conducted unto any towre Castle highe place or hill to view that countrey and that he may be accompanied wth ij or iij [two or three] honest men such as do best know the cuntrey for the better accomplishment of that service, and that his depture [departure] from any towne or place that he hath taken the view of . . . do set forth a horseman to safe conduct him to the next market Towne, etc."

His later visits to Dr John Dee, at Chetham's Hospital, Manchester (then a priests' college), evoke a picture of the mathematician and astrologer—with his "long beard white as milk"—poring over some of Saxton's charts. To fill out the picture one may regard the figure holding globe and compasses, in the afore-mentioned atlas, as a mirror of Saxton's own self and place him, imaginatively, alongside the tall, slender astrologer. . . .

In Dee's diary one gets a rare mixture of superstition, talks with angels conjured down from Heaven—and cartographical matters. One minute he is drinking "a draught of white wyne and salet ayle", fortified by crab's eyes, for a kidney attack; and the next, writing to his learned friends on scientific affairs. Saxton's recorded visits to Dr Dee were in the summer of 1596. The diary entries create an interesting picture: 15th June, "I wrote . . . to Christopher Saxton at Denningley;" 21st June, "Mr Christopher Saxton cam to me . . .;" 5th July, "Mr Savill [an antiquary] and Mr Saxton cam;" 6th July, "I, Mr Saxton [and others] to Howgh Hall;" 10th July, "Manchester town described and measured by Mr Christopher Saxton;" 14th July, "Mr Saxton rode away." One hopes that, in between times, Saxton was spared his host's queer concoctions. Yet the map-maker had been accustomed to colourful characters. Thomas Seckford of Woodbridge, Suffolk,—Court Surveyor and Master of Requests under Elizabeth— was one of them. Seckford smuggled on a large scale, but had also sponsored Saxton's great atlas and financed it!

Of an early edition of this atlas Dr Whitaker remarked:

> The engraved plates for a number of counties were undoubtedly prepared for an edition of 1665. If they were not actually published, that might easily be explained by the confusion and mortality caused by the Plague in that year. A suggestion that the stock of newly printed maps was destroyed in the Great Fire in the following year is equally reasonable as an explanation of the non-existence of any copies. A definite fact, however, is that the engraved plates for Saxton's maps of Northumberland and Devonshire disappeared about this period. I can only suggest that they were actually in the hands of a London engraver at the time of the Great Fire and were destroyed.

I was shown maps by other famous men, including John Speed, whose atlas, *The Theatre of the Empire of Great Britaine* (1611-12), assiduously depicts hundreds, wapentakes and plans of the county town on all but the maps of Northumberland, Durham, Cumberland and Westmorland. I wonder why? Did his courage fail him in those northern parts?

Speed's map of Lancashire makes some amends, from the Northerner's point of view, by including "The portraitures of all those kings sprunge from ye royall families of Lancaster and Yorke which with variable success got and enjoyed ye Crown and Kingdom." One side of the map "showeth them of Lancaster, the other syde them of the house of York". The York portraits include that of Richard III, who was always popular in the county, despite evil rumours about two princes murdered in a tower. And Speed also bows his way into Northerners' esteem by referring to the "most famous and fayre Citie of Yorke . . .".

Dr Whitaker's map oddities were something else in which I revelled. Perhaps the most attractive are the playing-card maps designed by Robert Morden in 1676. Many of the Restoration gentry and their ladies must have run card parties with these ingenious packs. Each king in the cardboard court is Charles II, wearing a full-bottomed wig, while the queens portray a rather naive Catherine of Braganza, his Portuguese princess. The knaves are a well-mixed variety of courtiers and others. Each of the fifty-two cards displays in its centre portion a different county map, which, though necessarily small, does show a few important towns, hills and rivers. Below, a narrow strip gives such details as "length, bredth [sic], and circumference" of the particular county. The Yorkshire card shows the Merry Monarch as King of Clubs; he looks down, rather glumly, on a county of sparse towns and villages, which surprisingly include Crake (Crayke) and Kilham, though Bradford and fine old towns like Scarborough and Knaresborough are altogether omitted. The one road on the map, from Doncaster via York and Yarum (Yarm), continues on the Durham card, linking Darlington and Durham City to Newcastle. As Queen of Clubs, Catherine of Braganza surveys the Durham scene with ill-concealed surprise.

Another set of playing-card maps, published later the same year by W. Redmayne, are even stranger to handle today. Charles and Catherine still reign, though in more regal attire, over the appropriate cards, but each county is nearly obliterated—'trumped' so to speak—by the suit sign. Redmayne announced that this "recreative pastime by Card-play" was "very useful for all Travellers . . .". In view of the scrappy maps, this is hard to take, unless one finds the accompanying notes some compensation. The notes, however, communicate little more than the maps, stating epigrammatically, for example, that Yorkshire is "temperate and fruitful, woods or Trees adorn it", and that in Durham "ye Soyle is barren, it hath Great Store of Sea Cole" and that "Tine [Tyne] Runs along with ye Picts Wall [Hadrian's Wall]". To add point to the coal reference, Redmayne's thumb-nail map shows little else but a couple of pygmy-sized coal-heavers, and two collier brigs off shore. Each miner is wearing a bowler hat, true to the times.

Redmayne speaks pithily of "Lanca-shire": "it lyes Westward, under the Mountains that run through the Midst of England . . . it yelds [yields] store of Barley and wheate . . . in it is the Greatest Lake in all England, viz. Winander Mere,* allso heers [here is] store of sal-mon-fish."

One day Dr Whitaker invited me to go over and see another

* Windermere was spoken of in this way until early in the nineteenth century.

exceedingly rare treasure he had just acquired for his collection. It was *The British Monarchy* (1749–54). This sober title conveys nothing of the phantasmagoria within. Perhaps after the Jacobite rebellion of 1745 and its attendant horrors the English milords were ready to be entertained. Or perhaps it was their own gay temperament that prompted George Bickham and his son to produce this atlas of 'birds'-eye-view' maps. Whatever the reason, one can only sit back and enjoy their effusions.

In the Northumberland vista, probably obtained from Kilhope Law in the south-west of the county, a wayfarer carrying staff and knapsack hastens towards this antiquarian paradise as though it were some lost Herculaneum. Hadrian's Wall, here again described as the Picts' Wall*, careers across the county, and beyond is the authors' idealised version of Warkworth and Alnwick Castles. The Durham map is prefaced with a row of dead birds and stoats suspended forlornly from tree branches, while rabbits scamper merrily below. Yorkshire, according to the Bickhams, has the River Ouse flowing (far from its proper course!) through a Sheffield of gabled houses dominated by a rustic fountain and turreted market hall. From that springboard, the county continues dreamily through fertile pastures until Yarum (Yarm), on the Durham border, is reached in a sort of Elysian ambience.

Westmorland is a scene dominated by a horsewoman, with man and dog companions, riding through a landscape in which the towns and villages are half lost amongst foliage; while Cumberland is viewed through a lofty ruined arch, with the Picts' Wall beyond, and the blacklead, or wad, mines indicated above Borrowdale. The Lakeland mountains were still considered vulgar; best ignored.

The Bickhams' accompanying comments, engraved in fine copper-plate script, are equally entertaining, though at times snobbish and often wide of the truth.

Thus, the "worst parts" of the East Riding "breed great quantities of sheep", while the North Riding "wants Fertility except in its Bowels, which produce Pit Coal, Marble and Several minerals". The North Riding's rich agricultural land is entirely overlooked. Of Lancashire it is written that "Chatmosse is famous for the subterranean Trees . . . which serve the Country People both for Fewel and Candle." Liverpool and its people are singled out for praise: ". . . and what at present ought not to be forgotten, they distinguish'd themselves by their Loyalty in the late [1745] Rebellion. We should be glad to say with Truth ye same of the other great Trading Town in this County, Manchester", whose chief "Manufactures" incidentally, "are brought to London upon Pack-horses".

* The first Northumberland map to name the Roman Wall as such, and to show it ending at Wallsend, on the east, was by A. Armstrong (1769).

Hadrian's Wall near Housesteads

A Roman aqueduct exposed at Corbridge, Northumberland

In Northumberland "The Inhabitants are commonly healthy and many of them live to a great Age without Sickness." Then, focusing upon Newcastle: "The politer Inhabitants live at ye Top of the Hill. . . . The Town has a stone wall [part of Hadrian's Wall], but not so strong as to keep us from Apprehensions during the late Rebellion. . . ." A further comment in this section outlines a curious custom from Alnwick. "At Alnwick whoever takes up his Freedom must go through the odd ceremony of jumping into a certain miry bog, which is said to be a penalty imposed by King John, whose royal Person stuck fast in that very hole" (see pages 271–2).

As Dr Whitaker would remark, Bickham's amazing atlas was the chief breakaway from normal map-making since Michael Drayton published his *Poly-Olbion* in 1622. This is a medley of songs in praise of different counties, illustrated by 'maps' that partake of the same gay mood. Yorkshire, his "Most Renowned of Shires", is given "The Eight-And-Twentieth Song" in this medley, and a merry song it is, compounded of rivers and mountains, antiquities and customs, also scenic oddities like Knaresborough Dropping Well and the East Riding Gypsey streams, all trilled over with obvious delight. His 'maps' have to be regarded in the same light-hearted manner. He invests the sea areas with mythical creatures and employs hordes of nymphs and shepherds as 'sign-posts' for hills, rivers and towns. In his Yorkshire map one nymph sits on the ground, near Goole, to indicate a swamp; another woman wields an axe to represent the old Halifax gibbet— often called the Sharp Maiden of Halifax; and a portly dame walks like a somnambulist while balancing York Minster on her head.

The Bishoprick of Durham is included with "Northumberlande", and rivers are again its chief topographical features; that is, rivers according to our map jester. Water nymphs abound, as usual, but St Cuthbert—who disliked the fairer sex—would have been horrified to see what a jaunty lass stands for Durham; she actually carries on her head, like a milkmaid with a pail, the three-spired edifice representing the cathedral that is Cuthbert's own shrine. He would have disapproved, also, of the nude youngster dancing on his beloved Holy Island (Lindisfarne). The Cheviots are a group of eight molehills at the top left corner, and on each sits a shepherd or other rustic figure. Some of the hills, for example, "Flodden hill" and "Cheuitt hill" are wrongly placed to the *north* of the Tweed, and a huntress sums up "The Forest of Lowes". The Picts' Wall appears as a rope stretching across the map from Newcastle, and a place is found for "Helkettell" (Hell Kettles) near Darlington. This gives Drayton a fine opportunity to draw three demons performing some hellish ritual.

The Bickhams had blandly stated that on their birds'-eye-view maps towns and villages were "interspersed according to their Apparent

5

Situation". 'Apparent' to the birds, perhaps, but hardly to any travelled person. Drayton's sense of scale and situation was even more haphazard, but then he had no desire to instruct, only to divert. Even later map-makers seemed unable to decide what their true function was.

A serious purpose informs Matthew Simons' work, *A Direction for for the English Traviller* (1636); it was designed to enable the "traviller" to "Coast about all England and Wales"; yet for all that, oddity creeps in. A triangular distance table occupies the greater part of each page, but the amusing feature is the "thumb-nail" map in the bottom right-hand corner. These maps are well-named; limited space allows important place-names to be indicated by initial letters only. To add to one's confusion, some initial letters represent towns, others castles. The map is, in effect, a puzzle of no practical value whatever. On the York-shire thumb-nail map the L for Leeds is omitted. A later edition put the L where it should be, and restores a dolphin to "The Germaine Ocean" for good measure.

It took a long time for English folk to get either a reliable map of their country or of their own area. Between 1759–85 Emanuel Bowen made various attempts to provide a dependable atlas for his countrymen. Many of the maps, however, were borrowed, and were too wide from east to west, giving a strangely distorted effect. One attractive feature is the set of historical notes that surround the county boundaries. On the Yorkshire map there is this comment: "Ackham or Accome [Acomb, near York], noted for a Mount called Sivers from Severus, who dying at his Palace at York, his Body was buried here after the Roman manner, and his ashes being put in a Golden Urn, was carried to Rome and laid in the Monument of Antoninus". Bowen simply quotes the current tradition, though actually the site of the emperor's funeral pyre outside York is not properly known. Prior to his death Severus is said to have "contemplated the urn which was to contain his ashes, with the words, 'Thou art about to hold a man for whom the world was too small'".

A few years earlier (1724) Herman Moll of London had produced a somewhat similar effort, which he called "A New Description of England and Wales . . . To which is added, a New and correct Set of Maps of each County, their Roads and Distances; and, to render 'em the more acceptable to the Curious, their Margins are adorn'd with great Variety of very remarkable Antiquities, &c." Thus, some of the maps are strewn round the edges with ancient coins, Roman altars, etc. Northumberland gave him plenty of scope in this wise, but his West Riding map is particularly instructive. The left margin is devoted to Roman tablets unearthed in various places. Adle (Adel, near Leeds) is represented by the wreathed head of a statue found there, and York by a facsimile of a "Monument of Conjugal Affection". The right margin is taken up entirely by a sketch of the Halifax gibbet in action. For the benefit of those not familiar with "the manner of execution according to the Halifax Law", the whole grisly procedure is elabora ted, each part of the guillotine being described below. The axe is about to drop on a victim's neck, and a woman nearby calls out in protest.

Another novelty, though on a smaller scale, was John Luffman's *Pocket Atlas* (1806). All the maps are circular and seem to portray each county as through a fortune-teller's crystal bowl. The West Riding enjoys a map to itself and must have vastly amused the children for whom the atlas was intended. This and other bygone Yorkshire maps from the Whitaker collection were reproduced on stiff card, some years ago, for the School Museum Service in the area.

To reprint William Green's *Picture of England* (1804) today would cause great hilarity among schoolchildren, for the maps are tilted at curious angles. Thus on the general map of England, our six northern counties are at the *bottom*. The southern counties, from Kent to Cornwall, have usurped our usual location at the top. In other words, Green made England stand on its head, with Carlisle and Berwick-upon-Tweed taking the full weight along an inverted Scottish Border! The individual maps are just as crazy. Cumberland, Northumberland, Yorkshire and Lancashire are all upside down, but County Durham and Westmorland recline sideways, with the north to the left. In Dr Whitaker's copy an attempt has been made to rectify the different orientations, but this has the dizzy effect of showing place-names sideways on, or inverted.

These rather silly maps had first been published by R. Butters in his *Atlas of England*, a year earlier. Why Green should perpetuate them, with modifications that are just as confusing, was known only to himself. In his hands, England had indeed become a Green and pleasant(?) land.

Even as late as 1828 new and strange ways of presenting county geography were being exploited. In that year G. B. Depping produced *L'Angleterre*, a French pocket atlas. Sporting trophies, waterfalls and overhanging rocks give him the setting for some of the microscopic maps, of the northern counties as elsewhere, though Yorkshire fares rather better in this respect, because of its size. Apparently snipped from a large chart, this map rests against an anchor; displayed from some oak branches are the names Walton and Tillotson to represent two notable county families. An eel peeps mournfully from the base of the map, and for some obscure artistic purpose a jug and basin occupy the left corner. One glaring topographical error is the substitution of the Tyne for the Tees, on the Yorkshire–Durham border.

John Warburton was a map-maker of the more orthodox type. His surveys were more factual and less dependant upon mere hearsay.

Clearly, he wanted to give good value, especially to the gentry who patronised his enterprise in return for their coats-of-arms appearing in full heraldic colours, on the relevant maps. He must have enjoyed himself immensely on this job. It was he who actually visited the various gentry, such as the Inglibys of Ripley Castle, near Harrogate, and the Hawksworths of Hawksworth Hall, near Otley, dining with them, sampling their wine and gloating over their family treasures—while his men did the road-measuring! This they did with the aid of a way-wiser. For his survey of Leeds, Warburton sought the help of Ralph Thoresby, the famous antiquary, and personally made calculations from the tower of St John's Church, Briggate.

The result of all this was his map of Yorkshire (1720), a fine production and popular about that time. When Dr Whitaker was building up his collection, Warburton's maps had become extremely rare. How he acquired one by accident makes a good story. While attending a sale of household effects at Hornby Castle, in the North Riding, he wandered down a gloomy back passage—away from the crowds—and noticed a chart high on the wall. Striking a match, he peered up and saw some of the tell-tale coats-of-arms, grimy by this time, and somewhat the worse for long exposure. But it was a genuine Warburton. After being cleaned and mounted on linen, it soon joined all his other maps and charts and road-books which in their various ways had attempted to hold up a mirror to our northern counties.

The Whitaker collection even contains some 'phantom' maps. Earlier map-makers sometimes relied on rumour for their topographical details, or copied another's mistakes. But those who drew up some of the transport maps of last century deliberately inserted *non-existent* features. Railways and canals are shown that were figments of the imagination. What was the reason? Simply this. Parliamentary powers might have been granted for some projected railway line or canal but the plans miscarried, probably through lack of funds. Meanwhile the maps produced in anticipation by over-zealous local authorities circulated a series of 'might-have-beens'. And these were repeated over and over again, on subsequent maps.

One such map (1845) shows the Liverpool-Newcastle line passing through Colne, Gargrave, Threshfield, Kettlewell, Kidstones Pass, Leyburn and Catterick; that is, through Upper Wharfedale and Wensleydale. Another map, in Walker's *British Atlas* (1879) shows a branch line from Allendale turning south into County Durham. A Lancashire map of the same period indicates a canal going through Haslingden.

Should any industrial archaeologist in the remote future search—on the 'clear evidence' of these maps—for relics of these particular transport facilities, he will go singularly unrewarded!

ON THE MAP 69

On Dr Whitaker's death, several years ago, his entire map collection passed to the Brotherton Library at Leeds University, where it can be consulted by arrangement. There, the more scientific map-makers come fully into their own: Saxton, Speed, Ogilby, Cary, and so many others, not forgetting the pioneer Ordnance Survey efforts after the 1745 Jacobite rising, when the lack of reliable maps had hindered the ghastly 'mopping up' of returning, disillusioned rebels. But I shall always feel glad that I saw the Whitaker collection—oddities and all— while it was still being compiled in Drayton's "wide West Riding".

It is a unique record of the many side-tracks and deviations and sheer burlesque our ancestors had to put up with (though often to their infinite pleasure) before a true, cartographical picture of the North (and other parts of England) could emerge.

But even now, with certain boundary changes in the offing, the carto-graphical picture is taking on the character of a kaleidoscope. One hears of Cumberland, Westmorland, and the Furness area of Lancashire uniting as Cumbria, as it was named about 1,000 years ago. The present Tees-side entities in North Yorkshire and County Durham envisage themselves as an entirely new county, to be called Cleveland. But, as yet, the whole process is in the melting pot, awaiting government action. What is certain is that nearly all our current maps will have to be re-drawn.

In this book, however, it will be simpler throughout to use prevailing county names and references, and let who will shape the new bounda-ries and fashion fresh designations for them.

4

Matins and Vespers

> Dry-shod, o'er sands, twice every day,
> The pilgrims to the shrine find way;
> Twice every day the waves efface,
> Of staves and sandalled feet the trace.

Sir Walter Scott's words still ring true, even though most tourists, whether pilgrims or otherwise, now cross over to Holy Island (Lindisfarne) by car at low tide. My own first visit to this sacred spot off the Northumbrian coast was by pony and trap. 'Booner' Cromarty, one of the islanders, met my train at Beal station, on the mainland, and took me over the three-mile strip of water and sand to the place that is forever hallowed by the memory of Aidan and Cuthbert.

As we crossed the sands the 1,300 years since their sojourn here seemed as nothing. We were the only persons on that wide, gleaming strand. The kittiwakes and guillemots that greeted us, the cormorants, the pink-footed geese and so many other island birds, echoed the greeting known to those pioneers of Christianity. There were eider duck, too, which the islanders still name Cuddy's Duck with lingering affection. It had companioned Cuthbert during his lonely hours of vigil.

In recent years there have been several official pilgrimages to Holy Island. Sometimes they are organized by the Roman Catholic Church, sometimes by Anglicans. In 1935 Dr William Temple, Archbishop of York, led about 2,000 pilgrims on foot over the sands. On reaching the semi-ruined priory they assembled near the 'rainbow arch' to sing "For all the saints who from their labours rest . . .". A wonderful setting for such praise.

Once, however, my family and I witnessed a silent pilgrimage. A small group of nuns gathered on Beal shore, tucked up their habits and waded barefoot past the long line of guide posts to the hallowed spot. It was half tide and as they waded slowly forward their lips moved in prayer. Later we saw them again, kneeling at different places within the priory ruins. . . .

The original priory was destroyed by invading Danes, but although the present building is of Norman date, it is still redolent of Aidan and his successor, Cuthbert, who with their devoted followers evangelised much of Northern England. When Aidan had arrived here from Iona, in A.D. 635, no emblem of Christianity was to be seen in all Northumbria. In his *History of England*, G. M. Trevelyan refers to the "ascetic yet cheerful life of these ardent, lovable, unworldly apostles of the moorland, who tramped the heather all day to preach by the burnside at evening [and] won the hearts of the men of the North. Indeed, Christianity had never, since its earliest years, appeared in a more attractive guise."

Later, we shall see something of Cuthbert preaching on the mainland. Meanwhile, Lindisfarne Priory speaks through its warm, red stones of the monastic heritage to which everybody, believer and unbeliever alike, owes so much. Lindisfarne Priory has been called 'Durham Cathedral in miniature'. Here are the same huge pillars with chevron mouldings, the same bold arcading, the same thick walls that characterize Cuthbert's posthumous shrine at Durham. From the central tower of the Norman church only the so-called 'rainbow arch' survives, like a soaring dream, but the west doorway is still impressive with its arched hood of dog-tooth mouldings, flanked on each side by a couple of blind arches.

The sound of the sea and the screeching of gulls break the vast silences of time. When the monks were here, children's voices would add their little cadences as they received instruction at the school provided in the priory courtyard. Their stone bench still runs along the eastern wall.

In *Marmion*, Walter Scott injected his own brand of romance into this place, with Constance of Beverley immured alive in the watchtower for having broken her monastic vows. But at Lindisfarne Priory romance needs no such dubious spur. It is implicit in all one sees and senses—the romance of a piety and a skill that could produce the Lindisfarne Gospels,* that could soften pagan hearts and breathe a new

---

* This beautiful and priceless book, with Lindisfarne birds as part of the ornamentation, is now preserved at the British Museum.

spirit over the North. The romance, too, of Cuthbert's body, after his death, being carried around the North Country by his Congregation of monks, year upon year, until the final bourne was reached at Durham. . . .

No visit to Lindisfarne is complete without a moment or two spent on the tiny islet where Cuthbert sometimes withdrew from the main island for meditation. Bede referred to this rock, for it is little more, as "a place more distant from the monastery, surrounded on every side by the returning waves of the sea". Here, from amongst patches of sea-lavender, the scant foundations of Cuthbert's oratory take the rhythmic baptism of spume, and one thinks of the sea otters who, with their furry bodies, dried and warmed the good man's limbs after his nightly vigils offshore, nearby or at Farne Island, in the penitential waters. . . .

It is not necessary here to elaborate upon all the monasteries that have graced the North Country. But their number was legion, and in most instances they have left an eloquence, dimmed by the sound and fury of the intervening centuries, yet still softly vibrant for those with ears to hear and a sense of heritage.

The sea still echoes amongst the fragmentary walls of Tynemouth Priory, but the sea-borne traffic it overlooks from its sandstone cliff has changed. Repeatedly the Danes hove to in their serpent-prowed vessels and ransacked the place. In A.D. 865 they set fire to the building and several nuns who had fled from Hartlepool to Tynemouth for safety were "translated by martyrdom to Heaven". Rebuilding only served to attract the pirate ships once more; they seemed to forge an unerring path through the coastal mists.

Today, from the battered priory, ships laden with merchandise can be seen peaceably sailing away or coming home again, and sailors still use the priory as a sea-mark. The priory's fortified headland no longer stirs with martial echoes. Yet Tynemouth Priory has witnessed much during its 1,300 years; much of the human story with its finest aspirations and deepest woe. Perhaps there is a special future dispensation for those who toiled and kept faith in such vulnerable outposts. Yet comparatively few monasteries were left unscathed by one foe or another, and none fully escaped the Great Pillage of the Dissolution engineered by Henry VIII.

Take Brinkburn Priory, enclosed by a loop of the River Coquet, not far from Rothbury. 'On the brink of the burn'—so it was named. The Augustinian canons could not have found a more delightful spot for their order in all Northumberland. And peaceful too.

I remember walking that way once in a storm. A curtain of rain fell around the old pile, and the surrounding trees, thick like a mantle, enveloped everything. Only the rain, and the splashing river and an occasional bird broke the silence. I felt quite envious of the brotherhood who first settled here in the twelfth century.

Yet even this Eden was not safe. It was so well concealed within its leafy bower that a party of marauding Scots missed it on their first reconnoitre. The canons rang their bells for joy—but too soon! Thick foliage might hide a 'plum' like Brinkburn, but *sound* travels. Turning on their tracks, the Scots followed the jubilant peal and made full amends for their initial oversight. The priory was sacked and then set on fire. The canons had to rebuild.

When J. M. W. Turner came along, early in the nineteenth century, the ruins he saw and painted were the aftermath of another menace—the Dissolution. In 1858, however, the place was restored by Thomas Austin for the Cadogan family. Dr Pevsner regards the restoration as "archaeologically almost entirely reliable". If William Bertram, who had founded the priory 700 years before, could see the restored building with its lancetted chancel, vaulted transept aisles, and late Norman carving, he would miss the black-robed canons at their offices, but otherwise he could rest, satisfied, that his God is still worshipped here in a fitting shrine.

At Blanchland, also, according to an old story, the Premonstratensian, or white, canons were too precipitate when the Scots were prowling in the neighbourhood. Their abbey basked in a fold of the moors, a few miles south of Hexham. Trees would probably hide this little hive of activity from all sides, but it was a mist descending on Grey Friars Hill, between Blanchland and Stanhope, that traditionally led the Scots astray when searching for monastic booty that day. And they might have gone off empty-handed, but for the sound of bells—abbey bells which the monks in their joy had started ringing because of their deliverance! But this story has been applied rather differently. It was another set of marauders, Henry VIII's commissioners, some say, who had floundered in the mist. Sent round in 1535 to assess the prospective monastic spoils, their first approach to lonely Blanchland was foiled by this exasperating moorland mist, which can descend like a blanket or roll along the ground like so many wraiths. If only those bells had kept silent a bit longer!

But in one sense the Dissolution of the Monasteries brought a blessing to Blanchland. The abbey church and other buildings fell into ruin, true, and the canons were scattered. Yet out of the chaos the present village of Blanchland was created. The village church is the choir where the canons sang their praises. The abbot's house is now the village inn. The canons' refectory became a row of mellowed cottages, and the Warder's Gate houses a shop. Blanchland went through the fire but has been born again.

Hexham Priory began as a Saxon cathedral, built with stone from Corstopitum nearly 300 years after the Romans had departed. Roman inscriptions strike an odd note in this place, especially in the crypt, which has an altar to Manopus embedded in the masonry, also an inscription originally bearing the names of Emperor Severus and his two sons, Caracalla and Geta; Geta's name was erased after Caracalla had murdered him out of jealousy.

The atmosphere of Lindisfarne is in this priory, not only because in A.D. 684 Cuthbert had been offered the Bishopric of Hexham (afterwards exchanged for that of Lindisfarne), but because Wilfrid, who built the Saxon church about 675–80, had spent part of his boyhood in the missionary school at Lindisfarne. Another thing that influenced Wilfrid during his youth was the sight of so much surviving evidence of the Roman occupation before the Dark Ages set in. Perhaps he had played amongst some of the ruined camps of Northumbria, and listened to tales of Roman prowess that had drifted down the centuries. After studying at Canterbury he spent a few years in the Imperial City and on the Continent, in the company of another youth, Benedict Biscop, filling his head with grand ideas which later fructified in this Church of St Andrew at Hexham. His biographer, Eddius, stated that no church this side of the Alps could compare with it.

This, then, was the splendid cathedral church which sprang up, stone by Roman stone, beside the River Tyne. But in A.D. 875 the Danes pounced again. They drove out all the inhabitants, of monastery and town alike, and left a trail of fire which reduced Wilfrid's temple of God to heaps of smouldering ruins. Of all that magnificence, only the crypt remained intact. Wilfrid's stone throne, or Frith Stool, now stands above the entrance to this underground oratory, and in the south transept a tall cross, showing many signs of mutilation, commemorates Acca (709–33) who succeeded Wilfrid as bishop and befriended Bede in his lonely cell at Jarrow.

In 1113 the church became a priory for the Austin Canons, but the Scots were now the trouble-makers; the priory bore repeated marks of their visitations. The final blow, at the Dissolution, might not have been so severe if the canons had surrendered peaceably. Instead, they turned the priory into a garrison and armed people from the surrounding country came to their support. But disaster was only staved off for a short time. Eventually, Henry's commissioners triumphed. The prior, or sub-prior, was hanged at the priory gate and some of the more aggressive canons seem to have fallen into the Duke of Norfolk's hands and "were tied up".

Yet Hexham still has its lovely priory church. Thoroughly restored in recent times, it has become, once again, one of the finest churches in English Christendom.

Coast, moorland and riverside have thus provided the setting for monastic reverie and service, but at Alnwick there is a complete change of venue. Hulne Priory stands within a thick stone palisade on the summit of a hill in Alnwick Park. The hill is supposed to remind one of Mount Carmel in the Holy Land. From the flat meadows bordering the quiescent River Aln, one climbs up the grassy hill and enters by a gate in the wall where a monk carved in stone seems to be debating some point of doctrine. He and other cowled figures only date, however, from the time (*circa* 1771) when the first Duke of Northumberland erected a Gothick summer-house within this sacred enclosure. Perhaps the Duke wished to re-people the place—if only in effigy—with a few Carmelite monks to represent those who first established themselves in this charming spot about 1240. A pele tower erected about 1480 in the same, warm enclave suggests defensive preparations against the Scots. Whenever I have been up there, nothing more disturbing than a few children's voices broke the long silence. A monastery on a hill: to the youngsters it was half-way to Heaven.

Shap Abbey, the only monastic house in Westmorland, retains little of a special nature apart from its west tower in a fold of the hills. A forlorn requiem for a place begun by Premonstratensian canons with high hopes late in the twelfth century. Other abbeys had their granges in this county, however, and the Benedictine monks of St Mary's Abbey at York were responsible for the wooden bridge that preceded the present stone one over the Lune at Kirkby Lonsdale.

From a monastic point of view, Cumberland was better endowed, with beautiful monasteries at Carlisle, Lanercost, St Bees and Calder.

Carlisle Priory surrendered its church to the cathedral in 1133, but continued to function until the Dissolution. Priory and cathedral provide a rather tangled story, almost as tangled as Border history itself with Scottish raids adding their quota of destruction and confusion, but the two religious houses merged effectively when the last prior, Lancelot Salkeld, became the first dean. Salkeld erected a fine Renaissance screen in the north aisle, while his monastic predecessor, Prior Christopher Slee, built a gateway near the deanery. Though rather worn, the gateway inscription still begs visitors to pray for Slee's soul.

It seems probable that some of the darker stone of the Norman building, which offsets the red sandstone of later times, came from Hadrian's Wall. St Cuthbert was shown the Roman ruins and a splendid Roman fountain when he came here in 685. I wonder whether he would also see some of the Roman items that are now in Carlisle Museum—especially the tombstone showing a lady with her pet bird? Some authorities believe that Cuthbert founded a monastery in the town, which, along with fifteen miles of the surrounding countryside, was then presented to him. As we shall see later, such gifts were not uncommon. In the same year, Crayke in North Yorkshire was given to him as a resting place while journeying between Lindisfarne and York.

During that sojourn at Carlisle, did Cuthbert gaze longingly towards Scotland and sigh for the Lammermuir Hills, away to the north-east? He had been a shepherd boy there before training at Melrose Abbey for the missionary life. He had loved those early days, between Tweed and Forth. And here he was, now, on the English side of the Border, moving men's hearts with his sublime message as he trudged over the fells. . . .

Lanercost Priory was also built beside the ruins of Hadrian's Wall, though a few miles east of Carlisle and having the River Irthing for company. An altar to Jupiter is embedded in the masonry, but 1,000 years had passed since this god was considered "best and greatest", for Lanercost was born of Norman patronage, about 1166. The nave of the priory church has become the parish church, and very fine it is, with various tombs and wall monuments doing their best to remind us of different members of the Dacre family who acquired the place after the Dissolution. Sir Thomas Dacre turned the west range of the monastic quarters into a house for himself. From his windows he could look down upon the old cloisters, and a pele tower where the prior had lived in as much safety as could be expected of this turbulent area. In another pele tower, now the vicarage, Edward I is said to have slept (if he did sleep!) before going off to hammer the Scots. Retribution soon came. In 1311 Robert the Bruce sacked the priory because Edward had stayed there. King David of Scotland followed suit in 1346, stealing the abbey treasure as a further reprisal and reducing the building "into nothingness".

When the monks of Holme Cultram Abbey, between Carlisle and Silloth, were threatened with closure, at the Reformation, their twelfth-century nave (now the parish church of Abbey Town) was spared because it afforded some refuge and protection when the Scots came swooping over the Solway.

St Bees is lower down the coast, near Whitehaven. The Benedictine monks of St Mary's, York, evidently felt reasonably safe in building a priory here, about 1120, for the Border was far to the north and Danish raids were a thing of the past. It was the Danes who, in the tenth century, had destroyed the nunnery whose founder the monks wished to commemorate. She was St Bega, an Irish princess of the seventh century who had determined to devote her life to the sick and poor. Her father scouted the idea and summarily betrothed her to a Norwegian prince. She escaped her father's vigilance, however, and sailed across to Cumberland, carrying with her a bracelet she claimed to have received from an angel. The bracelet was a token of her pledge to live as a nun and help others. Part of this story is doubtless mythical, but the nunnery was certainly established, slightly inland from St Bees Headland, about A.D. 650, and became the inspiration for the fine parish church of today, with its fascinating mixture of Norman, Early English and Victorian architecture.

Calder Abbey, still farther down the Cumberland coast—yet *not* beyond the range of the insatiable Scots, despite the optimism shown by the monks of St Bees—had a strange parentage. It was founded in 1134 and colonized by monks from Furness Abbey. Soon after, the Scots arrived! The brethren hastily returned to Furness but, finding no welcome there, Abbot Gerald and twelve monks trailed over hill and dale to North Yorkshire and founded the first Byland Abbey. Ill-luck was still with them. Because of disagreement with the monks of neighbouring Rievaulx Abbey about the clashing of their respective bells, a new site had to be sought. They wandered around for thirty years and at length settled beneath the Hambleton Hills, near present-day Coxwold.

Meanwhile, Calder Abbey was colonized afresh, and the cause prospered, resulting in the Cistercian edifice one sees today while going the roundabout way, via Ennerdale and Egremont, to Wastwater. A fine, if difficult, country for grazing monastic flocks.

Now Furness Abbey (1127) grew rich on its flocks and other produce. Some of the herds were grazed as far afield as Hardknott Pass. The fleeces were actually exported from the monks' fortified depot on Piel Island. The monks built their own ships, and Walney Island became their iron foundry. The abbey, at the centre of all this activity, enjoyed a certain glamour in being sited at Bekansgill, or the 'Vale of the Deadly Nightshade', a little way out of modern Barrow. Indeed, it is from one of the abbey's many granges that Barrow, the shipping and industrial centre of today, has developed.

Even now, the ruined Furness Abbey—second only in extent to Fountains in Yorkshire—sufficiently indicates its former influence and wealth. The abbey was powerful enough to forget its monastic ideals and raise an army, comprising 400 cavalry and 800 infantry, which fought at Flodden! At Dalton, nearby, a castle was built as an outer defence in case of attack. The abbot was his own monarch and the Furness peninsula his kingdom. And what a kingdom it was, with water on three sides, the long, narrow island of Walney as seaward defence, and Piel Island with its Norman keep conveniently placed at the mouth of Walney Channel.

A warm glow seems to envelope the abbey itself, for soft red sandstone went to its making. William Wordsworth and George Romney would both see the place before modern industry began to encroach. Wordsworth's beloved Duddon Valley opens into the estuary north of Barrow, while Romney—born at neighbouring Dalton—painted his juvenile pictures hereabouts before going south to fame and fortune. But Furness Abbey is still a delight and a place one could write sonnets about. Trees throw a thick curtain around the precincts; in autumn the foliage seems part of the very fabric. Norman arches recede from the cloister, a fifteenth-century belfry rises silently aloft, and the monastic church stretches out for 275 feet, like an endless chant. A closer look reveals something of its inner beauty—soaring arches, a row of lancet windows, a carved head with flowing tresses, and, best of all, the fifteenth-century sedilia with stone canopies as delicate as lace. And through the green places a little stream wriggles along with its faint water music towards the sea.

To reach Cartmel from Furness one no longer needs to cross the perilous sands of Morecambe Bay. The coast-road passes through Aldingham, where Cuthbert's body was rested during that long peregrination; skirts the modernized Conishead Priory; and then loops round the Leven estuary to link up with another road bordered with trees and wild flowers. It is a fitting approach to the priory that for so long kept watch and ward over the Kent Sands and provided the guide service already mentioned.

The Cartmel given to St Cuthbert by King Egfrith of Northumbria, was probably administered by a reeve from Lindisfarne. And it has grown old gracefully. A preaching cross stands in the square opposite the priory gatehouse (now an artist's studio), and swans parade the tiny River Eea as it prattles towards the priory. When the bells ring here, the old peaceful order seems to creep stealthily upon one. . . .

Yet this is part of Lancashire "across the Sands"; part of the domain which Robert Bruce's army overran in 1322, as recorded only too accurately in the Lanercost Chronicle. Translated from the Latin the account reads:

The King [Edward I] mustered an army in order to approach Scotland . . . hearing which Robert de Brus invaded England with an army by way of Carlisle . . . and plundered the monastery of Holme Cultrum . . . and then proceeded to waste and plunder Copeland and so beyond the sands of Duddon, to Furness.

But the Abbot of Furness went to meet him and paid ransoms for the district of Furness that it should not be again burnt or plundered, and [brave man!] took him to Furness Abbey. Notwithstanding, the Scots set fire to several places and lifted spoil.

Also they went further beyond the sands of Leven to Cartmell, and burnt the lands round the Priory of the Black Canons, taking away cattle and spoil. And so they crossed the sands of Kent, as far as the town of Lancaster, which they burnt. . . .

Cartmel's peace, therefore, was not inviolable. And there was always that dread responsibility for safe conduct of travellers over the treacherous Kent Sands. Many perished and were buried in the priory churchyard. Even as late as 1820 a plan was evolved for erecting raised wooden platforms as places of refuge across the Kent Sands. Actual records of these refuges seem to be absent, but I cannot help wondering whether the idea originated from the wooden refuges, reached by fixed ladders, which still punctuate the tidal crossing from Beal to Cuthbert's Lindisfarne.

Externally, the most striking feature of Cartmel Priory is its belfry. This is set corner-wise on the low, supporting tower. Fortunately, at the Dissolution, the 'Town Choir' was spared, for, as the local people argued, this was their own place of worship. Because of those protests, over 400 years ago, we can now enjoy some of the splendid monastic furnishings, in particular, the carved choir stalls. Enclosed on three sides by a fine seventeenth-century oak screen given by George Preston of Holker Hall nearby, the stall misericords betray their medieval carvers in almost hilarious mood. Even sacred themes are given playful treatment, as when the Trinity appears as a kingly person with three curly-bearded heads. The two side heads seem to be looking askance at the surrounding pleasantries—a mermaid preening herself with comb and mirror, a satanic dragon, three dogs chasing a deer, and a few comic devils.

Several miles south of Morecambe, Cockersand Abbey once stood with its feet almost in the sea. I like to think that flocks of dunlin might then have performed their curious aerobatics there, above the sandy beach, as they do across the Lune at Sunderland Point. From the point I have sometimes gazed over the Lune, hoping to catch a glimpse of this old abbey. But history was against me. The closure under Henry VIII had been too thorough, though the thirteenth-century chapter house still survives like a ghost from the past, and the canopied stalls have taken their exquisite beauty to the Priory Church at Lancaster.

Whalley Abbey, near Clitheroe, has fared better than many others. Entering by an imposing gateway, you find yourself first in a lovely courtyard, fragrant with flowers. Tall trees grow there like stately pillars, and a flight of steps leads upwards, invitingly, but no longer to the monks' dormitory. For ruin fell upon the place, after the Reformation, yet not so completely as to debar further occupation. The last abbot, John Paslew, must have paced this courtyard in deep thought before deciding to join the Pilgrimage of Grace. For this he was later hung, drawn and quartered at Lancaster. But the abbot's lodging is lived in once more, and the cellarer's building, roofed afresh, provides a conference hall for Roman Catholics. The carved woodwork in which the monks took such delight, survives in several places. The stalls can be seen in Whalley parish church; and a reredos replete with saints and mitred abbots, along with some curious stained glass, in Browsholme Hall.

Both Whalley Abbey and Church figure repeatedly in Harrison Ainsworth's romance, *The Lancashire Witches*. Richard Assheton, one of two local gentry who had helped to suppress the Pilgrimage of Grace, later acquired part of the abbey for his own use. Hence the curse on the Asshetons, to the effect that any of the family who chanced to stand on Paslew's (supposed) grave in Whalley Church, would die within a twelvemonth.

William Trafford, Abbot of Sawley, Whalley's neighbour, suffered the same fate as John Paslew and for the same 'offence'. Yet whereas Whalley Abbey has found new life and purpose, Sawley has crumbled to a mere figment of its former glory. There is no justice in these things! One can saunter in the shades of Whalley and read its past with little difficulty. At Sawley, on the contrary, one has to search diligently for anything more than its couple of roadside arches. Yet the abbey had had its great days and must have felt very important when one of its monks, William de Rymington, who was also Chancellor of Oxford, openly opposed John Wycliffe and his reforming views. The fragmentary ruins here at Sawley seem to show who got the better of the argument.

I have beside me a map that indicates the chief monastic sites in Yorkshire after the Norman Conquest. There are over eighty! Today, most of them are known only to students of history and a few antiquaries. Because of their extensive remains, others are bywords amongst modern tourists. Their very names ring like poetry: Fountains, Jervaulx, Mount Grace, Rievaulx, Byland, Kirkham, Roche, Kirkstall, Easby, Egglestone. To enjoy the appeal of Bolton Priory, sequestered in a loop of the River Wharfe; Whitby Abbey, high among the circling gulls on its sea-cliff; or St Mary's Abbey in the heart of York, one needs nothing but a mind attuned to sacred architecture, and a pair of sound, exploratory legs. Each place strikes deep chords of time, so that at Fountains, say, one can overhear (through modern artifice) the monks singing their own composition, the *Ave Mundi Rosa;* and at Whitby (with the aid of a carved stone cross) Caedmon's Song of Creation. At St Mary's, York, the piety and buffoonery of the Mystery Plays, probably written here in medieval times and now being performed again—to vast audiences— are helping to demonstrate just one more phase of England's undying monastic heritage.

Let us saunter in the grounds of St Mary's Abbey. All the life of modern York is shut off, so that one can enter into the spirit of a Benedictine house, founded nearly 900 years ago by William Rufus.

Beautiful trees and flowering shrubs now cast their shade on lawns that hide some of the abbey foundations. But one almost complete wall of the abbey church still stands, braced at the east end by a massive arch with clustered columns. It is in this corner that, every third year, the

(*above*) A wild boar emblem of the
20th Roman Legion, found at
Corbridge. (*right*) A playing-card
map from a set made in 1676 by
Robert Morden

Fountains Abbey, Yorkshire: looking north-east into the presbytery

revived Mystery Plays are re-enacted. The centre window of that wall becomes the Eye of Heaven. God appears there in majesty with his angels; first at the Creation of Man, then at intervals as Man—on the green sward below—goes through many of the incidents related in the Bible. The impact is tremendous, especially as night falls and the various figures become lustrous with concealed lighting. Here, one feels, is Man's pitiful story in a nutshell. The glorious beginning, with Adam made in God's image, and then the Fall, until Christ appears like a shaft of Heaven's own light.

Medieval outlook and humour inform these plays, but their deeper spiritual content is paramount. The crowds who gather to see them usually go away strangely subdued. Forms and beliefs may change with time, but Man's dilemma remains. . . .

Some remarkable finds made in these abbey grounds are now accommodated in the adjoining museum. It is a natural step from St Mary's to Fountains. In 1132 a small band of monks seceded from St Mary's and helped to found this Cistercian house farther north, near Ripon. And from very humble beginnings the Fountains brotherhood fashioned an abbey which became one of the chief pearls of the Cistercian movement.

Its alternating story of holy poverty, piety, public service, wealth and power is implicit in much of the monastery that visitors now see, despite partial ruin. There are guest houses for rich and poor; the usual infirmary for sick and aged monks, also a stone bench in the cloisters where, at Easter, the abbot would follow Christ's example and wash the feet of his brethren. The cellarium is a long, low building where foodstuffs, produce from the extensive abbey farms, and agricultural tools were stored. Here, too, the lay brothers could take some exercise or listen to the River Skell flowing beneath, echoing the deeper tones of one of their psalms. Today, the cellarium's vaulted roof, supported by central pillars like branching trees, excites everybody, especially architects. Huge Norman pillars stand like stalwarts of the Faith down each side of the monastic church and, beyond, the Chapel of the Nine Altars sends its slender arches up to the skies.

But there is also a four-storeyed tower, which no Cistercian monastery should have. Though shiningly beautiful in itself, and Perpendicular in style, it marks a complete departure from Cistercian simplicity. Marmaduke Huby, the abbot who built it as much for his own glory as his Maker's, lived in personal comfort and prestige; his successors lived to see the monastery fall to Layton and Legh, two of Henry VIII's sour commissioners.

Again one must remark upon the fine setting of these Yorkshire monasteries. Fountains resides in a wooded hollow watered by the Skell and flanked by crags which yielded the abbey masons their first

6

stone. Jervaulx is laved by the Ure, in a quiet reach of Wensleydale. Kirkstall—a daughter house of Fountains—still manages to give industrial Leeds something of the beauty that inspired J. M. W. Turner, and prompted the Reverend Patrick Brontë to write a poem on the place while he was courting Maria Branwell.

At Kirkham, near Malton, the River Derwent can now reflect little of the Augustinian priory founded here in 1122-30; all too little, and yet the richly-carved entrance gateway invites one to stand and ponder and walk beyond to what is left of the chapter house, then to the refectory doorway—surely as perfect today as when Walter L'Espec was still mourning the loss of his son. While out hunting, the youth fell from his horse and was killed. The priory is his memorial. One of the modern windows in Helmsley Church, towards Pickering, illustrates the story with verve, colour and imagination.

A tour of the Yorkshire monasteries ensures that one sees the most enchanting parts of the county. Roche, almost on the southern border, is still an oasis of serenity, with the almost inevitable stream gliding along, past gatehouse, transepts and cloister and, in spring, a host of daffodils. From Guisborough, in the north-east, almost everything has gone from sight except the huge east wall of the priory church, a charming dovecot, and an enclave of trees, mostly limes, arranged in the shape of a coffin. A lofty chestnut tree, at one end, has lifted its bright candles, century after century, beside this burial place of the monks.

And so one could go on, still finding enrichment for mind and soul in such places. For sheer, stark romance I myself would always turn to Whitby, where St Hilda, the first abbess, transformed the snakes that once infested the East Cliff, her domain, into stone—hence the ammonites still found on the beach below! If the story seems fanciful, one can only blame the 1,300 years that have intervened since Hilda came with her small community to this cliff-top far above the crashing waves, where sea mists moved about like phantoms.

For quietude and a sense of reverence I would turn to Bolton Priory in Wharfedale (but *not* on bank holidays!) and walk again down that sublime nave which frames the landscape in its shorn windows. For a touch of austerity, Mount Grace would be my choice, for this was a Carthusian priory where each monk lived alone in his cell and tended his own garden plot. Some of those cells, though now open to the sky, are otherwise intact, even to the food hatch, beside the door, that gave him no glimpse of the server. Each monk was virtually a hermit. But for *everything* that a monastery represented—beauty, serenity, peace, toil, worship, prayer—who need go farther than Rievaulx?

Walter L'Espec, whom we encountered at Kirkham, gave land in Ryedale for the building of this abbey, the first Cistercian house in

Yorkshire (1132). Aelred, the third abbot, describes this Norman knight for us. He was "passing tall, with black hair and long flowing beard. His forehead was wide and noble and his eyes large and bright. His voice was like the sound of a trumpet." In 1151 this aged warrior, whose ancestors had come over with the Conqueror, expressed a desire

> For time enough to make my peace with God,
> And train my soul for better things.

This he did by entering Rievaulx Abbey as a novice—a novice amongst 140 monks and 600 lay brothers. He died there while gratifying his desire, about two years later, and was buried within Aelred's 'holy mansion'.

The later developments of this 'holy mansion', which was also a Cistercian mission centre, blessed from the start by Bernard of Clairvaulx, gave us the glorious place we see today in a kind of earthly Elysium. Not even Fountains can quite provide the same blissful shock. Half hidden amongst wooded hills, it is the Shangri La of English monasteries—an impression even enhanced if the abbey first breaks upon your vision from the Terrace, which an obliging landowner created for this very purpose in the eighteenth century.

Yet it was indeed an *earthly* Elysium—not proof against disaster. The Scots—referred to by one contemporary as "satellites of Satan, unmindful of salvation"—avenged their defeat at Bannockburn by taking their toll of Rievaulx and other northern abbeys. Then, in 1349, the Black Death carried off their abbot, Richard II. The final blow was delivered by Henry VIII. To some extent, however, Henry was here *deprived* of spoil. Much of the lead melted from the roofs and then cast into ingots, ready for despatch, was either forgotten or deliberately hidden beneath debris at the west end of the nave. These ingots, each bearing the royal seal, lay there for almost 400 years, only being discovered about 1920 when the Office of Works (now included in the Department of the Environment) started to reclaim the extensive abbey ruins from further decay. Five of the ingots were given to York Minster for the re-leading of the famous Five Sisters Window, one went to the British Museum, and one is kept in the small though fascinating museum in the grounds of the parent abbey.

Out there in the sunshine stand the monastic church and choir, the refectory and other claustral buildings, all pathetically roofless, yet still impressive in size, form and graceful outline. But that little museum hut in the grounds also cherishes much that should be seen. It contains monastic jokes carved in stone; other pleasantries, like the farmer taking a pannier-load of corn, on his horse, to be ground at the mill; also the keystone—carved with the Lamb of God—of a shrine still standing in the chapter house. The shrine is believed to be that of William, first abbot of Rievaulx, he who had been sent over by Bernard of Clairvaulx to set alight the Cistercian torch in Yorkshire.

Was it entirely by chance that the modern Abbey of St Lawrence rooted itself at Ampleforth, in this same hallowed part of Yorkshire? The French monks who found refuge on this site at the time of the Revolution must have been doubly grateful to their benefactor, Ann Fairfax of Gilling (across the valley), for Ampleforth is roughly at the centre of a ring of ancient monasteries. Perhaps Rievaulx, Byland, Newburgh, Kirkham and Fountains, despite their occasional short-comings, had between them bestowed a spiritual aura on the neigh-bourhood? Some philosophers assure us that *nothing* ever dies!

Nothing really dies! This became truly apparent during the industrial depression of the 1930s. Commander Clare Vyner and Lady Doris Vyner of Fountains Hall, which is built largely from parts of the adjoin-ing abbey, launched the Fountains Abbey Settlers' Society. This move-ment provided for the training of youths in gardening, farming and forestry. The youths lived in a specially prepared camp above the ruins of the abbey which, in its heyday, had fostered the same pursuits. Some of those lads came from Jarrow, one of the worst affected towns in the Great Depression, The Settlers' Society was surely a flowering of the seed sown, in a spirit of service for others, by the first Cistercians of Fountains.

But there was another and much older monastic link. At Jarrow, long before the shipyard era, there had been a monastery where Bede studied and prayed and wrote his many books. The Jarrow lads trained at Fountains must often have seen St Paul's Church and a few other remains from that Saxon monastery, where Bede himself had been trained while yet a boy.

Bede spent practically all his life between the monasteries at Jarrow and Monkwearmouth. He is commemorated in St Peter's Church, the only surviving relic of Monkwearmouth monastery, by a stone cross with carvings that illustrate various episodes of his life, such as the eager boy first arriving at the gate of Jarrow monastery, the scholar writing his *Historia Ecclesiastica*, and the dying man translating with his last breath the final verses of St John's Gospel. I have a special interest in this cross, for it was carved by my old sculptor friends, the Milburns, under the shadow of York Minster.

Bede died at Jarrow, but many years later his remains were put with those of Cuthbert and interred at Durham Cathedral. Eventually the two saints were parted, Bede being given a fairly plain tomb in the Galilee Chapel, and Cuthbert a shrine behind the High Altar.

This chapter began with Cuthbert's time on Lindisfarne and ends with his final bourne at Durham. Between the two nodal points there had been that long, faithful procession through various parts of the North Country in search of a permanent home for the beloved leader.

Carrying his body and a few precious relics in a wooden coffin, Cuthbert's Congregation wandered for seven years through Lancashire, Westmorland and Yorkshire, and then came to Chester-le-Street. The body rested there for over a century. When the Danes became active again, the quest was resumed.

During this second phase of the protracted journey, the Congregation is said to have been made aware, by the long-deceased saint, of the actual destination he desired. Its name was given as Dunholme. None of the monks had ever heard of it. Then, one of them happened to overhear a milkmaid tell her companion that the lost cow she sought had been seen heading for Dunholme. Hence according to the old tradition, which it would be churlish to doubt, an errant cow was instrumental in leading the monks to the chosen place: Dunholme, the 'island hill', now known as Durham.

The monastery and cathedral which gradually grew up on this peninsula, formed by a sharp bend of the River Wear, now provide one of the finest sights in Europe. Guide-books must be left to recount its story in detail, but some features tell their own story: the majestic Norman church with its rotund pillars supporting a stone vault; zigzag arches that bound like choppy waves along the roof of the Galilee Chapel; the sanctuary knocker, resembling the head of a dragon, at the north door; cloisters where children of the present diocese sometimes enact episodes from the life of Cuthbert; the Prior's Kitchen overlooking College Green with benevolent regard for the inner man and still furnished, inside, with smoke-jacks, roasting spits, and fish-kettle. Then, not least, there is the monks' fourteenth-century dormitory, still roofed with rough-hewn timbers from the prior's woods at Beaurepaire.

Within this dormitory and its annexe, called the Loft, the life of the old monastery becomes palpable. But first one must see the Cuthbert relics brought from Lindisfarne so long ago. Here is his pectoral cross of gold studded with garnets. Perhaps one can imagine it swinging on his chest and catching the sunlight as he strode over the Northumbrian moors and fells during his preaching missions. When found in 1827 it was hidden on the saint's body beneath three thicknesses of silk wrappings. What may have been his portable altar is also here: a small square of oak plated with silver. Nobody seems sure, today, whether another treasure, the ivory comb, actually belonged to Cuthbert, though it could have been used for dressing his hair and beard on ritual occasions. The vestments are of later date, though still over 1,000 years old. I seem to recall a few sea-birds worked into one of the needlework designs. Certainly, the song of the sea is in this place, though for its hearing one needs to be attuned to the epic story of Cuthbert, as performed today by those children in the cloister garth.

In one of their mimed scenes a boat leaves Lindisfarne with a coffin placed across the thwarts. The original coffin is in the Loft, beside the other relics. Made about A.D. 698 specially for the purpose, it carried Cuthbert's remains and all those treasures on that long trek through the northern shires. Though now in fragments, the coffin still bears incised representations of Our Lord, the Virgin and Child, and several saints and apostles, together with a litany. It is amazing to think of this very reliquary being carried by the monks through our northern valleys, across the sands of Morecambe Bay, and being rested at such places as Aldingham, Kentmere, Crayke, Ripon and Chester-le-Street, before Cuthbert reached journey's end 'until the resurrection' here at Durham.

Beneath the huge rafters of the main dormitory, fashioned by Bishop Walter Skirlaw, another story unfolds. It recalls the first group of monks, under Bishop Aldhun. Although following the Benedictine rule up to a point, they were allowed to marry and rear a family. When William de Saint Carileph came on the scene, in 1081, he objected to this arrangement and gave the monks an option. They could remain in the monastery if they renounced their wives and children. Otherwise they must depart. Only one accepted his terms. The rest were scattered and the memorials of their predecessors destroyed or buried as if to efface their memory. Carileph then replaced those stalwarts, still known as the Congregation of St Cuthbert, with monks from Jarrow and Monkwearmouth. Some of the despised memorials were recovered last century and are now displayed, like so many "prodigals", in the old dormitory (see also page 187).

Lower down the River Wear, 3 miles from Durham, a monk named Godric established a hermitage, which became the present priory, with the blessing of Ranulph Flambard, who succeeded the clean-sweeping Carileph as Bishop of Durham. A mighty man, this Flambard, and a great builder. His signet ring is preserved at Durham, and his pastoral staff. But I like to think of him perhaps forgetting his expansive schemes and his personal dignity, on occasion, and seeking momentary peace where the waters of the Wear flow beside Finchale.

5

Sermons in Stones

MANY of our older cathedrals and parish churches began as monastic foundations. Some still bear the older name. Selby Abbey on the west bank of the Yorkshire Ouse is really a monastic church that survived the Dissolution. The same applies to Malton Priory and Bolton Priory, and to those already mentioned at Carlisle and Cartmel. They form a bridge between pre-Reformation and post-Reformation times, between monk and parson, or wherever the watershed variously occurred. Chaucer's "poor parson" who was "riche . . . in holy thoght and word" would fit into both dispensations, though of course some churches have come through from very early times, unscathed by the Reformation.

I shall not attempt to cover all the abbeys, cathedrals and churches in our area, but simply give a brief picture of my own favourites, for the English church is inseparable from the English scene, visually and for deeper reasons too. A man can even be a professed atheist and yet have a high regard for church architecture (if it is good) and for the fine setting of a place like St Mary's, on its cliff-top at Whitby, the little fane amongst limestone outcrops on Cartmel Fell, or even of such a homely Quaker meeting house as the one that secretes itself beside the River Rawthey at Brigflatts, near Sedbergh.

Nowhere in the North is there a finer monastic cathedral than that at Durham. Its lordly position overlooking the River Wear has sent many people—writers, artists and others—into rhapsodies. It almost spans the neck of the peninsula and seems to spring from the rock on which it stands; but as a wide belt of trees, when in foliage, hides the rock from view on the western side, the impression is given of a vast cathedral resting on a frieze of greenery, with the river far below. Daffodils clothe the banks in springtime, and the erstwhile water-mill—once dedicated, along with its neighbour mill across the river, to the Jesus Altar in the cathedral—now serves meals for those with a taste for the romance of history.

During the last war, when cathedral towns became as vulnerable to aerial attack as centres of industry, I was sent post-haste to Durham. As photographer to the National Buildings Record, it was my job to record almost every feature of the cathedral and its precincts, so that in the event of damage, architects would have a detailed visual guide for eventual repair or reconstruction.*

Several weeks and nearly 200 photographs were needed for this urgent task. During that perilous time, visitors would come from a distance to see whether the 'dear old cathedral' was still intact! Some days I would overhear Dean Alington using the occasion to show them round the huge building and speak of its continuing place in the life of English people. His serene imperturbability, just then, must have been one of the finest things from which those visitors profited.

To walk through the cathedral with my camera, and the resident architect's keys in my pocket, was a stirring experience. Those keys opened up unique vistas: from the fine triforium arches into the ribbed roof vault; from the central tower gallery down into the Norman nave and transepts; from the clerestory gallery of the thirteenth-century Nine Altars Chapel on to the feretory platform that supports Cuthbert's shrine and the stones on which pilgrims once knelt in prayer; from the roof of the Slype—where a group of faces one might have seen in the old narrow streets of medieval Durham, were carved in stone—into the silent cloisters, and so on. From one of my exalted viewpoints I could admire Prior Castell's clock afresh; that lofty fourteenth-century clock, with its multiple dials, which fills one end of the south transept and, through its painted doors, admits the choristers on their way to the choir for evensong.

One event I did not see, from any angle, was the Bishop of Durham ascending to his throne, the highest throne in Christendom. As James Wall says, in his fine book on the cathedral, this "bishopp's seate", erected by Bishop Hatfield in the fourteenth century, "is but a reflection of the conditions under which it was built, for the bishop was also

* Luckily, there was no damage at Durham.

a Count Palatine, and his throne represents the secular dignity of the head of the palatinate, as well as his spiritual eminence."

The Selby Abbey Rolls contain many curious entries, some of them being records of payments made to various persons for services rendered. From the fifteenth century, for example, one reads the following:

to Robert [the] Hunter for his trouble in catching rabbits and partridges at Crowle [North Lincolnshire], 2s; to William Swallow and others with him bringing fish by water from Crowle to Selby, 3s 4d; to John Watton, bringing the Lord Abbot a ferret, 12d; to a man bringing 2 fish called grampus from York, 20d; to the servant of Thomas Smith of Lound, driving one boar to Selby, given to the Lord Abbot by him, 12d; to a certain servant at Fryston bringing 2 herons to the Lord Abbott, 20d; to the son of John Burnhill, bringing to the Lord Abbott a fawn from Crowle on the eve of the Ascension, 8d.

The wide range of the abbot's domain, and the kind of sport and food he enjoyed, are here amply suggested. When, 500 years later (in 1935) a garden was planted within the abbey churchyard, some of the same districts—first bestowed on the abbey by William the Conqueror —gave plants and shrubs. One was a *Berberis wilsonii* from Crowle. Formerly, this Lincolnshire village in the Isle of Axholme was surrounded by a marsh abounding in fish and waterfowl, which explains those references to Crowle in the abbey rolls. Crowle Church is dedicated to St Oswald, King of Northumbria, whose head accompanied St Cuthbert's remains in that much-travelled coffin we have seen in Durham Cathedral library.

Several reasons have been advanced to account for the Conqueror granting a charter to Selby. Perhaps the most cogent is this: as Battle Abbey was built to commemorate the Norman Conquest, in the south, Selby—where Benedict, a monk from Auxerre in France already had a cell—should perform a like service for the north. The great south window in Selby Abbey illustrates the sequence of events, which include Abbot Benedict planting his cross beside the River Ouse in 1069, William the Conqueror granting his charter later that same year, Abbot Hugh and his monks building the abbey, about 1100, and Queen Matilda working away at Battle of Hastings scenes on the Bayeux Tapestry.

There is no doubt that William I did found Selby Abbey, but any feelings of gratitude must have been offset by his harrying of the north—a scorched-earth policy which left practically the whole area between York and Durham 'waste', as tersely recorded in Domesday Book.

Henry VIII's 'waste' policy, nearly 500 years later, spared the abbey church, which became the parish church in the reign of James I.

Selby Abbey is still avowedly Norman in its magnificent nave, though later times added their particular architectural glories. One of the best books about the abbey is that written by the late Canon John Solloway, who had the old abbey quarries at Monk Fryston, nearby, opened again in 1935 to provide some of the familiar magnesian limestone for external restoration of the church to something like its original plan.

Canon Solloway's face, modelled in stone, now smiles benignantly from a side doorway, recalling the way in which he greeted everybody. And what a sense of humour he had! Some palimpsest tomb-stones in the abbey church were, for him, "bargains in tombstones" because, according to their inscriptions, they had been used repeatedly for different persons through the centuries. "Look at this one," he would say. "It was first inscribed to the memory of 'John de Pontefract of this monastery, monk.' " In 1723 Mary Pickering was evidently buried in the same grave. Then, in 1790—as if one female intruder was not enough to shock John de Pontefract's celibate soul—Mary Aslabie followed. A Benedictine monk, with two women of future times atop of him! I can hear the dear old canon laughing at the economy and incongruity of it, even now.

One church that escaped William's Harrying of the North had been founded by John of Beverley as early as A.D. 693, in the place from which this good man derived his name. William would have done his worst here, too, but for a mysterious malady that suddenly seized Toustain, one of William's henchmen, as he arrogantly spurred his horse through the church doorway. He was picked up, writhing in agony and with a broken neck. Superstitious fear gripped the other would-be violaters. St John of Beverley had reached out in displeasure from his grave!

Whether one can credit this old story or not, the church was certainly reprieved, with the result that Beverley became a 'city of refuge' for those whom William burnt out of their homes farther afield.

The present minster at Beverley is a splendid eye-catcher. From Westwood, one of the common pastures that encircle the town, its twin west towers rise from the plain like two fingers of a priestly hand raised in blessing. A nearer view reveals the excellence of its Gothic lines despite the absence of a balancing, central tower. Neighbouring streets give enchanting vistas of the great white edifice, and a certain garden I know, in Keldgate, ensures for its fortunate owner many a private communion, for the silvery bell-tower and its twin seem to rise, though at a short distance, from his vestibule of begonias and roses.

Beverley Minster is noted, amongst many other splendid features, for its carvings. You can begin, on the west front, with Adam and Eve, he with his spade in the Garden of Eden, she a demure little person, also cloaked in animal skin, holding her distaff. Inside the building you can see the wimpled head of a queen, a medieval packman almost collapsing under his load, a couple of choristers singing lustily, and a man playing the bagpipes as though he, as well as his instrument, must burst at any moment. On the choir misericords, a farmer puts his cart *before* the horse, a boy rides a pig, and a fox robed as a cleric preaches to a congregation of geese.

Without such pleasantries, so stately a church might become overpowering, yet one could spend many days in sheer enjoyment of its finer architectural features. Near the High Altar stands the stone chair used in medieval times by malefactors seeking sanctuary. Today, one need not commit any legal offence to sit there awhile. Indeed, it is a privilege to do so, in the midst of so much chaste splendour.

About Ripon Cathedral, there is, I always feel, a strong note of austerity. The stolid west front, though pierced with tall lancets, seems almost too heavy for the three small entrance doors huddled together at the base. But come here during a Song Festival, when five or more diocesan choirs give of their best, and the huge pile seems to 'relent' a little and the nave arcades to take wing.

Here, too, the choir misericords are of outstanding interest. Like those at Beverley, they were the work of the famous Ripon School of Woodcarvers a few years before the Reformation. You see Jonah being swallowed by the whale and, on another seat, being ejected on to a desert island. Samson is here, walking off with the gates of Gaza; also a figure clutching a bag of money who was long thought to be Judas being taken away, in a wheelbarrow, to perdition. An elephant standing on a giant tortoise accompanies the bishop in his stall, and a prating monkey peers across from the opposite side of the choir.

All the saints of northern Christendom are here, too, unaffected by all this show of humour, and regal enough as they look down the length of the church from the war-memorial reredos. It is a roll-call of faith: Wilfrid, Aidan, Cuthbert, Hilda of Whitby, the Venerable Bede, John of Beverley. Alcuin, the great scholar of Saxon York also has a place, together with Caedmon, the Whitby herdsman who turned poet and singer overnight.

St Wilfrid holds the key, as it were, to Ripon's greatest treasure. This is the crypt below the present church. Earlier churches on the site have come and gone, but Wilfrid's crypt remains, like a hoarse whisper from Saxon times. The passages leading to the crypt could be compared with the devious, uncertain ways of history. You enter by a trap-door in the nave choir, and descend a flight of narrow stone steps reminiscent of many a castle dungeon. A passage just as narrow then branches left, then right, dipping as you move slowly forward. You wonder, perhaps, whether it wouldn't have been wiser to act like Theseus when he took a guide-thread with him through the labyrinth leading to the Minotaur's den. Today, however, the dark, cold passages are illuminated. When I first went down, some fifty years ago, there was no such help. You simply groped and stumbled until at length a small chamber opened up on your left, a chamber that can hold about a dozen or fifteen persons, no more. This is Wilfrid's crypt.

Beneath its low barrel roof there are no furnishings. You provide your own 'furnishing', from any knowledge of ecclesiastical history you may possess, aided perhaps by an obliging verger. . . .

Pilgrims of old came down here with their gifts, though by a different route which has vanished with time. They gazed with rapture at the holy relics kept there, and then tried to pass the test of virtue by squeezing through a hole in one wall, a hole reached by a side passage and still known as St Wilfrid's Needle. What penance or scorn they invoked if they could not thread that difficult 'needle' we can only surmise.

During the last war, as I have related in *Secret Britain*, precious books and manuscripts from the British Museum and other places were stored in this dark catacomb, which has remained inviolate and almost unchanged since the seventh century.

About the same time, in the year A.D. 627 to be exact, King Edwin of Northumbria rode into York with Bishop Paulinus and many others in his train. At the Council of Northumbria, held just previously and probably at Londesborough in the East Riding, he had resolved to follow his Queen, Ethelburga's example and become a Christian. Bede tells the story with great power. On arrival at York a crude wooden church was hastily erected and Paulinus baptised Edwin there on Easter Day of that momentous year.

The wooden hut marked the beginning of York Minster, and the well that traditionally served for the royal baptism is now to be seen within the east crypt. Did anybody in Edwin's company that Easter Day, know or sense that the Roman Praetorium, with its regimental chapel, had stood thereabouts? A Christian baptism on virtually the same spot, marking a distinct departure from the paganism of Rome, as partly represented by its crumbling memorials all around, would appeal to a man like Paulinus. Was not the pagan temple at Goodmanham, near Londesborough—which comes dramatically into Bede's narrative—also replaced by a Christian church!

The architectural progression from those Saxon days is a constant source of interest and speculation. One building replaced another as the centuries went by. Even the least historically minded visitor can follow the different periods, beginning with the now truncated Norman pillars in Archbishop Roger's west crypt, then through the thirteenth-century transepts, the fourteenth-century chapter house and nave, and so on, until the fifteenth century appears with its soaring west towers.

In rather more detail the story runs like this. A Saxon cathedral seems to have altogether perished by fire. The same disaster awaited the next building, but this fire was premeditated—by William the Conqueror. It was part of his revenge for the northern rebellion that followed the Conquest. He had the nerve to celebrate Christmas at York that same year! His seasonal 'gift' to the citizens was a general wreckage. The whole city had been burned down, including the cathedral and its famous library. It recalls the sack of Rome.

William's conscience—apparently in complete abeyance during that season of goodwill—troubled him soon after. That is probably why, the very next year, he appointed his own chaplain, Thomas of Bayeux, as Archbishop of York. Thomas was a Norman, true, but apparently just the man to win the confidence of the scattered clergy and transform the smouldering cathedral ruins into a worthy successor.

Practically all Thomas's handiwork has long been superseded, but it is thought that the pillars once supporting his tower are enclosed by the huge columns of masonry beneath the present lantern tower. Lack of funds so delayed the erection of the next nave that deep pools of water collected in the roofless building; there are records of workmen having been drowned in them.

And so the chequered story of York Minster continued.

Great builders like Roger Pont l'Evêque and Walter de Gray came and went. There were periods of intense building activity, interspersed too often by neglect. When Charles I brought his court to York in 1641 he distributed that year's Maundy Money in the Minster and chose the chapter house for a brilliant Garter ceremony. But there were many things that incurred his royal displeasure. A subsidiary building had somehow intruded into one of the transepts. He ordered its removal. The choir stalls were re-arranged at his bidding, so that the splendid woodcarving could be seen to advantage. Using the proceeds of a fine imposed on Edward Thoraldby for some moral offence, Charles then gave £1,000 to the Chapter, towards fabric repairs and a new organ.

This organ, made rather surprisingly by a London *blacksmith*, perished in the fire of 1829. Jonathan Martin, the lunatic responsible for that fire, had fancied that the organ 'buzzed' at him. He nourished other grievances too. They drove him into the Minster one day and, after hiding until the place was closed for the night, he started a bonfire, feeding it with service books, music MSS, stall hangings etc. Before the alarm was raised next morning, the flames had spread their trail of destruction. Martin, who escaped from the inferno by climbing through a window in the north transept, had only one regret—that the damage he caused was not even greater.

The cost of restoration, £65,000 (a very large sum for those days), was chiefly met by public subscription. In addition, Sir Edward Vavasour—following the example of his medieval forbears—gave fresh supplies of magnesian limestone from the family quarries near Tadcaster. One of the casualties in this terrible fire was the choir roof. The heavy stone vaulting crashed through the pavement below, yet during subsequent restorations something was discovered that had been hidden for centuries—the western crypt. As already indicated, this still contains a few pillars of the Norman building; their incised lozenge and zigzag ornament can be construed as Archbishop Roger's signature, though such ornament—seen to great advantage at Durham Cathedral—was then in vogue. Of the carved choir stalls which Charles had admired, only two survived Martin's fire. They are now in the vestry adjoining the Zouche Chapel.

Yet another fire was to take its toll. In 1840 a workman carelessly left a candle alight on the bell-frame in the south-west tower. As before, there was plenty of time for the blaze to spread before discovery. Result? The south-west tower was gutted, the bells melted in the heat, and the roof of the majestic nave collapsed. Cost of repairs and renewals? £23,000, raised again largely by a sympathetic public.

The two world wars brought their own peculiar perils.

In both wars the priceless stained-glass windows were removed for safety and hidden in various places. But in the 1939-45 war there was an additional precaution. Every architectural feature was photographed in detail, to facilitate repair or renewal in the event of damage by bombing. After the 1829 fire, plaster replicas were begun of the Minster's remaining sculptures and decorations; but photographs are more thorough and can be stored in much smaller space.

This brings the present writer into the story. Suddenly, in the middle of 1942, the National Buildings Record switched me over from other urgent record work to this even greater task; the Minster had to be photographed down to the last niche and corbel. All this had to be done speedily, for the so-called Baedeker raids had already assailed other cathedral towns. The Minster was in greater danger than ever before.

And yet, as I got to work with my camera in this enormous, vulnerable pile, never a word or gesture of fear reached me, from cathedral staff or visitor. The place seemed 'possessed'.

And so the photographs accumulated, day by day, in the middle of that glorious summer. They took me on a remarkable tour of history: from the royal well of the 627 ceremony in the eastern crypt, to the wooden vaulting of the choir and nave necessitated by the fires of 1829 and 1840; from the fourteenth-century chapter house and its sculpture gallery of comic faces, to the triforium passage that seems to give an 'angel's-eye-view' of everything in the main church. Once I was 'trapped' up there for half an hour; Evensong had begun far below and decency compelled me to sit still, and wait until it was over. Has anybody else ever followed Evensong from that exalted position, 60 feet above the robed choristers?

The next great peril was revealed, in 1967, by the discovery of cracks in the masonry of the great central tower, by shifting foundations, and the east wall being nearly 3 feet out of plumb. The enormous and costly task of repair is nearing completion, as I write. York Minster has added another thrilling chapter to is fascinating biography.

Apparently, one of the chief causes of the tower's instability was due to the north-west pier having been built over a Roman well! Part of the extensive 'surgery' performed at the Minster under the direction of Bernard Fielden, chief surveyor, has been the insertion of stainless steel rods and huge concrete plinths to support the tower. The excavation necessary for this operation has provided a new undercroft. Here, future generations will be able to see many interesting features found during repairs. One is a coffin lid bearing the 'portrait' of the thirteenth-century Archbishop, Walter de Gray, together with his insignia—a chalice, patten, crozier and ring. The archaeologists taking advantage of this unique 'dig' have many other treasures to display in that under-croft. The Minster has never before given up so much of its hidden past.*

Manchester Cathedral is one of a number of churches given cathedral status during the last 100 years or so. Newcastle, Bradford, Wakefield, Sheffield and Blackburn are others, and all merit the visitor's regard. But as Manchester Cathedral was badly knocked about during the last war, it deserves special mention here, if only to point a contrast with what the visitor will see today, after that period of sore trial.

The collegiate church has stood in the heart of Manchester since the fifteenth century. Its history is well recorded, from the time when Tudor craftsmen gave it one of the finest sets of choir stalls in the country, to the setting up, rather belatedly, of a statue of Humphrey Chetham, one of Manchester's great benefactors. The story of Manchester itself also unfolded in this beautiful building, with John Byrom—the local man who wrote the carol, "Christians Awake"—and others, commemorated in a window of the Ely Chapel.

When the air raids started, in 1940-41, Sir Hubert Worthington, architect in charge, had those wonderful choir stalls encased in steel. This meant that 'for the duration' the two fellows playing backgammon,

* One further discovery is a stone column, found in sections, from the Roman Praetorium that once occupied the Minster site.

the hunting fox, the dancing pigs, the thieving monkeys, and so many other artful creatures, had to re-enact their little dramas without any audience, and in total darkness. But their 'lives' were safe. They had their own air-raid shelter. Not so the rest of the building!

When John (now Sir John) Summerson of the National Buildings Record sent me to Manchester, the cathedral had already suffered badly. I stepped past the grey steel shrouds that covered the choir stalls, into a perfect shambles of fallen masonry and shattered woodwork. One carved screen had been damaged by bullets during the Civil Wars. What I now beheld was infinitely worse. Much of the east end was roofless and shored up with timbers. Pools of rain-water had formed on the floor. I recall William Theed's statue of Sir Humphrey Chetham (since removed to the west end) peering at me through a forest of scaffolding. Both he and the bluecoat boy at his feet looked woefully deserted.

Later, with photographs of the then fragmentary Lady Chapel Screen, the Ely Chapel window tracery, and many other features, safely in my camera case, I spoke to the policeman who had been on duty outside the cathedral during the night raid responsible for this destruction. He told me that bomb blast had stripped off most of his uniform, and that when he returned, properly clothed again, the great west doors of the cathedral had burst open and were swinging wildly on their hinges. . . . All this, and much else of the same horrific kind, makes a chapter of cathedral history which, due to wartime regulations, the local newspapers could not report.

Even Liverpool's embryonic Anglican cathedral—the only one to be built in the Northern Province since the Reformation—was not entirely immune during those terrible years, when, for a time, so widespread was the destruction, local rail communication was cut off and one had to travel the last few miles to the unhappy city by bus.

Many Liverpudlians must have looked anxiously, as each morning broke, towards the ridge overlooking the city on which both their cathedrals—the Anglican Gothic one, designed by Sir Giles Gilbert Scott, and Sir Edwin Lutyen's Byzantine edifice for Roman Catholics—were gradually taking shape.

The Roman Catholic cathedral was not far advanced; the real wreckage of its plans came in post-war years. Rising costs have made that truly noble building, which would have yielded in size and majesty only to St Peter's in Rome, a 'might-have-been'. The cathedral that has taken its place, more modest in scale and design, is surmounted by a glass tower which, when illuminated from within, resembles a glowing crown shining over the whole city.

The neo-Gothic cathedral has overcome its wartime scars—shattered windows and damaged masonry—and has for many years been able to enfold worshippers in the warmth of its red sandstone, though the

(*top*) Roche Abbey near Maltby, South Yorkshire. (*bottom*) Norman masonry
at Lindisfarne Priory, Holy Island, Northumberland

(*left*) St Cuthbert's Cross in Durham Cathedral Library. (*below*) Trinity design on medieval misericord in Cartmel Priory Church, Lancashire

building will not be finished, and the inspiration fully realized, until
1975.

Inspiration finds expression in smaller churches too, or wherever men
and women gather for worship. Here I shall simply mention a few from
different parts of our area, choosing some that agreeably reflect their
natural surroundings or hold a mirror to some important historic event.

By every right the parish church on Holy Island comes first, echoing
as it does the very sounds of wave and sea-bird that Aidan and Cuthbert
knew. The priory ruins seem almost an extension of this little church
with its massive Norman pillars. The red and white stones, used to
ornamental effect on these pillars, somehow remind me of the sea-
stained rock by the shore on which, according to an old legend,

> St Cuthbert sits and toils to frame,
> The sea-borne beads that bear his name.

Visitors to the island formerly spent much time looking for such
'beads', which, I believe, are actually fossil remains of extinct marine
creatures. Near the church door Cuthbert is recalled by the remnants of
a stone cross that also "bears his name". At village weddings, however,
this Petting Stone (its alternative name) is leaped over by the bridal
couple to ensure good luck for their future. But, as anybody at Durham
Cathedral will tell you, Cuthbert—that saintly celibate and lover of
quietude—so disliked womenfolk that his posthumous spirit even had
the Lady Chapel removed to the opposite end of the cathedral, far from
his mortal remains. Perhaps, by this time, his kindly soul has seen the
light!

Looking south from Holy Island one can easily discern the Farne
Islands, dotted offshore like so many grey seals though full of potential
menace. From its lofty rock pedestal, Bamburgh Castle faces them with
a brave front and, on the landward side, presides with fatherly air over
Bamburgh's peaceful village. The church at the far end of the long street
offers a commentary on this pregnant theme, and on others too.

Aidan is said to have died (A.D. 651) within a Saxon church that stood
on this same spot. The present church, especially the chancel, is a fine
tribute to its thirteenth-century builders. Below one side of the chancel
there is a vaulted crypt which became a kind of mausoleum for the
Forster family, well known in Northumbrian history. General Tom
Forster, implicated in the 1715 Jacobite rebellion, was rescued from
Newgate prison by his sister Dorothy. Here it is sufficient to recall that
Dorothy's secret manoeuvre on her brother's behalf involved the use of
a dummy corpse placed in a coffin. The real Tom was spirited away to
France. Yet one of the coffins found in this crypt, in 1837, was supposed
to be his. Could it have been the one that bamboozled the authorities?

7

In the church overhead one monument—by Francis Chantrey—commemorates Dr John Sharp, Archdeacon of Northumberland (died 1792). He restored Bamburgh Castle, making it into a school, a home for shipwrecked mariners and—such is the size of the place—a signalling station linked with Holy Island.

Shipwreck also casts a mantle of fame over another monument, the one erected to the memory of Grace Darling. On the morning of 7th September, 1838 she and her father, lighthouse-keeper on Longstone, one of the Farnes, had pushed off in their little coble to the rescue of survivors from the *Forfarshire*. The terrible gale that had forced this steamship on to the rocks did not daunt Grace, as they went backwards and forwards until all the survivors were rescued. Many repercussions of this epic piece of bravery, including Grace Darling's premature death, will be recounted later. Meanwhile it is perhaps enough to look upon her effigy here, beneath a stone canopy in the churchyard. An oar rests beside her as, from her stone pillow, she looks out towards the treacherous Farnes.

I have a great liking for the parish church at Berwick-upon-Tweed—a rare seventeenth-century building flanked on one side by an exhilarating stretch of the Elizabethan town walls. But my final choice from Northumberland must be the Norman church dedicated to St Laurence at Warkworth. It stands quite close to Warkworth's fortified bridge over the River Coquet, and looks uphill—as if for extra protection—to the imposing castle of the Percies.

One would hardly be surprised to find the church occupied by kneeling soldiery from the old castle, during some Sabbath break, or frequented at intervals by the guardians of the bridge if the road from Scotland seemed clear. Indeed, the church with its thick walls, rotund pillars and narrow chancel door and windows seems to share the general air of defence. One relieving note is the modern pulpit. In colourful panels this shows many familiar episodes from Northumbrian history, such as Benedict Biscop preaching to his band of monks, St Hilda of Whitby conversing with Caedmon, and St Cuthbert sailing across the narrow bight of water to Coquet Island, seen so well from the castle. Some say that it was on this sea-bound rock, then a gathering ground for monks, that Cuthbert was at length persuaded to leave his lonely Lindisfarne, and the even lonelier Farne, and accept King Egfrith's offer of the Bishopric of Hexham.

The antiquity of many churches in County Durham is most impressive. At Escomb Church, near Bishop Auckland, the mind runs back to Saxon times and even beyond, for built into its structure there is Roman masonry, probably from the neighbouring fort of Binchester. Winston Church, in Teesdale, also incorporates a few Roman stones, from the fort at Piercebridge. But I cherish fond memories of the Saxon church at Norton-on-Tees, partly perhaps because I was introduced to it by an architect who lived just opposite, in The Hermitage.

The oldest part of this house was built for the first priest, about 900 years ago. With the building Mr Harrison, the architect, had acquired some of the former clerical privileges, such as the right "to keep two ducks on the village pond" and "to have children play on the Hermitage Green"—a triangular patch beyond the garden, and quite distinct from the large, village green. When the new vicarage was built, even nearer the church, in Georgian times, the old priest house was enlarged and became a grammar school.

Mr Harrison seemed to have found his house almost as intriguing as the church it once served. Amongst other things, he discovered a concealed window that had kept a 'secret eye' on the church, also part of a fireplace with adzed beams where the priest would derive some winter cheer. He also discovered the terms arranged with a certain John Walker for making the eighteenth-century alterations. Walker was requested to "build a schoolroom on the north side of Hermitage Green, 10 yards long, 6 yards wide, 4 yards high, for which he was to receive a whole sheep per week during the job, and a quartern of wheat for each carpenter he employed".

This slight digression is inserted to provide a cameo of life in what was then a secluded village centred upon its venerable church. In imagination one can see the grammar-school boys file across and take their places beneath the lofty roof. A wandering eye might rest upon the fine tower with its Saxon windows, or upon the effigy of a fourteenth-century knight and his lady far below. The knight's earthly campaigns seem to be represented by the lion and dog in fierce combat at his feet, but the lady beside him—doubtless sick of battle ardours—finds refuge in a book.

Another attractive feature is a stained-glass window illustrating the life of Bernard Gilpin, the 'Apostle of the North'. As vicar of this church (1552-3) he must have taken his rest, sometimes, in that little house adjoining Hermitage Green.

Norton is now part of the newly-formed county borough of Teesside (1968). In the same amalgam comes Stockton-on-Tees, whose eighteenth-century parish church may not be outwardly as attractive as that at Norton, but was built near enough to the present day to reflect the beginnings of modern progress. The story is entrusted to the carved pew-ends. Some deal with the impact of Stockton and its neighbourhood on discovery and invention. A few are adapted as personal memorials: thus Captain James Cook is recalled by a carved replica of his ship, the *Resolution*, and many emblems of his historic voyages.

Cook was born in 1728 at Marton-in-Cleveland, about 5 miles south of Stockton. When four great-grandsons of Captain William Christopher were killed in action during the First World War, they were commemorated here by a pew-head that provides another link with Captain Cook. The design refers to the explorations of Captain William Christopher, a local man, who became a commodore of the Hudson Bay Company's fleet and accompanied Cook on his last voyage. From some driftwood he picked up on that voyage Captain Christopher himself made the communion rails in this church.

Yet another pew-head depicts Locomotion No. One—the 1825 pioneer locomotive of the Stockton and Darlington Railway. One could hardly expect the carving to show the fellow who had to wave a warning flag while preceding the new contraption on his white horse; but it does give a faithful impression of this engine, which could rattle along at 15 m.p.h. and which now rests, with veteran's dignity, in Darlington Railway Station. In 1925, to mark the centenary of the Stockton and Darlington Railway, Locomotion No. One chugged out of Darlington again—and this replica was made for Stockton Parish Church.

Yorkshire is so vast and its interesting churches are so many that a native of the county, like myself, can but give a nod of recognition all around, and then try to pick out a few of some special merit. With apologies therefore to the Norman church at Adel, near Leeds; the fifteenth-century church at Dent, where Adam Sedgwick, the famous geologist both preached and worshipped; to St Cuthbert's Church at Crayke, near York, which has many associations with this ubiquitous saint; and to many others in town and village, I turn to three which help to sum up religious activity in the county before and after the rise of Nonconformity.

One little-visited church that recalls great events is All Hallows at Goodmanham, near Market Weighton. I once spent several days in the vicinity, trying to recapture the sense of time and place that here needs over 1,300 years for its fulfilment. The oldest part of the building dates from the early twelfth century, but the only visual clue to the great significance of this site is a small, modern window in the chancel. It shows a grey-robed figure brandishing a flaring torch and standing on a fallen idol. "Just another saint," might well be some casual visitor's remark, yet Coifi—of whom the stained-glass figure is an imaginary portrait—far exceeds any conventional notions of sainthood.

To evoke his epic story I like to stand beside the church tower and look towards Londesborough, 2 miles to the north-west. In A.D. 627 a famous Council of Northumbria was held in King Edwin's summer palace, probably situated at Londesborough. The proceedings, during which Christianity was being vigorously championed against paganism, were—as stated earlier—vividly described by Bede. Finally, the issue was decided by the courageous action of Coifi, High Priest of Woden at Godmundingham (Goodmanham). Converted like the King by Paulinus's exposition of the new faith, supported by the wise counsel of some unknown aged warrior, Coifi rode off dramatically to his temple of Woden, flung its idols to the ground and set fire to the place. Even now, it is stirring to imagine him galloping hence through this quiet pastoral countryside, for the pagan temple he came to destroy—a temple whose gods had no further meaning for him—stood on the small hill now occupied by Goodmanham Church. The chancel window to the memory of Coifi is also, therefore, a memorial of this pivotal event that led directly to Edwin's baptism at York and the founding of York Minster in the same year (see page 92).

St Mary's Church, perched like a beacon near the abbey on the east cliff at Whitby, has a very long story, full of incident, as when, during the seventeenth and eighteenth centuries, the local shipwrights remodelled the building on nautical lines. Here, however, only one theme can be followed.

The memory of the Reverend William Scoresby, F.R.S. (1789-1857), is preserved at several places in the North Country, notably here at Whitby, which became the family's home town. A large wing of Whitby Museum is devoted to mementoes of Captain Cook and the two Scoresbys, father and son. In this section one may see numerous nautical instruments designed and made by Scoresby junior, the one who eventually became a clergyman. Amongst the instruments are his chronological compass, his compound four-bar magnetic needle, and his "largest horse-shoe magnet . . . from whose sources", wrote Scoresby, "the magnetism of all my other magnets has been derived". To get the story neatly rounded off, one is inevitably drawn to St Mary's Church. Here, in the Norman chancel, stands a chair that was surely never intended for seating purposes. It is only too eloquent of Scoresby's famous voyage in 1856, undertaken for "magnetical research", in the *Royal Charter*.

This was an iron vessel, and Scoresby successfully demonstrated that on such a ship the only feasible place for a compass—in view of the prevalence of metal—was at the masthead. Consequently, on this commemorative chair, the back panel is carved *in deep relief* with a couple of anchors, surmounted by a compass. Below the anchors a separate carving illustrates the subsequent wreck, in 1859, of the *Royal Charter*. The owners of the vessel had this chair made from the wreckage.

One very sober church carving embodies an oft-told story that hits off village life to a nicety. The carving is a bust of John Wesley portrayed in the act of preaching. During a visit to Bishop Burton, near Beverley, Wesley led a service beneath the boughs of a great wych-elm on the village green. The anniversary of this event was celebrated by his followers at the same spot until 1836, when the tree was uprooted in a storm. Nothing daunted, these good folk got a local craftsman to carve a bust of Wesley from some of the wood and it was joyfully set up in the new Wesley Chapel nearby. During renovations, almost sixty years later, the bust was found to be badly worm-eaten and put outside.

Soon after, the vicar of Bishop Burton's lovely old parish church happened to pass; he took pity on the outcast and bought it for £2, chaffing his Wesleyan neighbours then and later about having "sold their Master for forty pieces of silver". The bust was given paraffin oil treatment by a well-known Beverley craftsman, who must have sensed the piquancy of the situation, for he submitted the following account to the vicar: "To re-baptizing John Wesley, and curing him of the worms—25s."

Wesley looks much healthier for this treatment; after languishing for many years in a vestry, he was recently given a place of some prominence in the main church, with Saints Augustine, Francis, Christopher, and other stalwarts of the Faith, all carved to the life on different bench-ends, for company. What a dialogue must ensue during the night hours!

In Lancashire, Whalley Church stands for something almost sinister, because of its unfortunate associations with the notorious Lancashire Witches. Harrison Ainsworth's novel with this title is creepy enough on the subject, but in recent years Robert Neill's *Mist Over Pendle* has let the fiends of fear loose again, especially when Mistress Alice Nutter of Roughlee, one of the evil sisterhood, fixes her gaze upon a charming young lady worshipper seated in an imposing family pew. . . .

A church stood on this site in A.D. 628, long before the neighbouring abbey became a ripple of creative thought in somebody's mind. The present church is of much later date, but sufficiently ancient to mesmerize any stranger to these parts. Pendle Hill, rendezvous of the seventeenth-century witches, lifts up its head to the east, and lovely old villages gather round on all sides.

The chief glory of the church interior is its woodwork. As the twenty-two choir stalls came from the abbey church it is particularly interesting to notice the kind of humour that appealed to the monks who once sat in them, beneath the tall decorated canopies. The misericord of the abbot's stall is carved with bunches of luscious grapes, accompanied by the remark (in Latin), "May they be always joyful who sit in this seat." The prior allowed himself something more playful—a satyr weeping in front of a laughing girl. On yet another stall a woman beats her husband with a frying pan; one of the scenes which prompted Dr Whitaker, a bygone vicar of this church and historian of Whalley, to observe, "These [carvings] perhaps might be intended to console the monks for the loss of love and marriage."

The big family pew, near the choir stalls, is understandably called The Cage, enclosed as it is within tall wooden bars and capped with an ornate cornice. It was originally made, in the seventeenth century, for Roger Nowell, Lord of the Manor of Read (who comes into Robert Neill's story), but long after his death a dispute arose as to who had the right to occupy this 'cage' during public worship, John Taylor of Moreton Hall or John Fort of Read. Even a law suit costing thousands of pounds could not resolve the issue. At length, in 1830, the 'cage' was divided by a wooden partition; the two parties to the dispute could then beseech the mercy of God from their respective halves!

Sefton Church, near Liverpool, may also stagger visitors because of its amazing wealth of wood-carving. This spreads like so many folds of lace across the chancel screen and decorates the choir stalls and other seats with a perfect little menagerie. Almost everything in the church—screens, pew-ends, pulpit etc., is graced by the carver's art. The craftsmen responsible, during various periods from the sixteenth century onwards, must surely have heard the voice that speaks in T. E. Brown's poem, "Opifex":

> This is thy life: indulge its natural flow,
> And carve these forms . . .
> I bid thee carve them, knowing what I know.

Farther north, and high above the Kent estuary, there is a small woodland church which should be seen. One might travel through this countryside of tangled knolls and limestone outcrops for a week, however, and never find it—but, once found, St Anthony's Chapel on Cartmel Fell will long abide in the memory.

My wife and I could have wished to arrive on horseback, like so many of the bygone Huttons of Thorphinsty Hall nearby, or the Brigg family, or indeed the Gilpins after whom the neighbouring valley is named. The wooden post over which they would all fling their horses' bridles before entering church is still waiting for them, in the graveyard, and is conveniently enclosed by a circular mounting block. Within doors, the same sense of another age prevails. Modern notions recede before the three-decker pulpit of 1698, the quaint, family pews allocated to Thorphinsty, Cowmire, and Burblethwaite Halls, and some lovely fifteenth-century glass. One window fragment declares the dangers of travelling far afield in such times, in these words: "Wilm

Brigg goeth to London upon tusday, 12th day of Aprill, God Save hym."

The thick coppices that nowadays embrace the chapel sufficiently recall the traditional wilderness where St Anthony lived:

> . . . xxll yere and more
> Without any company bot the wilde brooe [boar].

Anthony and the boar appear in the ancient stained glass, providing an apt object for the Kentmere Gilpins to gaze upon when they first settled hereabouts, for one of their ancestors, Richard de Gylpyn, was given the manor of Kentmere about 1206 for having slain a wild boar "which did great mischief in the adjoining mountains".

As briefly mentioned in the first chapter, the waterside church at Aldingham, on the Furness peninsula, marks one of the monks' resting places suggested in the old rhyme about Cuthbert's posthumous journey:

> O'er northern mountain, marsh and moor,
> From sea to sea, from shore to shore,
> Seven years St Cuthbert's corpse they bore.

To reach this haven the monks would have to cross the notorious sands of Morecambe Bay, taking turns no doubt to shoulder the coffin that held Cuthbert's mortal remains and such treasures as the Lindisfarne Gospels and his pectoral cross of gold.

On safely landing, the Congregation probably decided to build a small shrine to their lost leader, but the present church here goes no farther back than the twelfth century, as evidenced by the south arcade, with its stout pillars. There is a staunchness about the church that seems to defy time. And assembled before it, on the shining sandbars of the bay, there is usually a delightfully varied consortium of sea-birds, as befits a place dedicated to Cuthbert.

On the afternoon of my recent visit the water had tamely withdrawn into half-hidden channels a mile or so from shore. But the church has reason to know its changing moods. One bygone rector took certain precautions which were favourably commented upon during Queen Victoria's visit to Aldingham in 1848. A letter is preserved at the rectory describing this occasion. It was written by the Queen's companion, Lady Augusta Bruce. After first visiting Furness Abbey, "which far surpassed anything I had anticipated", their open carriage drew up at Aldingham rectory and soon they were enthusing about the lovely old church and "parsonage" which "are on the water's edge and very picturesque". Dr Stonard, the venerable rector, showed them his fine collection of books, and conducted them through the church. But Lady Augusta spotted something else: "He [the rector] has built an addition to the church at his own expense." The 'addition' was the crenellated sea-wall that protects the building from the boisterous floodwaters of Morecambe Bay. It seems a pity that the tiny parochial school, with its tall chimney and round-headed casements, at the seaward corner of the churchyard, has fallen into disuse. One could have envied the children being on the very edge of this natural bird sanctuary.

How can one choose among the churches of Lakeland? Nearly all of them are beautifully situated and place their own little 'signatures' on the Lakeland scene. Indeed, many of them tell their own story of this matchless area.

Wordsworth saw Hawkshead Church

> . . . upon her hill,
> Sit like a thronèd lady sending out
> A gracious look all over her domain.

Despite certain changes since then, it is still exciting to wander through the strange alleys Wordsworth knew as a schoolboy here until the "thronèd lady" is reached.

Buttermere Church stands on a rock far above the lake, and is small enough to give the impression of having lodged there, like a boulder, after rolling down Buttermere Pass.

It seems natural that most of the lakes are neighboured by the grey stone of a church, with perhaps a little bellcote to scatter its music over the water. At Patterdale, Ullswater has the curious building designed by Anthony Salvin in 1853. It adds little to the appeal of Lakeland architecture, seeming content to play in a minor key to the glorious surroundings, here dominated by Helvellyn. Salvin was better inspired at Keswick, where St John's, his church of 1838, is magnificently seen from Derwentwater, its spire sending a tall shaft of beauty against the interfolding background of Skiddaw and Saddleback. John Marshall, the man who provided this stately church, was a Leeds flax-spinner of whom we shall hear more later. One branch of the family lived on Derwent Island. It is perhaps significant that their boat-house, on the lake shore, resembles a small church, even to the bellcote which became vocal when a boat was required to take the family home from Sunday service at St John's.

In springtime, Rydal Church looks towards its small lake over a field of wild daffodils known as Dora's Field, after Wordsworth's daughter, Dora. Wasdale and the Vale of St John almost hide their respective houses of God, while at Troutbeck above Windermere the small eighteenth-century church stands aloof from the village, the better, perhaps, to emphasize its glorious setting amongst the hills.

The design of its east window by Burne-Jones owes something to William Morris and Ford Madox Brown, who were fishing nearby at the time. Dr Pevsner remarks: "Brown's figures are more agitated than Burne-Jones's, and he uses more perspective, too."

St Martin's Church at Windermere is full of good things, not least the fragments of stained glass from Cartmel Priory, and a fifteenth century window commemorating the Bowness carrier who conveyed the roofing lead to this site on his pack-horses.

Three churches are especially notable because of associations with men who helped to enrich Lakeland and life itself, in some way.

At Grasmere the spirit of Wordsworth presides over everything, and one sees the riverside church with fresh eyes and feeling on reading the poet's description:

> Not raised in nice proportions was the pile,
> But large and massy, for duration built;
> With pillars crowded, and the roof upheld
> By naked rafters intricately crossed,
> Like leafless underboughs, mid some thick grove,
> All withered by the depth of shade above.

Every year, usually on the Sunday nearest 5th August (St Oswald's Day), those "naked rafters" looked down on a floor strewn with rushes, for this was rush-bearing Sunday. Wordsworth and his family always joined the rush-bearing procession through the village, with a fiddler leading the way. The poet, who now rests in the churchyard above the swirling River Rothay, would rejoice to know that the custom is still observed, as we shall notice later.

At Coniston, John Ruskin lives again on a churchyard memorial cross designed by Professor Collingwood. Ruskin's great interests—music, art, work and Nature, are beautifully symbolised on the cross, to remind everybody who passes that a great man once lived nearby, at Brantwood, across the lake.

In his abounding love of the countryside, John Ruskin had much in common with H. D. Rawnsley, a canon of Carlisle Cathedral, who spent many happy years as vicar of Crosthwaite Church on the fringe of Keswick. Towering behind the church is Skiddaw. From Greta Hall, nearby, S. T. Coleridge—who lived here for a time with Robert Southey—would watch the clouds on Skiddaw with rapture. To him a sky without clouds was "like a theatre at noon". When Southey died he was laid to rest in this churchyard and Wordsworth, in writing his epitaph, referred to Southey's joys and griefs vanishing

> ... like a cloud
> from Skiddaw's top.

Coleridge's 'theatre' had lost something of its soul.

Today there is a special joy in sauntering within this church, for all its interesting features, including a white marble figure of Southey, must have been lovingly touched and explained to hundreds of visitors by the man who helped to found the National Trust, in 1895: Canon Rawnsley.

Near Ruskin's memorial on Friar's Crag, overlooking Derwentwater, a slab of local slate bears this inscription: "To the honoured memory of Hardwicke Drummond Rawnsley, 1851–1920, who greatly loving the fair things of Nature and of Art set all his love to the service of God and Man. He was Canon of Carlisle, Chaplain to the King, Vicar of Crosthwaite 1883–1917, and one of the founders of the National Trust, into whose care Friar's Crag, Lord's Island, and a part of Great Wood were given by subscribers who desired that his name should not be forgotten. 7 September 1922."

One might say, with truth, that Rawnsley's church had two local habitations: one, in that grand old place at Crosthwaite, dedicated to St Kentigern, a sixth-century pioneer of Christianity; the other amid the mountain altars surrounding his beloved Derwentwater.

An earlier benefactor in this neighbourhood was Lady Anne Clifford. She is remembered in several churches, notably, in St Lawrence's at Appleby, for there she rests, beside her mother, not far from the Castle Pew, still carved with her emblems. The devout, if proud, lady used to sit here in state when in residence at Appleby Castle.

All that was long ago, but in the little chapel attached to the almshouses she endowed here, in 1653, the 'mother' and 'sisters' of the community speak as though Lady Anne is still amongst them, ready— as it were—to walk across the courtyard, bright with geraniums, as soon as the vicar of St Lawrence's rings the bell at the gate for morning service. Barrel-roofed, the chapel measures 20 feet by 10 feet and is furnished with oak pews down each side and a pulpit in one corner. The walls carry Biblical texts and the Ten Commandments, which doubtless strengthen the injunction that the 'mother' and twelve 'sisters' shall "endeavour to live quietly and peaceably amongst themselves".

Another of Lady Anne's many castles was at Brougham, beside the River Eamont. Two of her churches stand nearby; one, St Wilfrid's, a little way to the south-west, the other, St Ninian's, to the north-east. Both are well worth seeing; St Wilfrid's because of its splendid seventeenth-century woodwork from the Continent; St Ninian's, or Ninekirks, because of its utter simplicity and isolation. In 1660 Lady Anne caused Ninekirks "to be built up again . . . larger and bigger than it was before". It "would have in all likelihood have fallen down", she confided to her diary, "it was soe ruinous, if it had not bin repaired by me".

To reach St Ninian's one has to cross five fields, almost pilgrim-wise, which suits the local Quakers very well when they are occasionally invited to hold their meetings for worship in this secluded spot in a loop of the Eamont, where the only sounds are the singing of birds, the bleating of sheep, the prattle of the river, and the soughing of the wind.

The puritan aspect of this church should not disguise the fact that here we have one of the earliest Christian sites in England. St Ninian is thought to have founded the first church here, about A.D. 400—a counterblast to the worship of Mithras as practised by the Romans at their neighbouring camp, Brocavum (Brougham). With the departure of the legions, 1,500 years ago, Brougham and especially St Ninian's little kirk dropped back into a silence that seems palpable.

Cumberland and Westmorland have been called the 'Galilee of Quakerism' because it was in these parts that the movement sprang to birth. Lancashire provided the initial springboard, however, for it was on Pendle Hill that George Fox, founder of Quakerism, had his vision. That was on a sunny day in 1652.

Of the many Quaker meeting houses that have since established themselves among the eternal hills, in this area, two may be mentioned here. Plain, simple, but strangely moving is the one dated 1692 at Yealand Conyers, high above the southern shores of Morecambe Bay. The Friends' Old School, adjoining, is a later building, founded in 1709 by the will of Robert Withers, of whom it was said that "he ever preferred the Lord's business before his own and never lost an inch of ground".

Even nearer in time to Fox's missionary vision is the Brigflatts meeting house (1675), secluded beside the River Rawthey, near Sedbergh. Its quaint furnishings include an open gallery and a dog pen at the foot of the steps. The place seems to tap the very essence of life.

6

On Guard

IT is always satisfying to follow some countryside route described by a celebrated bygone traveller, like Thomas Gray who, some years after writing the famous "Elegy", toured the Lakes on foot, beholding the mountain scenery through a 'Claude glass'—a plano-convex mirror, bound up like a pocket book and best used, said one contemporary, by suspending it by the upper part and *turning one's back* on the object being viewed, whether mountain, waterfall, or some mouldering castle mantled with ivy.

But the traveller whom I have followed with ever-increasing pleasure and profit is Lady Anne Clifford, Countess of Pembroke—a proud though admirable woman who could defy James I and Oliver Cromwell with equal impunity, and yet ride about the North of England with all the pomp and dignity of a crowned queen.

In her copious diary she thus describes her birth, on 30th January 1589: "my blessed mother brought me forth in one of my father's chief houses, called Skipton Castle in Craven". Her father was absent at the time, engaged in one of those buccaneering expeditions against the Spaniards which Queen Elizabeth publicly reproved but privily supported. Looking back from the mature years in which her diary was written, Lady Anne simply records that her father was then "in great perill at sea".

The travels which chiefly concern us here are those undertaken by Lady Anne in visiting her various castles in the northern shires. Her own words help us to picture this great lady: "The collour of myne eyes was Black lyke my ffather's and the forme and aspect of them was quick and Lively, like my mother's. The Haire of myne head was Browne and thick, and so long as that it reached to the Calfe of my Legges when I stood upright, with a peake of Haire on my forehead and a Dimple in my Chynne lyke my Father, full Cheekes and round faced lyke my mother, and an exquisite shape of Bodie resembling my Father."

An ornate tomb in Skipton parish church enshrines the memory of this bold adventurer, George, third Earl of Cumberland, but a monument more to my liking is the grotto in the gateway of the adjoining castle; it is made up of shells, mother-of-pearl and other marine treasures picked up by this 'Sailor Earl' on foreign shores. The gateway itself is sandwiched between two massive drum towers and, from the cresting, the family motto "Desormais", meaning 'Henceforward', places its seal on the market town over which the castle still seems to exert feudal oversight.

But for Lady Anne, ruin and decay would have reduced the castle to a shapeless pile by today. What a good preservationist she was! Her own surveyor, too, and Department of the Environment. 'Restorer of the Breeches' was a tag which suited her admirably. The inscription on a tablet she set up over the entrance shows her mettle, and gives a string of titles that would daunt anybody:

> This Skipton Castle was repayred
> by The Lady Anne Clifford, Countess
> Dowager of Pembrookee, Dorsett, and
> Montogomerie, Baronesse Clifford, West
> Merland [Westmorland], and Vescie, Ladye of the Honour
> of Skipton in Craven, and High Sheriff
> Esse [Sheriffess] by inheritance of the Countie
> of Westmorland, in the yeares 1657
> and 1658, after this maine part of itt had
> layne ruinous ever since December 16
> 48 [1648], and the january followinge, when
> itt was then pulled downe and demol
> isht, almost to the foundacon, by the
> Command of Parliament, then
> sitting at Westminster, because
> itt had bin a garrison in the then
> Civill Warres in England.
> Isa. Chap. 58. Ver. 12. God's name be praised.

Evidence of Lady Anne's restoration zeal is all about you as you pass through the outer gateway on to the lawns that spread like a thick carpet up to the main range. The extensive Tudor work, which hides a little of the Norman castle, and contains a fine banqueting hall, is best approached by an entrance at the west end provided by Lady Anne after the 'slighting'. This leads through to the Conduit Court, as graceful now as when first created in the time of Henry III, and even improved by the yew tree at the centre which Lady Anne planted. Its tall, fluted trunk adds something almost architectural to the quadrangular assembly of sunlit windows, and doorways emblazoned with highly pictorial coats of arms.

One place near Skipton which Lady Anne enjoyed visiting is Barden Tower in Wharfedale. Perhaps it was the solitude that appealed to her, coupled with the knowledge that one of her ancestors, the 'Shepherd Lord,' often forsook Skipton Castle to study the stars, here, with some canons from Bolton Priory. A pike hanging from the oak rafters of the retainer's house at Barden is shown (though with only inherited tradition to support the claim) as the very one carried by Sylvester Lister when he accompanied the 'Shepherd Lord's' contigent to Flodden.

A small church adjoins this house. Its bedrooms are accommodated in the squat church tower, and at one time it was customary for the gentry in residence at Barden Tower to walk through the retainer's house to reach the Lord's Gallery at the back of the church. Lady Anne repaired this gallery and the rest of the building, but some alterations last century robbed the church of its unique character. Lady Anne, thou shouldst have been there, at that fateful hour!

She once committed the following remark to her diary: "In these three houses of mine inheritance, Appleby Castle and Brougham Castle in Westmorland, and Skipton Castle in Craven, I do more and more fall in love with the contentments of a country life. . . ."

Each of her castles was visited in turn; after a long sojourn, now at Brough, now at Appleby, and so on, her cavalcade would proceed to the next place. She sometimes rode in a horse-litter, sometimes in her coach, but always there was an impressive retinue comprising her ladies-in-waiting, accommodated in a second coach; officials and men-servants on horseback; maidservants in yet another coach; and, bringing up the rear, all the domestic paraphernalia of this amazing household.

She would vary her routes and despite the above-mentioned encumbrances rejoiced in little-used tracks through the dales and across the inhospitable Pennines. Sometimes her itinerary would involve crossing Stainmore Common, then a wild, desolate region but now considerably tamed. Occasionally it would be her whim to pass through Ravenstonedale while travelling north towards Brough, Appleby and Brougham.

I like to think of her planning one delightful route she was to use on two occasions while travelling from Skipton to Pendragon Castle. After a first night spent at Kilnsey, Upper Wharfedale, she rode "through Kettlewell Dale up Buckden Rakes, and over the Staks [the Stake Pass] into Wensleydale to stay with cousin Thomas Metcalfe at Nappa". Mary Queen of Scots had slept here years before; the memory would probably be distasteful to Lady Anne, for her father had been one of the four peers charged to see Mary executed. However, after spending two nights in the fortress-like Nappa Hall, which is as charming today as it would be in Lady Anne's time, the party continued, 'crocodiling' over Cotter "where", to quote the diary again, "I think never did coach went before", and thence to Pendragon after crossing Hell Gill bridge.

This small bridge which spans the infant River Eden on Abbotside Common seems to have captivated our intrepid traveller. Perhaps it was the grandeur of its moorland setting, together with the eerie chasm beneath the stone arch, that impressed her. Anyhow, she told her nephew to go and see it for himself. The advice is still worth taking, for to the west you have Wild Boar Fell rearing its massive, leonine form; Baugh Fell to the south-west; and, in front of you, the way over Mallerstang by which Lady Anne descended to Pendragon Castle. She had restored this place in 1660, years after the Scots had given it their too-close attention. Today, the castle looks as though the Scots had been at it again!

Nowadays, Lady Anne's route from Cotterdale to Pendragon would hardly be reckoned as a track at all, yet much of it marked the way by which Scottish raiders had often swooped upon Yorkshire. Mary Stuart herself travelled by this same upland track when being led to Bolton Castle in Wensleydale. That some of the wildest, least hospitable (and grandest!) country of northern England thus spread itself across Lady Anne's vast domains—a 'great divide' which few but cattle drovers or armed soldiery ever tackled—seems never to have troubled her. And by this time she was getting on in years, for only with the failure of the male line of Cliffords, when she was approaching sixty years of age, had she inherited the family estates.

Like Pendragon, Brough Castle has also paid the toll of time, weather and neglect, despite Lady Anne's efforts to keep the place in good order. From its walls, however, you can still obtain splendid views eastwards to Stainmore, southwards to Mallerstang and the Pennine massif beyond, and northwards along the fertile Eden Valley. How well did the Normans site this fortress, and the Romans their fort, Verterae, which preceded it!

Beverley Minster, East Yorkshire: nineteenth-century choir screen by J. E. Elwell

St Anthony's Chapel, Cartmel Fell: the Burblethwaite Hall pew and the
seventeenth-century three-decker pulpit

As Lady Anne always named Appleby and Brougham Castles as her favourite residences, there is good reason for pushing on through the ever-delightful Eden Valley so that ample time can be given to them. The countess must have found this part of her journey comparatively easy, yet none-the-less gratifying to the senses, with Roman Fell, Dufton Pike and Cross Fell rising out of the mists on her right, and the Lakeland hills glimpsed far over to the west. . . .

At Appleby the memory of Lady Anne is part of the very air you breathe. Sometimes she would climb up to the castle by Bondgate and Scattergate; at other times the triumphal entry would bring her and all her minions in by the main bridge and Boroughgate. Beautiful lime trees now line Boroughgate where this ascends to the castle gates, and the only regret is that permission to enter the castle grounds has for some time been withheld, due to acts of vandalism.

The castle occupies a lobe of high ground in a dramatic loop of the Eden. When the countess first came here she found the place in scandalous condition. No small part of the joy of wandering around the castle buildings comes from trying to see her hand, in the restorations she effected in 1653. The partition wall in the Norman keep, known as Caesar's Tower, and the four turret heads surmounting the tower, are her work. So, too, are the steading in the western bailey, and the charming bee house. The view from the top of Caesar's Tower is stupendous, taking in all the northern Pennines and changing almost every moment because of the pageant of the clouds or the mysterious shifting of morning mist.

The posthumous re-union of mother and daughter, in Appleby Church (mentioned in the last chapter) seems doubly appropriate and satisfying after one has seen the Countess's Pillar on the roadside near Brougham Castle. Brougham marks the northernmost limit of her repeated itineraries. The 10 miles that separate Appleby and Brougham (pronounced Broom) are therefore well worth covering, preferably by some of the by-roads on the west side of the Penrith highway.

The Countess's Pillar, half a mile south of the castle, on the Penrith road, is an impressive bit of finery bearing sundials, Lady Anne's coat-of-arms, and the following inscription (here abbreviated): "This pillar was erected by Anne Countess Dowager of Pembroke . . . for a memorial of her last parting with her good and pious mother . . . ye 2nd April 1616, in memory whereof she also left an annuity of Four Pounds for the poor of Brougham parish every 2nd April for ever upon ye stone table here hard by."

Today, the vicar of St Ninian's Church, near Brougham, who superintends the charity, has difficulty in finding suitable beneficiaries for the Brougham Dole. "Nobody comes", he says, "so the fund accumulates." Some years ago, however, a few children came along on

8

the appointed day, stepped expectantly on to the said 'stone table'—really a couple of stone slabs let into the ground—and received 'crumbs' of the bounty in the form of sixpences.

Brougham Castle, delightfully situated above the banks of the River Eamont, would need another Lady Anne to make the place habitable again. Yet there is much to see and admire. You can climb to the 'roof' and enjoy glorious views in all directions, the northward view with Penrith Beacon on the skyline being particularly good. From the same vantage point you can peer within the now roofless chamber "wherein", wrote Lady Anne, "my noble father was born and my blessed mother died". I wonder whether this was near the Painted Chamber where Christopher Dalston of Acorn Bank (now known as Temple Sowerby Manor)—"oldest son to my Cousin Mr John Dalston", wrote the diarist—once dined with his wife? Their hostess, we also read, was (for once) too indisposed to be with them. At length, she herself died in the chamber where her mother had expired, years before; today its wall crannies grow for her a continuing memorial of stonecrop, aubretia and dainty, many-hued fern.

Other castles in this beautiful neighbourhood have a stunted eloquence in these days. Norman lords had given Kendal a fine castle on a hill overlooking the town, but when Camden came along with his note-book in 1586, he reported that it was "ready to drop down with age". A swift decline for a castle which, only forty years earlier, had seen its master's daughter, Katherine Parr, leave to become Henry VIII's last, and most fortunate queen. It was this rise in the family fortunes that caused the Parrs of Kendal to put their ancient heritage aside in favour of life at court. The town still cherishes Katherine's Book of Devotions.

To the castle ruins, many years ago, came a travelling hardware merchant, claiming the right, as a self-styled descendant of Katherine Parr, to settle there—which he did, attracting to himself many who were curious, and, one supposes, doing a good trade in pots and pans into the bargain.

Scaleby Castle, north of Carlisle, has had a rather better fate. Its sombre ruins are probably haunted by the Gilpins who once lived here, but at least the shell of the castle now harbours a modern house. Dacre Castle, above Ullswater, has matured into a farmhouse, so that cattle can now graze its pastures peacefully, without danger of being seized and driven over the Scottish border.

Lowther Castle, seen across its fine park, stirs all that is romantic within one's veins, though the habitable building dates only from the early nineteenth century, its progenitor being a picturesque ruin nearby. Wordsworth, who knew the place well, dedicated his *Excursion* to Sir William Lowther. The poet's words:

Oft through thy domain, illustrious Peer,
In youth I roamed on youthful pleasures bent

can be echoed by many, today, because of the Wild Life Park that
brings visitors by the hundred to these ancient acres. It seems fitting
that amongst the animals given sanctuary here, one sees Highland
cattle, a few St Kilda sheep, and the red deer—that beautiful creature
whose remote ancestors roamed these parts and gave their human
contemporaries an abundant supply of picks and other tools made from
their antlers.

Perhaps Henry VI startled a few deer while he was wandering these
fells after fleeing from the Battle of Hexham. A shepherd eventually
found the hunted king and led him to safe refuge at Muncaster Castle.

The whole story leaps to mind as one first sees this finely sited castle,
high on its wooded hill above the River Esk, after taking that adventurous road from the Duddon Valley to Ravenglass. For nine days
did Henry stay up there, before moving off to other sanctuaries, farther
south, in the Bowland area.* Anthony Salvin was to rebuild the castle
in the 1860s, giving it, amongst other features, a new pele tower to
match the original one. But nothing can efface that old story while the
Luck of Muncaster is preserved here, or while the three-storeyed tower
stands, nearly a mile to the north-east, to mark the spot where that
shepherd stumbled upon the distraught king, in 1461. The Luck, a
shallow glass bowl barely a handspan in width, was given by Henry
to his host "with the prayer that the family might prosper so long as the
glass remained unbroken".

Henry Hornyhold-Strickland, F.S.A., refers to his home, Sizergh
Castle, as having developed from a Border pele tower of the fourteenth
century. This description places the Scottish Border much farther south
that what was generally acknowledged as such after the Union of the
two kingdoms in 1603. A large tract of country, therefore, was previously regarded as debatable land, "which became the scene of endless
warfare, pillaging and burning. Any building within it, such as Sizergh,
had to be of massive structure to discourage the attentions of raiders,
and to act as a place of refuge within whose barmekin neighbouring
farmers might drive their stock and find temporary refuge whenever
the beacon fires were lit to give warning of a border foray."

Some pele towers, however, were that and nothing else. Small
bastilles of this kind still form a chain over the Northumbrian countryside. In the churchyard at Corbridge a stout pele now provides the vicar
with a convenient parish room!†

* See the author's *Yorkshire Villages* (Robert Hale).

† Further examples are mentioned by Dr Pevsner in the introduction to his Northumberland volume in the *Buildings of England* series (Penguin).

But to return to Sizergh. A good approach—now that National Trust ownership opens its doors to everybody—is via the Kendal road heading north from the Kent estuary, or along the by-lane that wanders in the same direction, but through the charming Brigsteer Woods. The utter peace of Brigsteer is in marked contrast with what Sizergh, and neighbouring peles like Hazelslack and Arnside Towers, also the core of Levens Hall, stood for. Some of these peles have barely changed in appearance since the days of the raiders. At Sizergh, Levens and Dallam, however, the pele has become the nucleus of a graceful home, each furnished in a manner that the old order of things would never have allowed.

Sizergh Castle has Tudor and Elizabethan embellishments, with an outer staircase that leads down in stages, with almost regal panache, to the lake. Levens also donned Elizabethan garb, but here one hardly knows which to admire most, the glorious oak panelling and chimney-pieces, and a room hung with Cordova leather; or the topiary work of the garden, as devised about 1700 by M. Beaumont, the King's gardener. The shapes of these trees include pyramids and pagodas, crowns and stove-pipe hats, animals and birds, also a maid-in-waiting. "The finest topiary garden in England" is the justifiable boast of the owners, Mr and Mrs Bagot.

Dallam Tower waited until the eighteenth century for its meta-morphosis—a lovely Georgian staircase with inlaid treads taking the place of a narrow, spiral stair that probably served the original pele. My wife and I were once privileged to ascend this fine staircase and take tea with the kindly owners, Brigadier Tryon-Wilson and his family. As we sat on some Chippendale ribbon-back chairs, the Kent estuary gleamed through the windows and the nearer Lakeland hills rose beyond like a hazy dream. In another age, we should all have been looking and listening, fearfully, in about the same direction, for the sign of oncoming marauders.

The Border country itself bristles with castles, like spines on a porcupine. Dr Pevsner rightly points out that in Northumberland, 'the castle county of England', such fortifications continued in regular use long after the rest of England was taking things easier, on a manor-house basis.

In the fulness of time, places like Norham Castle kindled all that was romantic in the soul of Sir Walter Scott, and that of Turner the water-colourist. In Turner's study, Norham Castle and the ford over the Tweed which it guarded, are seen in the gloaming; a faery scene, innocent of menace. Scott's *Marmion* peoples the fortress with warriors, captives weep in its "donjon keep" and as night falls and the castle gates are barred . . .

The Warder kept his guard,
Low humming as he paced along,
Some ancient Border gathering song.

Today, the romance is of another order. After climbing the long, steep village street, we approach the fortress unchallenged, and catch a glimpse through the trees of the Tweed far below, with perhaps a tiny boat sculling peacefully by. The only living things within the castle's roofless walls are the birds, which make a mockery of all this show of defiance, chirping and trilling in and around the kitchen quarters and the hall, where so many have dined before shaking the mailed fist, yet again, at the ancient foe. It all seems rather farcical today, like a bit of play-acting. But when Bishop Flambard of Durham built the first castle here, and his successor, Hugh Pudsay, started building the present fortress, the Church had turned militant in earnest, entering the lists with zest.

Wark Castle, which glowered over the Tweed farther to the west, opposite Coldstream, now provides little substance to the old threat, being a dismal ruin. Visually, there are far better rewards at Ford, 8 miles to the east. Immediately prior to the Battle of Flodden (9th September, 1513) the Scottish army crossed the Tweed at Coldstream, beseiged Wark and Norham Castles in their stride, and then attacked Ford Castle. Here, the word 'attacked' has amorous overtones, for it was at Ford that James IV of Scotland dallied with the fascinating Lady Heron, chatelaine at the castle, before his men set the place on fire!

Ford has taken a beating at the hands of the Scots several times, but the castle always 'shook itself' and rose again, to become in due course the attractive range of buildings one sees today, high above the River Till. Some of the original towers still stand. One of them, the Flag Tower, was used by Lady Waterford last century as her art studio. In the eighteenth century somebody had Gothicized the castle, providing gateways, for example, that would serve well as a stage set but offer no resistance whatever to a foe. They are prettily rusticated and even boast a (fixed) portcullis and mock crenellations. In her turn, Lady Waterford gave the place a baronial appearance, and at a medieval tournament suggested by the ever-resourceful Walter Scott she was chosen as the Queen of Beauty.

When I was there some years ago, all this pageantry had become the setting for youthful activities sponsored by the National Association of Boys' Clubs. Lady Waterford, herself childless, would have been delighted to see some of these lads practising archery in her forecourt, and elsewhere learning pottery, sculpture and woodcraft. A few went off at intervals to train as climbers on the Cheviots.

Those youths would pick up a lot of history, too, especially in one of the castle's older rooms. Here, in a glass case, one saw the ring, sword and dagger of James IV—all taken on Flodden Field by the victor, Thomas Earl of Surrey. The ring and dagger had been sent to James by the Queen of France with a letter asking him, as her knight, to "take three steps on to English soil" and "for her to break a lance". In losing the battle, and his own life in the process, he broke a lance indeed. To quote Sir John McEwen, Surrey's triumph "was greater than he knew; for never again was Scotland's voice to be heard, speaking as an equal among her peers, in the council of European nations".*

As for the Scots, they put their lament characteristically into poetry. One verse sobs out:

> Dool and wae for the order sent our lads to the Border!
> The English for ance by guile wan the day;
> The Flowers of the Forest, that fought aye the foremost,
> The prime of our land, are cauld in the clay.

And so one can roam through Northumberland, storming castle after castle for the sake of some thrilling story, and reaping into the bargain much fine scenery. Aydon, Alnwick, Chipchase, Haughton, Warkworth; what an alphabet of military prowess, and it could be enhanced still further by the inclusion of castles which dot the Northumbrian coast and its hinterland, almost from Tweed to Tyne.

Berwick's castle had withstood many assaults but meekly surrendered to the demands of railway pioneers in Victorian times. The station platform usurped the site of the great hall in which kings have supped and taken great decisions. Practically all that now remains of this commanding fortress is the water tower, and the White Wall that reaches down to the Tweed beside the Royal Border (railway) Bridge which had stolen some of the castle masonry.

From some vantage point along the Elizabethan town walls in Berwick one can discern, in the hazy southern distance, a little pyramid lapped by the sea. This is the castle on Holy Island. It stands like some fabled keep on a tapering plinth of Whin Sill rock, and, like St Michael's Mount off the Cornish coast, gives a leap to the imagination. It seems to have sprouted upwards from the parent rock.

In such a place might some wizard have pored over his magic books and brewed strange elixirs. Actually, Fort Beblowe—its original name—was built in the reign of Elizabeth I to protect the harbour. By some chicanery, which lured the garrison on to a boat and made them drunk, the castle was seized for the Pretender in 1715. After a couple of days, however, the interlopers—who had expected reinforcements which never arrived—fled, only to be captured nearby amongst the island rocks, and marched off to Berwick gaol.

* From an article on Flodden published in *History Today*, May 1958.

Early this century the spell of the place laid hold of Edward Hulton, then proprietor of *Country Life*, and Sir Edwin Lutyens right thoroughly fulfilled the romantic potential of the castle for its new owner. Since 1944 the National Trust has thrown a mantle of protection around the castle, which means that anybody can now enter the spirit of the place and enjoy the fun of Lutyens' architectural conceits. After spiralling up the parent rock, and ringing a bell which sends eerie echoes within, like so many warbling sprites, you tread under low arches, through creepy passages and low-vaulted chambers. Surely, in one of those chambers, 'our wizard' lurks in the shadows. . . .

I often wonder what the nuns made of it all!—some nuns we had seen on their island pilgrimage. Their devotions complete, they were picnicking at the foot of the castle as we passed by, chuckling to themselves as at some new, unprecedented experience to come.

As seen from Holy Island, Bamburgh Castle is a giant reclining on another but much larger Whin Sill outcrop. Perhaps the best nearer view is that from the beach, on the northern approach, where dark bands of dolerite spread like tentacles over the shore. The village green affords another fine view of this imposing fortress, partly Norman, which Lord Crewe's trustees rescued from decay in 1757, and Lord Armstrong over-restored about seventy years ago. Even so, it must be grand for the present tenants, living as they do within the context of so much stirring history and enjoying such superb views up and down the coast and out to the Farne Islands. An arrangement entirely in tune with these days of stately home 'collecting' occasionally allows visitors some share in these visual excitements.

It is best to approach our next coastal castle from the north, also, and on *foot*, for from this angle Dunstanborough Castle looks impregnable and demands from everybody a stiff, zigzag climb up the dolerite bastion on which—before it fell into decay in Elizabethan times—the castle stood so proudly. Historical records enable one to see the place in its prime, with the highest in the land contending here for favours or engaging in some treachery. J. M. W. Turner saw it in very different light—a place for dreams, legends (there are plenty of them at Dunstanborough!), and haunting memories. But there is no substitute for an actual visit. Where else in Britain can you feel such sadness at departed glory, framed in so wild a setting! The ruined walls paraphrase the tumbled boulders far below; even in the castle's heyday it needed a savage sea-chasm to provide an escape route for Queen Margaret. Gulls and fulmars now weave around the ruins their own continual lament.

A tour of *all* our northern castles would tick away at least half of any normal life span. Some tourists have eyes for little else, just as others specialize in country houses, or churches, or cathedrals. Once, in a

Durham hotel, I overheard a middle-aged man say to his dining-table companions, "This is my *cathedral* suit." He was making a leisurely survey of all our English cathedrals. The suit he wore was a loose-fitting tweed outfit that had evidently rubbed against scores of tombs, climbed many a dusty newel stair, and polished much ancient seating. I have yet to hear of an outfit given over exclusively to *castle* exploration. But when you think of some of the places already mentioned in this chapter, and others to come, such an outfit would have to be hard-wearing indeed.

The ivy-clad walls and towers of Barnard Castle, high above the River Tees; Hylton Castle, near Sunderland, inhabited—so they say—by nobody but its 'cauld lad' of ancient legend; Raby, still favoured by Lord Barnard's family, though as defiant as ever; Bowes, Pickering, Helmsley, and so many others. Many of them have towers to climb, narrow passages that challenge man and boy alike, or dungeons dark and drear. The appeal of an old castle is that you can either take it at face value, enjoying all its visual and hidden enchantments; or regard it chiefly as a 'history book', replete with all the paraphernalia of siege, battle and foray, laced with illustrious names.

But those dungeons! In the exuberance of youth, I once made a brief tally of what Yorkshire castles provide in this vein. Skipton Castle has two dungeons, one reached by sixteen steps that disappear into the gloom, the other a horrible hole minus any source of light. Richmond's dungeon lies beneath the Gold Hold Tower, named after a hoard of treasure supposed to have been found there long ago, so tantalizingly near the prisoners. The governor of Scarborough Castle, which stands magnificently on its sea cliff between the town's two bays, could consign his captives to a dungeon hewn in the rock, where the constant booming of the waves would add something sinister to their terrors.

A 'popular' feature at Bolton Castle in Wensleydale is the dungeon in the floor of the north turret. When I first looked down, many years ago, the only means of entry was by *falling* in, with peril to limbs and clothing alike. Today, wooden steps afford some help to the curious. My friend George Jackson thus describes the dungeon in his admirable history of the castle: "Originally the unfortunate prisoners were *dropped* through the square trap in the vaulting to alight on a damp floor some eight feet below. A heavy flag, which sealed the cell, and a guard in the small chamber above, precluded all opportunities of escape. The two small comforts provided—a latrine and an air-vent in the north wall—were probably considered advanced prison reforms by the fourteenth-century humanitarians. The air-vent, in addition to providing ventilation, gave sympathetic friends an opportunity to supply prisoners with food and messages of consolation." In such a loathsome pit, I'm thinking, consolation would seem superfluous!

St Mary's, Whitby: a Norman church remodelled by local shipwrights in the seventeenth and eighteenth centuries

Liverpool: part of the university precinct, looking towards the city centre and the river and flanked by the two cathedrals

(*above*) Locomotion No. 1 carved on a pew-end at Stockton-on-Tees parish church to mark the centenary of the Stockton and Darlington Railway. (*right*) The Vicar's Pele within the churchyard at Corbridge

Even worse is the dungeon at Knaresborough Castle. The sight and feel of it could always darken the next hour for me, in my early days, yet it held a macabre fascination. Only a few yards away the limestone crag, on which the castle keep stands, falls precipitately to the River Nidd, helping to create a view comparable with that enjoyed by Richmond's castle, similarly situated above the River Swale.

Such pleasant surroundings must have emphasized the tragic lot of those incarcerated within the castle walls. But at Knaresborough the dungeon is no rude pit. The official guide-book even understates the case in describing it as "a fine specimen of good workmanship". In some ways it resembles a church crypt, having a flight of steps that descend from the castle yard, and a circular pillar—9 feet 6 inches in circumference—supporting a vaulted roof. But there the resemblance ends. Iron hoops embedded in one wall show where the prisoners were chained, all in a row, awaiting release by liberation (most rare!), or by death.

The custodian whom I knew best had the histrionic sense well developed. After admitting a few visitors, he would close the oak-studded entrance door, switch off the (recently installed) electric light, and then move across to that central pillar. When a fresh prisoner was bundled in, he would say, room was found for him along that line of shackled men by shifting the others down the wall in order of ghastly precedence, thus releasing the first one for the executioner's attention. From the one small window in the 15-feet-thick wall, a narrow shaft of light falls dramatically on to the block where the unfortunates came to their end, in full sight of the others. At this point the guide would wave his arm or leg in that one beam of light, and everybody gasped in horror. A gruesome bit of 'theatre'. I always suspected that the guide was enjoying himself immensely!

My elder brother-in-law, a Lancashire man, used to fill my boyhood mind with horrifying pictures of the dungeons in Lancaster Castle. Years later, when the Lancashire Witches seized my imagination, I could see them—Mother Demdike, Chattox, and all the rest of them—mouldering in those cells, where no devilish chicanery could deliver them. I heard them muttering ancient spells and curses; appealing to their 'familiars', repeating Scripture backwards. All in vain. Lancaster Castle had them in its irrevocable grip.

The reality was not far removed from my imaginings, as anybody may judge for himself today, on visiting this huge threat grimly fashioned in stone. George Fox and Margaret Fell were put on trial in the same room that had seen those witches sentenced to death. Far above, on the roof of the keep, 'John o' Gaunt's Chair' still stands to its full 10 feet, as it did when news of the approach of the Spanish

Armada was flashed abroad and "Skiddaw saw the fire that burned on Gaunt's embattled pile". From Roman times onward, Lancaster Castle has performed almost every role that such a place is capable of. In 1858, here in the Shire Hall, Jenny Lind even sang to an enraptured audience!

The history of Carlisle Castle is almost as varied, with Scottish and English elements in about equal proportions, for, like Berwick-upon-Tweed, Carlisle was a 'shuttlecock' between the two warring countries. Royal palace, seat of parliament, prison—the castle has been all these things. It figures repeatedly in the Border ballads, the outwitting of its captain being a popular theme.

One of the ballads sings the praises of those who rescued William Armstrong of Kinmont from Carlisle Castle on the night of 14th April 1596. 'Kinmont Willie', his usual tag, was one of the best-known cattle thieves, or reivers, who then plagued the Border country. His capture during a mutually recognized period of truce along the Border, was like a red rag to a bull. The 'bull' was none other than the Laird of Buccleuch. With a body of men as incensed as himself at such treachery, he set off to "herry a corbie's nest"—Carlisle Castle. Such a dash and a plother they made as they stormed the prison which held their reiving brother, that the Warden of the English Marches and his garrison "did keip thamselffis close", for what were they against 500 wild Scots? The number had been judiciously multiplied five times over, to make reason with Queen Elizabeth when she heard of the affair, and to soften her anger.

Thus was Kinmont Willie delivered from his chains. But there was no escape for another from over the Border—Mary Stuart. In 1568 she fled from Scotland and flung herself on the mercy of 'cousin Elizabeth', Queen of England. A friendly-disposed Richard Lowther, deputy Warden of the Marches, met her as she crossed the Solway and escorted her in good faith to Carlisle Castle. But Elizabeth had given orders that Mary was to be kept under close watch. Worship at the cathedral was permitted her, and for her amusement football matches and a few hunts were arranged. When it was feared that Mary's supporters in the town might effect her escape, the warm-hearted Richard Lowther invited her to his home, Lowther Castle. Her welcome there was short-lived. After only one night at this fine country residence (now in ruins) she was moved to Bolton Castle in Wensleydale. Her "long heart-ache road to Fotheringhay" had begun. As for Sir Richard Lowther, he was despatched, under a cloud, to the Tower of London.

7

Ancestral Homes

IT is almost trite to say that many a country house has an ancestry worth probing. In the North that ancestry will often reach back to the times of Border warfare. A few examples have already been cited. On visiting such houses, one may be impressed at first by the overlaying Tudor or Jacobean work, or perhaps a Georgian scheme of things, with its rich display of Adam 'prettiness' and Chippendale grace. Yet beneath that elegant garb there may well be a coat of mail.

Chillingham Castle does little to hide its ancestry as a fourteenth-century tower house, and the famous herd of wild cattle in the adjoining park serve admirably to emphasize the ancient character of the place. No cattle thieves from over the Border dare tackle *them*; not for nothing were these beasts descended from the original British wild ox! Even Thomas Bewick and Landseer, there only on artistic bent, had to cope with the animals' ferocious attentions.

Chipchase Castle, too, still looks formidable and defiant, though its present role is peaceful enough. But Wallington is in this respect deceptive. What you see here, alongside that attractive road (B 6342) leading north from Kirkharle to Rothbury, is something resembling a French château: seventeenth-century elegance in a setting of far-spreading parkland. The interior sustains the same artistic role and also derives something from safe and secure Victorian times. The *full* truth is much broader. A castle stood here in medieval times but the sole remains are tucked away beneath the present house. To quote the late Sir Charles Trevelyan, "Down there are still to be seen the bottom storey of the castle, several doorways hinged for heavy gates, vaulted ceilings, narrow windows, and the well which must have supplied water when the moss-troopers were abroad."

Yet those turbulent days are echoed in the more sophisticated house above.

In Victorian times the central courtyard, part of Sir William Blackett's seventeenth-century building, was reduced in size, roofed over, and at John Ruskin's suggestion turned into a gallery of art devoted to Northumbrian history. The fifth of these paintings deals with an episode during Border warfare, but it is best to confront them in proper order. A pleasing feature of the paintings is that some of the chief characters portrayed, almost life size, were modelled on contemporary persons known to, and even including, members of the Trevelyan family.

Sir Charles Trevelyan once acted as my personal guide to these 'windows of history'. Although he described them effectually in his own book on Wallington, I got the overspill of his wide knowledge.

First comes the building of Hadrian's Wall—a vigorous composition, with a Roman centurion overseeing a cohort of foreign workers. The section of wall shown is that which careers over the Whin Sill crags, near Borcovicium, Crag Lough being far below. Very aptly, the centurion is a likeness of John Clayton, one of the first to conduct excavations in this prolific area, while "the striking face of a soldier with black hair and an aquiline nose was Dr Bruce", the famous authority on the Roman Wall.

The Dark Ages pass by, and then Cuthbert emerges from the womb of time. King Egfrith has landed with his retinue on Farne Island to persuade the hermit to accept the Bishopric of Hexham. Cuthbert's reluctance to leave the island—where he is observed digging onions for his next meal—is plain to see; an eider duck at his feet and the sea-swallows overhead seem to companion his thought. For this portrait of Cuthbert the model was the Reverend G. Cooper-Abbs, whose descendants now live at Mount Grace Priory, in North Yorkshire. King Egfrith was another local personality, and a prominent figure in the King's retinue turns out to have been "Mr Gow, one of the finest estate agents in the North country".

In episode number three, the marauding Danes materialize in their 'serpent boats' out of the morning mist, and land near Tynemouth Priory. All the terror of their coming is here suggested, as the inhabitants scramble away, up the cliffs. We see the tonsured monk with his holy vessels, books and altar candles; a little lad with his toy wind-mill; and, amongst others, a fine-looking woman laden with hastily gathered household effects; she was impersonated by Pauline, Lady Trevelyan, who was largely instrumental in having this 'gallery of time' created.

Another side-step, and we are witnessing Bede on his deathbed in the monastery at Jarrow. He has lived "just long enough to dictate the end of his translation of the Gospel of St John". In a sand-glass nearby the sand has almost run out.

Then dawn the Middle Ages with their tale of Border reivers. Regarding this episode Sir Charles must be quoted at some length: "A scene in a Border castle . . . when 'riding and reiving' was a main occupation in the Tyne and Rede valleys. The men are seated waiting their meal. One of the retainers has the Northumberland pipes under his arm. The lady of the house enters, holding up the Spur in the Dish, to show the larder is empty and that they [the raiders] must ride before another sirloin smokes on the board."

Now follows the characterisation. "William Henry Charlton, of Hesleyside, is portrayed as the master of the house; the Dame is probably Miss Dodd. . . . The old man on the left is Andrew Pearson of Cambo; the monk, Wilson, the Hesleyside gamekeeper." Sir Charles adds that the piper was that well-known character, William Armstrong of Linacres. In imagination, the blaring of pipes will stir the assembled menfolk to heed the matron's challenge and ride off to replenish the larder at the expense of some neighbour's cattle, or, better still, a few from over the Border.

Feud and foray are still in the air, in the next scene, which shows Bernard Gilpin attempting to reconcile two opposing factions in Rothbury Church. Bell Scott, the painter of this series, introduces himself into the episode as one of the knights in armour, while Sir Walter Trevelyan is the calm figure at the lectern.

The masquerade concludes with a graphic representation of Grace Darling and her father rescuing the survivors of the *Forfarshire*; and another of Newcastle quayside in all its busyness, soon after the erection of the High Level Bridge. The three figures wielding hammers in the foreground of the painting are portraits of actual men employed in George Stephenson's works.

I have described this gallery in some detail because it makes of Northumbrian history a continuing pageant. And from the spandrils above, other notable men look on, among them Emperor Hadrian who built the famous Wall; Alcuin the great Saxon scholar; James, Earl of Derwentwater, so tragically implicated in the 1715 Jacobite rebellion; Thomas Bewick, naturalist and engraver; Earl Grey of the

Reform Bill (1832); several of the Trevelyan family; and George Stephenson, 'father of modern railways'.

All these scenes and figures, portrayed beneath a spirited version of the Border ballad of Chevy Chase, seem particularly appropriate in a house associated with several eminent historians.

Lord Macaulay is himself represented here by a collection of his annotated books, the table at which he wrote his famous *History of England*, and his four-poster. His nephew, Sir George Otto Trevelyan, partly wrote the *History of the American Revolution* in the Wallington 'study'. Sir George's youngest son, George Macaulay Trevelyan, drew inspiration even from the set of toy soldiers kept in the house.

These lead soldiers were the favourite playthings of Sir Charles and his brothers, when boys. There are over 6,000 of them, in British, French and German uniforms. In later days G. M. Trevelyan ascribed "his own capacity for so vividly describing battles", in his historical works, to the 'war games' played out so often on the floor of the house museum, in the golden days of youth. The soldiers, now disposed as for the armies of Napoleon, Blucher and Wellington, are displayed in a glass case for all National Trust visitors to see. And Mrs Pauline Dower, Sir Charles' daughter, has painted a suitable background for them.

Country houses that reflect their own district, and local history also, are not too plentiful in County Durham. Perhaps Lumley Castle might be cited, though it is still of distinctly militant aspect and no longer a private home. It is a hall of residence for Durham University. I have no doubt that one of the first things that students learn, after their arrival, is an old story about James I and the Lumley family pedigree. The pedigree was being elaborated at great length for the King's benefit. Nothing of personal glory and achievement was being omitted. The rigmarole went on so long, and reached so far back in time, that at last a bored James protested, "Oh, mon, gang nae further; let me digest the knowledge I hae gained, for I didna ken Adam's other name was Lumley."

The founder of the family was Liulph, whom Camden described as "a man of right great nobility in the time of King Edward the Confessour". St Cuthbert, dead for well-nigh 400 years, had frequently appeared to Liulph, advising him in many things. Eventually, the "noble generous man"—Liulph's usual description in the Red Velvet Book—was murdered by the Bishop of Durham's chaplain, through jealousy of Liulph's superior wisdom. Surely an unusual motive? It seems fitting that Morcar, the younger of Liulph's sons, should later join the monks of Jarrow where Bede—Cuthbert's biographer—had lived and died.

When Lumley Castle was turned over to Durham University many of the furnishings went to Sandbeck Park, in South Yorkshire, home of later members of the Lumley family, the Earls of Scarbrough. No greater contrast could be imagined than that between the baronial castle overlooking Chester-le-Street, and this Palladian home designed about 1760 by James Paine. Because of those transferred furnishings and family documents, the castle lives again to some extent in the Georgian mansion.

The late Earl of Scarbrough once showed me, with veneration, the Red Velvet Book compiled for Baron John Lumley in Elizabethan times. A huge volume, it contains a detailed inventory of the Baron's "monumentes of Marbles, Pictures and tables in Paynture, with other [of] his Lordshippes Howsholde stuffe . . . Anno 1590". There are many strange references; one, for example, to a painting of Sir John Lutterel (of Hooten Pagnell, near Doncaster, and Dunster Castle, Somerset), "who died of the sweat in K. Edw. 6 tyme", and to another showing "an old man fancying a yong woman".

Great personages are represented amongst the pictures, some of which now hang at Sandbeck Park. Among them are "Queen Elizabeth as she was comying first to the Crowne; Erasmus of Roterdame; Sir Gefferey Chaucer, knight; Ignatius de Loyola, first founder of the societie of Jesus; and Thomas, the first Lord Crumwell", Henry VIII's vicar-general for the suppression of the monasteries.

One memorable portrait shows John, Lord Lumley, who fought at Flodden though he had barely reached manhood. The artist has portrayed him in pensive mood, which reflects, perhaps, a lingering memory of Flodden's butchery. . . .

Sandbeck's own records strike a happier note, though there are some odd things too. When the house was being built, for instance, Richard Marshall, one of the masons, agreed to make the chimneys "so that they shall cause no offence when fires are made therein". Coal fires were long considered 'offensive' because of possible damage to my lord's tapestry hangings and other decorations. The owner, on his part, agreed "to allow unto the said Marshall [while the work was being done] one roome about the said house for him and his people to lay their bedds in". An endorsement on this document shows that the chief masons turned out to be "arrant knaves, both, for they performed nothing accordingly but gott my money and wold never mesure their work".

Despite these annoyances, the place grew into one of Yorkshire's fine houses, where Richard, the sixth Lord, could stage memorable concerts. Himself an accomplished violinist, he would often get "two or three of the best players at Sandbeck to play for him a week at a time". It was he, probably, who adapted one large room for these concerts by raising the ceiling and decorating it with birds, flowers and musical emblems. The Lumleys had come a long way from that grim fortress home, with its battle echoes, in County Durham.

In the way of country houses, Yorkshire presents an *embarras des richesses*. Great and small, they run through every building period and exemplify the work of many of the more famous architects, with our own, Yorkshire-born John Carr and William Kent frequently offsetting the Brobdingnagian mannerisms of Vanburgh (as at Castle Howard) and the dainty effusions of the Adam brothers.

Even when making a selection of houses that have an eloquence beyond purely family affairs, the choice is wide.

At Burton Constable Hall one enters into the heart of the Seigniory of Holderness, in Yorkshire's farthest east. This Jacobean house with Georgian refinements is set in spacious parkland, and the present owner, John Chichester-Constable, is forty-sixth Lord Paramount of the Seigniory. This high-sounding office goes back to Norman times, but most of the privileges have gone. Formerly, I was told, "if anybody within the far-spreading Seigniory died intestate his property came by right to the Lord Paramount; also the estate of any Holderness suicide".

The Lord Paramount can still claim everything washed up on his shoreline, which covers 70 miles of coast and [Humber] estuary. But there is a snag. He has to dispose of any whale that may be stranded on that shore—a costly obligation, with none of the old whaling rewards as compensation. Hence the family's concern, some years back, when a 'school' of whales, numbering about 150, was sighted not far away in the North Sea. In a dream, the late Lord Paramount told me, he saw them all strewing his beaches with their expensive bulk. Fortunately, the dream did not materialize!

How wonderful it was to have had the freedom of these extensive grounds for a whole day, and a set of state rooms which blend history, art and architecture in quite enchanting manner! Personally, having seen much of the vast interior in the company of the late Brigadier Chichester-Constable, I would relish the unique experience that Fred Elwell, R.A., of Beverley once described for me.

He was painting a water-colour of the Long Gallery. Lined with oak panelling and hung with portraits that are in themselves a history of England—Mary Stuart, Thomas Cromwell, Chancellor Thomas More are just a few of the characters—this room alone could keep anybody fascinated for hours. Because the family were absent that day, Fred Elwell was locked in the room so that he should not be disturbed. But as the servants completely forgot his presence, the artist's long session in a chamber that could almost reproduce the ghost scene in *Ruddygore*, supported by a few family spectres, had somehow to be terminated. Our Royal Academician assumed the skill of a cat burglar and climbed out of a window. Many years later, he showed me that

Ford Castle, Northumberland

Warkworth Castle, Northumberland

painting. It seemed as though the domestic ghost of a nun must have materialized in *duplicate*, on that memorable occasion, for *two* nuns are stepping determinedly towards his standpoint through this evocative corridor of time.

Somehow, Harewood House, near Harrogate, seems altogether too grand for such pleasantries, though many a humorous titbit could be recounted, as when one wealthy American visitor, after rhapsodizing his way through the mansion, pressed into the guide's palm a gratuity which turned out to be—one penny! A mistake, obviously, but the late Princess Royal enjoyed the joke as much as anybody, especially when the guide laughingly said that a penny was evidently all that a tour of Harewood House seemed worth!

Harewood is indeed one of England's finest flowerings of all that was best in eighteenth-century elegance. Many great names mingled their brilliance here. John Carr designed the house, in 1759. Robert Adam came two months later, "dazzled the eyes of the squire", Edwin Lascelles, with his own schemes and set to work on the interior. Rose and Collins filled the ceilings with exquisite plaster work. Angelica Kaufmann, Antonio Zucchi and Biago Rebecca painted them with classical mythology, Chippendale made the furniture, and the surrounding park was landscaped by Capability Brown. What a team!

And then came the pictures, priceless ones by many of the world's greatest painters. Yet Tintoretto, Bellini, El Greco, Veronese and the rest must, for our immediate purpose, yield to the artists through whose works we can see the local countryside.

Thomas Girtin lingered during his North Country tours to portray Edwin Lascelles' new house, also the neighbouring bridge over the River Wharfe. Turner came over from Farnley and lavished his skill, not only on scenes of the palatial house, but also on the ruined castle where the first lords of Harewood had lived, in medieval times. Another 'Turner' evokes all the witchery of Plompton Rocks, near Knaresborough, for which Edwin Lascelles had provided a lake-mirror, before transferring his affections to Harewood. But lonely Plompton with its grotesque crags and grottoes still exercises its magic, like a dream that never came to fruition.

John Varley left an incomplete water-colour of the model village of Harewood, so different from what one sees now, with the avenue grown to maturity and all the buildings complete, but nevertheless a charming peep of Harewood in its promising infancy. George Richmond, whose portrait of Charlotte Brontë is so well known, came to Harewood to paint Louisa, Lady Harewood, and evidently snatched a few moments, while changing for dinner one day, to sketch Capability Brown's lake and woodland vistas as seen from his bedroom window. And then Sir Alfred Munnings, who used to go on painting holidays

9

with Fred Elwell of Beverley, made hunters and hounds come alive in his study of the Bramham Moor Hunt.

But an estate like Harewood has never fully exhausted its potential, especially now that the public are admitted. In 1970, therefore, the Earl of Harewood introduced a bird garden, siting it near Capability Brown's landscape effects. Whether Brown himself ever visualized such 'capabilities' is more than doubtful, but surely his heart would rejoice and his solemn face light up could he see his ornamental lake supplemented by ponds devoted to king penguins, Chilean flamingoes, snow geese from Alaska, and mandarin duck from China and Japan. Multi-coloured macaws fly overhead, crowned cranes from East Africa go through their amusing paces, and gay toucans nest in the trees.

Capability Brown's ambitious scheme has surely reached its apotheosis.

If anybody desired to peer into the past he couldn't do better than visit Browsholme Hall, near Clitheroe. The hall is an epitome of English history, though with its own special overtones. When I was conducted through the place privily, some years ago, by the owner, Colonel Robert Parker, I began to feel rather like one of those characters in Harrison Ainsworth's novel, *The Lancashire Witches*, who could momentarily invest bygone people with renewed life and purpose. It is an odd feeling.

Browsholme is on the Yorkshire side of the River Ribble, but the hall is mentioned frequently in Ainsworth's romance. When Alison Device is crowned May Queen she tells her mother what she would do if she were a real queen: "I'd make you rich, mother, and build you a grand house to live in, much grander than Browsholme, or Downham, or Middleton." Alison had named the finest mansions of the district; it is not surprising that Browsholme aroused her chief envy and headed the list.

Richard Parker had built the original house of timber and daub, but soon after 1507 this was supplanted by a stone dwelling which a later owner enriched by having it re-fronted with red sandstone. Further improvements occurred in Georgian and Regency times, when the present landscape garden came into being, Pendle Hill acting as backcloth 7 or 8 miles to the south.

The countryside to which Browsholme is the key, however, is not Pendle but the surrounding Forest of Bowland, for the owners have long been hereditary bow-bearers of this fascinating area. The name, Parker—first adopted in the fourteenth century—signifies the office of park-keeper. "To hold this office," says the colonel, "the Parker had to be well versed in reading, writing, accountancy and the law, and many of the succeeding owners of the hall have been graduates of Cambridge and trained in the law, and have held such distinctions as High Sheriff, Deputy Lieutenant, and Justice of the Peace".

No longer do herds of deer and wild cattle roam through the former royal hunting ground. Yet all is not lost. Presiding from one end of the Tudor hall (the entrance room) there is a challenging portrait of Thomas Parker, Bowbearer in 1592, wearing a magistrate's outfit of that period. Nearby, Edward Parker, Bowbearer about 1690, holds a staff tipped with a buck's head and a bugle horn hangs from his girdle. And on a side wall hangs the actual iron stirrup gauge used by the bowbearer to test a dog's girth. If any dog belonging to a local farmer or tenant could not squeeze through the ring—9 inches at its widest—the dog might have to be mutilated, or even killed; a device to protect the king's precious deer.

Moving slowly through the hall, beneath deer antlers, ancient pieces of armour and several monastic emblems, we came at length to a remarkable display of woodcarving at the far end of the long room. It comprises two Charles II oak chests, a family manuscript cupboard, dated 1681, and, above, part of a late thirteenth-century reredos from Whalley Abbey. "The whole feature was created by Thomas Lister Parker in 1817", I was told, "to replace a water organ whose maintenance he could no longer afford." The saints enthroned on the reredos suggest a music of their own, in plainsong and chant, and set me thinking of the vital part Whalley Abbey has played in North Country history. In particular, I thought of John Paslew, the last abbot, who fired a beacon on Pendle Hill to signalize the Pilgrimage of Grace—and was later executed for treason.

Then I discovered something macabre.

Only a few yards away from the Whalley reredos the family have preserved the skull of one who was martyred after the same insurrection. The strange sequel of this incident is best told in Colonel Parker's own words: "When the top storey of the house was removed in 1703 the skull was brought down from the family chapel. It was always treated with great reverence until in the late 1850s Edward Parker, then a boy, buried it in the garden as a practical joke. Disaster followed disaster; the façade began to fall away from the Tudor walls behind it, fires broke out from smouldering beams, and there were many deaths in the family. Finally, the frightened youngster confessed, and the skull was dug up and returned to its cupboard. Everything became normal again, but the family had to move to Alkincoates until the house was once again habitable."

"Where is the skull now?" was my natural rejoinder.

"Safely locked in that court cupboard," came the reassuring answer.

Another curious item is the porter's hooded chair of James I's time. It resembles a watchman's hut and has lately come into its own again.

"It was always placed in this position, near the main entrance", said the colonel, "so that an eye could be kept on callers. Since I opened the house to the public, the porter's chair has been used by the man who collects the entrance fees."

During my own visit a group of young schoolboys filed past the porter's seat; how entertaining it was to observe their several reactions as the house gradually unfolded its past. For them, as for me, figures emerged from the Wars of the Roses; from the Civil War period—when the place was ransacked by Roundheads and a 7-year-old boy of the house was seized as hostage; and from Regency times, too, one memorable figure being J. M. W. Turner newly arrived to paint some of his charming water-colours. Every boyhood instinct, however, was aroused by the sight of so many mementoes of the chase, from hunting horns and spurs to deer antlers and many other trophies. Bowland Forest in a nutshell.

At one point in their tour of the house the boys had their school history lessons revitalized by Colonel Parker's illuminating references to Jane Lane, "the resourceful lady who helped Charles II to escape after the Battle of Worcester; there she is in that portrait"; also to Bonnie Prince Charlie, whose portrait on silk was one of those smuggled into England in somebody's boot-heel, when the Stuart cause was still *sub rosa*.

Colonel Parker clearly loves to share with his visitors these and other personalities who have helped to make Browsholme Hall what it is— one of the most rewarding country houses in the North. I left him entering up the latest visit in a register, beneath the quizzical glance of John Parker, a bow-bearing ancestor painted in hunting attire by a cousin, Arthur Devis, in 1750.

On moving farther west we soon encounter some of the black-and-white houses for which this district is famous. In Cheshire they are called 'magpie' houses, for obvious reasons. Little Moreton Hall, near Congleton, is an outstanding example. The exterior is a multi-patterned design of timbers with plaster infillings. Long and short, curved and straight, the timbers seem at first sight to pose some riddle. In bright sunshine the effect is certainly dazzling, but one must admire the ingenuity behind it all.

Chester city abounds with such buildings. George Lloyd, Bishop of Chester from 1604 to 1615, lived in one of the best. Here, the rural version of the style is elaborated to include on the Watergate Row frontage a panel of Biblical scenes, plus a few animals. Leche House, next door, chimes in with its own sixteenth-century variations, and even preserves, within, a fireplace priest hole big enough to hide two persons. And then, not many yards away, Stanley Palace presents itself as the one-time town house of the Stanleys of Alderley, with a bold façade of timbered circles and half-circles, and tree-bough shapes thrusting upwards in the dormer gables. The town also has its 'magpie' inns.

Lancashire corners a few 'magpies' too, and fine 'birds' they are. Think of Speke Hall, near Liverpool! Fortunately, one of them reaches beyond its own context, as a typical fifteenth-century manor house, and reflects something that happened here to transform life for thousands of people. The house bears a rather charming name, Hall-i'-th'-Wood, and stands on the fringe of industrial Bolton.

When the earlier part of the hall was built, in post and plaster, it was surrounded by woodland and important people began to call. In 1591 a great-grandson of the family added the stone portion with its fine tower porch and lofty chimney stacks. The Brownlows now had the best of two architectural fashions, distinct from each other yet blended by some alchemy known only to the builders. I never know which to admire most, the older house, with its façades made up of wavy lines in oak, carved brackets, crosses, squares and a fenestration to match; or the Elizabethan portion, stately and dignified under its cresting of spiked finials.

As the house never seems busy with visitors, the sense of past times is almost overpowering. Echoes from one's own footsteps on the bare boards awaken other echoes—of Christopher Norris, a prosperous Bolton clothier who bought the place from the Brownlows; and of the Cromptons too, farmers and cotton manufacturers.

Soon after, Hall-i'-th'-Wood came down in the world, and was split up into tenements. Poverty resided here in a framework of affluence. And it is as an impoverished son that we hear Samuel Crompton working away at his secret invention that should have put him and his wife on the path to fortune . . .

There are musical overtones, also, for Samuel played hymn tunes on a chamber organ probably made by himself. One of his own compositions was a hymn written to celebrate the Jubilee of George III. But neither the King nor any of his ministers had any idea of the revolution that was germinating in this little corner of the North.

Cotton had not then become 'king' in Lancashire. Samuel Crompton's part in the enthronement was the invention of the mule, which spun cotton like gossamer. Yet such were the suspicions of neighbours that at first he had to hide his contrivance, by night, in a hole in the attic floor.

Later, jealousy and trickery robbed him of that fortune, but the machine had won its way into the cotton industry. To everybody concerned it is now simply 'the mule', but its original name—the Hall-i'-th'-Wood Wheel—recalls this delightful old house and spins an even fuller story.

Size and prestige are not everything in this matter of country houses. Some of the smaller ones are rich in history and architectural appeal. In Northumberland we could have paused with pleasure before the eighteenth-century house at Chesters in which John Clayton, the antiquary, could gloat over the adjoining Roman camp he helped to excavate. The visual excitement here was provided by Norman Shaw, who in 1891 enlarged the house and added a curved frontage centring upon a colonnade of huge Ionic columns—his own version, perhaps, of a Roman commandant's residence. How Shaw loved such evocations!

Mount Grace Priory, near Northallerton, shows how part of a Carthusian monastery could be adapted to secular usage in the seventeenth century, and yet remain in complete harmony with the medieval priory and its glorious setting at the foot of the Cleveland Hills. The Dissolution played havoc with the church and its courtyard of cells, but today Nicholas Love, one of the priors, could still find many a quiet corner here for his meditations. Devised from the former priory guest-house, the seventeenth-century dwelling is in spirit blessedly close to its origins. And it was no mischance that he who understudied St Cuthbert in the Wallington paintings was a member of the family who now live here.

Then one might profitably visit Hodge Hill, a small sixteenth-century house on the wooded slopes of Cartmel Fell, far above Morecambe Bay. Its attractions are many. An open gallery over the entrance speaks of long summertime sessions of spinning, mixed no doubt with shreds of local scandal. The oak staircase indoors is guarded by gates to keep the dogs of the house from roaming where they were not wanted. At the head of the stairs the family's black page-boy awaited orders in a narrow closet as dark as himself. And just beyond, in a discreet corner of the bedroom corridor, a simple courting seat exists—just a plank for two. From the spinning gallery a girl could easily escape, unobserved(?), to its promise of seclusion and whoever was waiting there, in the shadows.

Hodge Hill's former link with the outer world was also of a clandestine nature, for the Phillipson family who lived here in the eighteenth century indulged in smuggling. The house was a convenient distribution centre for contraband landed at Flookburgh, on the nearer shore of Morecambe Bay.

John Blades, the owner, who several times welcomed me to this sequestered spot, told me how, as a schoolboy at Sedbergh, he and his pals explored part of the smugglers' traditional track amongst the hills: up the Winster Valley, from Hodge Hill, and on via Winder to the back of Sedbergh Calf. A tradition he heard later spoke of an underground passage from Hodge Hill to the vestry of Cartmel Fell Chapel.

In these sceptical days tales of underground passages are generally discredited, often with good reason, but in this district I am never in the mood to spoil a good story. Somebody might yet find evidence of that passage. And the distance between house and chapel cannot be more than 300-400 yards.

It was a lovely spring morning when, after speeding through North Westmorland, I turned aside at Temple Sowerby village to keep a long-standing invitation. How good it had been to anticipate this tryst with Dorothy Una Ratcliffe (the late Mrs McGrigor Phillips), whose many travel books, dialect plays and poems enriched my generation, and will surely continue to enrich others, with an almost indefinable charm.

Before me stretched the massive Pennine ridge, to which Cross Fell, its highest summit and gathering ground of the Helm Wind, contrived to give the appearance of some vivid Turner landscape. Somewhere at the foot of those mountains, I recalled, Mary Queen of Scots had ridden by, after her Scottish experiences. In her one-act play, *Mary of Scotland in Wensleydale*, 'D. U. R.' tells how the Queen fared at her Yorkshire destination, Bolton Castle. So it was an historic countryside I had entered, as well as one of impressive natural grandeur.

At length, Temple Sowerby Manor came into view—a flush of rose-coloured sandstone set in the emerald of encompassing trees. A Queen Anne house, I thought at first. Then, on approaching nearer, across the fields, a Tudor wing appeared on the west, and some Regency work, culminating in a clock tower on the garden side. It all looked so inviting.

The indoor welcome was even more memorable. The housekeeper showed me to a seat in the spacious entrance hall and then vanished with my card. . . . Flowers filled the room with soft fragrance. A Dutch clock ticked away the minutes. Sunlight streamed through the sash-bar windows, putting a glow on the polished refectory table and even penetrating the shadows of an enormous fireplace in which three or four persons could have sat, ruminatively, in comfort. There were portraits, too. Who could that stern Dutchman be, near the tub of hydrangeas? And what was the story behind that Buddhist shrine?

But my reverie was cut short by the swishing of a silken gown. 'D. U. R.' was descending the seventeenth-century staircase that debouches into the entrance hall. Tall and stately, she glided straight across to the hooded fireplace, and arranged herself with consummate elegance on a Charles I high-back chair. Her sense of drama thus satisfied, she then smiled in the way that captivated everybody, and began to speak as though we two were the only persons who mattered, just then, in all Westmorland.

Our conversation drifted at first around this lovely old house, formerly called Acorn Bank, which she had rescued from dilapidation twenty years before. "On this very fireplace", she said, "there are masons' marks identical with some at Aigues Mortes, that town in south-east France linked with the Second Crusade." Eight centuries spanned in no time at all! The first settlers on this site were apparently the Knights Templars who held the manor until the Dissolution. Henry VIII cannot have realized what a 'plum' he was parting with when he granted the place to Thomas Dalston!

It has seemed appropriate to mention my welcome to Temple Sowerby Manor in some personal detail, because 'D. U. R.' made the place *dance* for everybody who came—artists, poets, dialect writers and others from all over the North. National Trust ownership, though it became desirable, can never keep in step with her blithe spirit. Yet the manor is still a treasure house, with strange corners too, especially where a Tudor staircase penetrates the comparative gloom of the former approach to a family chapel and to a hiding-place for fugitive priests. Up this same stairway something else came for safety, during the Second World War—various works of art from Manchester Art Gallery.

On a later visit I watched some Westmorland folk-dancers perform on the manor lawns; how satisfying it was to see "Rufty Tufty", "Gathering Peascods", and so many other dainty measures tripped out against a far-flung background that swept across from Shap Fell to Blencathra and other Lakeland hills, all silvered in the distance. On the braes above Crowdundle Beck, behind the house, 'D. U. R.' naturalised the Lenten Lily and planted innumerable varieties of daffodil. Many people called her, affectionately, 'The Lady of a Thousand Daffodils'. 'T' Croodle Beck', fond name for that flower-bordered stream, seems to sing again in one of her poems in which she anticipated the Beyond:

> . . . when I gits to Gowden Yats
> An' t' saint lifts up yat-sneck
> I hope I feel a suther wind
> An' hear a tantril [vagabond] beck.
> An' aboon douce seraph music—
> Harp, flute an' violin—
> T' saint say to me in a hamely way,
> 'Noo! Missus, coom thi ways in!'.

8

In Community: Amongst the Towns

"GOD made the country, but man made the towns."
The criticism of town life implied in the old saying needs modifying, in varying degree, when one begins to consider some of our great northern centres. Here, however, it is impossible to give any of them full justice. A short briefing of a few more important places is all that space will permit. Let us allow certain secular buildings and a few personalities to speak for each town or city, leaving other aspects to later chapters and to the reader's own investigation.

Leeds, the second largest town in Yorkshire, is situated on the River Aire, as I discovered afresh and with some excitement when a youth, for the back windows of the woollen warehouse that employed me at 6s per week gave a private view of the river as it swept noisily beneath the main railway station. Secret pleasure was obtained by dropping broken bits of cloth-board into the swirling water and watching them disappear, like so many doomed rafts, into the great gloomy tunnels. . . .

The station and its river tunnels were an outstanding engineering triumph of Victorian times. About the same period Cuthbert Brodrick, a popular architect, gave Leeds two buildings which registered a distinct advance from the days when green fields encircled the town and its merchants sold their cloth on Leeds Bridge. One building was the Corn Exchange, which, despite Dr Pevsner's remarks, can still delight the beholder because of its eliptical dome of steel ribs far overhead, like some gigantic spider-web. *In toto* the building was supposed to recall a Roman ampitheatre!

Brodrick's other riposte to Victorian affluence was the imposing town hall, flanked with four sculptured lions. Pevsner speaks well of this building, with its classical Greek frontage of massive columns, which nicely offset those tame, recumbent lions. To many of us the town hall recalls great exhibitions, pageants and orchestral concerts, but few people who have heard its famous organ thundering out choruses from *The Messiah*, or accompanying the Leeds Symphony Orchestra, will know of a strange incident that preceded its installation.

As the swell-box was considered the largest ever made, a local enthusiast proposed that a dinner should be given *inside* it. "To be sure," said one of the illustrious guests, "it was a sort of pic-nic business, but it was none the less enjoyable. . . ." The fare included some choice entrées, fresh salmon, a haunch of venison, and six bottles of vintage port. Even more enjoyable, apparently, was "the intellectual feast— the feast of reason and the flow of soul. . . . We had jokes about the 'box' we had got into, the 'swells' that occupied it", and much else of like nature. When somebody remarked upon the resemblance of this novel 'dining-room' to a ship's cabin, George Cooper of St Paul's Cathedral and the Chapel Royal exclaimed, "Of course, it's going to be a *C* organ".

With its tower-blocks of flats and offices, pedestrian precincts, and a motor-way that runs through the very heart of the city, Leeds has now moved far beyond its Victorian and Edwardian confines. But to me, the thought of that meal inside the town hall organ is a succulent titbit to serve up, on the right occasion, to some of the younger generation.

Since the last war Bradford, near neighbour to Leeds, has been so thoroughly transformed in general appearance that any old-timer returning to the city today would feel like Rip Van Winkle. Many of the once-familiar landmarks have vanished: quaint little back streets beloved by generations of bargaining wool-men; tall Italianate warehouses that sprang up in the German quarter during Victorian times; several town houses of the bygone elite of the city. Even Bradford Exchange, once a holy of holies to local merchants, seems to be threatened by winds of change. To find his way about, our Rip Van Winkle would have to take his bearings from the cathedral, say, or St George's Hall which the Hallé Orchestra made its second home, or, even better, from the Victorian town hall whose 200-foot tower, modelled on the campanile of the Palazzo Vecchio at Florence, still soars above the city like an upraised finger.

Sheffield is no whit behind other cities in changing its outward garb for something considered more stylish. My parents, who brought up some of their family here, would gaze incredulously at the new shopping centres overlooked by sky-scraping blocks of flats, and at other recent innovations. And the suburb where I was born—of which my maternal uncle, the late G. R. Vine, could write* nostalgically about the local salmon pastures, cutlers' grinding wheels, strange characters, and the coming of the first horse-drawn tramcars—is now spanned by a section of the M1, high on its two-tiered viaduct over the Don Valley.

But the older Sheffield is not easily by-passed by modernity. One can still see the Elizabethan Turret House, where for a time Mary Queen of Scots was held in custody; or enjoy the peculiar tranquility of Paradise Square (near the cathedral) where, at one time, the master cutler would publicly destroy any product considered unworthy of the city. The present Cutlers' Hall, nearby, dates only from 1832, yet it is full of history relating to the Lordship and Liberty of Hallamshire, an ancient industrial 'kingdom' not found on any map, yet covering a large area. At the Cutlers' Feast, held annually, one of the chief dishes is a concoction known as brewis, traditional fare of the early apprentices to Sheffield's staple trade.

Sheffield is evidently determined to preserve every vital link in its chain of time.

Kingston-upon-Hull's transformation act was rendered essential by the damage and destruction the port suffered during the last war. Contrary to popular opinion there was always much for tourists to admire in this old town on Humberside. Its docks and shipping had and still have unfailing appeal. A central boulevard contrived from an obsolete dock, fine parks and several splendid buildings added to the attractions. Some of these buildings, such as the parish church, Trinity House and Wilberforce House, survived the holocaust of war; others perished.

One day in 1941 John (now Sir John) Summerson and I went over to launch our own campaign, on behalf of the National Buildings Record. As elsewhere, every architecturally important building would have to be photographed in detail. Some places had already gone up in flames, or hung together by mere shreds of timber or masonry. High Street— once the preserve of merchant princes—showed great gaps in its parade of Georgian houses. Other houses had been hastily evacuated and left to any stray cat. John Summerson bending down to stroke one such 'stray', while I photographed what remained of an elegant staircase, is a memory full of pathos for me. That house with its fine ceilings and fireplaces had once been the pride of the influential Etherington family!

Another evacuated building was the Charterhouse, founded in 1384 by Sir Michael de la Pole and rebuilt in the eighteenth century. Its

* In *The Story of Old Attercliffe* (Ward of Sheffield, 1932).

aged tenants had moved into the country, leaving the Master in sole charge. After the Master had conducted me through his damaged house, across the way, we stepped into the large garden, pitted not long before by six incendiary bombs. In each cavity he later planted a standard rose tree, naming them after different members of his family.

This spirit has fashioned post-war Hull!

None but the older generation today can have any conception of the havoc to which several of our northern towns were reduced between 1940 and 1944. Yet just as Christopher Wren planned a new London after the Great Fire, so have architects, planners and enterprising councils seized the golden opportunity to sweep away any surviving eyesores, such as slum dwellings, and build anew.

Manchester has no hesitation in calling its own, post-war changes a *Renaissance*. From Mancenion, the Celtic 'place of tents' (*circa* 38 B..C.) to a busy town created by the Industrial Revolution, was a fair stride. In 1653 Humphrey Chetham had founded his famous hospital, which recently achieved the status of a grammar school and has since become a school of music. Between times it had tasted the fire of modern war, though many of its fascinating rooms escaped damage—notably, the library where Harrison Ainsworth, author of many historical romances, studied and wrote, and the muniment room with its amusing roof-boss showing the Giant of Notting Hill swallowing a boy—a Chetham boy, insist the youths who show you round! It was in this same room that Dr John Dee summoned his angels, caused weird lights to flash through the windows at night, practised sorcery, and served 'wizard' cordials to inquisitive guests.

Manchester got fully into its stride, culturally, with the opening, in 1900, of the glorious library given by the widow of John Rylands, a prosperous cotton manufacturer who had started his working life as a weaver at Wigan. The library was so designed by Basil Champneys that one treads through its corridors and main, nave-like sanctuary as though walking within a Gothic cathedral almost in expectation of matins or evensong.

Books and manuscripts often put on display here provide links not only with Lancashire, but with the Orient and other distant places. World-famous scholars browse here in a state of bliss, ordinary folk come to gloat over illuminated books once owned by kings and queens, or the unique collection of finely-bound Bibles. A local merchant may even pop in to search through appropriate treatises in the hope of identifying some pest of the cotton plantations.

And now, as one further leap forward, Manchester plans an education precinct—the joint effort of city council, university, Institute of Science and Technology and the local hospitals. The brochure setting forth this unique venture is a feast of promise that will take at least twenty years to materialize. In his wildest dreams, old John Dee could never have foreseen such a future.

Peering into a city's origins is always entertaining. Who would think that Liverpool, now the largest city in the north, sprang out of forest glades where Druids performed their rites within stone circles not unlike Stonehenge? Development came slowly. The Cheshire banks of the Mersey were bristling with life and activity while Liverpool was still a mere fishing community, poor and decayed. Even by Elizabethan times its inhabitants referred to their township as "very poor and mean", a subtle attempt, perhaps, to play things down and thus evade corporate taxation!

The building which chiefly epitomises Liverpool's eventual growth from obscurity is the town hall. Completed in 1754 to the design of John Wood of Bath, it replaces several earlier buildings and still houses various mementoes of old times. Here, for example, are a couple of stakes replacing the levers once used "by the running footmen to prise the wheels of the Lord Mayor's coach out of roadside ruts in pre-paving days". A silver oar, dated 1785, was the insignia of office formerly borne by the water bailiff, a role which continued until the formation of the Mersey Docks and Harbour Board in 1858. Similar emblematic oars, though fashioned in wood, are still preserved at Kingston-upon-Hull.

What the Humber is to Kingston-upon-Hull, the Mersey is to Liverpool—a great highway leading to all parts of the world. A promising post-war development of Liverpool's dock system is the Seaforth Project, which the city's official guidebook describes in some detail. Historically, this project, which provides ten deep-water berths capable of handling the largest vessels that sail the seas, throws into amusing contrast the old ferry traffic which operated with adventure and not a little peril* up and down and across the Mersey in days before the Mersey Tunnel materialized, early this century. Up-to-date ferries still work between the Lancashire and Cheshire banks of the Mersey. The tunnel offers speedier transit, but some of us prefer, even now, the breezy way across this mile-wide 'arm of the sea'. By either route, the Cheshire Wirral always beckons with compelling allure. Its lovely old villages and the bird sanctuary at Hilbre Island, opposite Hoylake, offer Liverpudlians rest and peace from daily toil.

By comparison, the port of Lancaster may seem small fry, yet it could once boast a greater tonnage of shipping than Liverpool and a goodly trade with the West Indies, which involved much traffic in slaves. Although Lancaster has lived down that unfortunate connection, the old maritime days are still recalled by a quiet saunter beside the

* See the author's *Ferries and Ferrymen* (Cassell 1969).

River Lune, especially in the region where this joins the Irish Sea between Sunderland Point and Glasson Dock.

Today it seems incredible that Sunderland Point, a mere hamlet with a fascinating bird-life preening its shores, could once provide mooring for ships too large to negotiate the narrow, winding river to Lancaster. Sunderland Point itself is none too easy to approach overland. It demands from would-be visitors a careful watch of the tides, for virtually the only means of access is by a narrow causeway covered periodically by the sea. A brief show of weather-beaten cottages and warehouses is now the only token of bygone prosperity. I once lost all sense of time while watching the amazingly concerted aerobatics of a flock of dunlin, where West Indian cargoes formerly came ashore.

Glasson Dock, on the opposite water-front, developed later as an out-rider to Lancaster because of its safer anchorage. But this place, too, is gradually slipping into the realm of make-believe, which the café-barge now moored there permanently only serves to enhance.

Before the Romans established their *castrum* on a bend of the Lune (hence the name Lancaster), the river seems to have shifted course somewhat. But St George's Quay marks the original Port of Lancaster and is now a rather quaint backwater, though still set about with tall warehouses and a custom house, erected in 1764 to the design of Richard Gillow. Gillow's connection with the famous cabinet firm, Waring and Gillow, will come into our narrative later. The first venue of Lancaster University (1961) had been part of the firm's early premises.

During the great cotton famine in the mid-nineteenth century attention was focused on Lancaster Moor, site of stone quarries from which much of the old town had been built. Alderman James Williamson provided work for the local unemployed by converting the area into one of England's finest public parks. The kindly alderman presented the park to the town in 1878. Its highest point surmounted by the Ashton Memorial from which Morecambe Bay and Lakeland can be seen in clear weather, came to be known as 'Top of Hard Times'. Charles Dickens, who once stayed at a local inn used as an overnight stopping place for coaches bound for the Furness area via the 'Sands' of Morecambe Bay, would surely have smiled an acknowledgement of the echo of one of his own novels.

The growth of Barrow-in-Furness from a seaport village, in mid-Victorian times, to the great shipping and industrial centre of today is the sort of romance that might have appealed to an Arnold Bennett. The monks of Furness Abbey, nearby, had smelted local iron ore away back in medieval times, yet until a hundred years ago most of the population hereabouts—a mere 700—were engaged in agriculture; the small coastal trade was limited to wool, slate and iron ore.

To enlarge further upon Barrow's rapid industrial progress would take us out of our present context. As for notable buildings which might register that growth there seem to be few, apart from the town hall. Yet Barrow deserves commendation for preserving so much of the local countryside, especially Walney Island. Its nearer shore supports the model village of Vickerstown, but beyond, all is as nature made it, with miles of sand-dunes, open countryside, and a concentration of bird life —gulls, eider duck, terns, shelduck, mallard, oystercatcher and many other species—which has created for South Walney a perfect nature reserve. Barrow's ships may sail the Seven Seas, but some of Walney's migrant birds perform even greater navigational feats. Long may the citizens of this upstart town remain content to leave Walney as it is!

Sunderland, at the mouth of the River Wear, on the Durham coast has been building ships for at least 600 years. The earliest known record (1346), here translated from the Latin, states that "Thomas Menvill occupied a certain place called Hendon [part of Sunderland], for the building of ships, for which he paid to the bishop an annual rent of two shillings." This was Bishop Hatfield of Durham, whose grant to Menvill included the fishing rights on the Wear.

From Menvill's enterprise sprang an industry that gradually lifted little monastic Wearmouth into a world context. This pageant of centuries is abundantly set forth in the local museum and art gallery. It shows how—after the Scots had been temporarily subdued—a small fishing village met a King's demand for ships, and yet more ships. By the seventeenth and eighteenth centuries Sunderland had several ship-builders and great names like Havelock, Laing, and Crown emerged, with many others to follow.

In 1891 one of Laing's vessels, the *Torrens*, had Joseph Conrad as second mate. On this ship, "tall and slender, with a long jibboom and beautiful bows, graced by the figurehead of a woman", Conrad may have prepared notes for some of his nautical romances.

Lewis Carroll's association with Sunderland led him into different seas—the rich seas of whimsy and humour. While visiting relations nearby he was evidently stimulated by a stuffed walrus, in the local museum, to write some of his famous verses. The walrus had been brought home from one of his Arctic voyages by Captain Joseph Wiggins. Carroll, having also noticed ships' carpenters walking the streets of Sunderland in their white aprons and queer square white hats, probably made rough sketches from which Tenniel later illustrated those haunting verses, which pair the walrus and the tearful carpenter and invest them with curious immortality:

> The Walrus and the Carpenter
> Were walking close at hand:
> They wept like anything to see

Such quantities of sand:
"If this were only cleared away",
They said, "it would be grand!"
"The time has come", the Walrus said,
"To talk of many things:
Of shoes—and ships—and sealing-wax—
Of cabbages—and kings—
And why the sea is boiling hot—
And whether pigs have wings."

An earlier generation of Sunderland folk must have felt strangely gratified to have been lifted out of their docks and launchingways for a while by such inspired nonsense.

South Shields, which punctuates the northward coastal route to Newcastle, has a magic of its own. Marsden Bay with its magnificent limestone cliffs, and a miniature Bass Rock off shore, supplies much of that magic; and eerie those bird-haunted rocks, tunnelled by the sea, must have seemed to the first Celtic settlers here. Their word *shiel* or *shieling* simply meant 'a fisherman's hut'. From the fort which the Romans built nearby, the local museum displays many fine relics, but of all its achievements South Shields is perhaps proudest of having produced the first reliable lifeboat. A clock-tower near the pier is a monument to the two men, William Wouldhave and Henry Greathead, who pioneered this vessel, towards the end of the eighteenth century.

And so we sail up the Tyne to Newcastle.

Whether approached by river or land the city is visually exciting. The river bridges alone provide a pattern of joy, most of them soaring far above the Tyne with a panache one would hardly expect from a great industrial and commercial centre. But wherever you tread in Newcastle, there are buildings and other pleasing features (such as Jesmond Dene park) which transcend mundane affairs. The lantern tower of the cathedral, hanging high over the city, is symbolic of an inner nobility, while the streets designed last century by Grainger and Dobson declare a love of architectural symmetry and imaginative planning which modern developments will but enhance. Grey Street, culminating in the Grey Monument, is still one of the finest streets in the country, while Northumberland Street—once thronged with traffic —has become a pedestrian refuge with seats spaced invitingly down its centre.

The cathedral's crowned lantern tower is now offset by the Carillon Tower, decorated with symbolic sea-horses, rising from the new civic centre designed by George Kenyon, the city architect. There is, in fact, a distinct affinity between the old and new towers. In former times a burning brazier of coals in the cathedral lantern helped the keelmen to navigate the River Tyne and also guided citizens through

The Tudor Courtyard at Skipton Castle, West Yorkshire

Topiary work in the grounds of Levens Hall, Westmorland

the town before the advent of street lighting. The 248-feet-high Carillon Tower takes up the tradition by having its own beacon and, of course, a chime of bells, which periodically ring out Northumbrian tunes, and carols at Christmas and New Year. Recitals are also given at set times by visiting campanologists. And far below, on one wall of the civic centre, the river god, Tyne—which the Romans acknowledged 1,800 years ago—re-assumes his age-old presidency in a striking sculpture with water pouring like a continuing libation from his upraised hand.

A 'flight of swans' by the same artist, David Wynne, rise from a pool in the Civic Centre Garth. This fine piece of symbolism, based on Seedorf Pedersen's poem, "The Swans from the North", represents the five Nordic countries in the order of their creation as independent states, and imaginatively reflects Newcastle's long established associations with Scandinavia.

In limited space it is impossible to do justice to other contributions that make the civic centre such an outstanding aesthetic achievement. A tapestry by John Piper evokes the geological structure of Northumbria and its typical flora; while a glazed screen engraved by John Hutton portrays the story of Northumbria from early times onward. Mithras is there, also Coventina, goddess of the well already noticed beside Hadrian's Wall. Solid fact settles elsewhere upon the screen with representations of such gifts to civilisation—by sons of the city— as George Stephenson's steam locomotive, Parson's marine steam turbine and Swan's incandescent electric lamp-bulb.

From the Pons Aelius of Roman times to modern Newcastle is a mighty leap, or series of leaps, and it is always interesting to pick out a few surviving 'milestones' in that progression.

The Black Gate of the castle that was 'new' in Norman times houses almost enough Roman remains to re-furnish a whole era. Thus it is possible to remain in this corner of old Newcastle and yet feel the winds blowing over Hadrian's Wall in its heyday and hear the tramp of the legions. . . .

Down by the municipally-owned quay, a blackened eighteenth-century façade hides the guildhall—ancient centre of local government. The hammerbeams in the court room are emblazoned with the arms of the various city guilds, accompanied by a medley of grinning masks that nicely reflect the medieval outlook. Yet even in Charles II's reign the tailors of Newcastle could here accuse a certain fairground dealer with having made a petticoat in the town, an indictable offence because he was not one of their company. Strange matters have also been discussed in the former mayor's parlour. Here, beneath a lovely plaster ceiling, mayor and council sat on cushioned seats around a large fireplace flanked with tiers of document boxes, while from the inner wall painted panels illustrating scenes of old Newcastle gave excuse for wandering attention. The Merchant Adventurers' Court, at the other end of the larger room, is a feast of fine wood carving, especially on the tall chimney-piece. This is decorated with Biblical subjects, including the judgement of Solomon, in which the rival mothers wear dress that would be familiar in the fashionable quarters of seventeenth-century Newcastle; and the miraculous draught of fishes, another scene given a humorous twist by what appears to be a sea monster trapped in the Disciples' net.

Mermaids and strange marine creatures abound in Trinity House, which stands in one of the narrow chares, or alleys, leading down to the Tyne. Established originally at Berwick-upon-Tweed, when border raids were rife, this charitable mission for distressed seamen and aged mariners soon moved down to Newcastle, but found itself still hampered by raiders. Local seamen were none too friendly, either, but in time the Guild or Fraternity of the Blessed Trinity was 'accepted' and support given to its aims, which included improved navigation of the Tyne.

The guild's first requisite was a chapel. Designed on the 'between decks' of an ancient wooden ship, it was furnished with pews made of oak brought from Bede's monastery at Jarrow, and illuminated by stained-glass windows, one of which bears the crest of Trinity House—a broken mast signifying that "God giveth the wind." A beautiful calm settles upon the place during divine service. On Trinity Sunday others beside brethren and pensioners are invited to service, male guests being privily handed a half-crown (now ten pence) for the collection! Ladies are not so endowed but have the privilege of sitting opposite their menfolk, with the aisle between them.

In 1637, while badgered by his enemies, Charles I found refuge at Trinity House. Later, master and brethren arranged for the king's passage to Holy Island, for greater security. Though he evidently enjoyed his sojourn there, Charles soon returned, being short of cash and anxious to collect moneys accruing to him from ship dues, then deposited at Trinity House. It is recorded that Charles spent much of his time here concealed in a room in a buttress where by means of a small window used as a spy-hole he could check the arrival and departure of the collector of those dues!

Plough beacon, fixed at a treacherous spot off Holy Island, was provided by Trinity House. It came into view during the visit of Queen Elizabeth and the Duke of Edinburgh to Holy Island in June 1958. As the island is one of the 'creeks or members' of the Port of Newcastle-upon-Tyne under the jurisdiction of Trinity House, brethren from this ancient establishment exercised their right of piloting the royal yacht on the last stages of the voyage. While on the island the

Queen and Prince Philip were regaled with the story of St Cuthbert.
I wonder whether they were also told about King Charles hiding under
the chapel of Trinity House?

Of the smaller towns in the North there is a splendid choice.

One could spend a week or so at Berwick-upon-Tweed without
exhausting its charms. An unforgettable view of the town is gained
from the railway-carriage window as one crosses the Royal Border
Bridge—a view in no way marred by the new housing estate at Tweed-
mouth and Spittal on the southern bank of the broad river. The web
of bridges, old and new, across the Tweed is one of the town's chief
attractions.

Berwick long enjoyed a unique position in the realm. Long after the
Act of Union, indeed until 1885, its independent status was recognized
in all Acts of Parliament. The citation of "England, Scotland, Ireland
and Wales" always ended with a flourish, "and our town of Berwick-
on-Tweed". Even today Berwick is a county in its own right, though
for administrative purposes deemed to be in Northumberland. This
proud distinction evidently stemmed from the uncomfortable period
when the town was bandied about like a shuttlecock between England
and Scotland. It changed hands no fewer than thirteen times! Today
the town shows commendable impartiality. Its youth plays football in
Scotland (Scottish football league) and county cricket in *England*!

The eighteenth-century town hall is a fine eye-catcher, which
Professor A. E. Richardson, R.A., once described as "a building which
would not disgrace the university towns of Oxford or Cambridge and
one which would be welcomed in London". Its similarity to St
Martin-in-the-Fields has often been noted. Indeed, its ecclesiastical
appearance is such that strangers often mistake it for the parish church.
How else could they regard the building when they hear a peal of bells
ringing from its lofty steeple on Sundays calling people to divine
service? This is an act of grace, however, for the real parish church,
nearby, has no carillon of its own.

Some years ago the gaol on the top storey was restored, not for any
punitive purpose, but so that visitors might either shiver up there with
horror, at the sight of different torture cells, or share the outlook
described so feelingly by Fuller, the local historian, in 1799. From its
many large windows, he wrote, "the prisoners enjoy several excellent
views of the Town, the German Ocean, Bambro' Castle and Holy
Island . . .".

Amongst those once lodged in Berwick gaol were fishermen who
had transgressed against certain regulations, as indicated in the following
complaint of bygone days: "Some lay with their [fishing] cobyll on
other men's watters"; for the second such offence "the cobyll [was] to be

brokyn and ther bodys to prison XL days". Salmon fishing, ancient staple trade of Berwick, still has its fascination for visitors, who assemble on Crabwater pier, at the mouth of the Tweed, to watch the fishermen battle with marauding seals as the draw-nets are hauled in.

Over to the west, Carlisle, that corresponding town situated on the shifting sands of Border history, enshrines much of its romance in cathedral and castle, as mentioned earlier. The town's Roman ancestry has also been evoked, to some small extent. Kenneth Smith, in his recently published history of Carlisle, indicates many changes that threaten the ancient corpus of the place. Its importance as a communication centre, for road and rail between Scotland and England seems to be reaping modern rewards (frowned upon by many) in the form of "swathes of dual carriageway around the city's heart". No doubt these new roads will blend with the eleven-storied civic centre opened in 1964. But the city centre from Roman times onwards is still marked by the Carlisle Cross, a handsome stone column beside which Bonnie Prince Charlie—accompanied by his "hundred pipers an' a' " —proclaimed his father to be the true king, in 1745; and from which the opening of the Great Fair is still announced at 8 a.m. every 26th August.

One is never long in Carlisle without hearing of Margery Jackson, an eighteenth-century miser of great wealth who lived in a fine house (still standing) near the town hall. On first arriving in the town, it is said, "she had the body of her carriage taken off the wheels and suspended by ropes . . . to secure exemption from the tax on carriages". She was so niggardly that never did anybody see her wear anything but the same dark fustian outfit. It was left to posterity to admire her fine wardrobe of blue, pink and primrose dresses; they are displayed in the local Tullie House Museum!

Such a character was bound to become a butt for everybody, especially the local lads, who would attach a piece of string to her knocker and rattle this from the safe distance of the town hall steps. Some say that her ghost still seeks out her tormentors.

One writer has remarked that Margery Jackson would be a young lady of 23 when Carlisle capitulated to the Young Pretender and his Highlanders; "if she was in the city at that time she must have witnessed some stirring scenes; and would later see the rebels' heads adorning the pikes over the Scotch gate . . .". Her favourite expression, "Trash," delivered contemptuously, might well have issued again from her tightened lips as she beheld this grisly scene.

Carlisle's fame as Cumberland's chief port declined when Whitehaven, on the Cumberland coast, seized that honour, with Maryport a close second. A friend has supplied some interesting notes about her Maryport ancestors, all staunch Quakers, who built trading ships there. One of them, named *Christian*, and another called *Christian Pilgrim* took pioneers to America. One of this ship-owning family became the mother of Lord Lister, who revolutionized surgery by his discovery of antiseptics. Another, William Harris, brought back from the Arctic a young polar bear which he kept in his garden, much to the delight of the younger generation. Eventually, so the family annals record, "Uncle William's pet bear died at sea... and was buried in the manner proper to seafarers."

It is customary for most tourists to flash through Appleby on the way to Scotland, or through Kendal (traffic permitting!) *en route* for the Lake District. How much they miss by such haste!

The *real* Appleby, the town known to Lady Anne Clifford and her contemporaries, is reserved for those who turn off the A66 and cross the Eden Bridge—into the seventeenth century. That, at least, seems to be the prevailing atmosphere, until the castle at one end of Boroughgate and St Lawrence's Church at the lower end, are noticed, like a couple of ancestors of even more hoary vintage. The Moot Hall enjoys an island site near the church; lime trees cast their shade on green verges. Red stone cottages on either side seem to form a processional route for the great ones at the castle. Over the cottage roofs morning mist rises slowly to reveal Murton Pike, Dufton Pike, Cross Fell and the challenging High Cup Nick, to the north-east—all parts of the Pennine Range as it lunges farther up country—untamed, inviolate and biding its time for yet another unleashing of the malignant Helm Wind. . . . An Eden settlement overlooked by Fiend's Fell, Cross Fell's all-too expressive by-name! Yet, withal, still the pleasant county town of Westmorland.

Although Kendal is the mouthpiece for *south* Westmorland, the threat of Border raids had much to do with its older street planning. Liddesdale and Redesdale, amongst the chief lairs of bygone reivers, might indeed be 50 miles or so the north, yet Kendal had reason to build many of its houses around a central yard, to which a single narrow entry, easily defended, was the sole means of access. Kendal's main through street gives little hint of these small domestic citadels, often linked together by cobbled pavements; but traces of a few bolts and bars at the entrances tell their own grim tale.

When another Scot came down, in 1745, he was welcomed by the Royalist owners of a house near the present general post office. This visitor was the Young Pretender. After the dismal retreat from Derby he again slept beneath Thomas Shepherd's roof, that is, if failure in his bid for the English crown allowed him any sleep. "Two nights later", one reads, "the Duke of Cumberland, in pursuit, occupied the same house and bed." Fate, adding insult to injury, was being perverse indeed!

Along with Queen Katherine Parr's Book of Devotions, in Kendal's town hall, there are seven of George Romney's portraits. Though he was born at Dalton-in-Furness, Kendal claims him as one of her own sons, even naming a bridge in Ford Park after him, and cherishing his simple house in Kirkland as a kind of shrine. In 1762, leaving his young wife and their two children behind, he sought fame in London and eventually found it. Nearly forty years later, sick in body and mind, he returned, to find his wife as loving as ever and a faithful nurse until his death in 1802. Innumerable portraits of Lady Hamilton are just one part of Romney's title to renown. But I always think that Mary Romney, for her devotion, deserves a laurel of her own!

Many of our more graceful towns insinuate themselves as such into other parts of this book. Keswick, Cartmel, Hawkshead and Kirkby Stephen are among the élite and Barnard Castle, though larger again, is of the same company. In them, town and country seem to merge. At one moment you may be in the main street, rubbing shoulders with tradesmen, chatting with neighbours, or commiserating with the vicar because of his dwindling congregation—or his poor crop of tomatoes. The next moment you can be musing with Wordsworth beside a lake, casting a line hopefully in the trout stream, or taking a quiet walk in the woods. The very buildings may share this affinity with nature. While dodging holiday crowds in Keswick's narrow main thorough-fare, it always gives me pleasure to know that the slender town hall—almost toy-like in appearance—was built from stones taken from the former house of the Derwentwater family on Lord's Island, a short distance away in Lake Derwentwater.

Durham City is one of Britain's great surprises. Most people expect this provincial capital to share the industrial grime and depressing aspect of certain satellite towns and villages. But this only applies to one section of the city. In its oldest parts, Durham provides an oasis for which people of an industrial age should be especially grateful. That is why it is included here, among the country towns.

Nature seems to have intended Durham to play this redemptive role for modern society. Her endowments are simple; a well-wooded plateau encompassed on three sides by the lordly River Wear—yet out of these, man, in quest of an ideal, has fashioned a paradise. Durham citizens of today can still describe the core of their city without unduly trimming the words of Robert Hegge who, writing in 1626, declared, "He that hath seen the situation of this city hath seen the map of Zion and may save a journey to Jerusalem."

Durham's history, obscure in its earlier stages, began to take definite shape with the arrival of the Congregation of St Cuthbert in A.D. 955. The story of the wanderings of those faithful monks who sought a safe hiding place for the sacred remains of Cuthbert has already been told.

The monks first ascended Dun-holme—the 'island hill', and now known as Durham—by means of a track marked by Bow Lane, and the church at its head, St Mary-le-Bow, is believed to occupy the site of the White Church temporarily erected to house Cuthbert's remains until a more fitting shrine could be built. This shrine is, of course, Durham Cathedral.

The beautifully-wooded and steep-sided 'banks' which reach down to the Wear originated in the wilderness which the Congregation found here so long ago. Referring to this 'island hill', or peninsula, one early writer speaks of the "thick woods [which] both hindred the Starres from viewing the Earth, and the Earth from the prospect of Heaven".

Approaching the cathedral along North Bailey—the neck of the peninsula—you suddenly enter the spacious Palace Green. The keep of the castle, erected by Bishop Walcher in the eleventh century, commands the north side of the green, while the east and west sides are dotted with lovely old buildings—museums and libraries for the most part, whose cultural purposes are now augmented by their having become an integral part of Durham University.

Prior to the Dissolution of the Monasteries, the numerous trade guilds of the town annually marched in liveried procession to Palace Green, where they displayed their colourful banners before approaching the cathedral door. Today, it is the sombre robes—touched with ermine, scarlet and lavender—of college professors that flit across the green.

A steep, narrow track on the west side of Palace Green leads to the Wear via St Cuthbert's Well. A local doctor, early this century, used water from the well for mixing his medicines. Every morning and evening he would send a boy with ladle and pail to collect further supplies.

On the southern side of the cathedral you enter the serenity of College Green, a quadrangle of exquisite charm and beauty. Here are the Choristers' School, St Mary's College and the residences of the Dean and Canons. Tree-shaded lawns form the green itself, and in one place, adjoining the cathedral library, there is a fine survival from monastic days—the prior's kitchen. Though reminiscent of the abbot's kitchen at Glastonbury, it is distinctive in having an amazing system of roof-gables, within the parapet.

Leave College Green either by the passage on the west side, or by the College Gate, South Bailey and the Water Gate, and you come to Prebends Bridge, which spans the river at its most luxuriant reach.

While standing on this bridge you feel the full impact of Durham's ancient peace. Around you is a sylvan Arcady, and rising from the very treetops—so it seems—is the shrine that men have nobly built to the memory of Cuthbert and the glory of God.

Not even Salisbury, Lincoln or Norwich have a finer setting for their cathedrals.

To come upon Richmond, in north Yorkshire, for the first time, is another surprise. What a grand situation it enjoys above the steep, rugged north bank of the River Swale! A man might look down from Castle Walk on this fair scene and wish for no other blessedness. The Swale provides the town's signature tune, and part of its very life. . . .

The cobbled, circular market place—probably the largest of its kind in England—is under the sole control of the mayor, as clerk of the market. Every Saturday two halberds are placed outside his residence or place of business to show that he is available to conduct market affairs.

But those cobbles! They pattern other thoroughfares in Richmond, too, and have often come up for weighty consideration before the corporation. Richmond folk dearly cherish their traditional cobbles. Didn't Leland mention them with respect in the sixteenth century? And it is whispered that in recent times one applicant for the post of borough engineer ruined his chances by daring to suggest that the cobbles be abolished.

True, concessions have been made in the form of narrow concrete strips across the market place, but the 'cobbler' of the borough still plies his trade, periodically going down to the river for fresh supplies and then setting the 'Swale rovers', as the cobbles are called, in a bedding of concrete. A compromise between old ways and new seems to suit all concerned.

Certain other features are rightly considered inviolate. Those who have known and loved Richmond in earlier years would easily recognize the older part of the town: the Norman castle, the market place and its fascinating network of alleys and wynds, the river banks and so on. But some years ago its Georgian theatre was completely restored.

The wide social range once catered for at Richmond Theatre is naively indicated by some of the old playbills hung in the corridor. One announces that "by desire, and under the immediate patronage of Mrs. Copley of Hanlaby Hall, on Friday June 14th 1833, will be presented for the first time here the fashionable petite Comedy of *John of Paris*". This was to be followed by *Hunt the Slipper*, a farce, and *Old and Young*, probably another farce. Admission charges were as usual—3s for the boxes, 2s for the pit, 1s for the gallery, and "half price at quarter past nine o'clock". Thus everybody was included, from the gentry to the humblest apprentice, who might have to dream of the leading lady's charms, that night, beneath his master's drapery counter.

Today, Shakespeare and the Georgian playwrights are performed here, in the same ambience once enjoyed by Edmund Kean, Sarah Siddons and Macready.

The market place boasts one other hoary feature—the island site occupied by Holy Trinity Church, where the corporation bellman, wearing peak cap and cloak, rings the various kinds of bell-reminders that Richmond folk have known for centuries: the 'prentice bell, the curfew, the pancake bell on Shrove Tuesday and the passing bell.

This church has served many secular purposes: town hall, court of justice, granary, school and prison. Shops (mostly of the eighteenth century) have grossly invaded its aisles, and the corporation actually has a suite of offices wedged between nave and tower. The sacrilege began so long ago that nobody would now think of reforming this astonishing state of affairs.

In 1945 Richmond was selected by the British Council as the typical English country town. Almost everything seems to justify this choice. Even the civic silver has an individuality of its own. I think in particular of Charles II's gift, the famous 'seal of two pieces'. The larger piece bears the borough arms and belongs to the mayor. The smaller piece, bearing the Richmond rose crest, fits into the larger piece with a silver pin and rightly belongs to the town clerk. Thus the seal could only be used when both gentlemen were together *and in agreement*!

The civic regalia and plate of our northern towns could keep us entertained for hours. Berwick-upon-Tweed has a comparatively new mace shaped like a flanged battle-club; an echo of bygone Border affrays, but decorated with motifs that represent eventual peace between England and Scotland. A steel halberd borne before Berwick's mayor on state occasions so far belies its ancient purpose as to be pierced with the initials of a seventeenth-century mayor and a comic version of the town's emblem—a bear and tree (a wych elm), which together complete the old pun, 'bear-wick'. Durham's nineteenth-century mace is capped by a bishop's mitre, and Bradford's with several ferocious boars' heads, referring to a certain beast that once terrorized the neighbourhood. A very small mace of 1671, treasured at Scarborough, has its own little snuff box and once fitted conveniently into the mayor's coat-lapel!

Bygone city waits are remembered by their chains of office at Beverley and York, but Ripon's baldric, a shoulder belt of purple velvet worn by the Serjeant-at-Mace, is unique.

Ripon's charter horn of A.D. 886, which hangs from this baldric, represents an age-old custom that will resound more appropriately in a later chapter. Meanwhile, it is sufficient to remark that the baldric itself carries the picturesque badges of mayors from the early sixteenth century to 1886, while a newer baldric continues this mayoral parade and carries a horn of its own—a splendid specimen taken from one of the bulls of the famous Chillingham herd of wild cattle and presented to the town in 1886.

Some of our old towns come vividly to life on market day. At Ripon the gay stalls cluster around the Obelisk, a tall stone column capped with a gilded version of the charter horn. This is the very centre of the town. The Wakeman's House stands to one side as it has done for seven hundred years; a delightful example of half-timbering with windows like bulging eyes. Its near neighbour is the Georgian town hall emblazoned with the old motto: "Except Ye Lord Keep Ye Citie, Ye Wakeman Waketh in Vain."

The enclosing streets by which townsfolk and farmers from surrounding villages came to market on Thursday ring the same ancient note: Priest Lane, Skellgate, Fishergate, Allhallowgate, Finkle Street. If one chose, one could approach the town via the River Skell from Barefoot Street—an old pilgrim route which provides a link with even older times when Ripon—despite its minster—was but a communal farm with its officially appointed pinder, swineherd and neatherd.

Preston's market place is another touchstone of history. Periodically it stages a fair known as the Guild Merchant, which stems from an old trade fair. Today the Guild Merchant lasts for a whole week, giving rise to much conviviality and back-slapping amongst Prestonians from all over the world.

Many important local events have centred upon this impressive market place. James I, during a journey from Scotland to London in August 1617, halted in the market place, and was presented with a most effusive address along with a purse of gold. "Cots' plutters!" the king is reported to have exclaimed, "What a set of liegemen have come to see Jamie!" In 1715 another group of onlookers heard the Old Pretender proclaimed at the cross in the market place, an event echoed with fresh overtones in 1745 when Bonnie Prince Charlie marched through the town to the tune of "The King shall have his own again".

In his *Two Thousand Miles in Wharfedale* (1904), the late Edmund Bogg gives a nostalgic word picture of Skipton's market place: "Old-world Skipton is becoming modernised. Yet on market days the main street leading to the upper dales, which is still unspoilt, presents a curious picture, when every kind of vehicle is to be seen, from a donkey-cart to a smart whitechapel [a two-wheeled spring cart]; herds of sheep and cattle, with the yelling of drovers, barking of curs, the bargaining of dealers and farmers . . . remind one forcibly of market scenes of olden days . . . the roadway for miles is lined with droves of sheep and cattle and carts laden with every kind of produce needed for consumption in the upper dales. . . ."

Today the scene has changed again but not the setting. Castle and parish church look down paternally from the head of the street, and narrow yards recalling those at Kendal branch off like so many sally-ports. And although the motor car has completely ousted older vehicles, Manby's ironmongery shop still stands nearby, like a voice from the past, though the products displayed outside on market day are fully in keeping with our times. Echoes from earlier days float around when the firm's ledgers and account books are opened again, for inquisitive persons like me to consult!

According to these records, scythes, sickles, spades etc., from Sheffield were sometimes held up for weeks because the canals were frozen. This could mean that a dale's farmer might come down to market in vain, and the lead-miners of Wharfedale be kept waiting for fresh tools. Fortunately, Manby's made many of their own goods, such as nails, pumps, land rollers, gas engines and once, early this century, a petrol-driven car. And it was quite customary for a few pounds of Wensleydale cheese to be supplied along with shovels, or a pound or two of horse-nails. About 100 years ago business life in Skipton was extremely versatile and a tradesman could have several irons in his workaday fire. At the back of one ledger, dated 1853, there are several notes about Manby's farming interests: "red cow bulled Thursday", "sheep went into Billy Platt field", "lambs sold to Mr. Phillips", "lamb went into William Platts field at 3s per week".

Much the same kind of enterprise once attracted hundreds of buyers to the Knaresborough market from a wide countryside, and the habit persists. The market place is within hailing distance of the castle but has features of its own that recall certain lively diversions, notably a cock-pit hidden in the attic chamber of a tall eighteenth-century house, now a café. Formerly, drapers coming to market with their panniered horses were guided through the darkness of surrounding woodland by a bell rung from the tower of the parish church. The bushel corn measure used in the market during Charles II's reign is now kept in the Court House, near the castle.

But the colourful blandishments of Knaresborough's historic market should never blind one to the town's other attractions. A steep path from the castle yard leads down to the River Nidd, which here cuts a broad channel below cliffs of magnesian limestone, creating a scene of great beauty. I once knew a lady who could always recover her voice, after some recurrent throat affliction, by walking up and down the banks of the Nidd. In former times that cure might have been attributed to the influence of Mother Shipton, whose prophetic life reputedly began in a riverside cave near the famous Dropping Well.

Cave dwellings were no great novelty in this town. Passages and vugs in the prevailing limestone honeycombed an extensive area now partly occupied by Georgian houses and shops.

At Beverley, as in most old towns, the local names repay study. The area of the market place has its share of them. Approached from the south by Toll Gavel, where some kind of toll was probably exacted at one time, the market place is in three sections. On the south side is Sou Market, Cornhill occupies the north side, while the narrow part in the centre—around the eighteenth-century market cross—is known as Butterdings Pavement, a name said to denote the sale of butter, coupled with the Scandinavian 'thing', or meeting place: a nice blending of the centuries that have helped to shape this town, which is surrounded by common pastures, originating as such in medieval times, and still supervised by pasture masters and a regular neatherd. Smart enough when it comes to business, Beverley is yet a place for antiquaries. Its old buildings—the Minster, St Mary's Church, the eighteenth-century guildhall and others, tend to be regarded by townsfolk almost as 'elder citizens', with every right to their own particular place in the sun. But it is never safe to assume 'senility'. The two churches have their staunch devotees, while the guildhall houses a court room that still deals effectively with offenders, under a central figure of Justice which, contrary to the usual custom, wears no bandage over the eyes. "In Beverley", the town clerk once assured me, with a grin, "justice is not blind."

And Beverley folk can turn from "making a living" to a flirtation with the past in enviable manner. Only a few years ago a lady of my acquaintance staged a Georgian rout in her seventeenth-century house near the Minster. All the guests arrived in period costume, were provided with a cold collation, and played parlour games by candlelight.

A well-known local architect appeared as a highwayman, and a schoolmaster as a coachman—fair game for a 'hold-up'. An eighteenth-century serving maid—"the picture of meekness"—was a cleverly disguised Beverley solicitor, now at the bidding of his own elegant wife and of the 'Duchess of Marlborough'. The host was a Regency beau in satin, lace and white wig, and the hostess a marvellous creation in grey pault dress, lace sleeves and coy side-ringlets. The lackey for the occasion was a doctor from Middleton-on-the-Wolds, suitably peppered up with gay waistcoat and cummerbund, and carrying a set of horse-brasses as his badge of service.

The slightly varying periods of dress were meant to represent different stages in the history of this house in Keldgate where the Minster bells chime pleasantly as though from a timepiece in the parlour. . . .

York is pretty good at such evocations, too. Indeed, this city was *made* for pageantry. It has everything that is essential: a long, thrilling history, old buildings in profusion, and an impressive roll-call that summons Roman emperors and their legionaires, Saxon scholars, medieval monks and pilgrims, Georgian belles and beaux, and present-day folk, prominent or otherwise, some of whom go to their daily work along streets like Stonegate and Goodramgate first trodden by those who served Imperial Rome.

An archway off St Helen's Square, at one end of Stonegate, leads to the guildhall, which is mellowing nicely again after being practically destroyed during the last war and then rebuilt. Before the war I would often persuade the custodian to let me loose in a locked side passage which tunnels beneath the building to the old water gate. It was always fascinating to stand near the spot where the Romans forded the River Ouse, and then to imagine the workmen's banter as in later centuries magnesian limestone from the Huddlestone quarries was unloaded, for use at the Minster and for secular buildings too. Succeeding archbishops stepped ashore here, also, after sailing down in state from Bishopthorpe Palace, 3 miles away. But the passage did not then enjoy its present mysterious guise; as Common Hall Street it was open to the sky as one of York's chief thoroughfares.

The guildhall dates from 1446 and replaces an even older one. Before incendiary bombs played havoc with the medieval hall on the night of 29th April, 1942, a set of stained-glass windows dealt, rather turgidly, with outstanding episodes in the story of York. One can still take a history lesson here, though now with the aid of a brilliant west window designed by Harry Harvey, in whom the medieval glass-painters of York have a worthy successor.

The first window panel extols the city's renowned architecture with choice vignettes of the four medieval gateways, the Merchant Adventurers' Hall in Fossgate, the Minster, and a twin-gabled Tudor dwelling in Pavement. Panel two shows the coming of the Romans and then the Vikings, the Siege of York in 1644 and the blazing guild-hall in 1942.

With the scenes depicted in panel four, York tastes the fruits of peaceful enterprise. Binoculars—which are necessary for full enjoyment of the window—will here pick out a medieval fair, a ship sailing on the then tidal Ouse, the old Ouse Bridge* supporting its row of houses, and an early Victorian train representing the activities of George Hudson, the 'Railway King'. Panel five also sweeps one through the centuries with three impressive tableaux: the baptism of King Edwin in A.D. 627; the scholar-priest, Alcuin, teaching his pupils far back in Saxon times; and a Georgian couple dancing in the Assembly Rooms nearby. The centre panel unifies the whole conception with a scene

* See the author's *Bridges in Britain* (Cassell, 1970).

from the medieval mystery plays, crowned by the city coat-of-arms.

I doubt whether the builders and restorers of modern York have produced anything finer than the 'new' guildhall. Its soaring oak pillars and cross-beams conceal colourful roof-bosses carved with droll little troubadours, jesters, and horrid devils that seem to have escaped from the Mouth of Hell in the mystery plays. The sunlight that falls upon this 'forest glade' falls also upon a wrought-iron balustrade near the committee room entrance. This was given as a token of restored friendship by the people of Munster in Germany, now York's twin city.

The coastal resorts in the north range from Morecambe, St Anne's, Southport and Blackpool on the west, to places like Whitley Bay, Saltburn, Whitby, Scarborough, Filey and Bridlington down the eastern seaboard. Each has its own devotees. Morecambe on a clear day shows the Lakeland hills as an exciting backdrop, while Southport has the graciousness of an old lady no longer lured by beach frivolities but in love with flower shows.

The wind may blow colder on the east coast and its sea-frets can be a nuisance. But it would take a lot to keep holiday-makers from Whitby or Scarborough, which are complementary to each other, yet so different.

The descent into old Whitby, from the East Cliff, is by means of a fantastic piece of fourteenth-century construction known as the Church Stairs, or the 199 Steps. They seem to bulge and twist out of the very hillside, and if their breath-taking awkwardness produces little but sighs and groans today, they were perfectly adapted to the swinging gait of old-time sailors as they climbed up to Sunday service at St Mary's. And devout fellows many of them must have been. Why else should one part of the harbourside be named Abraham's Bosom?

With a final lurch or two over a cobbled area that only a storm-tangled beach could equal, you are debouched from Church Stairs into Church Street, surely one of the most curious and rewarding streets in any British port.

Flanked by curious shops and cottages (now dwindling in number, alas), it is punctuated by narrow alleys which creep back to some hutment on the cliff side, or dip down to the harbour in an atmosphere reeking with herring, ship's rope and brine. Artists love these alleys. The street used to be the haunt of jet-workers. Up till forty or fifty years ago you could always be sure of finding a few 'jetties', wearing the traditional bowler, busy at their treadles in one of those huts. Today, the trade has so far declined that few 'jetties' remain, and those few in other parts of the town.

Jet-working is a very ancient craft. Using local jet, craftsmen have exploited every kind of feminine fashion through the centuries, making rosary beads for Whitby Abbey nuns, witch crosses as a protection against the 'evil eye', Victorian hat-pins in pairs that resemble a couple of masts complete with chain rigging, and brooches engraved with girls' names which fond sweethearts gave to their fishing cobles.

The shipyards that once lined Church Street have also gone, but one memorable house remains, the house which became William Scoresby's residence in 1819. Overlooking the upper harbour, it stands to one side of a narrow entry called Saltpan Steps. It was this Scoresby (the elder) who invented the 'crow's nest'. Mariners honour him for other achievements too, but the older generation of Whitby folk like to think of the pump he erected in his yard for public use. It bears a Latin inscription which means, "Water for the free use of all. Draw, and drink it, but don't gossip." Minus its handle, the pump now stands in Whitby Museum.

The house that attracts most visitors, however, is number 16 Grape Lane—a slip of a lane that connects Church Street with the harbour bridge. It was in this tall house that (Captain) James Cook studied and slept in the attic, a spacious if somewhat spartan chamber roofed with ship's timbers.

The swing bridge which spans the harbour, thus connecting the two halves of the town, is the successor of many bridges at this site. An old resident recalls a scene of activity at the penultimate bridge when Cornishmen and others arrived for the herring fishing. In addition to the Staithes yawls and the local mules and ploshers, there would invariably be a fleet of two-masted craft from Penzance, Mousehole, Fowey and other Cornish ports, all waiting to get mooring space. Today, because of the change from sail to steam or diesel, the opening of the bridge is much less frequent. It is a good viewing point for the harbour, and—happy touch!—a side gangway is reserved for children when fishing for dabs.

Scarborough is a mixture of the genteel (on the south cliff) and the bourgeois (beside the harbour). At times the two elements intermingle with benefit to both.

In my boyhood days part of the very essence of Scarborough's romance lay in the Lilliputian house hewn from a large boulder that had rolled down Castle Hill and stopped just short of the sea. Do children still try to squeeze their way in? I saw it again not long ago, beside the Marine Drive; it looked as enchanting as ever.

The Marine Drive is always exciting. It connects the North and South Bays by clinging to the rounded base of the castle headland. Rough seas are best enjoyed from this three-quarter-mile-long prome-nade, where plumes of water are sometimes flung to a height of 50 or 60 feet. I have had many a drenching while standing too near the edge, but what thrilled me even more—in those carefree days of youth—was the sight of two or three builders' cranes and several huge blocks of stone placed strategically along the drive. They were in readiness, we knew, for any break-through by the sea—the "pretty turbulent Sea" that had so impressed Celia Fiennes, the seventeenth-century diarist and traveller.

Through nature and artifice Scarborough provides for both old and young. Oddly enough, however, the beach was long considered an *adult* preserve. Celia Fiennes remarked that "all the diversion [of visitors] is ye walking on this sand twice a day, at ye Ebb of the tide and till high tide. . . ." A few years later sedan chairs, coaches, chariots and cumbrous phaetons had appeared in this fashionable whirligig. A contemporary drawing shows the 'quality' further amusing themselves on the south sands; there is horse-riding, landscape painting, bathing—but not a child anywhere! Almost another century had to pass before the youngsters came. In June 1803 a certain Mr Hutton brought his invalid daughter to Scarborough, and wrote: "To observe the little animals . . . fabricating their pies and castles in the sand, is a treat for a philosopher." Perhaps his young daughter was well enough later, to join "the little animals".

Sacheverell Sitwell, famous member of a famous Scarborough family, has recorded his own memories of these wonderful sands and their attractions, particularly the pierrot troupes, the sight of which decided Charles Laughton—another Scarborough man—to take up the stage as his career. Sitwell also recalls how the lifeboat coxswain taught his brother, Osbert, to dance the hornpipe.

Within the painting: "Blessed · are · the · Merciful · for · they · shall · obtain · Mercy"

GRACE DARLING and her FATHER

Bell Scott's painting of Grace Darling's rescue of the survivors of the *Forfarshire*, in the Central Hall at Wallington, Northumberland

Mulgrave Castle near Whitby, North Yorkshire

Wilberforce House, Kingston-upon-Hull: the Wilberforce eagle emblem in plasterwork

9

In Community: Amongst the Villages

> Far remote and retired from the noise of the Town;
> I'll change my brocade for a plain russet gown!
> My friends shall be few,
> But well chosen and true;
> And sweet recreation our evening shall crown!
> Henry Carey on "Mrs. Stuart's Retirement"

Many villages supply the *poetry* of community life. Here in the North we have them in great variety. They may be cupped in a fold of the moors, have a sparkling beck for music, echo to the rhythm of the sea, or bask in the shade of some Border castle.

A long-cherished memory sent me back, some time ago, to a small Northumbrian village. During my first visit to Ford fifteen years before, Mary Guthrie conducted me through the village school, explaining many things about the Scriptural paintings with which the Marchioness of Waterford, of Ford Castle, had decorated the schoolroom walls. Mary Guthrie was the caretaker of those days and I recall her pleasure at being able to point out her old schoolmaster, Mr Todd, who was aptly impersonated in one of the studies as Gamaliel.

The story of how these paintings came to be done, in this secluded part of the Cheviot country, has a timeless appeal. Hundreds of visitors call at the school building every year to see and hear about

Lady Waterford's handiwork. Yet in the telling of that story one aspect—to me a very important aspect—tends to be overlooked. Perhaps the raconteur feels that few callers would be sufficiently interested in the homelier side of the paintings. After all, these were completed nearly ninety years ago. The art is the thing; who wants to know about John Thompson, Andrew Trotter, Betsy Locke and the rest? Even the Reverend Hastings M. Neville, a late rector of Ford, who wrote his book, *Under a Border Tower*, as a memoir of the marchioness, touched but lightly on this aspect—and he was an actual onlooker.

Lest such humility should expunge this vital part of the story— for who can faithfully implement a beloved tradition when all its participants have died!—I felt impelled to discover and put on record the names and a few anecdotes of those whom the marchioness selected for her purpose.

No sooner had Louisa, Marchioness of Waterford, set foot in Ford than she planned to improve the place. In 1841 she had married the third Marquis of Waterford. They spent eighteen happy years together— —and then came tragedy. In 1859 the marquis—promising his wife that after the forthcoming hunt (at Curraghmore, Ireland) he would renounce the sport she so disliked—fell from his horse on that very meet, and was killed.

There were no children of the marriage, and to assuage her grief Lady Waterford furthered her aims of 'raising the village' of Ford by building a school and taking a hand in the spiritual welfare of the villagers' children. For their edification she essayed the task of painting a number of Scriptural studies, concentrating upon young people from Bible stories. The first was begun in 1861-2; the last, "Saul at the feet of Gamaliel", was completed in 1883.

Each figure portrayed is vital; each group has verve and compelling power. Round the room they go, and as large as life: Cain and Abel, Abraham and Isaac, Jacob and Esau (the deer hounds sniffing the mess of pottage belonged to Lady Waterford), Moses and Miriam. Samuel is here with his parents, David tends his sheep (long-haired Northumbrian sheep), Daniel instructs the three youths of royal descent. Then comes the New Testament series, with the Infant Saviour in the midst, that is, occupying the centre of one long wall. Jesus is seen again as a boy of 12 in the company of the rabbis. Nearby are the two Johns, the Baptist and the Evangelist, followed at length by Timothy receiving instruction at his mother's knee. The series is clinched, artistically and otherwise, by a fine study of Christ blessing the children, which spreads the full width of the west wall.

Lady Waterford's sketch-book was rarely out of her hands. Her studio was in the west wing of Ford Castle, and when engaged on the school murals it was to this part of the Border tower that she inveigled certain of the villagers and their children, one by one. For her models were the folk she knew and talked with almost daily in the village.

Who were these folk? Through their eyes one should get a fascinating homespun picture, not only of castle and village, but of the neighbourhood at a time when tourists were few. That is what I set out to discover.

My quest was probably too ambitious, but there were many rewards. For one thing I met Andrew Trotter, one of the last two living persons from that time of Ford's apotheosis.

A retired gamekeeper, he was living at Branxton, near Flodden Field. As a boy he helped his father in the castle grounds, and he told me how he and other lads would climb up the ivy to get peahen's eggs from the battlements. Mrs Heslop, Lady Waterford's housekeeper, knew him only too well, therefore, when he was eventually summoned to the studio to become one of the angelic boys brought forward to receive Christ's blessing, in the large terminal group. "I was then seven years old," said Mr Trotter. "I'm now 82."

He showed me a photograph of a drawing ("the original is now in Burlington House") done by the marchioness as a kind of cartoon for the bigger study; in it young Andrew wears a green tunic and holds a mandolin. In the mural he wears *black* velvet. But either way, a perfect pattern of a boy. "Eh, but Mrs Heslop had a bad time with us lads," corrected Mr Trotter with a twinkle. "She once told me that I would hang on the gallows yet!" Nevertheless, a glass of milk and a piece of cake usually accompanied such admonishments.

A few months before my second visit the Duke of Gloucester stayed at Ford Castle and Mr Trotter purposely trudged up from the valley to point himself out on the school murals for His Royal Highness's benefit. But I don't suppose the duke heard about the peahen's eggs, *or* the way in which Andrew and his chums recited their Scripture passages (with the aid of a concealed Bible) to the marchioness on Sunday afternoons. When Her Ladyship discovered the Bible the oratory would always cease abruptly!

The other model then still alive was Mrs Coxon; as Fanny Short she 'sat' for the Moses study. There was a family of Shorts in the district at that time, and most of them appear in the murals; Annie Short was Miriam, John Short was one of Joseph's brethren. Mr Short, the father, was a local preacher at Ford Moss, a neighbouring village which once had its rural coal mine. Joseph's remaining brethren eventually became miners at Ford Moss.

The model for the Infant Saviour was little Willie Lock, also from Ford Moss, which suggests that the marchioness gained a real and sympathetic insight into the lives of these mining folk. She had once accompanied her husband into this small country colliery. Her respect for the men of Ford Moss was considerable, and she probably knew the whole story of the retired miner who, when asked by Hastings Neville one day as to whether his wasn't a very lonely life, replied quite reverently, "No, Sir, I never feels dull. I'm aye divartin' mysel' convarsing with th' Almighty."

Mary Heslop, Lady Waterford's housekeeper, appears in the murals repeatedly—as Rebecca, as Lois in the Timothy group, and as one of the mothers in the scene of Christ blessing the children. The village blacksmith came along from his forge and made an admirable Abraham, and a small medallion of Isaac in old age is a likeness of the old marquis, Lady Waterford's father-in-law.

Anybody with the right features and expression was liable to find himself, later, in this remarkable pageant. Two guests at the castle became the Chief Baker and the Chief Butler in the story of Joseph. Two bearded brothers, Billy and Samuel Smith, were portrayed as Moses (in maturity) and Aaron. Samuel was a real village 'character'; his wife was noted for her toffee and no matter how often a child might go along to buy some, Samuel would be there to pipe out, "Now it's good toffee, it's Maggie's own make!"

Among those who provided the rabbis in the Temple scene were the Reverend F. H. Gooch, the curate, John Todd the schoolmaster, and several estate shepherds and foresters. Some of these appeared again in the culminating scene of Christ blessing the children, notably, the curate who, with a child on his knee, 'sat' as the chief figure; among the mothers were the schoolmaster's wife, the curate's wife, Miss Boardman, Lady Waterford's maid and, as already mentioned, the ubiquitous Mrs Heslop.

Alas, there is no Mrs Heslop to usher visitors into the castle today. She had served here with the Delaval and Waterford families for more than sixty years. An apparation of the last Lady Delaval is once said to have conversed with her in the castle court. Her knowledge of the castle's history almost equalled that of her later mistress, and questions were always being put to her by visitors. What was the spell that Lady Heron here cast upon James IV of Scotland, leading to the fatal delay and defeat of Flodden? Which was the room in which the ill-fated king slept?

When Lady Waterford was not sketching she was almost sure to be conducting some friend over Flodden Field, winding up her account with that lament for Flodden:

> The Flowers of the Forest, that fought aye the foremost,
> The prime of our land, are cauld in the clay. . . .

All this lent a deep significance to the marchioness's work for Ford and its school, for here she dedicated herself to the youth of her own day. It seems fitting, therefore, that—as indicated earlier—Ford Castle should now play its part in the education of another generation of England's youth.

In June 1957 the 'school' was transferred to a new building, and the older building—the venue of Lady Waterford's paintings, since restored and strip-lighted—leapt into fresh prominence as Waterford Hall. Open every day, the hall relates the paintings to their author, chiefly by a marble figure of the marchioness, also by her paint-box and brushes.

Another day, during the same tour of Northumberland, I called again at Glanton, about 7 miles west of Alnwick. It is a small village, situated between the Breamish and the Aln rivers, which I approached through the Vale of Whittingham while all the hedges were afroth with may blossom.

Itself a pretty village, Whittingham has a well-preserved pele tower and many strange tales to relate. But my mind was set, that day, upon Glanton, for I had a promising appointment to keep.

On Glanton Pike (695 ft) a beacon would be fired in times of Border forays and even much later. Down in the village people still talk about an 'alert' on the night of Tuesday, 31st January 1804, when Bonaparte was said to have landed on English soil. Surrounding beacons were soon ablaze and Glanton became a rallying point for the neighbour-hood, to the sound of drums and the clatter of the Cheviot Legion Volunteer Cavalry and the Coquetdale Rangers. When morning brought the news of a false alarm Glanton turned to rejoicing and feasting.

For some years now, Glanton has been a rallying point for orni-thologists because of its Bird Research Station—the first of its kind anywhere in the world—run by Noble Rollin, his wife and son. Birds have fascinated Noble Rollin ever since boyhood. Even at the age of five years he kept pet birds. Primrose Cottage—now an im-portant feature of the bird station—housed those pets; first, a tame jackdaw, later, owls and song birds. A scientific-minded father encouraged the boy; another influence was a retired gamekeeper. I envied Noble Rollin his good fortune as he told me how, in those tender years, he would trudge day after day to the keeper's cottage on the farther side of Glanton Pike and listen enthralled while Job Simpson —an impressive figure with waist-long silvery beard—initiated the boy into the secret ways of birds.

Swallows were darting back and forth as I was ushered into the main building—a spacious Regency house facing the village street. Almost every room is dedicated to the feathered creation. In charts and records you can follow the day-to-day story of many species, for the technique employed here is to observe birds continuously throughout the twenty-four hours; then a new method of bird study.

We stepped into the large garden. Away to the north-east is the hill called Jennie's Lantern footed by Crawley Dene. Glanton Pike rears up to the north-west. Altogether, an ideal setting for hearing the dawn chorus. "I first hear the lark over the Pike," said Rollin, "and the curlew, lapwing, redstart and others soon chime in from the field beyond the garden." "How sad", he continued, "that the dawn chorus of birds—most sublime expression of their vocal powers—should have been neglected by earlier naturalists. Even Gilbert White is silent on the daily chorus of the skies and hedgerows!" It was left to Rollin to organize the first synchronized survey of this amazing diurnal performance. That was on 4th June 1933. Since then, ever increasing numbers of voluntary observers in different parts of the British Isles rise uncomfortably early, on the appointed day, to make observations in their own locality, purely in the interests of science. Later, such observations were organized on a world basis. And all the results come back here, to this charming village in the Vale of Whittingham, to be tabulated, compared and filed away for future study.

If that sounds rather cold and scientific you should come over to Glanton, sometime, and peruse a few of those records. This is what I did, selecting some from my own native Yorkshire. Records had come from such places as 'Twenty Steps' below Castleberg Crag, at Settle; Saint Robert's Gardens, Knaresborough; Primrose Valley, Filey; the village of Thwaites Brow, near Keighley; a railway viaduct near Lightcliffe, Halifax; Langtoft on the Wolds. Two observers in the tiny valley below Fulneck Moravian School, near Pudsey, recorded what was required and then went into ecstasies about a certain blackbird—the first of its species to sing at dawn and the last at night—which "had a particular phrase which stood out clearly in his song and which did not occur in the song of other blackbirds".

Today, field studies and safaris are organized from Glanton that embrace the East African scene, southern Spain, Brittany, the Dordogne etc. Yet the teeming bird and animal life of the North Country is also covered: wild duck on the Northumbrian lakes, below Hadrian's Wall; geese on the Solway; sea birds and seals on the Farne Islands; and the Chillingham wild cattle. Ford Castle and Otterburn Tower are occasionally taken over as jumping-off grounds for further exploration.

What a continuing triumph for little, homespun Glanton, where a bull once chased me out of a hillside field while I was trying to photograph the place in its seductive vale.

One Northumbrian village with a natural bird sanctuary is Bamburgh, on the coast.

Bamburgh Castle and church have already coloured our story.

The castle is seen to great advantage from the village green, known as The Grove—a triangular piece of ground created from an old quarry which supplied stone for the building of the castle.

The appeal of Bamburgh is subtle. Outcrops of Whin Sill and the sea swirling around them have much to do with it; also the simple design of its mellow russet cottages, plus the knowledge that great events have shaken the place.

It was in one of these homesteads, Wyndings House, that some years ago I met William Dixon, great-nephew of Grace Darling. All accounts of this national heroine show her to have been of a reserved though determined disposition, which William Dixon seemed to have inherited. Yet, with only a little encouragement he was soon launched upon the old story for my benefit, and how fine it sounded in his rich Northumbrian burr!

The wreck of the *Forfarshire*, on Harcar Rock amongst the treacherous Farnes, was first noticed by Grace Darling herself. Peering through one of the windows of the Longstone lighthouse, where her father was keeper, she saw the sundered ship at 4.45 a.m., but not until 7 a.m. could she discern, with the aid of a telescope, a small group of survivors clinging to the rock.

Determined to make a bid for their rescue, she at once called her father. He, however, considered that such an attempt would be madness, so savage was the storm and mountainous the waves. But Grace seized an oar and declared that she would go alone if necessary, whereupon William Darling agreed to accompany her, while his wife, with much foreboding, helped to launch the frail coble.

Harcar Rock is only 300 yards from Longstone Island, yet Grace and her father had to make a detour of a mile before they could reach the scene of the wreck. As the coble would hold only five or six persons, Mr Darling leapt on to the rock to decide which of the nine survivors should embark first.

Meanwhile, Grace managed the boat, an almost superhuman feat in such a sea, for she had to keep clear of the rock to prevent the boat from being dashed to pieces, and sufficiently near to allow the first detachment to step aboard. Eventually, after a *second* trip, all the survivors were safely landed on the island. . . .

Mr Dixon then showed me the log kept by William Darling while at Longstone. Its entries are often full and detailed, but his report about the incident of 7th September 1838, is a model of brevity: "Nine persons held on by the wreck and were rescued by the Darlings."

When the facts concerning the rescue gradually drifted beyond Bamburgh, the Darling's onshore home, gifts began to shower upon Grace from admirers all over the country. Queen Victoria subscribed £50 to a congratulatory fund, the Duke of Northumberland sent a prayer-book and a silver-gilt watch, and the Duchess a paisley shawl. Mr Dixon spread some of these and many other gifts on his drawing-room table, for they had become treasured heirlooms, along with a grandfather clock at the foot of the staircase—the very clock, he thought, by which Grace read the time when she sighted the wreck. A tremor ran through me as I handled them all, one by one, even to the sole piece of intact china-ware—a prettily painted saucer—re-covered later from the wreckage by divers.

These heirlooms, together with the life-saving coble, are now displayed in Bamburgh's Grace Darling Museum nearby. Rather more personal are the gulls' eggs and sea-shells collected by Grace and her father on the Farnes.

Bamburgh's on-shore sanctuary, where Grace must often have marvelled at the antics of the wild fowl, when she was a girl, is known as The Slakes, a small estuary opening into Budle Bay. I have walked that way myself, within sight of oyster-catchers, dunlin, godwit, packs of widgeon, also St Cuthbert's favourite, the eider duck.

I sometimes dream of Bamburgh and itch to be back there again, with a soft breeze coming from the Farnes, the whistling of the red-shank piercing the air, and the whirring of many wings. . . .

Northumberland has other rewarding villages: Elsdon in Redesdale, nearly all the settlements up the Coquet Valley, and, of course, Blanch-land—lonely, serene, and watered by the Derwent on the Northumber-land-Durham boundary.

But one other Northumbrian village calls for more than passing mention. I first walked to Cambo in a blinding rain-storm, and found refuge in a small cottage which restored my good humour with a wholesome lunch and a chance to dry out! Only later did I discover the outward charm of this village, slightly raised on its ridge a few miles west of Morpeth. To my own impressions of the place Mrs Pauline Dower (*née* Trevelyan) of Cambo House has kindly added her own commentary.

It seems that in the thirteenth century, the village was called Camho, a name adopted by its chief landowner, Robert de Camho. His village stood a little to the east of the present one, which was created as an estate village in the eighteenth century by Sir Walter Blackett of Wallington nearby. With a sure eye for the fitness of things, derived from the prevailing mode of architecture, he built a row of single-storey cottages with thatched roofs, punctuated in the middle and at each end by graceful, two-storey dwellings like pavilions. In 1818 Sir John Trevelyan added another storey to the intermediate cottages, but the 'big houses' still bespeak their former status. In one of them, 'Two Queens', Geoffrey Winthrop Young and his wife, who come into our narrative later as mountaineering friends of the Trevelyan family, lived for six years, enriching their own times and ours, by poems and books in praise of mountains, and memoirs that embrace much of the North Country as well as other places of inspiration.

The 'character' of Camho is further shown by a much older building near the village shop, which dates from the 'troublesome times' of the sixteenth century, when a pele tower was vital to any Northumbrian community. The church came later (1843) as a gift of Sir John Trevelyan and his son. Still later, Sir Charles Edward Trevelyan maintained the family tradition for public service by adding the fine tower to the church, also providing a vicarage and further cottages, all in harmony with the existing scheme of things.

It must be delightful to live in such an atmosphere of homely elegance. The smithy still has its old forge and bellows handle tipped with sheep's-horn, and the green its drinking-fountain in the form of a dolphin. Tapped water came in due course, but the 'dolphin' still supplies clear running water and an iron cup to drink from. The local children would hardly be normal if they did not sometimes still patronize the 'dolphin'. This came just too late to refresh the boy who went to school here and later achieved a fame of his own as Capability Brown. . . .

It is now time to wander farther afield, into an area shared by three counties—Northumberland, Durham and Cumberland.

Some friends and I once stayed in this area, at Nenthead, a model village of the early nineteenth century. We were on the roof of England and spent all our days exploring the ramifications of that 'roof', descending often into valleys called 'hopes' dotted with small settlements once populated by men who worked the local lead mines.

The district often floods my memory with scenes of deep-cut ravines and splendid waterfalls, or linns, and of the grey stone villages and hamlets that crossed our path.

Much of this came back to me recently, through a Quaker friend's loan of some autobiographical notes written by her grandfather, whose youth was spent on a farm at High Studdon near Sinderhope, in the beautiful Allen Valley. Staward Pele, a ruined pele tower, stands near-by, and at the southern end of the valley a beacon at Allenheads once gave warning of raids to the neighbouring villages in Weardale and Upper Teesdale.

A runaway marriage at Gretna Green added some spice to family affairs, and it is remembered with glee that the prospective groom had part of his coat-tail ripped off—"grandmother's memorial protest"—as he rode away with his "bonny girl with bright red cheeks and black hair", a mere 16-year-old.

In the early part of the last century, to which these reminiscences apply, it was often said that to be successful a farmer "must marry the dairymaid". The Gretna Green episode seems to have lent swift wings to this theory, though when the couple returned, and were forgiven, the local clergyman insisted on marrying them 'properly'. This, in spite of the fact that the family were staunch Quakers and rode regularly to 'meeting' on their ponies or in a dogcart, and heard 'ministry'—not from any parson—but from some elder who spoke in 'thees' and 'thous' and dressed in the approved simple manner. One of these worthies, speaking at the meeting, would untie the strings of her Quaker bonnet and push this back from her head as she 'warmed up' to her subject.

Local village life in those days produced many interesting characters. One, the above writer's Aunt Sarah, was the first person in Allendale to be the proud owner of an umbrella. Whether she ever used it is questionable, for the story goes that when a shower came on, she hid the umbrella under her cloak to keep it dry. . . . The schoolmaster was another 'star', though anything but brilliant as a teacher of youth. Towards winter the scholars had a 'barring-out day', which meant that the master was locked out of school until he returned in the afternoon with 'toffy sticks', made from treacle, bought at the local shop. Two such sticks for each scholar was the price for his re-entry, but by then the day was almost done!

The youngsters seem to have got their best lessons, first hand, from the natural life of this Pennine country. Several pages of the autobiography are devoted to the birds of moorland and burn; peewits, golden plover, snipe, curlew, ring ousel and many others. In winter flocks of wild duck and geese gathered around moorland springs, which never froze. "In later years my brother Isaac brought these springs and unfluctuating streams to the notice of the Hexham authorities, and now they supply Hexham with abundant water."

The same writer's father used to say that "he had no recollection of illness in the dale until two competing Scotch doctors arrived on the scene—and then the pains and aches began to multiply"! Lead mining was then at its peak. All the dale's villages had their quota of miners, Sinderhope even having eighteen families who derived their meagre living from this industry, which yielded the owner, Wentworth Blackett Beaumont, as much as £100,000 per annum. The miners would keep two or three cows on their bit of land, and were allowed to cut peats for winter fuel freely. But, when at work, "they stood in water up to their knees . . . and the mines were ill-ventilated". Respiratory troubles and rheumatism were frequent complaints. So there was good work awaiting those Scotch doctors, after all.

What of today, in this area? After the bottom fell out of lead-mining, the population of the villages declined. But something else is attracting people here again, and cottages which could be bought for a song not very long ago are now commanding high prices. The magnet is fluorspar, found around the old lead workings. So the hill-farmers with their flocks of Swaledale sheep have village neighbours, once again.

When we move west into the Lake District the term 'village' usually means a small cluster of cottages, fashioned in local slate, beside some beck with steep fells on each flank. The Borrowdale settlements, Grange, Rosthwaite, Seatoller, are on this diminutive scale. To the initiated each is a gem in a mountain setting; to the speed hog, anxious to be over the Honister Pass, which begins at Seatoller, hardly worth a second glance. But that applies more or less to all Lakeland! Speed merchants should stick to the motorways and leave little places like St John's-in-the-Vale, near Keswick; Dacre, above Ullswater; Troutbeck on the Kirkstone Pass approach; Winster, near Cartmel Fell, and so many others, to those who love serenity. Penthouses, cylindrical chimneys and spinning galleries sometimes add their own distinctive architecture.

Watendlath, above the southern end of Derwentwater, is another of these serene 'pockets' of humanity. The name has a Norse ring about it, and how well did the late Sir Hugh Walpole distil its atmosphere! His brief description in *Judith Paris* still applies: "It was utterly remote, with some twenty dwellings, a dark tarn and Watendlath Beck that ran down the strath until it tumbled over the hill at Lodore." For motorists it is a cul-de-sac amongst the hills; remote, yes, though many tourists are now well content to climb that winding track from the lakeside, dip their toes in Watendlath Beck and—if they know their Walpole—try to conjure up the white witch, Mother West, who "gave the girls love potions and the men cures for the rheumatism".

A fairly recent by-pass has restored to Portinscale, at the northern tip of Derwentwater, something of its former peace. Its name recalls a Viking settlement, Port-Thing-Scales, signifying the huts of the Parliament by the ford. This, at any rate, was Canon H. D. Rawnsley's interpretation. Long before the canon helped to found the National Trust, he would spend hours in the company of Richard Mitchell, boatman and ropemaker of this place. When Mitchell was not ferrying people over to Keswick, or to St Herbert's Isle, he would be making ropes, especially for Maryport ships, and sometimes as he worked, chatting to "t'li'le parson" from Crosthwaite.

The two became such firm friends that when Mitchell died, in his ninety-third year, Rawnsley wrote a rhymed tribute which the ropemaker's grandson, Richard Gill—also of Portinscale—kindly allowed me to copy.

H. D. Rawnsley was no Wordsworth, but three of his verses are worth quoting for their personal allusions:

Just beyond the Derwent, friends,
Where the Viking once was feared,
And the road for Swinside bends,
Lived and laboured—early, late—
One to humble fortune reared,
One content with low estate.

Never more through shower and sun,
Shall we watch him at his trade,
While the hemp to strength was spun,
Pacing up and down "the walk"
Where the best of ropes were made,
He too busy for to talk.

For dark death, with solemn shears,
Cut at length his long life's rope,
With its two and ninety years;
All the wisdom, all the store
Of his memory and his hope,
These are vanished evermore!

Rawnsley buried his old friend in Crosthwaite churchyard, beneath a stone carved with a rope design and these words: "A threefold cord is not easily broken." Within five or six years, Rawnsley, having learned much local lore from Mitchell, was instrumental in securing Brandelhow Woods, near Portinscale, for the newly-formed National Trust.

'Dick' Gill, who continued here as ferryman for many years*, had his own rich store of tales. The following is a fair sample.

An American visitor once asked him if there were any *big* fish in Derwentwater. "Sometimes", replied Gill, "we catch seven-and-a half-pounders".

"Oh," said the Yankee scornfully, "we use *those* for bait. Are there no *really* big fish?"

Dick thought for a moment and then came up with the silencing rejoinder, "Yes; not here, but in Bassenthwaite Lake over yonder. The local sheep-farmers once got worried about the loss of lambs. So one night they kept watch and found that some pike left the water, climbed the lower slopes of Skiddaw, and *ate* the lambs."

It is never safe to try to catch one of these villagers out!

In later years Canon Rawnsley bought Allan Bank, Grasmere—a house formerly occupied by William Wordsworth, who here wrote part of *The Excursion*. Allan Bank stands aloof from the village, on the track to Easdale Tarn, with Helm Crag—capped by Wordsworth's imaginary astrologer and bent old woman—so much the nearer.

* See the author's *Ferries and Ferrymen*.

Not long ago my wife and I spent a holiday within daily sight of Allan Bank, and the pageant of clouds and mist rolling over Helm Crag made us think again of Coleridge, he to whom a sky without clouds was "like a theatre at noon". Coleridge and his family staying at Allan Bank with the Wordsworths was a pleasant thought for us, as we looked up to the house across the meadows, for Coleridge was such an interesting character. He would start a tour of the Lakes "with his nightcap packed up in a natty green oilskin", a few pens and paper and a stripped besom as staff. Once, after the echoes of a thunderstorm had died away, while he was on Scafell, he loosed a few echoes of his own, by calling aloud the names of his own children. . . .

Grasmere and Wordsworth are synonymous. You cannot see one without entering, however slightly, into the spirit of the other. At Dove Cottage, the poet's home before he moved to Allan Bank, thousands now pay their homage. A quaint little place, low-roofed, simple and squat; one room papered by sister Dorothy with newspapers, and all the rooms like small boxes; a garden-plot stepped up at the back of the cottage, rather secretively, as though designed for un-interrupted communion with kindred souls, such as Coleridge, De Quincey and Charles Lamb. Small even for a couple in these days, but big enough then to house Wordsworth's growing family and nourish thoughts that gave rise eventually to *The Prelude* and his "Ode on the Intimations of Immortality". He wrote:

> The lovely cottage in the guardian nook
> Hath stirred me deeply, with its own dear brook,
> Its own small pasture, almost its own sky!

The interior of Grasmere's fine old church, beside the River Rothay, is still as Wordsworth knew it.

To this church, during one Sunday every August, the rush-bearing procession comes after parading through the village. In his day, Wordsworth was "the chief supporter of these rustic ceremonies", which were enlivened by Jimmy Dawson, the fiddler, and were brought to a successful conclusion—for the children!—by gifts of specially made local gingerbread stamped with the image of St Oswald. In 1910 Canon Rawnsley wrote a new hymn for the rushbearing festival. Today, some bishop often heads the procession, which used to be beautifully represented on a signboard outside a local hotel. There one saw the leading girls, carrying a large, homespun linen sheet decorated with flowers, and bearing wands of rushes gathered from the shores of Grasmere lake. When I last went that way, the signboard had vanished. Will nobody have it replaced?

Downham is often regarded as Lancashire's prettiest village. Because of bygone witches, who held their covens and brewed their mischief on Pendle Hill, Downham had an evil reputation as well, along with Newchurch and other places on the south side of Pendle. But that story must wait. A much calmer outlook is induced if one goes along there on some bright, warm day when the villagers are sitting at their rose-bowered doors, ready to talk to strangers.

In one of these villagers I found an able raconteur who seemed to know everything about the place, past and present. As we sat on his doorstep, facing Pendle, Downham first shaped itself as a Saxon village fortified by a thick thorn fence, also by the male inhabitants, who took turns at night to guard the village against robbers. In 1910 the Saxon foundations of the church were exposed for a time, but my mentor's best church story evoked a lively picture of Downham Preaching Day (30th January), originally provided for in the will (1680) of Sir Ralph Assheton, Bart, of neighbouring Whalley. To ensure variety this annual sermon was never to be preached by the same parson. Gradually the event became more of a holiday than a holy day, and one year a football match was even arranged with the lads of Newchurch! The visiting preacher went down into the mêlée, seized the ball, took it with him into the pulpit and then, after conducting the service, let the game proceed, himself delivering the kick-off from the churchyard steps.

The church porch frames an uninterrupted view of Pendle, with its distinctive reef knolls in the mid-distance. One of these limestone knolls, known as Gerna, is the villagers' barometer. They tell you that if cows graze their way to the *top* of Gerna, the day's weather will be good.

At Downham Hall, beside the church, one branch of the Assheton family continues to live. They have squired the village for generations. One of them, Nicholas Assheton, kept a diary (1617-18) which Harrison Ainsworth was to draw upon when writing *The Lancashire Witches*. But the diary contains far more than fulminations against witchcraft, and the squire did not spare himself either, for he is continually going "to wyne" and often "maide more than merrie"—doubtless at the village inn. On 12th May 1618, despite the witches, he climbs to the top of Pendle. A few days later he has a "grene doublet" made. With a light heart he also goes off hunting, dancing, dicing; he listens to many sermons in the old church and once—as he blandly confesses—"plaid the bacchanalian".

Pendle (1832 ft) is like a polestar to Downham and neighbourhood. From its summit Abbot Paslew and his companions watched for the first gleam of beacon fires that signalized the beginning of the Pilgrimage of Grace. George Fox had a different kind of vision from Pendle: "We came near to a very great high hill," he wrote, "and I was moved of the Lord to go up to the top of it. When I came to the top I saw the sea bordering upon Lancashire." He also saw a bright light as from heaven and a great company of people "in white raiment"; then, "as I went down I found a spring of water in the side of the hill, with which I refreshed myself". Downham villagers know this place as George Fox's Well.

Because of the constant interplay of light and shade upon its flanks, Pendle always seems *alive*. All in one week I have seen it shrouded in mist, fiery red, black as jet, golden with evening sunshine, rampant like a monster waiting to pounce; and again, just a green, beckoning hill. No ugly pylons spoil this ever-changing panorama for in 1930, when electricity came to the village, Sir Ralph Assheton paid for the cables to go underground.

An afternoon spent in Wycollar, a few miles east of Pendle, used to be a rare delight. The place now only causes heartache! It is sad to see a beauty spot one has loved for a lifetime decaying through sheer neglect, and all but empty—almost like Oliver Goldsmith's *Deserted Village*.

Yet it was in this secluded spot that Charlotte Brontë found, at Wycollar Hall, the Ferndean Manor of *Jane Eyre*. On one of its squires, Henry Owen Cuncliffe, Charlotte is supposed to have modelled her brusque Rochester. But the Cunliffes departed from Wycollar long ago, and most of the farming families who peopled the surrounding cottages have followed suit. Yet Wycollar is no more isolated than dozens of other, well-favoured places. If it were in the Cotswolds, people would be outbidding each other for possession of one of these quaint cottages, with their attractive vernacular features and almost faery setting. Spruced up, cared for and lived in, Wycollar could easily hold its own with many more famous places that lack its picturesque bridges and the beautiful Dene which meanders a couple of miles before reaching the far-spreading Brontë moors. Can Brontë enthusiasts and lovers of the northern countryside generally, realize what is here at stake?

Haworth is but 5 moorland miles from Wycollar, yet how different is the prospect in this bygone home of the Brontë family! It gets thousands of visitors every year, all eager to pay their homage at that worthy shrine, the Brontë Parsonage Museum. In summer, the steep cobbled street swarms with sight-seers. Brontë mementoes of every conceivable kind are snapped up from the shops; even the cakes in the cafés seem to have the requisite flavour! And make no mistake, Haworth is indeed well worth visiting (especially on a quiet day!), for in most essentials it is still the place Charlotte, Emily and Anne knew; the place that listened to Patrick Brontë's searching homilies and looked on, sadly, as Branwell dissipated himself to death.

You can enjoy the same walks which the Brontë girls enjoyed—

out Oxenhope way, to the Sladen Valley, to Emily's Wuthering Heights—and also, be it remembered, to that little dene curling its way beyond the Yorkshire boundary, past waterfalls and coppices of alder and birch to the now ruined hall where Jane Eyre comforted the blinded Rochester.

In *Yorkshire Villages* I paid extensive tribute to the parochial aspect of my native county. Many of the villages are of outstanding interest and charm. From the Pennines to the coast, and all along the dales and plains they spread their little quotas of joy.

At Malham in upper Airedale the limestone scars are quite cyclopean, dwarfing the grey stone cottages that nod to each other across the beck far below. Constance Pearson, dales' artist, lived in one of those cottages, with the Cove almost at her back door. Once, for a Women's Institute exhibition at York, she represented the Yorkshire dales in appliqué, with sheep-shearers wearing check shirts, flocks of Swaledale sheep done in wool gathered from hedges, Ribblesdale quarries contrived from pieces of brown tweed, and the wrought-iron gates of Skipton church fashioned in coloured threads. All the salient features of dales' village life were there—the farmsteads, the dry-stone walls in their often crazy patterns, the green lanes, the pack-horse bridges, even the limestone caves. These panels were offset by a few actual treasures discovered in those caves, also reminders of that great dales' lover of the seventeenth century, Lady Anne Clifford, and of the lead-miners too.

Before the eighteenth century, such majestic scenery as that enfolding Malham generally provoked horror in the few visitors from the outer world. Even poet Thomas Gray could only take a fleeting glance at Gordale Scar, and pass on. Today, streams of humanity bubble from the local youth hostel and leave no corner of this Pennine village and its environs unexplored. One of my own finest memories of Malham is of a winter's day, when Gordale Scar—all 400 feet of it—was festooned with icicles and the frozen beck below resembled an alpine glacier. A wild, primitive, *unbelievable* scene, shared only, just then, by two solitary mortals. . . .

In the present context we must linger at only two other Yorkshire villages—two that illustrate widely different phases of North Country life. One village shall be Aldborough, to the north of York, and the other Staithes.

Aldborough's Roman background has been sketched in already (see page 52). History is Aldborough's main ingredient. Long after the Romans had departed, Aldborough continued to pulse with life and purpose.

In Elizabethan times Aldborough was Crown property, which explains why Good Queen Bess was, ostensibly, concerned as to when

Evening in Scarborough Harbour

(*left*) Headpiece of Berwick-upon-Tweed's Civic Mace. (*below*) Ripon's Charter Horn of A.D. 886 and silver badges representing past Wakemen. (*bottom*) Richmond's Seal of Two Pieces given by Charles II

the villagers shut up house for the night. In 1585 it was decreed "that from hensfurth no mans servant nor made servant . . . shal be owt of his or their howse any time after IX of the cloke without special lycence of his or their master, upon payne to forfeit for every time so being 5s".

All this seems very remote from our times, but when we try to spotlight a later period we enter the sphere of party politics—as keen then as now, and we see the village taking sides, encouraged by the gift of so-called election mugs. Two such mugs preserved at Aldborough Manor proclaim the Lawson interest in no uncertain way. Amid a pleasing design of flowers and leaves, one mug has this legend— "Lawson for ever". Presented by the candidate to his electors, these and similar beer mugs were meant to be filled up at any local pub at the donor's expense!

I cannot say whether such bribes helped to send William Pitt the Elder and Michael Sadler the reformer to Parliament as members for Aldborough, but they were probably replenished at many pubs in 1820 after the following letter was addressed to the electors of Aldborough:

Gentlemen,

You are desired not to engage your Votes for this Borough, until *Mr. Lawson's* Return from *LONDON*, when Two Candidates in his Interest will be proposed for your Consideration. And you are also Cautioned against paying the least Attention to the Threats or Menaces of *THE DUKE OF NEWCASTLE'S* Agents, as you will be legally and duly protected in all your Rights and Privileges, which is the sole Object of the proposed Opposition to the Newcastle interest.

After the Reform Bill of 1832 such 'rotten' boroughs were dissolved. A good thing for Aldborough, as it left this maypole village to pursue its own rural interests at last and bestow on posterity an utterly peaceful spot to which one would often be only too glad to flee when present-day electioneering methods get over-heated!

Of all Yorkshire's coastal villages, Staithes is the wildest, as Robin Hood's Bay and Runswick Bay are (with Staithes itself) the most quaint. Staithes has long been a hostage to the sea. The impertinence of man trying to get a footing in this narrow strand between two brooding, oolitic cliffs is continually avenged by lumps of the place being snatched away by the savage waves. That is why the little shop where (Captain) James Cook once worked can no longer be seen! It explains why the Cod and Lobster Inn is now but half its original size. In this place drama means nothing fanciful on a gaily-decorated stage, but a stark, protracted tussle with the forces of nature. And as such it seems to answer something deep in man's soul. Perhaps that is why some of us, whenever we are in the neighbourhood, go down that crazy street again and squeeze through its final bottle-neck to the brief water front, just to watch and wonder how long the battle can go on.

Only recently, an aged local fisherman confided to me that nowadays "more water than ever seems to be forcing its way ashore at high tide". That sounds ominous! Can it mean that the little alley on the seaward side of the 'Cod and Lobster'—the alley on which my artist friend, the late Fred Lawson of Wensleydale, stood three or four years ago to make a sketch of the Slipway Cottages—is the *next* 'lump' doomed to destruction?

Dame Laura Knight was another artist who loved the wildness of Steers, as Staithes becomes in the speech of its inhabitants. She lived here and married here, filling her sketchbooks with all the day-to-day minutiae of the fisherman's life: his grip of an oar, his deft mending of the nets, his sure handling of a coble. In later years she committed the following prose sketch to her memoirs; "The life and place were what I had yearned for: the freedom, the austerity, the savagery, the wildness. . . . A poet should have written his sagas there." Her easel on the shore at low water, or on the brief, wave-washed quay, was for years as familiar a sight as the bollards, and the rotting posts along the cobbled slipway. . . .

Erosion has claimed many places along the east coast, but the chief villain on some stretches of the Durham coast has been *industry*. The toll of natural beauty is frightful. I need say no more, except that King Coal has mercifully spared some inland villages, which are as poetry to the other region's black tragedy!

Raby Castle, once a stronghold of the proud Nevilles, seems now to protect the neighbouring village of Staindrop from desecration. Like several places in South Durham, Staindrop ranges its cottages around a large village green, and does so with an air of grace, for although the cottages are not particularly old they have the individuality of a group of ancients, comfortably ensconced between castle and church.

Today's peaceful atmosphere is, however, deceptive. Border raids probably forced bygone villagers to adopt this close-knit pattern for defensive purposes. Narrow wynds lead secretively from the green to join footpaths that encircle the village like so many escape routes.

But peace and order bring confidence. One of those wynds recalls in its name, Nicky Nack, the clatter of spinning wheels and leads on to Emmanuel Wells, probably an old gossip centre.

My favourite amongst these Durham 'green' settlements is Gainford. The River Tees flows by, just out of sight. In fact, here on the green, *everything* is out of sight except the white cottages, the pub at one corner, and patches of blue sky peeping through thick overarching foliage. A car suddenly appears through the trees and as suddenly vanishes from sight, leaving the cottages to their unruffled calm. I would never be surprised to see a squirrel or two amongst the tree-branches overhead, or a weasel shooting across the grass.

Here, in one of our chief industrial counties, survives the immemorial English village.

10

History in Little

I once planned to write a book about the fascinating contents of some of our northern museums. After considerable research along these lines, I realized that a whole *library* would be needed! If therefore, this chapter on certain museums should seem all too sketchy, the reader should himself try to pour a pint into a thimble, and remember that some of our poets have attempted to cup eternity, no less, in the chalice of a few brief verses!

All our big towns and cities, and many smaller ones, attempt to embody their own long history in a worthy shrine of time. With few exceptions, museums are no longer the fusty and unrelieved array of glass cases about whose dismal contents *my* school generation had, alas, to write descriptive essays. Instead, school parties may now imbibe the pleasures of social history, while dancing to the tune of an old tingle-airy, as at the Kirkstall Abbey House Museum; or wander through bygone streets and gaze enraptured through the bow windows of a sweet shop specializing in such delights as 'conversation lozenges', fairy rock and spice pigs, and then perhaps send a few postcards off, each stamped in part with a Victorian 'penny black'.

In the north, the 'living past' was never so attractively cornered as here, at York Castle, among the well-simulated streets and alleys in which one rubs shoulders with an apothecary, a cordwainer, tallowchandlers, handloom weavers and a host of other colourful characters who peopled the world of Laurence Sterne, Charles Dickens and Maria Edgeworth.

The buildings that accommodate the York Castle Museum, founded by a Pickering doctor in 1938, centre upon a grass circle known as the 'Eye of York'. The museum itself can now be construed as the 'Eye of Yorkshire', for almost every phase of life from the three Ridings, during the last two or three centuries, is reflected in its spectrum. In the fussy Victorian Parlour, it would be natural to chatter about Gladstone's latest speech, or make a dish of tea for Sydney Smith, that irrepressible wit of local society. The moorland cottage seems to carry a whiff of heather and peat from the North Riding, while the Jacobean room is arranged as for a secret conclave of Bonnie Prince Charlie's local supporters.

Kirkgate, named after the museum's founder, Dr John L. Kirk, is a cobbled street of old shops and houses, while Princess Mary Court and Half Moon Court charm one from the lurking shadows of highwaymen to the first days of motoring. And by dropping a coin in a slot, one can hear the different dialects spoken then and now, in the three Ridings. To add further reality one can even buy wholemeal bread made from corn ground in a water-mill that once stood in Raindale, near Pickering.

Kirkstall Abbey House Museum, which echoes to those gay tingle-airy tunes, is another medley of bygone streets, lined with shops that recall the old Leeds Pottery, and various trades inherited from dispossessed lay-brethren after the closure of Kirkstall Abbey across the way. A blacksmith's shop, here, contains the small forge at which Samuel Marsden (see pages 198-99) worked while at neighbouring Horsforth. The smithy's other gear preserves a link with the great industrial enterprise of Kirkstall Forge, which itself dates back to monastic times. All these associations would, I imagine, have gratified the practical farmer, blacksmith and wool pioneer that resided in the complex make-up of the Reverend Samuel Marsden; he would have been even more gratified could he have known that Gott's Mill (1809), nearby, is even now being acquired as a museum of industrial history. The adjoining riverside wharf is known as Botany Bay, for it was here that Marsden's first bales of Australian wool were unloaded, nearly two hundred years ago.

Sheffield's staple industries are represented in different phases. In the Weston Park Museum cutlery cuts its way through the centuries with an impressive variety of knives and forks; these, along with a fine collection of Sheffield plate and silver ware, provide a striking contrast with the Chinese ivories shown in a large section of Graves Art Gallery. Achieving their apotheosis in such charmingly naive figures as Kuan-

Yin, patron saint of mothers, and Four Heavenly Kings who guard the world from evil, at the four points of the compass, these seventeenth-century creations agreeably offset Sheffield's own ivory products, from knife-hafts and cuff-links to carved elephants and lions.

But Sheffield is not content with an historical 'shop window', attractive though this is. The open-air also has its rightful place. One of the old "cutlers' wheeles", beside the River Porter in Whiteley Woods, shows how the trade was formerly conducted, on a semi-rural basis, the hum of the grinding wheels providing a sort of tenor obligato for the song of woodland birds. Distinctly rural, too, is the setting of Abbeydale Works, an eighteenth-century scythe factory which Sheffield Corporation maintains with all its curious paraphernalia, from tilt-hammers to coke-fired steel-smelting furnaces.

The thrill of industrial history is catching, especially when, as at Huddersfield's Tolson Museum, one can see and feel what Charlotte Brontë was talking about in *Shirley*, also Phyllis Bentley when the Luddites come into her West Riding novels.

Here for example is a model of one of the cropping frames that aroused such violent opposition from weavers whose livelihood they seemed to threaten. Here also is a large hammer, curiously known as Enoch, said to have been used to break up the first cropping frame. At Wormald and Walkers' Mill at Dewsbury a gun was fired at 10 p.m. each night during the Luddite scare so that one of the partners who lived nearby would know that, so far, all was well. Until about 1968, long after the need ceased, the custom was still observed at the mill, by means of a 'firework'! Although the museum director was unfortunately too late to rescue that earlier blunderbuss for his Luddite section, he has secured (from the Wentworth Collection at Sheffield Public Library) something which the affected mill-owners would have been only too glad to possess. It is a copy of a handwritten account indicating how the Luddites, who worked in secret, recognized each other: "You must raise your right hand over your right eye, if there be another Luddite in company he will raise his left hand over his left eye —then you must raise the fore finger of your right hand to the right side of your mouth, the other will raise the little finger of his left hand to the left side of his mouth and will say What are you? The answer, Determined—he will say What for? Your answer, Free Liberty— then he will converse with you and tell you anything he knows."

The terror caused by this underground movement inspired the ladies of Huddersfield to present a sword to Captain Thomas Atkinson, in 1815, in appreciation of his services during the Luddite troubles. In the museum, that sword companions another that was said to have been carried by William Horsfall, a mill-owner of Marsden, when he was killed in a scuffle with Luddites.

Another phase of bygone industrial strife is represented at the Tolson Museum by a large flag, or banner, displayed in the Eye of York in support of Richard Oastler's demonstration there in 1832 against child slavery in the West Riding factories and mills. Oastler's spirited advocacy of a ten-hour day, in factories that exacted even longer hours, involving young children as well as adults, had spurred some workers at Rastrick near Huddersfield to prepare this banner: "Oastler is our champion. The Ten Hours Bill. And We are determined to have it." This rallying call is continued on the other side of the banner: "We hate Tyranny and Oppression." For her child to be able to say, in later years, that he had been present at that epoch-making demonstration, one Yorkshire woman walked 75 miles with the babe in her arms. She probably cheered with the rest on seeing this challenging flag.

These passions of a former day have a modern ring about them, and they crop up again at the Shibden Hall Folk Museum, on the outskirts of Halifax. The hall itself, which dates from the fifteenth century, has many associations with the local wool industry. Pack-ponies were once a familiar sight on the surrounding hills, and some of the harness bells are here as a reminder of the soft melody that floated over the air as they passed. To offset the elegant apartments of the hall, the outbuildings now embody a number of craft workshops, centring upon the bar of the Old Crispin Inn. The juxtaposition is significant. Across the yard, grace and affluence. Here in the inn, brought over from Halifax, some of the local Luddites met in 1812 to decide which mill they should attack first.

From early times at Halifax anybody found guilty of stealing his neighbour's cloth or sheep was summarily committed to Halifax gibbet, a forerunner of the French guillotine. The axe that severed the culprits' heads has fortunately gone into final 'retirement' in the town's Bankfield Museum. Yet it serves as a kind of macabre background, or the ghost of a threat, for those who once occupied some seventeenth-century weavers' cottages rescued and rebuilt here from the neighbouring countryside.

Over at Wakefield industry has left many curious relics on its way forward. The city's fine streets are still occasionally trodden by cloth-capped miners returning from a shift at some local pit, but they would be as surprised as anybody else at the bygone mining equipment preserved at the City Museum. Tallow candles to light up the old seams, wooden sledges, remnants of wooden bowls thought to have been used for scraping the coal face, also a couple of three-legged stools not unlike milking stools. What curious pictures they evoke, from the underworld, as known perhaps to a certain sixteenth-century miner whose boot, preserved here, was lost in the coal workings at Altofts! To him and his like a pricket holding several tallow candles— as discovered at a Shipley pit—might have been as ordinary as are safety-lamps to miners of today.

And so one can go through the industrial belt along the southern reaches of our area, calling at various museums to gain a glimpse of as many bygone trades.

There is something especially heart-warming in Tim Feather's Cottage, as reproduced at Keighley Museum. He was reputedly England's last hand-loom weaver. Looking around, one almost expects to see Tim, haloed with white hair and beard, step inside, put his hat on the peg, and resume work at his loom, humming perhaps to the clack of the shuttle. Actually, his cottage was at Stanbury, on the Brontë moors. Some moulds which the Feather family used for making spoons from locally mined lead have since found a home at the old Brontë Parsonage, which Timmy knew well. The Brontë sisters would often see him at work, in that little cottage at the brow of the moors. And in their own kitchen they certainly used one of his lead spoons. A pleasant thought!

Several Lancashire towns have their own way of commemorating the rise of 'King Cotton'. Although Manchester has brought treasures from the Orient into its museums, and many English and foreign works of art, there are fine textiles to be seen, also a dug-out canoe found when the famous Ship Canal was being excavated.

Preston's pride, the Harris Museum and Art Gallery, is full of good things. From various documents and relics one can follow the development of the Preston Guild Merchant from 1329. In 1802 John Horrocks and John Watson, pioneers of the town's cotton trade, headed the guild's procession of manufacturers, which also included some of the suspect mill machinery in motion. And Preston folk need never forget the part their ancestors played in the Jacobite rebellions, while there are commemorative medallions and basket-hilted swords to be gloated over, also a gold locket containing a miniature of Prince Charles Edward which he is supposed to have given to a Preston lady at a ball held in his honour. Add to these mementoes a Jacobite toast-firer, engraved with a head-and-shoulder portrait of the prince, wearing tartan cloak and beret, and the swirl of the bagpipes seems, once more, to fill the air.

Many Jacobite toasts to the 'King over the Water', and to Prince Charlie himself, must have been made also at Towneley Hall in Burnley. For his active support of Prince Charles Edward, Francis Towneley was beheaded in 1746. Even now, there is something clandestine about this beautiful museum in its own park. The eighteenth century saw much rebuilding here, but the secret room remains. It is a priest's hiding-hole, pitched between two floors, and rendered sound-proof by a covering of clay mixed with rushes. Food was traditionally passed to the man in hiding by removing a stone in the wall.

Judging by appearances, the Catholic Towneley family might still be in residence here, eager to show sympathetic friends their richly-furnished rooms, and their sumptuous early sixteenth-century chapel with its altar piece from the Netherlands. When Roman Catholicism became a proscribed faith, however, worship had to be conducted here in secret. Recusants of "more than ordinary perversity" was the tag attached to these Towneleys, one of whom even had to hide in a game-keeper's cottage nearby to evade capture during the Civil Wars.

At Lancaster Museum one is reminded of many developments since the Romans established a fort there, and also, be it said, since Julius Januarius, a retired decurion, settled on a farm near Skerton and sought prosperity for his crops by erecting an altar to Ialonius Contrebis. Julius would have had good reason to know the River Lune and its vagaries, which probably needed propitiation of other gods, too. The tidal Lune has always made history for Lancaster. As the museum display testifies, its shipping ranged from dug-out canoes to wooden vessels used in the eighteenth and early nineteenth centuries in the West Indian trade. Slavery was the dark side of such trading, but there were other aspects, as when Gillows of Lancaster imported mahogany from Jamaica, Cuba and Honduras for their famous furniture. Perhaps Gillows also made the case for a clock by Thomas Fayrer (1744-83), one of the town's horological craftsmen. Early in the nineteenth century, however, some of the local clock-makers kept pace with the times by changing to the manufacture of spindles and bobbins for the growing cotton industry.

Liverpool's time chart also has much to do with shipping. Yet long before any kind of craft sailed the Mersey, the neighbourhood supported amphibious life of the giant reptilian species. Seen in the comfortable atmosphere of the city museum, the spoor of such creatures, as found in the famous Footprint Bed of Storeton Quarry, near Birkenhead, may seem like a bit of prehistoric 'doodling', until life-size models of dinosaurs and ichthyosaurs, based on fossil remains, make one aware of the huge fantastic creatures that preceded Man around the Mersey estuary.

Even when various examples of Liverpool pottery meet our gaze, we are still engaged with the Mersey. Not only did many of the eighteenth-century potteries grow up nearby, but one of their specialities was the production of 'ship bowls'. These were decorated with pictures of sailing ships, accompanied by a suitable, well-wishing motto. On a share certificate issued in 1806, the Herculaneum Factory is attractively shown with its windmill, ovens and workers' cottages, along the shores of the Mersey. Three-masted ships sail by and, in the distance, the Cheshire bank—which long concealed the evidence of those giant reptiles—looms up like some Ultima Thule of the imagination.

Tullie House at Carlisle is another vivid touchstone of much that has transpired around this Border town since the Romans were here, and since Edward I, 'Hammer of the Scots', made the town the springboard for his Scottish forays. History contrived one of its many quirks when Bonnie Prince Charlie, moving south on the crest of his wave, appointed Sir John Arbuthnot as governor of the city, who then made his home in this attractive Jacobean house. One may try to visualize the new governor, inflated with short-lived pride, traipsing up and down the fine oak staircase, which now takes visitors through a pageant of time, covering all manner of change, from prehistoric ages onward. A local artist has designed two murals, one showing how Lakeland might have appeared about the end of the Ice Age, and the other re-creating the Keswick Stone Circle when new, some 4,000 years ago, with all its megaliths intact for some as yet undiscovered purpose.

But the Solway is also recalled—most amusingly, perhaps—by one of the 'belly canteens' used by certain women for smuggling contraband liquor over the Border into Carlisle.* Strapped beneath her clothing, such a bulky vessel seemed to give a woman the dignified status of an expectant mother, whom no customs officer would presume to challenge. As each 'canteen', made of sheet-iron, held about two gallons, it is easy to imagine the welcome awaiting these ladies in some shady quarters of thirsty Carlisle.

Hadrian's Wall, undulating across the neck of England, has its own museums *en route*. Some have been mentioned, but by far the biggest collection of antiquities from the Wall has found its way to the Black Gate Museum (part of the castle) in Newcastle, through which town Hadrian's fortification ran to its eastern limit at Wallsend.

When George Stephenson's son, Robert, rode on his donkey from Wallsend to school at Newcastle, many of the Black Gate treasures were still undiscovered; which makes one wonder how many more tooled altars, votive offerings, coins and trinkets of all kinds lie underground, for rabbits to burrow amongst, until some excavator stumbles upon them somewhere along that great outpost of Roman civilization. Whenever I see such antiquities, either at Black Gate, Housesteads, Chesters or Corstopitum, I try to rekindle the thrill experienced by the persons responsible for turning up something that has been concealed for seventeen or eighteen hundred years. This javelin from Carvoran, for example; a gold brooch; some Latin verse inscribed on a stone in honour of the Divine Mother; part of a shrine to Mithras; a third-century tombstone "to the memory of my daughter Pervica", whose charming little person—carved on the same stone—greeted

* See the author's *Smugglers' Britain*, (Cassell, 1966).

some fortunate finder in recent times at Great Chesters. This is part of the joy of archaeology, and the Black Gate Museum takes one, by proxy, on many similar 'digs'.

By comparison, the museum's collection of antique furniture seems of yesterday. One stout chest came from the Keelman's Hospital nearby, an early eighteenth-century building that recalls the ancient Newcastle 'anthem', *The Keel Row*. It extols the same broad Tyne that Emperor Hadrian had to bridge nearly nineteen hundred years ago. Although Newcastle is as modern in outlook as most go-ahead towns, it can never forget the formative past, with such a hoard of history at its very core.

Durham City takes up the story with a number of Roman altars and sculptured stones, some of which came from Hadrian's Wall and others from forts that guarded the important Roman road running north through Durham and Northumberland. These relics are housed in a section of Durham Cathedral library which was the monks' dormitory in monastic times. The library's historian, H. D. Hughes, M.A., spoke truly when he said that "anyone entering it [the Dormitory] for the first time realizes that he is looking at something outside of his experience". The long and lofty room is spanned by immense rafters made of oak taken from the Prior's Woods at Beaurepaire, nearby, in the fourteenth century. Each rafter is a solid tree-trunk, adzed roughly to shape and purpose. Beneath these forest timbers spread the sculptured stones and the artifacts from various places in the North Country.

The Cuthbert relics in the adjoining room, as already described, provide the necessary background for a group of grave crosses and other monuments set up in later years to commemorate the passing of successive members of the 'Congregation of Saint Cuthbert'. These men were a mixed body of clergy who sometimes married and reared a family. When Bishop Carileph (1081-96) came on the scene, those who remained from the old dispensation were given the choice of *renouncing* their families and becoming true celibate Benedictines, or leaving. All but one quitted. Carileph vented his spleen by destroying or scattering the memorials of their forebears. The few that survived provide their own variations of Christian symbolism. They date from the same period that produced the famous Bewcastle Cross, a wonderful grey sandstone cross, still standing, mutely eloquent of Saxon ideas and ideals, away there between the western reaches of Hadrian's Wall and the Border. From a plaster-cast in the Durham Cathedral library one can enjoy its rich carving, which ranges in subject from the risen Christ and other Christian emblems to a falconer with his hawk on wrist-gauntlet, and a quaint little menagerie of birds and animals.

The late Canon Greenwell, a keen local antiquary who was responsible for collecting many of the library's Anglo-Saxon stones, once said, "I got them in various ways, legitimate and illegitimate, by gift, purchase, and by felony!" All he meant by 'felony', however, was the surreptitious acquisition of a coveted stone from the land of somebody who cared about it not one hoot. A justifiable process, this, which goes on in one form or another even today. While living at Guisborough in north Yorkshire, for example, a lady of my acquaintance rescued from the roadside heather a beautifully carved stone, probably from Guisborough Priory. When council men working on that road told her that similar pieces they had found were either discarded, or used as filling material in the actual roadway, she had no scruples about preserving her 'find' in her own home, pending the interest of a suitable museum. In similar fashion, many an old church font, sometimes of Norman workmanship, has been 'lifted' from some farm where it had degenerated into use as a pig trough. Why allow some fragment of history to lapse, as though it had never been!

Kingston-upon-Hull is the fortunate custodian of several museums. In them one can trace the history of shipping, follow bygone whalers to Greenland waters, look on while William Wilberforce tackles the slavery problem, and 'travel around' by means of stage-coach, 'dandy-horse' or steam-car. A wide choice, still further enhanced by a display of silverware that put Hull craftsmen of the eighteenth century into the front rank.

A stranger to Hull, or Whitby, that other Yorkshire port linked with the Greenland whale fishery, might never associate whaling as such, with the arts, yet a form of art did flourish in those inhospitable waters. It was called scrimshaw work—a kind of etching on sperm whales' teeth, whalebone or walrus tusks. In *Moby Dick* (1851) Herman Melville calls the process "skrimshandering". Using the crudest of tools, perhaps only a jack-knife, a whaleman would etch his design on the hard surface and then rub into the incisions a little Indian ink, paint, or even soot. Two fine specimens in Hull's Pickering Park Museum show a whaling vessel in full sail, and some flensers (skinners) at work on a *Mysticetus*, or common whale. Simpler articles made from bits of baleen include cribbage boards and staybusks, the latter sometimes being covered with whaling scenes and love tokens, presumably to impress the lady, back home at Hull, for whom they were intended.

Again in *Moby Dick* Melville speaks of Hull's "Levianthic Museum", then of a sperm whale skeleton kept in the grounds of Burton Constable Hall, not far away. The museum has its whale skeletons, too, but the Burton Constable whale was "articulated throughout; so that, like a great chest of drawers, you can open and shut him, in all his bony cavities. . .". Melville goes on to say that locks were to be fixed on some of "his trap doors and shutters, and that a footman would hence-forth be in attendance, as required, with a bunch of keys". This skeleton has now collapsed, but such exhibitionism would have been quite foreign to a self-respecting museum. Hull is content to show how whalers went about their dangerous work and spent their time when the ship was ice-bound. A jewel box made of walrus ivory by a Hull silversmith, Katherine Mangie, shows again how certain products from Arctic seas were used to practical and artistic account.

William Wilberforce was born in the very house in High Street that now epitomizes all that he did, so assiduously and over a long period, to abolish the British slave trade. To feel the full impact of his achievement as emancipator one need go no further than the Slave Room. It might even be called a Chamber of Horrors, for displayed about the room is all the nauseating evidence of that damnable traffic in human beings.

There are branding irons, iron shackles and slave-drivers' whips. There are original posters offering slaves for sale—average price, £150 for a male, £75 for a female. One slave, 'Mary', was exchanged for salt, wine and brandy to the value of $48. Inventories of sugar planta-tions ennumerate slaves as though they were so many head of cattle. Reward notices concerning runaway slaves actually betray the injured feelings of the *owners*! . . . But from an alcove nearby a life-size figure sits in his Chippendale chair, wearing cravat, velvet jacket and knee breeches. He can look with wry satisfaction upon all this bestiality—for he and his supporters helped to banish it! The figure is that of Wilberforce, ostensibly in his own study, surrounded by pictures, books and a model slave ship used in his valiant campaign.

Other rewarding museums are scattered through towns and villages all over the North. Some have been given incidental mention in other chapters, but anybody who would probe beneath the surface of modern times, as a doctor probes to test the blood stream, can also enjoy many other adventures. He can become a temporary devotee of the Mithraic cult, at Newcastle University's Museum of Antiquity; enter as guest into old Teesdale farmhouses, as reconstructed at the Bowes Museum, Barnard Castle; toil over minutely written stories with the Brontë youngsters in Haworth's Parsonage Museum. At Harrogate he can take the waters in the imagined company of Laurence Sterne, William Wordsworth and Charles Dickens. At Keswick, Hugh Walpole's manuscripts and his pictures from Brackenburn, above Derwentwater, are on show. Bradford can give you many a ghostly thrill while walking through the strange rooms of Bolling Hall, and at the village museum at Hutton-le-Hole, near Pickering, witches weave their spells afresh amongst reconstructed moorland cottages and barns.

The museum at Berwick-upon-Tweed introduces you to Jimmy Strength, reputedly the last of the ill-fated Stuarts; and another local character, Robert Evans, the blind fiddler who became a freeman of the local Guild and Town Wait. Scarborough presents many interesting personalities, from the Sitwell family of Wood End, now a natural-history museum, to William Smith, the pioneer geologist—scholarly company for George Cayley, with his strange flying contraptions, at the round museum near the Spa Bridge.

York's Railway Museum will become of increasing wonder as the steam locomotive era recedes from living memory. Engines that careered so majestically at the head of a long line of carriages, now come to rest alongside 'old stagers' like the *Columbine* which had no cab at first, so that drivers wore beards to protect their faces! George Stephenson is represented by many features, none so impressive, however, as the diorama showing the opening of the Stockton and Darlington Railway in 1825, with over three hundred costumed figures looking on incredulously as Stephenson makes history by driving *Locomotion* from Shildon to Stockton.

In these days an increasing number of people seem anxious to trace their ancestors back for several generations, and are willing to pay substantial fees for the necessary research. Museums perform much the same service, though on a more general basis, and for little or no cost to the man in quest of his forebears.

At one of our newest museums, housed in the stable block of Abbot Hall, Kendal, Lakeland life and industry are being probed and exhibited for the public benefit. Ancestors, especially Victorian ones, are very much in evidence. Here you can meet the local farmers with their hay sleds and portable sheep dips; the men who quarried the fells for stone; and others who worked the iron mines in a region that had achieved fame a little earlier through the activities of John Wilkinson, who made the first iron boat and then went on to make bridges of iron. Wilkinson was buried in an iron coffin and has an iron obelisk to his memory at Lindale. But some Victorian miners found other ways of proclaiming their skill. Using the best quartz crystals unearthed by the spade, they made a kind of grotto, or spa box, as a profitable hobby. One of them is shown here, along with typical mining tackle, in an adit shored up by pit props.

Perhaps grandfather was one of Kendal's snuff-makers, or a weaver of 'Kendal green'? This fine, hard-wearing cloth, worn by the bowmen of medieval England, continued to be produced in the town, along with many other commodities, until much later times. The workaday life of these and other craftsmen takes shape before you as you move around. From neighbouring Staveley, Dorothy Wordsworth's first introduction to the Lake District, there is a machine used by makers of wooden bobbins for the Lancashire cotton trade. Winster, one of

William Wordsworth's favourite valleys, supplies a long-case clock by Jonas Barber, who required no town workshop to blandish his wares. Customers were glad enough to *walk* to his countryside retreat.

With these and many other tokens of the past a Lakelander need no longer bemoan lack of knowledge concerning his forebears. At Abbot Hall he can at least see how they earned their daily bread, and—by means of several period rooms—enter into their very mode of domestic life.

One room is devoted to Arthur Ransome, whose books for children have the Lakes for their background, also the Norfolk Broads. Here, through various personal items presented by his widow, the ambience of his early boyhood is revealed—holidays at the Swainson's farm at Nibthwaite by Coniston Water, camping on the lake's Peel Island, friendship with local shepherds and woodmen, and a chance encounter with W. G. Collingwood, Ruskin's friend, who had lately fired the boy's imagination with his romance *Thorstein of the Mere* (Coniston Lake). Ransome repaid the 'debt' of such an enviable upbringing by delighting generations of children with his *Swallows and Amazons* series of books.

While looking through this study, in the museum, it is amusing to recall that as a few-weeks-old baby Arthur Ransome had been carried by his father, a man steeped in Lakeland lore, to the top of Coniston Old Man.

Even as I write, my old friend Frank Atkinson—who helped to create the Halifax Folk Museum—tells me of his latest ploy—a regional open-air museum at Beamish, County Durham. Here, craftsmen will be seen at work with bygone implements; horses will plough the fields once again; engines will return steamily to service; and electric trams clatter nostalgically through this specially created village of eighteenth-century houses and shops.

The establishment of such a folk museum is rather like reviving an old play of many acts, all well loved in their own generation.

11

The Romance of Industry

THERE is indeed a romance in industry—a romance (often hidden) that can only be suggested in this chapter, for how can one forge any kind of unity from iron and steel, textiles and shipbuilding, lead and coal mining, stone quarrying, engineering, plastics, potash and North Sea gas!

In one of his poems John Masefield attempted to 'float' some of our many cargoes:

> . . . Tyne coal,
> Road rails, pig lead,
> Firewood, ironware, and cheap tin trays.

But in that poem one can barely hear, except in imagination, the rivetters, the loom-workers, the blasters, the furnace-men, or the hundred other skilled artisans who have helped and still help to build up Britain's national wealth and her usefulness to other peoples. Even a precis of northern industry would require a whole tome, and much of it would be in the prose of daily toil.

All I shall do here is to present several cameos of northern industry, letting the particular theme lead us where it will, often enough into unexpected byways, with many personal overtones.

Leeds Corn Exchange: detail of the nineteenth-century steel dome

Chetham's Hospital schoolboys with Manchester Cathedral behind them

Now that Britain's railways have been drastically curtailed I find an almost Gilbertian piquancy in the knowledge that the very first commercially successful steam railway recently staged a come-back. Steam locomotion was adopted on the Middleton Colliery Railway, near Leeds, as early as 1812—two years before Stephenson built a locomotive and seventeen years before his *Rocket* startled the world. Middleton's prior claim is recognised by few people besides railway historians, for the line always remained small and independent, whereas the Stockton and Darlington (1825) and the Liverpool and Manchester (1829) were boosted as outstandingly important lines by the large railway companies that eventually incorporated them.

It is thought that outcrop coal from Middleton and Beeston nearby was used for their iron forges by the monks of Kirkstall Abbey, on the other side of Leeds. In 1646 Sir Ferdinand Leigh owned a "coal myne" at Middleton, and by 1669 Francis Conyers of the same place was issuing halfpenny tokens "for the use of the Cole Pits". When Ralph Brandling married the Leigh heiress in 1697 there was a fusion of mining interests, for the Brandlings of Felling, County Durham, and later of Gosforth, Northumberland, had worked their Tyneside collieries long and successfully, despite the continuing influence of the "nice dames of London", who, according to Stowe, avoided "any house or room where sea-coles are burned". This "vile" product from the North—which the Earl of Northumberland deigned to use at Wressle Castle, in the East Riding, though sparingly, lest "the smoak of the seecoyls wold hurt myne arras"—was still, in the main, the poor man's fuel, when he could get it.

Gradually, the prejudice against coal was overcome. By 1717 Ralph Brandling owned "a wrought Colliery, or Coal Mine, with a Water Engine and Smithy" at Middleton, and local people doubtless began to acclaim him as a go-ahead lord of the manor.

From about 1755 the Brandlings secured rights to lay waggon ways that would facilitate the delivery of Middleton coal to the inhabitants of Leeds, 4 miles away. These rights, confirmed by Acts of Parliament (1757 and 1779), carried the obligation to supply a specified minimum tonnage of coal every year at fixed prices. Many of the waggon ways were fitted with flanged cast-iron rails. A few of them survived until early this century. I was brought up at Beeston, and some of my earliest memories concern those rather mysterious metals that wandered without apparent aim through our favourite meadows and country lanes. Childhood imagination linked them with some strange, unknown form of transport, for they had long fallen into disuse. The truth dawned later when my historically-minded elder brother became apprenticed to an engineer and our walks took us farther afield, to Middleton. Blenkinsop and Matthew Murray eventually became

13

by-words for us; locomotives bearing those magic names plied regularly along the Middleton railway track, reminding us of the part played in railway history by these two pioneers.

The earliest section of the railway was constructed in 1758. It extended from Belle Isle, near the east gate of the Brandling grounds, to the coal staithes at Leeds. Most of this track then ran through fields, and it must have been curious indeed to see Brandling's coal-waggons being pulled slowly along by horses through flowers and tall grasses, as also happened, of course, on the subsidiary waggon ways around Beeston. During the Napoleonic wars the price of horse fodder increased so alarmingly that Charles Brandling found himself unable to sell his coal at the contract price unless some cheaper form of transport was devised.

John Blenkinsop, who had become agent to Charles Brandling in 1808, provided the solution. Rightly estimating that steam traction would be better and cheaper than the old method, he designed and patented a rack, or toothed rail, for use on the steeper gradients of the existing track, and Matthew Murray—a rising young engineer— designed special locomotives having toothed wheels that engaged in Blenkinsop's rack rail. This rail was laid on one side of the track rather than down the middle, so as not to interfere with the horses, which continued to haul some of the waggons; the other rail was smooth.

In 1802 Murray had designed a four-storey building to resemble an engine cylinder, the entrance being the valve chest. It was in this peculiar Round Foundry, situated near the Leeds terminus of the Middleton Colliery Railway, that he built his engines on the Blenkinsop principle. The first two were named *Salamanca* (after a current British victory) and *Prince Regent*. They cost about £400 each, which included a royalty for the use of Trevithick's 'high-pressure' steam patent, and created a sensation when demonstrated before thousands of spectators on 24th June 1812. At length many foreign engineers and scientists came to inspect this "vast public utility" before introducing steam railways to their own countries.

Locally, the event was celebrated in various interesting ways. Part of the railway track ran through the yard of the Leeds Pottery, in Jack Lane, Hunslet. Because of this way-leave the pottery paid only 2s per ton for Middleton coal. Richard Humble, former agent at the colliery, had been a partner in the Leeds Pottery, and when Blenkinsop's rack railway was introduced the pottery responded by making Leeds-ware plaques bearing a faithful representation of Murray's first steam engine. In George Walker's *Costume of Yorkshire* (1814) one plate, entitled "The Collier", shows Middleton Colliery and one of the locomotives in operation. Walker tells us that the miner depicted in the foreground is returning from work "in his usual costume—white clothe bound with red", and that "by two of these machines [the steam engines] constantly employed, the labour of at least fourteen horses is saved".

After being successfully used for over twenty years, the rack-rail system gave place to ordinary steam traction, supplemented by horse-haulage, for horse feed was now cheap again. About 100 years ago the last of Murray's four locomotives was withdrawn from service, and *Blenkinsop* and *Matthew Murray*—the two tank locomotives that I knew as a boy—began to chug their way to and from the different pits.

The names of these pits rang with a peculiar cadence. There were Fanny, Jane and Henrietta, Broom and Venture, Bleachground and Gosforth—the latter, of course, reflecting the Brandling interests on Tyneside. Some of the pits are still operating, but the encroachment of housing estates and other industry has robbed most of the area of its semi-rural character. Fortunately, Charles Brandling's home and beautiful grounds survive. The grounds have become a public park covering some 316 acres, and the Lodge is now the Middleton Park golf-house. The last section of Blenkinsop's rack-rail was kept here for many years—a 3-foot section with hollow teeth as distinct from the solid teeth that characterised the longer sections. This unique feature is now displayed, along with fine models of the *Salamanca*, in Leeds City Museum.

Between Blenkinsop's day and the beginning of the present century, the Middleton Railway underwent several changes. At one end of the line, extensions were made to serve more pits, and at Hunslet valuable traffic links were established with the former Midland main line. In 1881 the gauge was altered from 4 ft 1 in., to 4 ft $8\frac{1}{2}$ in. (the Stephenson gauge). A change of ownership, about 1862, arrested a brief period of decline, but when Brandling's successors, the Middleton Colliery Company, began to lay a branch track over part of Hunslet Moor they encountered opposition from the local residents.

Hunslet Moor is common land—an oasis of green where children play and horses sometimes graze near rows of brick houses. One section of the new track was actually uprooted by the outraged mob. But the colliery company won the day. The branch line was eventually completed, safely fenced off, and soon Hunslet Moor folk learned to accept the closer proximity of this brave little railway.

It was near this contentious part of the track that I recently renewed my acquaintance with Middleton Railway, which, a few years before, had almost expired. It is now protected by the National Trust and run by a group of railway enthusiasts, many of them from the University of Leeds.

Although 7,500 passengers were carried as a triumphant gesture when the railway was re-opened on 20th June 1960, it is being used mainly for goods traffic. Several local firms have convenient sidings that enable a variety of freight to be loaded on to waggons loaned by British Railways. The freight has included coal (though most of this now goes by road), pit props, machinery and scrap iron. A few years ago an entire gas works was despatched piecemeal by one of these Hunslet firms to New Zealand. As the first stage of the journey was along our historic track the waggons were gallantly labelled, "To Christchurch, New Zealand, *via the Middleton Railway* ...".

And now for the *ships* that carried coal.

Earlier phases of England's coal-shipping trade are recalled nostalgically in many places in the North, particularly around Newcastle and Sunderland. On George Stephenson's fine memorial near Newcastle Central Station there is a life-size figure of a miner holding his safety lamp. He is reminiscent of the figurehead designed as a miner clutching his safety lamp which the collier *Wearmouth* once flaunted.

Not far away, in the old guildhall, an ancient fraternity known as the Hostmen's Company still foregathers, as if to perpetuate the memory of their early predecessors, whose chief function was to entertain foreign traders and supply them with cargoes of coal for their return trip. The latter service, jealously guarded, provided a profitable working arrangement between the hostmen and the keelmen, who plied their coal-carrying keels, or lighters, from the colliery staithes to the sea-going ships.

Newcastle was shipping coal to London as early as the time of Henry III. Trade made such a leap forward in Elizabeth I's reign that moss-troopers as well as women are believed to have been employed in the mines, to meet the new demand; by the early seventeenth century some 200 hoys, or sloops, were regularly conveying coal from the Tyne to the Thames.

Regarding the coal-ships of subsequent times nobody has written with greater knowledge and zest than the late Sir Walter Runciman, who had served as cabin boy on one of those vessels. In his fascinating book, *Collier Brigs and Their Sailors*, he stated that "some of the colliers built in the middle of last [19th] century were little removed in rig, appliances, types and design from those with which Drake carried on his successful commercial and piratical enterprises". His list of such ships included *Maid of Athens*, *Brotherly Love*, *Sundew*, *Kezia*, *Widdrington* (name of a famous North Country family associated with the 1715 Jacobite rebellion, and with the mining town of Blaydon), *Salem*, *Smiling Morn*, *Winsome*, *Ancient Promise* and *Vesper*.

One renowned collier was called *John Bowes*. It was built in the Jarrow shipyard of Charles Mark Palmer and commemorated John Bowes, who had inherited vast coal interests from his father, the tenth Earl of Strathmore. Bowes and his French wife, the Countess of Montalbo, founded and endowed the magnificent Bowes Museum at Barnard Castle, and it seems appropriate that the museum director is assembling a great variety of items here that will form a permanent exhibition illustrating the history of north-eastern coal-mining.

Another well-known coal magnate, the Earl of Lambton, ran a fleet of colliers which flaunted the names of some of his own family —*Lady Beatrix*, *Lady Eleanor* etc. It is said that the funnel markings on these vessels referred to the Lambton Worm, theme of a hoary folk tale which has since been set to a rollicking tune. To hear it sung by a few Durham miners is as stirring and hilarious as their rendering of "Blaydon Races". The black-and-red bands on the earl's ship-funnels were the sailors' reminders of "young Lambton's . . . feerful worm" that grew to an awful size and often fed "on calves an' lambs an' sheep, an' swally little bairns alive . . .".

In 1946 Sunderland Museum and Art Gallery staged a fine exhibition to mark the six hundredth anniversary of shipbuilding in Sunderland. The ship-model section was notable for the number of colliers represented, most of the prototypes having been made by S. P. Austin and Son Ltd.

I have already mentioned Lewis Carroll's famous verses, "The Walrus and the Carpenter", which Sunderland inspired. One topic of conversation between the Walrus and the Carpenter—"why the sea is boiling hot"—must surely be a fanciful reference to the then new steamships and their cargoes of sea-coal.

When Daniel Defoe visited the West Riding he was so astonished at the ramifications of the cloth industry that he wove around it some of his choicest remarks. He found Halifax "one continual village . . . at every house a tenter and on almost every tenter a piece of cloth". And again: "We saw the houses full of lusty fellows, some at the dye vat, some at the loom, others dressing the cloths, the women and the children carding or spinning, all employed from the youngest to the oldest. . . ."

At Leeds, continued Defoe, "The clothiers came early in the morning with their cloth, and as few bring more than one piece, the market days being so frequent, they go into inns and public-houses with it and there set it down." He noted further that "several considerable traders in Leeds go with droves of pack-horses loaden with these goods to all the fairs and market towns over the whole island. . . . 'Tis ordinary for one of these men to carry £1,000 worth of cloth with him at a time, and having sold that, to send his horses back for as much more. . . ."

Leland, Henry VIII's itinerant antiquary, had earlier described Bradford as "a praty quik market toune [which] standith much by clothing". A temporary decline in the woollen trade, due to Civil

War disturbances, put Bradford behind Leeds, but recovery came later and by Victorian times it could be boasted that, in one year, 17,135,704 pounds of wool were "consumed in the manufactures of the parish".

Perhaps the greatest factor in Bradford's prosperity was the introduction of Australian wool, mainly due to one man, and that man a clergyman—the Reverend Samuel Marsden—who sprang from an obscure though neighbouring hamlet.

Bagley is barely a spot on the map and has to be 'fathered' by adjoining Farsley to gain any kind of recognition today. Since Marsden's time Farsley has caught the full brunt of industry, yet it is the very industry that grew from his own foresight and zeal. A street memorial erected here in 1934 neatly summarises his story. One tablet states: "Samuel Marsden . . . received his education for the Ministry at Cambridge University. He was appointed Chaplain to the Settlement of Sydney and left for Parramatta, New South Wales, Australia, in the year 1793. In the year 1814 he equipped his own ship, *Active*, and landed in the Bay of Islands, New Zealand, the first missionary to this land. He preached the first sermon there on Christmas Day of the same year."

A second tablet continues: "In the year 1807 the Reverend Samuel Marsden brought from Australia to England the first wool for commercial use. This was stored in a warehouse on this site and afterwards manufactured into cloth by Messrs. W. J. Thompson at Park Mills, Rawdon [across the Aire valley]. He did much to foster the growing of wool in Australia and in 1809 took back there five Spanish Merino sheep given by King George III."

Marsden is himself represented on the memorial by a bronze portrait which reflects his university period; while a merino ram's head, above, indicates the vast wool trade he helped to create.

The memorial inscriptions, although adequate for ordinary purposes, are a challenge to anybody with historical momentum. It is known that Marsden's father had a small farm and blacksmith's forge here. Later the family moved across the Aire valley to Horsforth, where Samuel helped his uncle, another blacksmith. While working the bellows with one hand, young Samuel would seize a piece of chalk in the other and write out declensions on the fireboard of the forge. One day the vicar of Rawdon came in to have his horse shod, and, noticing Samuel's preoccupation, expressed great pleasure and asked the lad if he would like to learn more. Thus began his tuition at the Reverend Samuel Stone's 'night school'—held, presumably, in the large Georgian vicarage.

Thanks to the Rawdon vicar, Marsden went to Hull Grammar School soon after, and thence to Cambridge University. At Hull he had become acquainted with William Wilberforce, who later recommended him for the chaplaincy at Botany Bay. From this point forward Marsden's story is well documented: his settlement at Parramatta and practical aid for the convicts in his pastoral care; his development of the local wool industry and other agricultural schemes; his successful landing in the then cannibal country of New Zealand, and so on.

The few Bengal sheep Marsden found at first on his Australian farm had been introduced some years earlier by the Dutch. The sheep were reared chiefly for their meat, but Marsden soon began to experiment in cross-breeding, with a view to improving the fleeces. It was a sample of this cross-bred wool that came to Rawdon in 1807 to be made into cloth. A few years ago I met Mrs Ethel Gaunt of Harrogate, one of whose ancestors—William Lawson, a personal friend of Marsden— unpacked that first clip of Australian wool. Marsden had despatched about thirty fleeces in flour barrels.

William Thompson of Park Mills, Rawdon, for whom Lawson was manager, declared that he had never seen such "muck", yet when it was scoured and woven, the resultant broad-cloth delighted everybody concerned. Dressed in a suit made from this fabric, Marsden appeared before George III, who was deeply impressed with his vision of a great wool industry developing in Australia, if only better fleeces could be produced. It was then that the King presented the far-seeing missionary with some merino sheep from the royal flock at Windsor.

On sailing to Australia with the merino sheep (which included a ram), Marsden prayed fervently for their preservation on the long, difficult voyage. In time they certainly improved the breed, and within three years Marsden's flocks had doubled in size and quality. By 1815 the quantity of wool sent to England from Australia was nearly 33,000 pounds; by the year of his death (1838) it had reached 4 million pounds. Today wool exports to England are so enormous that one would hardly be surprised to find Samuel Marsden enshrined at Bradford Wool Exchange as the textile workers' patron saint.

Many years ago Mrs Gaunt visited Miss Elizabeth Betts—Marsden's grand-daughter—at Parramatta, who kindly gave her several personal treasures, including Marsden's turnip watch and a pair of his clerical bands. They are now displayed in Farsley library, along with samples of that first wool and a length of the material woven from it. Yet, to my mind, the most touching mementoes of all are the gay little Australian flowers that come as seeds in the bales of imported wool. The seeds flow downstream in the wool-washings from neighbouring mills and some of them flourish, as if by right, within walking distance of Marsden's humble birthplace.

Lancashire's great cotton industry has bestrewn the county with many tangible memories of the time when Manchester could be described (in 1642) as "the very London of these parts, the liver that sends blood into all the countries thereabouts".

It is sadly true that in the next century or so the cotton trade often went hand in glove with slavery. Two Liverpool merchants in particular are black-listed in this respect. One, named Sill, so profited from the West Indian trade that he was able to set up a fine establishment in the remote valley of Dentdale and there employ a retinue of black servants, whose early life had been spent in the African jungle. That house, Whernside Manor, lately redeemed its past, somewhat, by being taken over as local headquarters of the Boy Scout movement.

Colonel John Bolton of Storrs Hall (now an hotel) on the eastern shore of Windermere, developed an association with black boys. According to some notes displayed below this merchant's portrait in the hotel, "whenever Bolton noticed any young boys among the slaves in his ships at Liverpool he would extract them and put them on a smaller boat and sail [through Morecambe Bay] to Greenodd, where a local man smuggled them up the Leven valley to Windermere . . . the boys were then taken by rowing boat to Storrs Hall". They were later sold to neighbouring gentry as house-boys.*

At about the same time William Wilberforce, while staying with friends, would row himself over to one of Windermere's islands and there ponder on the slave problem and on ways to overcome it. Did he ever hear rumours of the goings-on at Storrs Hall, farther down the lake?

Lancaster's complex of erstwhile cotton and silk mills adds something rather grim—altogether at variance with their products—to the local canal side and to the banks of the Lune; yet to follow the Lune down to the coast makes a thrilling excursion into the beginnings of the cotton trade. It also provides another excuse for visiting Sunderland Point.

From Overton on the mainland the tidal causeway lands one at length on to a pebbly shore, which could be the strand of some forgotten isle. Mooring posts at the water's edge now seem to be a continuation of the metal rails and wooden stakes that keep users of the tidal road out of sea and river quagmires that glisten on either side with peculiar enchantment.

In this bird-haunted retreat it is difficult to imagine former trading activities of any kind. A slipway of old millstones; a few dreamy-looking cottages; a post office half hidden up a narrow side lane; fishermen handling baskets of freshly-caught whitebait; a patrol boat tying up for the night. That pretty well sums up Sunderland Point today, though one must not forget its cotton tree, or Sambo's grave.

The cotton tree on the quayside is said to have sprung from the first

* For a fuller account of this aspect of the slave trade see the author's *Secret Britain*, (Cassell, 1968.)

bale of cotton landed here, somewhere about 1700, when Robert Lawson started unloading his cargoes of cotton at this spot. Every July the tree mantles the ground below with a large covering of silky fibre. This tree must not be confused with the cotton *plant*, on which Lancashire's staple industry was founded. It has been identified as the kapok tree, known in the West Indies as the cotton tree, and must have taken firm root by the year 1736 when a West Indian merchant disembarked here with his cargoes, and with a negro servant, Sambo.

It seems that faithful Sambo was left at Sunderland Point while his master went forward to do business at Lancaster. Thinking he had been deserted, Sambo, simple soul, refused to take any food and died of a broken heart. A cairn-like grave in the middle of a field is his memorial. The epitaph, in verse, indicates how much he was mourned by his kindly master:

> . . . But still he sleeps, till the awakening Sounds
> Of the Archangel's Trump new life impart.
> Then the Great Judge, his Approbation founds,
> Not on Man's Colour but his Worth of Heart.

Sambo had earned his niche, however humble, in the romance of Lancashire industry.

Another industry that sprang from this same shore, where the Lune meets the ocean, to the antiphonal cries of widgeon and grey-lag geese, was the great furniture enterprise of Waring and Gillow. Early in the eighteenth century Robert Gillow's sea captains here unloaded cargoes of West Indian mahogany, and took some of it back again, later, in the shape of elegant furniture. By the 1870s the firm's name was of such standing that Gilbert and Sullivan could play upon it in *H.M.S. Pinafore*. Josephine, Captain Corcoran's daughter, compares the prospect of marrying a common sailor, for love, with papa's luxurious home "where everything that isn't old [is] from Gillows' ". Her dilemma was hardly fair to the sailor, but who—ran her feminine mind—could possibly forsake the compensating allurements of secretaires with secret drawers and sliding tops, a desk that concealed a bed, library chairs with swivelled book-rests, or tabourettes with scroll ends that looked like something exotic from ancient Herculaneum!

Several country houses in the North were furnished almost throughout by Gillows'. In one of them—Broughton Hall, near Skipton—the library and drawing room still seem to form a friendly compact between the Gillows, and the Tempests of Broughton, both families of long-standing Catholic persuasion.

William Wordsworth's circle of friends included various members of a mill-owning family which originated in my own part of the

West Riding and then gravitated, one by one, and largely under the poet's influence, to the Lake District. In the writings of William and Dorothy Wordsworth this association tends to be overshadowed by the more intimate friendships with Coleridge, Southey and others, but the Yorkshire strand was picked up again by W. G. Rimmer, then of the University of Leeds, a few years ago, in his fine economic study entitled *Marshalls of Leeds, Flax-Spinners, 1788-1886*.

Several generations of the Marshall family lived at Low Hall, Nether Yeadon, just across the fields from my former home. It is a lovely Tudor house, enriched with a charming porch and wicket rescued after the Dissolution of the Monasteries from Esholt Priory nearby. Despite a few inevitable changes, it is still at core the home of John Marshall (1661-1745), who showed his independent outlook by identifying himself, as church secretary, with the pioneer Baptist cause in mid-Airedale.

The second Baptist chapel (1765) was built at Rawdon, like the first one (1715), but on a different site. In this strange little meeting house, which had a sundial over the entrance, special box-pews for the fiddlers, and private ones for Bradford wool-merchants, John Marshall's grandson, another John (1765-1845), was instructed during his early years. When his flax-spinning interests needed a boost, later on, it was to this same Chapel that he turned for a small loan—£50. His Aunt Sarah at Low Hall lent him £100, and other members of the family also dipped into their pockets. Thus was set in train not only the famous flax mill, first established at Adel, north of Leeds, and later in the Holbeck area of the same city, but also the connection with Wordsworth.

In August 1795 the second John Marshall married a distant cousin, Jane Pollard of Halifax. She and Dorothy Wordsworth were already firm friends, and the friendship doubtless grew during the Marshalls' three-week honeymoon in the Lake District.

In her journal, Dorothy refers to many subsequent visits by John Marshall, whom she found "so gentle, so mild, and with so much genuine feeling, simplicity and good sense". On 9th September 1800, she entered in the journal: "Mr Marshall came—he dined with us. My brothers walked with him round the lakes after dinner. Windy. . . ." Next day she recorded: "After Breakfast Mr Marshall, William and John went on horseback to Keswick. . . . I wrote to Mrs Marshall."

The spell of the Lakes was already upon Marshall. Again and again Dorothy reported that he and William had gone off walking or riding together. Marshall had in fact become one of the 'Lakers', as those tourists were called who first 'discovered' the appeal of this incomparable district. How one envies him the experience of sauntering with a half-mystical William over Loughrigg Fell or beside the River Rothay near "Grasmere's peaceful vale".

In June 1807 the poet and his sister were the guests of Jane and John Marshall at their home at Headingley, a Leeds suburb; the flax trade was prospering and evidently warranted these interchanges. This particular visit had one notable literary result. The whole foursome rode horseback and by coach from Headingley into Wharfedale, and then up the valley to Bolton Priory. We know that Wordsworth was impressed with the witchery of the place, for it breathes through his "White Doe of Rylstone"—the poetic story of Emily Norton's regular trysts at Bolton—which appeared the following autumn.

Five years later the second John Marshall joined the ranks of those worthies who planned a home for their families amid the once 'horrid' fells and 'eerie' lakes. John Christian Curwen, a northern coal magnate, had pioneered the way by acquiring a circular house for himself on Belle Isle, Windermere. Marshall built with better taste, in the Regency manner, on the shores of Ullswater. His private "Book of Tours" reveals his growing passion for rowing on this and other lakes and tramping over the fells that had half terrified Thomas Gray. One day Marshall recorded: "From Keswick went through Wattenlath and Borrowdale and came down by the foot of Honiston Crag to the top of Buttermere...." Not a bad jaunt for an erstwhile townsman, though the correct spellings were yet to come.

The Wordsworths occasionally walked over from Grasmere to Hallsteads, the Ullswater house, and in their aura one can imagine John Marshall, and later his sons, acquiring Lakeland accents and an introduction to the Picturesque cult. Ullswater was already embroiled with Picturesque moods and fancies. Were not echoes awakened over the lake by strategically placed cannons and men playing French horns? We do not know how the Marshalls reacted to such exuberance, but I sometimes wonder whether the curious flax mill they were to add to their existing premises in Holbeck, Leeds, didn't owe something to the same flair for novelty.

By 1829 Wordsworth was on such good terms with the new Lakeland gentry that he was invited to accompany John and his son James on a five-week trip to Ireland. For John Marshall it was a business trip, but James repeatedly went off with Wordsworth, "each on a vile hack horse" and along "vile roads" into the hills of Kerry....

On 25th August 1825 the poet had been one of three celebrities (Canning and Walter Scott were the others) in whose honour Colonel John Bolton, the Liverpool merchant of Storrs Hall, staged a splendid regatta on Windermere. From the grounds of Storrs a causeway 116 feet long (recently restored for the National Trust) juts into the lake and terminates with a gazebo known as the Temple of the Heroes, built in 1804. Plying around this attractive causeway were the gaily-decorated barges carrying Bolton's numerous guests. I have little doubt that amongst the cheering onlookers there would be quite a few Marshalls, for other branches of this industrial family were now settling thereabouts. William, the flax-spinner's eldest son, was at Patterdale Hall, the third John at Keswick, while James, the third son had acquired Monk Coniston, an estate marked today for most tourists by Tarn Hows, with its magnificent mountain views.

A Lakeland home had also to be found for the fourth son, Henry, and as usual Wordsworth's advice was sought. The place eventually chosen was Derwent Isle in Derwentwater, almost opposite Friars' Crag. A previous owner, Mr Pocklington of local renown, had fitted his island retreat with all sorts of quaint conceits, such as a fort and battery for creating echoes over the water. He once objected to a scheme that threatened to lower the level of the lake, by declaring that "it would join his kingdom to England". When this delightful 'kingdom' was taken over by Henry Marshall he enlarged Pocklington's house, took up bird watching, studied weather symptoms, and made some protests of his own, chiefly against a projected railway alongside his beloved Derwentwater. In 1951 Denis Marshall, a master at Sedbergh School, presented Derwent Isle to the National Trust. But as yet there is no public access. The tree-girt isle seems permanently and secretively moored to its own idyllic past.

By the early nineteenth century various other branches of the Marshall family had found residence in the Lake District. W. G. Rimmer has counted 111 of them, on the male side alone! Besides the houses already mentioned there were Castlerigg Manor, Skelwith Fold and Hawse End. St Herbert's Isle in Derwentwater, to which some friends and I used to row for picnics and youthful sport, also came to the family. Wordsworth's influence was certainly far-reaching.

Most of these houses have in recent years become hotels, guest houses or schools, but one Marshall memento that does remain, largely unaffected by time (except its coating of grime) is the esoteric building within industrial Leeds which helped to provide and support the entire lineal ménage. It is the family's flax mill off Water Lane—originally fitted with Matthew Murray's newly-invented hackling machines. The building resembles an Egyptian temple and at first enjoyed a distinctly rural setting. By that time the John Marshall who used to listen to the fiddlers in Rawdon chapel was 70 years of age. It is odd to think of him and his sons poring over Ignatius Bonomi's plans for the Egyptian-style mill, with its winged-sun emblems and lavish use of lotus and papyrus motifs, beside those limpid Lakeland waters.

The new mill was opened in 1840. A few years earlier, Dorothy

Wordsworth had asked John Marshall if he could find employment in the existing Water Lane mills for a Lakeland youth she knew. A nice gesture of continuing friendship and mutual regard.

The production of cheap cotton in the 1880s reduced the demand for linen yarns, and by 1886 the Marshall concern had closed down. Another firm produced linen cloth here for the next ten years, after which period 'little Egypt' lost its original purpose altogether. Nevertheless, during the fifty years I have known the place, Marshall's Temple Mill has been—to observant passers-by—a source of wonder in an otherwise drab neighbourhood. Yet there is always the Wordsworth connection (for those few aware of it!) with the Marshalls to restore a stimulating sense of romance.

There is an echo of the Marshall enterprise, in the Castle Mills concern at Knaresborough. In this, the oldest linen mill in the country, one notable Egyptian process survives. The ancient linen-makers by the Nile beat their material with sticks to secure 'finish'. For the same reason a beetling machine was being used at Castle Mills when I called some years ago. In other words, rolls of linen, revolving on drums, were beaten by a series of wooden hammers, mechanically operated. Thus, beside the waters of the Nidd—whose power drives the looms and other machinery, harnessed to turbines—flax continues to be woven into fine linen.

Before the days of power looms, however, a large part of Knaresborough's population helped in this local industry. A handloom was to be found in almost every cottage. Weavers were supplied with warp and weft and the mill-owner employed a 'spy' whose task was to listen at the cottage doors. He had to satisfy himself that the weaver was working his loom in the approved manner—two blows of the slay to every throw of the shuttle. A unique form of eavesdropping which must have caused both listener and weaver some embarrassment. This forgotten bit of history provides an amusing background for some of the firm's more recent products, which include fine linen, bearing the appropriate insignia, for such royal households as Buckingham Palace, Windsor, Sandringham and Harewood.

From Wordsworth to Chaucer is a mighty backward leap, yet Sheffield's staple industry comes into *The Canterbury Tales*. Did not the Miller of Trumpington carry with him a Sheffield "thwitel", or meat knife? On the strength of that association a comparatively new stained-glass window in the chapter house at Sheffield Cathedral portrays the whole company of those loquacious pilgrims, including the miller himself, suitably equipped with a thwitel thrust into his waist-band, looking for all the world like a Falstaffian butcher. There he stands, in the top tracery light, lording it over a fair scene, and flanked by a knife-grinder and a bladesmith to suggest the continuing enterprise of Sheffield cutlers.

Perhaps the best way to capture the spirit of that enterprise is to step within the Cutlers' Hall, opposite the cathedral, and let the tiny 'seed' sown on an earlier page of this book mature, through the activities of this ancient fraternity, within the uncharted 'kingdom' of Hallamshire.

The Master Cutler is head of this industrial kingdom that is not shown on any map. As already hinted, you will search in vain for 'Hallamshire', yet this kingdom, together with a 6-mile outer fringe, embraces an extensive area centring upon Sheffield and including Rotherham, Barnsley and other well-known places. Its distinctive influence has been felt for at least 600 years. It has its own rules, customs, and officers; and, be it added, will remain unaffected by any government boundary commission's proposals.

About 1161 the Cistercian monks of Kirkstead Abbey, Lincolnshire, had been granted a plot of land at Kimberworth, near Rotherham, for the smelting and forging of iron, and the industry eventually spread through the neighbourhood. In 1297 Thomas de Furnival, Lord of Hallamshire, presented a charter of rights and privileges to his "free tenants . . . of Schefeld", who agreed to pay him as annual rent "£3, 8, 9¾p. of silver". Trade gradually expanded, but an infusion of fresh skill came with the arrival of Huguenots in the sixteenth century. The Earl of Shrewsbury was one of the commission appointed to welcome those refugees. . . .

By 1604 the Earl of Shrewsbury, Lord of the Manor of Sheffield, was drawing revenue in respect of twenty-eight "cutlers' wheeles," ranging from some on Sharrow Moor (now Hunter's Bar), to others in the neighbouring valleys of the Rivelin, the Don and the Sheaf. About 1624, when the Cutlers' Company came into being, the customary rent was £3 per wheel, and as 400 or 500 master workmen were then using the wheels for knife-grinding, one can readily see that, to quote a contemporary with a neat Biblical turn of phrase, they were "very profitable unto the Lord".

These 'apron men' also paid unto the lord one penny annual rent for the distinguishing mark stamped on their knives. The first known holder of a Sheffield trade-mark was William Elles, a maker of iron knives. His mark comprised two triangles placed apex to apex and separated by a narrow bar. Elles receiving this mark at the official court is the subject of one of the subsidiary chapter-house windows at Sheffield Cathedral—a window that aptly commemorates the origin of the Cutlers' Company. Not far from Elles, and in the same colourful medium, Benjamin Huntsman (1704-76) bends over his furnace where he had discovered the secret of producing molten steel. . . .

But to revert to those trade-marks. It is a privilege to glance through the Cutlers' Hall register and note some of the ingenious devices with which Sheffield traders have identified their wares.

Sport contributes many of the marks: an acrobat arched from the ground like a crawling caterpillar; two anglers seated back to back in a rowing boat; a swimmer; a tug of war; a leap-frog performance; a cricket bat; men playing bowls etc. Animals and birds are represented by an elephant, a cat in a boot, a walrus, a tortoise, a frog and a kingfisher. Music provides such tokens as a violin, bagpipes and an angel playing a trumpet. Then there are several vignettes—Samson trying his strength against a lion; Guy Fawkes as a bonfire effigy; a gipsy kettle suspended over a tripod; Mazeppa lying flat on his galloping horse; a witch riding her broomstick. They form a curious medley, these marks, and even embrace such characters as a university don, a bewigged judge, a bearded hermit and the Devil himself. Little wonder that they are regarded as "the true heraldry of Hallamshire".

The company's three great annual events are the installation of the new Master Cutler, the Cutlers' Feast and the Forfeit Feast. There have been many changes of procedure on installation day, but it would take a lot to induce the assembled cutlers to renounce their brewis. The recipe used today by the catering firm responsible is their own affair, but traditionally brewis is a thin broth to which oat-cake has been added. It is served to the members on the morning of installation day, and in partaking of it the influential cutlers of today—all spick and span in their dress suits—recognise their humble forebears in the craft, for, as already stated, brewis was the main item of the apprentices' diet in bygone days.

Public generosity has long been the hall-mark of members—and nowadays, of course, membership is not limited to those engaged in the cutlery trade, but includes many Hallamshire worthies from silver-smiths to those in the heavy steel industry. The Cutlers' Company now administers fourteen charities endowed by wealthy citizens. Some of the charities were established about 180 years ago, and have been providing comforts for aged persons ever since. The Cutlers' Hall has staged many a magnificent feast during its long history, but there is nothing finer, in its way, than this practical bit of work forged afresh every year on behalf of such benefactors as the Ashton brothers, Thomas Hanbey, Samuel Hadfield, and John Smith. If one were to strike a mark for their now united effort it would be an *outstretched hand*.

The many offshoots of Sheffield's cutlery trade would lead us into realms of unimagined romance. One would see the last of the city's ivory-cutters, importing elephant tusks from the Congo and shaping it into knife hafts and scales, teapot handles, serviette rings etc. One of these craftsmen told me that in his youth "some of the clean dust, created in the cutting processes, was sold to chemists, who made from it a highly nutritious preparation known as ivory-dust jelly. It was prescribed for invalids and was reputed to be even more beneficial than calves'-foot jelly"!

Or one might come across a horn-cutter; by day transforming buffalo and deer horn from India and Ceylon into knife hafts; and in the evenings giving rein to fancy by shaping the same material into penguins or birds of paradise.

At almost every turn—Romance, whether one witnesses a silver fruit-dish being saw-pierced with a lacy, vine-leaf design, or a piece of Australian or Burmese mother-of-pearl fashioned—as a change from knife handles—into ornamental dragon-flies and sea-horses.

One of our newer industries owes its origin to a lake formed by glacial moraines in the Kentmere valley, Westmorland, during the Ice Age. A local resident told me that her husband's grandfather used to fish on that mere from a raft. When it was drained about 1840, to provide agricultural land, two 16-foot boats of Norse design were dredged up, also a Norse spear-head. One of the boats is now shown in Kendal Museum.

But these were not the only finds. A rich deposit of diatomaceous clay, formed from marine algae, or skeletons of minute diatoms, was exposed. Dammed up by those moraines for untold centuries, the deposit—the only workable deposit of its kind in England—is now being utilised in the manufacture of fireproof board for the building trade.

Fortunately, the beautiful valley is not unduly affected by these workings. And something very like that old fishing raft, though fitted with a derrick, is used to lift the precious earth from its watery bed.

A modernized spinning gallery at Troutbeck, Westmorland

Robin Hood's Bay, North Yorkshire

Pendle Hill from Downham Village, Lancashire

12

Town and Country Craftsmanship

WATCHING men at work and trying to follow the intricacies of their skill—often to the accompaniment of piquant comments!—is one of the most pleasurable of hobbies! At Hawes, in Wensleydale, a certain rope-maker plies an ancient craft in a pastoral setting, using equipment of such antiquated appearance that some visiting schoolboys once became rather scornful. Old Outhwaite continued working at his rope-making frame, fitted with sledge-like adjustable supports and a queer twisting device, and then retorted with his accustomed humour, "Well, you all use two legs, just as Adam did—no better method has yet been found!"

Up till a few years ago a clogger was kept busy, nearby, supplying local dairy workers and farmers with damp-proof clogs, having soles of alder or beech; and exactly the same kind of footwear to local gentry and visiting artists. Even they dislike getting their feet wet while traipsing through a stackyard, or over the moors in search of inspiration!

We still have our thatchers, makers of wooden hay-sleds designed for hilly country, and blacksmiths who can turn their hands to anything in metal. A smith I once knew at Hawes showed me a 'boneshaker' made by one of his forebears; a fine, wrought-iron balustrade fashioned later, to ornament his own house; and a set of iron sheep-brands. A complete 'alphabet' of these brands burnt on the smithy door enabled farmers from far and near to identify any 'foreign' sheep which may have strayed into their fields. This blacksmith also makes 'budgets'—the peculiar back-cans that Wensleydale farmers use for milk-carrying over short distances. The sight of one of these 'budgets', strapped from a pair of broad, swinging shoulders, is as familiar in these parts as the dry-stone walls, the field-barns and the curlews overhead.

While in this district one should sample a slice of the real Wensleydale cheese. It seems to taste better up here, in the countryside which has produced it for centuries.

Almost every 'local' thinks and talks in terms of dairy produce. They even gave the name Buttertubs to those limestone fissures situated near the crest of the pass linking Wensleydale with Swaledale. But you could walk or drive over the Buttertubs Pass many times without realizing that one clue to the antiquity of this regional product is to be found in the sheep that solemnly graze these heights. Ewes, not cows, provided the milk for the first Wensleydale cheese, which was made by the Cistercian monks of Jervaulx Abbey, lower down the valley. Originally, however, the community was established at Fors Abbey, near the head of Wensleydale. I like to think of the abbey herdsmen at their labours up there, in such grand, open solitudes, rearing sheep, shearing them for wool, making blue-veined cheese for their community and the neighbourhood, and then joining in the monks' litanies accompanied by the descant of singing becks.

Today, Wensleydale cheese is made at many centres, some of them in neighbouring dales. Before the last war many a farmer's wife also produced good, wholesome, tasty cheeses of the same vintage, even though—when she ran short of rennet—she might use a black snail to curdle the milk. But whether produced in lonely farm or village dairy, Wensleydale cheese is part of our monastic heritage.

After the Dissolution of the Monasteries, the secret recipe passed to the Towler family of Cover Bridge Inn, near Middleham and Jervaulx. Only later, when others began to use the recipe, was the cheese specifically called *Wensleydale*. The substitution of cows' milk for ewes' probably came in gradually; otherwise the recipe has remained virtually the same. Ultimately, of course, the cheese owes much of its crisp, salty flavour to the rich grazing afforded by the limestone fells. These rise to a height of 1,700 or 1,800 feet; their contours are patterned by craggy outcrops on which sheep, and sometimes cattle, perch themselves with a sublime disregard for the laws of gravity.

It is always fascinating to watch the different cheese-making processes. At the Hawes Creamery, within actual sight of Abbotside Common, I once saw the morning's milk arrive—thousands of gallons of it, from local farms; I watched it being mechanically cooled, and then stepped indoors to see dairymaids and dairymen busy themselves at their huge vats, mixing and cutting the curd, and later grinding the curd, in readiness for filling the moulds that eventually go, looking like so many small hat boxes, into the hand presses. Several days later, after the cheeses have been neatly 'bandaged' and arranged in drying racks, a small gouge will be used to extract samples from two or three of them. This is the connoisseur's method of tasting *Wensleydale*. Once you have had a nibble, out of the gouge, you are blessed indeed. You are among the dale's elite! And can talk on terms of some understanding with Kit Calvert, the grand old man of Hawes, who is as much at home with the local dialect and history as with the Wensleydale cheese industry, which—but for his staunch efforts during the last war—would have become as extinct as some of those silly sheep that come to grief in the Buttertubs.

Some of our traditional crafts have indeed expired. The spinning galleries to be seen outside old homesteads at Hawkshead, Tilberthwaite and Yewdale above Conistone bear mute testimony to the days when old and young would sit till dark spinning away with distaff or wheel, squeezing the utmost from every bit of local gossip. So charming a feature are these spinning galleries, so pleasing to the eye, that the owner of Yew Tree Cottage, at Troutbeck above Windermere, has replaced one which occupied a kind of penthouse above the cobbled yard. But I'm afraid that such household spinning, and all that went with it—from the drying of the yarn and storage of peats under such useful cover—have departed as surely as the *domestic* phase of the linen trade at Knaresborough, and the weaving—in Nidderdale—of locally grown wool, coloured with vegetable dyes extracted from wayside plants.

Yet one country craft that everybody believed to be extinct enjoyed a revival about thirty years ago. It is the old craft of hand-quilting.

This is one of the few 'stay-at-home' crafts of Britain and, withal, a genuine survival of peasant art. Modern machinery has not affected its older form, which explains why you can still see beautiful handmade quilts, resembling those that were so fashionable during the sixteenth and seventeenth centuries, occasionally being produced in the cottage homes of County Durham.

The antiquity of quilting as a handicraft is impressive. As you watch nimble fingers stitching away at the goose-feather design, say, or the lover's knot, it is salutary to think that those same fingers could as easily have worked on any of Catherine Howard's twenty-three quilts, made in sarsenet, that were given to her as a sign of royal favour in 1540.

Quilts were being made as early as the thirteenth century, but it is in the inventories of the great families of the next three or four centuries that the products of the craft are really gloated upon. At Kenilworth, in 1584, Robert Dudley, Earl of Leicester, could boast of several elaborate bed-quilts. Yet none of them—I am convinced—not even one described as "A faire quilte of crymson sattin . . . all lozenged over with silver twists, in the midst of a cinquefoil within a garland of ragged staves", would cause the more proficient Durham quilter of today to hang her head.

Before trying to locate one of these modern quilters, let us glance once again at the historic background of the craft. Such a preview will serve to illuminate, not only the strange origins of quilting, but the remarkable thing that has happened with the resurgence of the craft in modern times.

Many Elizabethan paintings show figures clad in quilted garments, made in satin, taffeta or silk. Plain diamond-quilting provided soldiers with an under jerkin or doublet that made the carrying of their heavy suits of armour more comfortable; for more courtly purposes quilted wear became highly decorative.

This was the hey-day of hand-quilting. The craft never really died out, though quilted garments went out of fashion, but latterly, in almost clandestine manner, it has made surprising advances. Just as quilting began in a humble way, with the peasants seeking means of warmth by padding pieces of rough material with any available bits of rag, wool or thistledown, so it has in recent times returned to the cottage hearths of Durham and to some extent, of Northumberland.

During a pre-war period of industrial depression and unemployment, a few women interested in needlecraft discovered that, to make ends meet, miners' wives and daughters were selling quilts which they had made in genuine Tudor style in their own sparsely furnished homes. And in this skill, those onlookers thought, there was a means of helping the miners' families on a bigger scale. So it was that the old craft—enriched here and there during the 'forgotten years' by designs of regional significance—was sponsored and taught to others by the Women's Institute Movement, backed by the Rural Industries Bureau. They organised centres where young girls could be trained in this craft of quilting. Though the last war scattered the trainees, those centres have done something towards ensuring the craft of its future and of a wider circle of admirers.

Ordinary domestic objects like wine-glasses and saucers provided quilters with their design units before cardboard templates came into general use. It is wonderful to see how many elaborate designs can be built up, by either method. The feather or fern readily lends itself to multiple treatment; with a scroll added at one end it becomes the traditional goose-wing design, while a different orientation of the design-elements produces the much-loved fan pattern.

The materials mostly used today are silk, linen or poplin for the covers, which, after being stretched out on and taped to a wooden frame, are padded with scoured sheep's wool, or cotton wool. It is the stitchery, of course, which keeps the padding in position, and the quilters sew in such a way that the underneath side is worked into the same design which the top cover bears. This none too easy task is accomplished by using a running stitch and keeping the left hand under the work to feel for the needle as it comes through and then pushing it back to the top again. In a good piece of quilting it should be impossible to say which side was uppermost on the frame.

My own first sight of the Durham quilters at work was at a Barnard Castle training centre, before the war. I found the girls in high glee, just then, for some of their silk quilts, worked in a traditional design of shell, rose and feather, had recently been bought for use in the royal apartments at Windsor. Later, I met a lady in the mining village of West Auckland who conducted classes in the craft all over the neighbourhood. It was a joy to examine some of her designs, particularly the true lover's knot; the cable and feather which, when continuous (as on a marriage quilt) denotes long life; the Weardale 'wheel'; and the tulip. Another popular motif is the 'Pagebank feather'—so named because the women of neighbouring Pagebank first used it on their quilts. The goose-wing is another traditional Weardale pattern.

With the upsurging of this craft, history is repeating itself, for once more many of the great houses of England have been fitted out with hand-made quilts. Some have gone, through trade channels, to Switzerland and others to America. But I think Mrs Black, my West Auckland informant, was most proud of having helped to furnish the 'Durham Room' at the Women's Institute's Denham College, in Berkshire, with quilts that should guarantee a permanent place in the history of English needlecraft for this delightful folk art of her county.

Wood-carving and cabinet-making have long flourished in our northern towns and countryside. In the sixteenth century Ripon had a famous school of carvers which furnished several cathedrals and churches with oak screens, choir stalls and humorous misericords that still delight visitors. Thomas Chippendale and Thomas Sheraton both came from the North—Chippendale from Otley in Wharfedale, and Sheraton from Stockton-on-Tees. Little is known about the youth of either craftsman, for both had to wait until fashionable London placed a premium on their handiwork and ensured for them an enviable immortality.

Hepplewhite also left his mark in the North, and although his supposed apprenticeship to Gillows of Lancaster lacks documentary confirmation, one can see something of his ingenuity and skill in a rare altar table at Whalley church, and an equally fine bit of craftsmanship in the round pulpit at Pickering parish church.

James Edward Elwell of Beverley was in a class to himself. His *magnum opus* was the Gothic-style screen in Beverley Minster, yet he could turn with equal facility to domestic carving. A painting of him poring over some design in his workshop provided his son, the late Fred Elwell, R.A., with one of his more intimate studies, but anybody can appreciate the master craftsman's flair for crisp humour by sauntering along Beverley's lovely street, North Bar Without, and gazing up at one or two house frontages.

A house once occupied by James Elwell presents a feast of quaint carving. A fine oak panel appears above each doorway, the subject of each panel being taken from a famous *Punch* cartoon of that day. They created quite a stir, locally, when first erected. Politically-minded townsfolk here found their national leader clearly and graphically delineated, for one cartoon features Disraeli speaking from the back of an electioneering cart to an audience of mesmerised farmers; and the other, Gladstone meditating over one of his grandiose schemes. There is no doubt as to Elwell's own political views, for the Disraeli cartoon portrays its central, gesticulating figure as "The Political Cheap Jack"!

Across the road is another exhibition of Elwell's pleasantries. Scaly monsters and grotesque creatures that thrive only in legend are here given vitality, but the *chef d'oeuvre* is a panel over the main door. Mr Elwell derived especial pleasure in fashioning this panel. He nourished a great love for the theatre, and after seeing his friend, John L. Toole, act the part of Caleb Plummer in *The Cricket on the Hearth*, he decided to perpetuate one of the outstanding scenes. So it is that this famous actor is here portrayed in the dolls'-eye-maker episode. The accompanying inscription, "We like to go as near nature as we can for sixpence," puts the final touch to a life-like reproduction. The Beverley woodcarver had paid his tribute to the actor, and, incidentally, to the author himself, Charles Dickens.

And so we come to modern times.

Kilburn, a few miles north of York, was a very quiet, aloof place when Bob Thompson was born there, in the village hall, on 7th May 1876. His father was the local joiner and wheelwright. Today, coachloads of visitors call at Kilburn every summer, not only to enjoy the surrounding scenery of the Hambletons, but to step within the village workshop and see some of the mouse-signed handiwork being fashioned.

Thompson trained some of his craftsmen from their youth. Indeed, his earliest trainees were village schoolboys who would pop in after school hours and try their hand at carving. With a rueful backward glance at his own youth, when he spent "five years' penal servitude" at Cleckheaton as a mechanic, he always encouraged local boys who showed any promise in woodcarving. Some of his protégés later set up as woodcarvers on their own account. Thus, through the years, has the 'seed' of his enthusiasm grown. Not only did he pioneer the woodcarver's craft in our day, rescuing it from virtual extinction; he has also been the means of spreading the craft itself and fostering in the general public a love of, and a desire for, beautiful, hand-made furniture. Fortunately, the village enterprise, begun with so much faith and determination early this century, now has worthy continuators in his two grandsons.

Bob Thompson's first inspiration sprang from his study of the medieval woodwork that survives in some of our northern churches and cathedrals. Anybody who would fully appraise the man and his achievement should follow in his early footsteps, as he peered among the choir stalls of Ripon and Beverley Minsters, admiring in turn the exquisite carving on the misericords, the bench-ends, the tabernacle work; the sheer beauty of mature, grained oak fashioned by master craftsmen. Look again at the Bishop's throne bench-end at Ripon, with the elephant standing on a tortoise, or at the Beverley misericord showing a boy cooking sausages, and the humour that informs so much of the Kilburn work can be traced to its fount. Not that Thompson and his successors are copyists. Far from it. A painter can derive inspiration from past masters and yet build up his own metier. So it was with Thompson.

Some of his finest work can be seen at Ampleforth Abbey, not far from Kilburn. Other buildings in which Thompson and his fellow craftsmen have placed their famous 'creeping mouse' signature include Westminster Abbey, York Minster, St Peter's School at York, Workington Priory and many charming, out-of-the-way churches like those at Hubberholme in Chippendale's Wharfedale, and Castleton on the north-eastern moors. Before starting to design furniture for a particular church he would visit the place and absorb its atmosphere. He could not tolerate incongruity. Equally objectionable to him was mere repetition. Once, a visitor to Kilburn, after admiring a certain piece of work, offered to buy a large quantity of the articles if they were all made to the same pattern and at a reduced price. Thompson's scornful reply is still quoted with glee in the neighbourhood: "Why, that would be mass production. *Get out of my workshop*!"

When I first met Thomas Whittaker, the woodcarver of Littlebeck, near Whitby, he began the conversation by saying, "Although I was born in York the Whittakers are a Lancashire family, hailing from the St Helens area." My interest was quickened when he added that woodcarving and carpentry had been in the family for five successive generations. One of them became a Roman Catholic priest, after first following the family craft, and was eventually hung, drawn and quartered at Lancaster Castle. Some of these forebears were probably responsible for certain woodwork in Lancashire's grand old churches; which was rather prophetic, for today Mr Whittaker is an ecclesiastical craftsman and woodcarver of wide renown.

Settling here at Littlebeck, to work for a living, must have been a real venture of faith. "The population when we came numbered just two," he told me. "It is now about twenty-six." But the true measure of success is the esteem in which his work is held, both in this country and overseas. In what terms, save those of romance, can one describe the faldstools he makes, recalling those used long ago in palace and convent; the credences, as used before the Reformation; the kists, or chests, to hold family documents or, maybe, a girl's trousseau; or, say, the carved book-ends ranging in subject from Guthrum, an invading Dane, to George Bernard Shaw?

And then there is the gnome. This little fellow has been adopted by Whittaker as his craft-sign; at least one of them is carved on every piece of his handiwork. According to Scandinavian folklore every acorn has its gnome guardian, who remains on duty while the acorn becomes a sapling and the sapling a full-grown tree. The gnome is, therefore, a very appropriate 'signature' for this craftsman who uses oak exclusively for his work. True, it is *English* oak, but when Scandinavian visitors laughingly foreswear their ancestors' piratical propensities and call on Whittaker, they hail his craft-sign with delighted recognition. "Ah, the little gnome," they will say, just as though he were a little peace-maker implanted on our coast!

On a signboard at the woodcarver's workshop a company of gnomes —borrowed from one of Grieg's Norwegian folk pieces, it would seem —have overrun the place, taking it upon themselves to saw the wood, carry the oak planks, and carve various items of furniture in the approved Whittaker manner.

Indoors, the master craftsman can be seen making his rich contribution to the churches, colleges and homes of our day. His methods are old ones that have stood the test of centuries. Traditional also are his tools: for example, the bow-saw, the draw-knife and the adze, which emphasises the grain of the wood and leaves a beautiful wavy surface.

One can be inspired by a fine tradition without falling into the error of making mere copies of some historic piece. Whittaker does not 'reproduce'; he *creates*—and believes that what he creates will become the antiques and heirlooms of tomorrow.

Sometimes extraneous circumstances lend a hand. Thus it was that an old family tradition determined the character of one of his oak kists. In the reign of King John, Richard de Gylpyn "Slew a wild boar which did great mischief in the adjoining mountains [of Westmorland], and as

reward the Baron of Kendal gave him the manor of Kentmere".
Accordingly, Gylpyn "took for his arms . . . a Boar sable armed and
tusked gules". The said kist, made as a muniment chest for the hero's
present-day descendant, has a front panel carved with that belligerent
boar—reputedly England's very last one, although that point would
be difficult to substantiate.

One day Thomas Whittaker bought some oak trees from Marston
Moor, scene of the great Civil War battle of 1644. Seven musket balls
were embedded in the timber and by counting the tree rings it was
possible to date the balls as probable relics of the battle. With his sure
feeling for history, the craftsman made a commemorative bed for a
client who collects antique weapons. One of the musket balls rests as
it was found, in what is now the bed-head, with a Cavalier and a Round-
head carved on each side. It isn't often, I understand, that such
'woodworm's eggs'—as my craftsman friend jestingly calls them—
can be made to serve some quasi-artistic purpose!

Almost 100 years ago a certain Accrington gentleman with a distinguished ancestry renounced his banking career to open a sports
shop. Cricket, golf, bowls and billiards meant far more to him than
handling other people's cheques. Perhaps the frequent sight of Pendle to
the north and the vast moors dipping west from the Pennines had
quickened his love for the great out-of-doors. Anyhow, he was
resolved to *share* his enthusiasms, and within a few years E. J. Riley,
joined by J. T. Kenyon, was actually making sports equipment at the
Willow Mills. This factory is 120 yards long; Max Whittenburgh, a
local professional sprinter, symbolized his approval of the place by
practising 100-yard sprints on the uninterrupted level of the first floor,
where billiard tables and accessories, then other sporting equipment,
began to take shape.

Some lines contributed by Mabel Potter over thirty years ago to a
well-known literary journal (now alas defunct) have a particular
application to each of the craftsmen then employed here:

> His are the grave discerning eyes, that see
> In rugged trunks the hidden symmetry
> Flexure and sinew of the subtle grain
> Disclosing beauty of the ruthless plane
> And penetrating chisel; his, the will
> Seasoned in frosted thought, that follows still
> To a hair's-breadth, the clean unfaltering line,
> The lonely vision of the soul's design.

"To a hair's-breadth"—thus does the maker of a billiard-table work,
his inward eye envisaging some future champion building up a mighty

break, his hands fulfilling a trust placed in his skill by hundreds of unknown players down the years to come. How thrilling it is to watch those dexterous hands! The tools they use are but an extension of each man's skill, as the slate-bed is prepared, then the table-frame, the pockets and the cushion-boards. Not far away another man will be shaping the cues on a machine which, though ingenious, still demands as much watchfulness as is given in a different room to the preparation of billiard balls.

It was the same with the other pieces of equipment. I saw a grizzled elderly man pick up one of the cricket bats and execute graceful leg-glances, or impeccable off-drives, for some valiant youth he might never see, by giving it that final scrupulous finish, using as his tool the shin-bone of a reindeer!

With equal wonder and admiration I looked on as a youth tested the 'woods', shaped earlier from blocks of *lignum vitae*. At one time, I was told, a drain-pipe was considered a sufficient gauge for such crown-green bowls. But not today! Imagine a miniature table-green, measuring 35 feet by 12 feet, covered with smooth billiard cloth. One end was fitted with a chute, whose two metal slides projected over the 'green' for 3 or 4 feet. At the beginning of each working day a master 'wood' was released from the chute, its swerving course being registered lower down the table by means of an adjustable metal flag on a projecting bar.

As the 'wood' passed beneath the bar a boy placed the point of the flag over its highest arc. Then, one by one, other 'woods' made to the same bias were sent down the chute; should any of them deviate from the 'master's' registered course, by the slightest fraction, correction was administered at once by a gentle rubbing with sandpaper. Occasionally the 'master' had to be 'shot' several times in one day, for any variation in the weather immediately affected the run of a bowl here, as on an actual green.

Crown-green bowling is a popular sport throughout the north. Periodic matches between one club and another are keen affairs, producing much banter, applause and racy comment. "Tha's narrer [narrow], Bill," says one supporter, as his pal's wood swerves away from the jack. "Tha's a yard short," says another; or, "Ah, good wood, Ted!" as the gap between wood and jack is gratifyingly reduced to nothing as by some hidden magnetism.

Although Rileys no longer make bowls and cricket bats the sporting fraternity will not soon forget the erstwhile source of so many pleasures!

In Sheffield we caught a glimpse of some workers in animal horn. The same craft flourishes in the Lakeland countryside, at Kendal, one of the termini of the old cattle drovers' routes through England. At one time, York too had its community of 'horners', but here at Kendal the trade that once produced lanthorns, horn-books, powder horns and drinking horns, now turns its attention to such articles as egg-spoons, salad-servers, shoe-horns, decorative jewellery, spatulas, pen-holders etc., and sometimes potters even use horn for shaping their clay. Yet the horn products of former times have found a new market— across the Atlantic, where reproductions are in demand of simple horn utensils, even horn windows, as used by the first settlers in the American colonies.

Out-of-door activities became favourite decorative subjects used by various North Country potteries. In these subjects one is granted many a glimpse of rural life in the seventeenth and eighteenth centuries. The chief criterion of any given product lies elsewhere, of course, but connoisseur and layman alike must enjoy such pleasantries!

By 1760 Liverpool, though still only a small town of about 30,000 inhabitants, could keep over twenty factories busy with fine products in earthenware and, to a lesser extent, in porcelain. Peat from the bogs at neighbouring Kirkby was used at first to fire many a potter's kiln, and a windmill would often provide power for grinding the materials. For delftware, some of the clay might have to be imported from Northern Ireland, a circumstance which seems to be neatly reflected in those Liverpool ship bowls. While serving punch from such a bowl, a merchant or ship's master could look fondly upon one of his own sailing vessels, hand-painted upon the surface. "Success to the *Gainsborough*" is the legend beneath one such vessel. On one creamware jug, *circa* 1785, Jemmy's Farewell before joining an ocean-going ship in the background is phrased in these touching words:

> Young Jemmy loved me well
> And sought me for his bride.
> But, saving a crown,
> He had nothing beside.
>
> To make that crown a pund [pound]
> My Jemmy gade to sea,
> And the crown and the pund
> Were both for me.

A certain Andrew Jones, captain of the steamer *John McAdam*, did himself proud with one of the Herculaneum factory's earthenware jugs decorated with black transfer prints that mediated both sides of a sailor's life. On the outside, a picture of boats moored invitingly on the Mersey near George's Parade; inside, a vignette of domestic tribulation, when ashore for a few days!

There were farming and pastoral scenes, too, including a delightful

Harvest Home that reflects a simpler age; and a boating idyll in some never-never land created by John Sadler for his Georgian clients. Even at the famous Rockingham Works, at Swinton near Rotherham, fabulous creations in the familiar brown china made for royalty, could be pleasantly offset by simple, rural scenes in which a peasant's cottage is his palace.

The heyday of Leeds ware was during the factory's first forty or fifty years, and a collector always hopes to acquire some of the early pieces with the characteristic yellow glaze. While these were being produced, in their Jack Lane premises, the proprietors ran into a peculiar trouble. A local record states: "On Sunday, July 31st, 1774, the sails of the windmill belonging to the Leeds pottery fell down with a tremendous crash; which being looked upon as a judgement for the desecration of the Sabbath, the proprietors resolved that the mill should never be allowed to be worked afterwards on the Lord's Day."

To gain an all-round appreciation of this ware, citizens of Leeds are fortunately placed; they have ready access to an outstanding and representative collection, shared between the Leeds Art Gallery and Temple Newsam House.

This dual display ranges from the early enamelled cream-ware, as produced before 1771, to the so-called 'imitations' of the last seventy years. Some of these 'imitations' are, however, of excellent design and finish, as I can testify after seeing much of the work done by the late J. W. Senior and his father. One notable piece is the puzzle jug (popular also in Liverpool). Late eighteenth-century in style, this jug with multiple spouts challenges the drinker to slake his thirst without spilling the contents. The secret is to put a finger tip over all the spouts but one. Another piece modelled to an old design is the many-gabled house profusely decorated with flowers in Staffordshire colours. It has an adjustable porch containing a pastille burner from which perfumes issued, sending pleasant fumes also through the hollow chimneys. For Catholics, such cottages sometimes became incense burners.

Fanciful designs are by no means absent from the vintage period. The pottery's chief output comprised conventional tableware in a variety of glazes and decorative embellishment, but there were also fabulous creations such as the centre pieces known as Grand Platt Menage.

Some of these centre pieces have female figures, dolphins and other creatures adorning tiers of shell-shaped dessert dishes branching out like limbs of a tree. A fine centre piece standing in the reproduction of G. W. Senior's shop window at Kirkstall Abbey House Museum is a cistern of the kind often used in fashionable households during the eighteenth century before tapped water was available. It is about 2½ feet high and runs riot with nautical emblems, such as mermaid attendants, dolphin spout, conch-shell finial and seaweed embellishments, all glistening creamy-white—a charming and very serviceable ornament for the Georgian or Regency sideboard.

The Leeds potters had their own artistic conceits that are well worth studying. One is a printed transfer showing Moses leading a vicar by candle-light. Another popular transfer depicts a pair of lovers surprised by an angry father. Knobs of coffee-pot lids were often shaped to resemble the widow of the Old Testament story with her barrel of meal and cruse of oil.

Painted inscriptions are also entertaining. A teapot in the Leeds Art Gallery collection bears a portrait of John Wesley, with the words: "The Rev. John Wesley, A.M. Fellow of Lincoln College, Oxford." On the other side "Love and Obedience" is inscribed, between a couple of cherubs that might have come out of some stained-glass window to join Wesley's new movement. . . .

Satisfying in their own right, pottery and porcelain in the modern idiom have little if any use for religious allusions. But for the artist in stained glass they may still be foundational. And stained-glass artistry has several gifted masters in the North, as gifted as York's Stonegate fraternity of medieval times.

From their own particular alcove in the hereafter, those Stonegate craftsmen—Thomas Benefield, John Chamber, Matthew Petty, William Inglish and the rest—surely breathed a heavenly sigh of relief when their own famous creations in York Minster and neighbouring churches were dismantled and buried for safety during the last war, and later restored to their allotted frames of tracery with loving patience and skill.

And what imaginative and colourful creations they were! In the Minster's "Te Deum" window, the Almighty appears as the Supreme Architect. Surrounded by Gothic niches and mosaic pavements, He sits there enthroned in majesty, holding a pair of architect's dividers, as if about to design fresh wonders. Other windows declare the miraculous performances of St Cuthbert and of St William of York. There is a Bell-founders' window, too, dedicated to Richard Tunnoc; also, it would seem, to a surge of musical monkeys. The great east window, designed for a change by a Coventry craftsman, has its own pageant of saints and such Old Testament characters as Noah looking over the flood waters from the prow of his ark, with a whippet and a red cow as visible companions.

Easily the most dramatic window in any of York's city churches is the Doom Window at All Saints', North Street. Here, a fourteenth-century conception of the last fifteen days of earth's sad story is presented with mounting horror.

The doom it foreshadows, although reflecting the lurid outlook of 600 years ago, is not altogether inapt in this atomic age. After preliminary convulsions in the world's oceans, fishes and frightful marine monsters take refuge on land. The sea then becomes one vast furnace. The flames spread, and by the sixth day the trees are all being devoured by fire. Earthquakes then cause widespread terror and ruin; buildings crash to the ground and people hide in caves from the all-pervading fury. The graves give up their dead. Stars fall from the vault of heaven. Fire consumes everything.

The epilogue is given in two tracery lights. On the left, St Peter receives the souls of the saved; on the right, as in the York Mystery Plays, Satan pitchforks the damned into Hell.

Today's stained-glass artists need no such Apocalyptic vision, but their creations can be just as compelling.

It was a bright autumn day when I once called upon Harry Stammers. The trees were in full colour. Late flowers bloomed in the garden beneath the city wall. The stonework of the Minster was touched to a delicate pink. All this I soon exchanged for the no less lovely colourings that were coming to life and purpose in this glass-painter's studio.

I had long wondered just how those glorious windows that bejewel nave and choir of so many cathedrals and churches were fashioned. Of course, one can read books on the subject, but if only one could have actually observed a medieval glass-painter at work! I was soon to realize that, in the main, the craft has changed little with the passing centuries. Allow for better tools, better equipment and so on, and that smocked figure over there might well have been Matthew Petty, Thomas Benefield or some other member of the old Stonegate fraternity, engaged on a window for the Minster. . . .

The first step is to make the actual design. Generally, this is drawn to the scale of one inch to the foot, and coloured as the final window will eventually appear. An historical subject—such as the trial of Archbishop Scrope—is rendered in symbolic manner.

A full-size black-and-white drawing, or cartoon, is then prepared, and on this, thick black lines are painted to indicate the exact position of the 'leads'. Then, using the cartoon as basis, a 'cut-line' drawing is made; this shows the 'leads' only—in other words, the shape of each piece of glass. Later, with this drawing as guide, each piece is cut. Benefield and his like would probably have chipped out the glass shapes, piece by piece. Today, an ordinary wheel-cutter is used. "And the glass itself?" I asked. This is specially made by hand for the glass-painters and supplied in a wide variety of colours. As in bygone times, 'reams' and bubbles give the glass its texture.

Tracing is the next process. The craftsman takes each piece of glass in turn, places it in proper position on the cartoon, and then with brush and pigment marks in such features as the lines of a suit of armour, or the folds of drapery. This done, the pieces are arranged to design on a sheet of plain glass laid over the 'cut line' drawing. A blob of beeswax is applied to each corner to secure the pieces in position, then the skeleton window is reared on an easel. The narrow, regular spaces which isolate each piece from the next—and seen now so clearly—are, of course, the craftsman's provision for the 'leads'.

Gradually now, the window takes pictorial form. Each piece of glass in the 'skeleton' is matted over with pigment. While still wet this is treated with a badger-hair brush, and then smaller, dry brushes are used to give the necessary texture to face, garment, or some architectural detail in the design.

Later, the 'skeleton' is dismantled, for each piece of glass has to be fired. Some medieval workers, I was told, used wood to heat their kilns. Here, the firing was done in a gas-heated kiln. The pieces are arranged, painted-side upwards, on a 'firing tray' spread evenly with a mixture of plaster of paris and whitening. To avoid breakage of the glass, the kiln is heated slowly. The temperature mounts to a maximum of 750 degrees Centigrade, and then—the fusing of pigment with glass having been effected—the kiln and its contents cool down overnight. Later, the silver stain is applied—that is, the clear yellow so useful for decorative effects. A further firing, at 700 degrees this time, is necessary to make the stain permanent.

Glazing is the process by which the window is 'leaded' together. When this is completed, the joints are soldered, and after the application of cement to make the window rigid and weatherproof, the craftsman can feel justifiable pride in his handiwork and arrange for the insertion of the window. The lead should last for 100–150 years and the glass indefinitely.

Something should now be said about the *story* represented in some of the designs. Mr Stammers' work is to be seen in many churches, but one at Hedon's fine old church, in the East Riding, deserves special mention for, amongst other features, it presents Augustine denouncing ancient forms of paganism, and modern forms, too; Aphrodite, Cybele, Neptune and Pan on the one hand, and on the other, totalitarianism symbolized as a skeleton wearing tin helmet and rifle, the quest for power through wealth, self-centredness, and the worship of the machine, symbolized by a man and a woman fettered to a piece of machinery.

The subject I saw in the making, at the Stammers' studio, was the trial of Archbishop Scrope, which took place at his own palace at Bishopthorne, 3 miles from York. For their share in the rebellion headed by Scrope, Henry IV caused the citizens to beseech his pardon by kneeling with ropes around their necks. This window can now be seen in Bishopthorpe Church. The versatility of Stammers' work is shown in the spandrel paintings of mythological creatures that adorn the astronomical clock standing in the north transept of York Minster.

Fortunately the craft so ably renewed in recent years by Harry Stammers, within the shadow of the great, Gothic Minster, is now carried on in almost the same historic ambience by one of his former pupils, Harry Harvey, one of whose fine windows we saw earlier at York Guildhall.

Such is the continuing joy of "painting on light".

The Carillon Tower on the Civic Centre, Newcastle-upon-Tyne

Rushbearers portrayed on a hotel sign at Grasmere

One of Lady Waterford's Biblical paintings in Ford School, Northumberland

13

At Leisure Through the Centuries

IT is interesting to observe how public and private
pleasures and amusements have changed since the
seventeenth century, to go no farther back in time.
Progress from dancing bears and tight-rope feats, to the early experiments in motoring and aviation constitute an amazing performance
in itself, although we shall also find that certain pastimes run through
the centuries with little abatement.

In George Bickham's atlas, *The British Monarchy* (1754), the author's
commentary on Yorkshire is headed by a remarkable drawing that
depicts a typical North Country fair of those days. The commentary
begins, aptly enough, with a slice of history, but I imagine that for
every person who plodded through that account, when the atlas first
appeared, scores would rest content with this charming vignette of
North Country people seeking amusement.

An inn bearing the sign of the elephant supports a balcony on which
an archbishop is being fanfared to the assembled company below. In one
corner a game of roulette(?) is already in progress, and over to the right
a performing dog goes through its tricks to the tunes of an itinerant
piper. An elegant couple in the foreground, practising with violin and
drum, could well be the local squire and his up-and-coming daughter.
Overhead, an acrobat balances on a perilously slack rope, but he is

getting as little attention as the pick-pocket furtively at work immediately below. The prevailing hubbub will tone down, one feels, when
gentry and peasants step into one or other of the pavilions that carry
posters proclaiming some of the wonders on show within.

Contemporary newspapers help to fill in some details at this point.
For example, in the short space of one year, the *Leeds Intelligencer* and
the *Leeds Mercury* informed their respective readers of several tempting
shows then available in local fair or public hall. There was "the amazing
Woman in Miniature, whose small Stature, true make and shape, at
once please and astonish every Beholder. . . . She is now in the 21st
Year of her Age [but] is not Eighteen Pounds Weight." Another
attraction was the company of "Famous Italian Patagonian Performers"
whose programme included the "Transformation of a Sheperdess into
a Flower-Pot, then into a Fountain". Again, "That curious Animal,
the Ethiopian Savage", was evidently drawing "the Curious of all
Degrees" in crowds to the 'Red Bear', in Briggate, Leeds. Then there
were Signor Rossi's "Surprising Feats on the Stiff Rope", which meant
that for a shilling or so one could watch, heart in mouth, while this
Venetian artist played his violin "on the Rope, in six different
Positions . . .".

It will be seen, therefore, that despite the prevalence of footpads and
highwaymen, public entertainment lacked nothing in variety or gaiety
at this period.

Then and later small country towns received their share of such
excitements. At Settle, in the Pennine area, limestone crags that in
prehistoric times had harboured mammoth, rhinoceros, bison and
long-tusked elephant, echoed afresh with strange noises when the
greatest menagerie of the age came along. Of this event I found an
amusing contemporary account in the pages of an unpublished diary,
now kept at the local Pig Yard Club Museum. I had just been handling
the skull of a great cave bear, found locally, when William Lodge
Paley's diary was put into my hands; before long I was reading this
schoolmaster's reactions to the visit of Wombwell's menagerie in 1843.

Under the date 27th May, he wrote: "Wombwell's menagerie came,
drawn by 45 stout horses in 14 caravans, the largest collection in Settle
since I came. They had many grand pictures [posters] larger than life.
It was 6d to see the beasts." When Paley beheld the show for himself,
two nights later, he seems to have been rather disappointed: "I went
to see the lions and got a [hand] bill *wh*[*ich*] *mentions more than they
showed.* [My italics]"

Performing horses and dancing bears were popular forms of amusement as long ago as the fourteenth century. Spirited renderings of
each are given on the borders of an illuminated MS., the *Romance of
Alexander* (*circa* 1340) at the Bodleian Library. Another peep at the

dancing bear visitations that delighted our medieval ancestors is afforded by one of the stained-glass window subjects in the Zouche Chapel at York Minster. Here the bear is apparently being led by its attendant to the next place of performance. With his horn, staff, and almost regal bearing, the custodian looks every inch the important showman he once was in town and village.

Another Zouche Chapel window subject gives a lively rendering of the one-man band. A wandering player is conjuring music simultaneously from drum, flute and the bells that fringe his cloak and hose. I am impressed by the wonderful continuity of these two types— the man with the performing bear, and the one-man band. Although they reach far back into the past, they survived in my home town (and probably in other places too) until the early years of the present century.

One of my earliest memories is of a bear prancing its way through our side streets. It was tethered on a long chain, after the manner of the one illustrated in the *Romance of Alexander*, and created wonder tinged with fear as its owner came round for our pennies. One could show more real affection for the tiny monkey, wearing red cap and coloured ruff, which performed the same acquisitive service for the tingle-airy man. The tingle-airy is a street barrel organ. A resplendent one often came down our way, and as the little monkey went round with the collecting tin, his master would be churning out sprightly tunes emphasised by co-ordinated cymbals and other musical effects. Tingle-airys continued to be made, in a certain back street of Leeds, until a few years ago. Indeed, despite the allurements of television and radio, they seem to possess a survival value as persistent as the town or country fair, with its fat woman displays, hoop-la stalls and roundabouts that oscillate children and adults on fierce-looking steeds to the gay tunes of a centrally-placed organ.

Many of our North Country diversions have a similar antiquity. At Grasmere and Haworth we have our rush-bearing festivals. Archery is by no means confined to the north, yet the village of Scorton near Richmond gave birth to what is probably England's oldest archery club, which awards annual trophies dating back to Elizabethan times. It is always a delight to see the annual contests, for which some village green, public park or recreation ground provides the setting—a pleasant change, in fact, from cricket or football, or the ancient game of bowls.

Several of our country houses preserve a bowling green in their grounds, on which historic personages have tried their skill. Because it diverted men from the practice of archery, bowling was long forbidden by law. But that did not deter Charles I, when Prince of Wales, from spending most of his five-day sojourn at Norton Conyers, near Ripon, on the owner's fine green to the north of the house.

One of the many books and pamphlets that poured scorn on the game traduced the players in these words: "Never did mimmicke screw his body into half the forms that these men do theirs," as they deliver a wood, and follow its course with "senseless crying". Anybody who patronises the game today, on those lovely crown greens of the North Country, will recognise the symptoms! I knew one keen player who, after delivering each wood, swivelled and swayed on the mat for several seconds with one leg drawn up, like a flamingo, until his wood came to rest, for weal or woe. To many of us the flat greens of southern and other parts of England seem tame affairs.

Another ancient game, although known to comparatively few, today, is merrils (spelt about six different ways). The traditional merrils board is marked with three squares, one receding within the other and all connected by cross lines and having a peg hole at each corner and intersection. To quote a keen player, "the game requires two opponents, each starting with nine pegs which they place in the holes, trying to prevent the other from placing three pegs in a row. The player who achieves a row of three is entitled to remove one of his opponent's pieces from the board," and so on to the bitter end. It sounds as simple as it is difficult, for I am assured that the game can last a day or two!

There are many variations of the game. To some it is known as Nine Men's Morris, a name recognised by Shakespeare in *A Midsummer Nights' Dream*, which probably explains why a certain kind of merrils board is now on sale opposite Shakespeare's birthplace.

My friend, Frank Weatherill of Danby-in-Cleveland, who makes the kind of board traditional to his neighbourhood, has delved deeply into the history of the game, tracing it back to Germany and even to Jerusalem, where—he says—a merrils board was once excavated in Pilate's courtyard!

In the north of England the game still has many devotees. On one East Riding farm a merrils board was actually marked out on the wooden lid of a corn bin. At a Howden chemical works a few years ago, merrils became a handicap game at Christmas and one would often see a board chalked on the floor, pieces of copper ore and coal being used as pegs. It would seem that wherever men were likely to have time on their hands, merrils was often indulged in. A merrils board incised on the wall of Kirkby Underdale Church on the Yorkshire Wolds, suggests all kinds of possibilities—a sexton resting from his labours and practising his skill with some villager; a couple of old cronies puzzling over their pegs after morning service; perhaps even the parson found occasional relaxation in this sunny corner. Another board, cut in a stone slab at Helmsley Castle in the North Riding, could well have been used by the garrison there, during the Civil

Wars. Perhaps those tell-tale lines were incised soon after the fortress was begun by Walter L'Espec in late Norman times. As L'Espec was the man who also founded Rievaulx Abbey nearby, it seems somehow fitting that the game which evidently gave much amusement at L'Espec's castle should only recently have provided the basis of a tournament at Rievaulx.

Although merrils, and a companion game called fox and geese, or reynardo, are now featured amongst the 'bygones' in Hutton-le-Hole Folk Museum, near Pickering, both games are very much 'alive', although only in small 'pockets' of the countryside. I would never be altogether surprised to come upon a couple of ardent merril players in some Lakeland village, say, or in a Lancashire backyard. Anywhere will serve. Along the Durham coast men will even scratch the requisite lines on the sand and use pebbles as pegs.

Some years ago I watched a few villagers by the beck-side at Thwaite in Swaledale, who seemed to be emulating the disc-throwers of ancient Greece. Actually, they were competing against each other in the game of quoits. At one time many dales' villages, and nearly every village around the Esk Valley, near Whitby, had its quoit champion. Frank Weatherill can recall some of those champions: 'Chower' Pearson of Whitby, Timmy Duck of Loftus and the Gallons menfolk of Fryup. Once, Timmy Duck beat 'Chower' Pearson and won a pair of trousers, although the more usual prize was a copper kettle.

The terminology of the quoits player includes such strange words as 'gater', 'cue', 'pot' and 'ringer', and all come freely into use as each player tries to ring the 'hob' with his quoit, or prevent his opponent from doing so—a tricky performance. Mr Weatherill remembers from boyhood the clatter of quoits on many a summer evening, resounding across the Esk at Lealholm with all the villagers looking on. And if he and others have their way the game will soon enjoy a 'come-back'. The antiquity of the game is suggested by a few iron rings found some thirty years ago near Whitby Abbey. They were much too large for horse or ox shoes, which prompted the excavators to believe they had hit upon some quoits used by monks at the abbey, who may have inherited the game from Danish settlers in that area. At their annual jamboree and maypole displays, the proprietors of Hutton-le-Hole Museum usually hold a quoit competition to promote interest and a revival of the game that once sent its peculiar echoes through so many North Country villages.

One of my early memories is of a group of men with sleeves rolled up, smiting a tiny wooden or pot ball on the poppy fields near my home. The ball, or 'knur', was first released from a metal spring and then struck in mid-air with a long knobbed stick, the 'spell'. Sometimes a wedge-shaped piece of wood was struck to fling the ball upwards.

Then again, the knur might be suspended from a gibbet-like frame while the man made his strike. Knur and spell, or nipsy, are the general names for this pastime, which, like quoits, always drew crowds of onlookers and still does so, especially in coal-mining areas, where the game is often called 'poor man's golf'. Each player, of course, tries to clout the knur farther than his challenger does, 200 yards being considered a very good strike, capable of drawing many choice expletives from the cloth-capped assembly.

Knur and spell has suffered many ups and downs since the dawn of this fast-moving century. One or two museums keep moving in like undertakers to seize any mortal remains of the game. But it is not 'dead' yet. Long may it elude the final obsequies!

The North Country miners' biggest annual event is the Durham Gala. To the uninitiated this gala may suggest just another semi-political rally. Actually it is a gay, carnival affair without parallel in England, not even excepting Preston Guild.

From early morning of the appointed day in July, until late at night, the streets of beautiful Durham city are thronged with miners and their families. At first, the general trend is towards the racecourse for the big meeting, but there are always many hold-ups in the narrow streets as the 100 or so colliery bands shoulder their way through. When small clearings occur some brass band will strike up with a bit of dance music, and everybody, young and old, immediately responds. As tradesmen find normal business impossible, one may see newsagents selling sandwiches, greengrocers serving cups of tea, or a music shop offering 'hot dogs'.

To quote Mr L. Scollen, who keeps the records at the Durham Miners' Hall, "a crowd of up to 300,000 joins the streets, fills the racecourse, and even takes to the water [the River Wear] in boats. On a fine day there is not sufficient room to swing a cat, let alone toss a caber."

During early years the miners went to Durham, on the great day, mainly to claim 'their reets'. At the 1961 gala, Sam Watson, then general secretary of the National Union of Mineworkers, referred to the big changes he had seen in his own lifetime, especially during the previous twenty years. He said, "The Gala—the greatest demonstration of free people in the world—is more carefree and colourful than it was before the war because of the change in the miners' lives. It is a sign of the progress we have made." He himself first worked in the Boldon Pit at 1s. 4d. per day. It is now quite usual to see miners' cars parked around the city outskirts when they come with the 'missus and kids' for the annual spree.

The lodge banners carried by the miners' bands are a study in themselves, as each bears a different design. Some will portray political leaders, from Keir Hardie onwards. There are also representations of the miner at his daily work, and various allegorical figures signifying the miners' solidarity and their concern for the welfare of the aged and for those bereaved through pit accidents. In addition there are banners showing Conishead Priory, the Durham Miners' erstwhile convalescent home near Ulverston, in Furness; Durham Miners' Hall; and—perhaps surprisingly—Durham Cathedral.

By extolling the great Norman cathedral in this way, members of the lodge concerned are assuredly not thinking of those bygone prince-bishops of Durham who occasionally took a high hand with local mine leases. Most of the miners have a deep respect for the cathedral, and older men remember the sympathy shown to them, or their fathers, by one bishop in particular, Dr B. F. Westcott (1890-1901). In 1955-6 several lodges made substantial contributions to the fund for restoring Prebends Bridge, which belongs to the dean and chapter.

But the gala itself provides the closest link between cathedral and miners, for the day's climax is a cathedral service usually attended by some 2,500 persons, mostly miners and their families. Preceded by one of the colliery bands, three lodge banners are taken in procession up the stately nave and then placed in the transepts for the duration of the service. Later, a collection is taken for the aged miners' homes, and after the last hymn, the bands mass and move out—still playing—into the Tudor setting of Palace Green. Much of this ceremony echoes pre-Reformation days, when various trade guilds held an annual assembly at Palace Green, each guild carrying its own distinctive banner.

Durham's annual gala may be the highlight of such events today, but the neighbourhood has others, notably Houghton-le-Spring Fair (October) which originated in the days of Elizabeth I and is now kept alive by local miners and their families. Historically, this fair is associated with Bernard Gilpin, the 'Apostle of the North', whose generosity to the poor of his parish was proverbial. He gave free dinners to any who called at his rectory on Sundays between Michaelmas and Easter. The swings and roundabouts of today's fair should not entirely efface his memory.

Even older is Lee Gap Fair, held near Wakefield on St Bartholemew's Day (August). The charter authorizing this fair was granted by Henry I to the Priory of St Oswald at Nostell, on the other side of Wakefield. Since then, Nostell has become famous for its collieries, and the miners employed there now help to maintain Lee Gap Fair. Today this is mainly a fun fair, but it was long noted for the sale of horses. Originally, the Nostell canons performed mystery plays here for the benefit of the crowds, and married any suitable couples in the adjacent church at Woodkirk.

Now that miners' sons are often well educated it is perhaps fortunate that one nineteenth-century custom is no longer observed. Boys from Leeds and Wakefield grammar schools were taken to Lee Gap Fair, and for some obscure reason they actually sat for their examinations among the fairground ponies and gypsy caravans.

In Northumberland, miners' holidays were sometimes rendered compulsory by adverse winds up the River Tyne. Around Christmas, particularly, the collier brigs could rarely pick up their cargoes. To mark the temporary closure of the pits, miners would decorate their last corfe of coal with lighted candles, and then give small presents to the lads working with them. These lads, however, were always ready for a 'break'. They would frequently observe what they called a 'gaudy day' to celebrate some pleasing event, like hearing the first cuckoo in spring. . . .

Love for the open air—a natural love often blasted by industry in some places—has long found liberal expression in the outdoor wrestling matches and fell-racing contests of Lakeland. Both are seen to great advantage at Grasmere Sports, with the Rothay tossing by, and great fells lifting up their heads to the skies like giant spectators of human effort.

One could profitably look upon and discuss these events until the sun goes down, and the last contestant plods wearily to his bed. Indeed, such discussion never seems to abate very much in Grasmere. There is simply a lull between one year's set of events and the next. They set the local calendar as surely as Rushbearing Sunday, and the first influx of holiday makers.

Of course the shape of holiday-making is now very different from what it was in Wordsworth's day, or even at the beginning of the present century. People now have ready access to the remote parts of the Pennines, say, or the Lake counties.

One great step forward, into this timeless heritage, is marked by the love of mountaineering, as first promoted by such lithe, knicker-bockered figures as the Abraham brothers of Keswick, Cecil Slingsby, the Trevelyans of Northumberland, and Geoffrey Winthrop Young.

Mrs Pauline Dower, of Cambo, Northumberland, has kindly recalled for me something of the pioneering spirit, as shown by a few of that select company. Her father, Sir Charles Trevelyan, with G. M. Trevelyan, the historian, and Winthrop Young blazed many a new trail in their youth. They climbed Rothley Castle, a fine mock ruin erected by Sir Walter Blackett of Wallington in the mid-eighteenth century. The castle with its square tower crowns those beetling crags and offers a challenge that *had* to be met. For Winthrop Young it recalled student days when the roofs of Trinity College, Cambridge, tested his agile daring. With nobler motives than the Picts and Scots of old history, these mountaineers forged a way up the steep Whin Sill crags that carry long undulating stretches of Hadrian's Wall. And, of course, they paid continual homage to the Lakeland hills, which earlier travellers had found so forbidding.

In several captivating books, Winthrop Young shared with his many readers the magic of those days. With a generosity that is characteristic of all who know and love the great mountain solitudes, his widow has 'belayed' me to some of the higher pinnacles of her husband's prose,* so that I may look around, as it were, and take my pick from those enchanting vistas. . . .

Here is Geoffrey Winthrop Young in his youth, making "a very frightening one-man ascent of the Napes Needle [on Great Gable] in thick mist . . . using a hay rope borrowed from Mrs. Wilson of Watendlath"; or involving himself and Richard Feetham "in a tangle of incompetence on the West Wall of the Pillar Rock and a hair-raising new line of descent never afterwards identifiable . . .".

Several adventurous climbs around Napes Needle, in later days, set him musing again about those Cambridge manoeuvres: "It was diverting to be climbing up clefts and chimneys well inside the rock body of the tower. Indeed, the type of rock had much the feel and look, and much too of the satisfaction, which I can remember when I made the first exploration of the Trinity College roofs, and there learned the fallaciousness of perpendicular cement, and Gothic carving, and the deciduousness of aged slates."

Then there were Christmas and New Year parties at Wasdale Head, convivial climax to great days on the neighbouring fells with Cecil Slingsby and the Trevelyans. First, the enchantment of winter climbing:

Time and again we arrived on the summit ridge of Scafell, after cutting up the ice of Deep Ghyll, or the hard snow of Cust's Gully, or the ice glaze of some chimney, and as we stepped out on to the freezing snow, blue-trodden over the crags, saw ourselves encircled by the last bands of copper and crimson light burning like cold fire round the whole horizon.

Then, the afterglow at Wasdale Village, where a few children performed for us Jack and the Beanstalk in soft broad Cumbrian. . . .

Upon Christmas night we gave our musical show in return, in which all the company by different routes became benighted on the Napes Needle. It was built up in the dining room, a cubist erection of empty ginger-beer and wine cases. Charles Trevelyan sang from the Shoulder, and George Trevelyan recited from the summit; and Evans, dressed as a topical suffragette, arrived there with him in a then topical aeroplane, ingeniously flown from the top of the cottage piano. Chorus succeeded

* In *Mountains with a Difference*, (Eyre & Spottiswoode, 1951.)

chorus from the benighted party statuesquely spread over the piled boxes. As no rescue arrived, the escape was dramatically effected at the close by the whole company uniting, in a thunderous destruction and downfall of the Needle, to a suitable chant. Upon which the gay-hearted Slingsby, most liberal of Tory royalists, leapt to his feet among the audience, exclaiming, "Just like you Radicals!—you insist on destroying *all* our Greatest Institutions!"

Winthrop Young wrote also of "solitary ascents" of Almscliffe Crag in Wharfedale—a fine landmark whose northern face affords chimneys and overhangs that have helped to train several climbers for the Alps and even the Himalayas. In *Helvellyn to Himalaya,** F. Spencer Chapman has paid his own tribute to our northern rock hazards by recounting one climber's progress from the Cow and Calf Rocks at Ilkley, Wharfedale, and the fells around Sedbergh School, to Chomolhari's 24,000-foot summit on the Tibetan border.

Pioneering on high hills was soon to be followed by pioneering of a very different sort—that enjoyed by the early motorists. Incidentally, Mancunians like to recall that the first Royce precision-built motor-car, leading to the famous partnership with Charles Rolls, came to birth in a small workshop at Hulme.

When the present century dawned it was still possible for any artist to take a camp stool and sit for an hour or two on some main road so as to draw or paint a given object. Thus in her student days did my older sister once sit, with nothing to distract her as she transferred the shape and character of a Tudor cottage—overlooking the A639 to be —to her sketching pad. The chances of a new-fangled motor-car of any make passing by, in clouds of dust, were almost negligible. If a car had rumbled along it would probably have been driven by that intrepid Leeds pioneer, the late Rowland Winn; or by one of the surrounding gentry he was then initiating into the crazy sport of motoring.

Rowland Winn came to know this road well, for he travelled often to the Dukeries. Clad in his chauffeur's uniform—peak cap, leggings and an ankle-length fur coat designed to combat all the rigours of 'roofless' motoring—he would periodically turn up at Clumber to give driving lessons to the Duke of Newcastle, after selling his noble client a sparkling new car. He once met three foreign princesses there, and gave them driving lessons, too.

Along with the few other pioneers, Rowland Winn fought a protracted campaign against the 12 m.p.h. speed limit. Some years were to pass before motor cars were regarded as anything except 'death machines'. But emancipation eventually came, and it must have been

* Chatto & Windus, 1940.

a very happy Rowland Winn who could stage the first 'motor wedding' in Leeds. It was his own. The car was an open one, bedecked for the occasion with a fringed awning.

Concessions like this must have been rare, however. All the early petrol-driven cars were wide open to the elements. Miss Gladys Winn once told me that for many years her mother wore a special motoring bonnet, rather like a turban. "It is a very elaborate affair in purple, with yards of material to wrap round the neck. I still have that bonnet," she added; "also father's straw benji, which he always donned for motor racing."

Unfortunately, an old photograph loaned to me which shows Mr Winn in one of his racing cars omits the gay benji. Yet the picture is a period piece of unique interest. Despite an oncoming car, our pioneer has swung his 'racer' across the road, to give the photographer a better angle for his time-exposure. This was taken on the sea-front at Saltburn, a well known North-east resort. Judging by the driver's smart, un-ruffled appearance, he probably posed for the study just before the annual contest on Saltburn beach. Copies of this vintage photograph could be bought, that year, at the local 'bazaar'.

On going through other photographs of Rowland Winn from that early period I get a composite picture of a man for whom life was a tremendous adventure, laced with abundant humour—as it continued to be to the end of his days. One photograph shows this future Lord Mayor of Leeds perched aloft in an open car, surrounded by a bristling array of fishing nets, rods and other sporting gear. He must have enjoyed the comical sight this assemblage provided as much as did the onlookers. It was a good advertisement for cars, too.

Once when I called upon him at his Leeds office, he and his business manager both became boys again as they recalled the sheer fun of those exploratory years. Even then, Rowland Winn foresaw the time when motoring would become so popular that private cars would be banned from city centres. Meanwhile, 'Rowly' could, and did, exploit the novelty of motoring, notably with his car organ.

The idea struck him just before the First World War. You would be walking through some busy shopping street, or perhaps a country lane, and suddenly catch the mellow strains of "The Rosary" or "When Loves Creeps in your Heart". No tingle-airy would be in sight, and the century was still too young for radio. I remember being caught up in the general wonder this phenomenon caused. But the secret eventu-ally leaked out. Rowland Winn was up to his tricks again. Musical tricks, contrived with the aid of a miniature organ he made himself and concealed beneath the car bonnet. It was powered from the engine, and the keyboard—a mere octave of shiny finger buttons—spread conveniently in front of the driving wheel.

In these noise-ridden days it is difficult to measure the delight which those simple tunes, and others in Winn's homely repertoire, gave to so many. He had all the makings of a showman, and was, in a way, a novel version of the one-man band!

Yorkshire even had a pioneer of the space age—nearly 300 years ago. This was John Mitchell of Scout Hall, near Halifax, who experimented with a (supposed) flying machine from the hill above his home—and broke his neck. No drawing of his contraption seems to have survived. Fortunately, other early aerial ventures are suitably documented, particularly the pioneer efforts of Sir George Cayley of Brompton Hall, near Scarborough.

Even though Cayley is now regarded as the inventor of the aeroplane, the sketches of his various contrivances—displayed with appropriate models in Scarborough museum—cause a shudder of apprehension. When his coachman stepped from the wreckage of the first man-carrying glider, remarking "Please, Sir George, I wish to give notice—I was hired to drive and not to fly," the aggrieved fellow little knew that he had become, in effect, the progenitor of space travel.

The year was 1852 or 1853—just about the time when a contributor to the *Quarterly Review* protested against the running of a 20 m.p.h. railway service between London and Woolwich, saying, "People would as soon suffer themselves to be fired off upon one of Congreve's ricochet rockets as trust themselves to the mercy of such a machine and go at such a rate." That remark about being projected into space, although poised as the absolute of nonsense, was surely tinged with unintended prophecy!

In his notebook found at Brompton Hall in 1928, Cayley states that "the first idea I ever had on the subject of mechanical flight was at Southgate about 1792, and two hours after, I made the little machine [a model] of eight feathers, two corks and whale-bone bow"—a machine probably based on the Launoy and Bienvenu helicopter of 1784.

The notebook 'scrawls' of his different flying devices are very instructive, although highly amusing too, especially that of his "ornithopter machine" which the experimenter wore as so much personal gear. It is almost as if the man were struggling with an outsize umbrella rent by the winds. About thirty-five years ago one of Cayley's gliders —referred to as "Cayley's first model aeroplane, 1804"—was incorporated in the design of the gold medal awarded for aeronautics. Another sketch shows his 'flying top' by which he demonstrated the action of the screw propeller in the air. When rotated rapidly by means of a cord, the propeller flew upwards to a height of 90 feet; a far more promising augury for future 'aerial navigation' than flapping wings.

All these and many other experiments were carried out by Cayley in or near a workshop attached to the Hall.

England's first aviation meeting was held at Doncaster, in 1909. Even then, with such aviators demonstrating their prowess as Delegrange, Sommer, Le Blon and Colonel Cody, all their machines were regarded as 'flying toys'—little different from some of the amusing devices seen at a typical country fair. This is not surprising if one turns up a few contemporary photographs. Some of the bi-planes were but enlarged box-kites. And now, only sixty years on, the moon itself has become a regular target and landfall!

Outer space, as a possible region for exploration, might already have engaged the brilliant mind of (Sir) William Herschell when he was appointed organist at Halifax Parish Church, in 1765, and began teaching music to the children of local gentry. With him, music and astronomy were handmaidens—which may account for a stained-glass window panel, showing his famous telescope, in the library at Low Hall, Nether Yeadon, near Leeds. I have never been able to discover whether Herschell actually visited the Marshalls for tutorial purposes at any of their homes, but the window panel is the kind of tribute that an appreciative owner, or some descendant, would provide in honour of such a remarkable man.

Before the telescope was finished, Herschell had invited distinguished personages to walk through the 40-foot tube. One admiring visitor was George III who, after viewing the instrument for himself, turned to the Archbishop of Canterbury and said, playfully, "Come, my Lord Archbishop; I will show *you* the way to Heaven!"

With this telescope Herschell was to discover the new planet, Uranus, thus partly fulfilling his ambition 'to leave no spot of the heavens unexamined". At first the planet was named Georgius Sidus, after a nurse called Georgiana he had known in Leeds. Although most authorities declare that the name commemorated George III, who knighted the astronomer, some of us have our own reasons for preferring the story of the nurse. A miniature instrument given to him by a blind friend was thrown by a pretty but deformed admirer into the River Aire; she evidently thought her action might keep Herschell in the neighbourhood of her (rather warped) affection. In trying to recover the instrument, Georgiana, the girl's nurse, was drowned.

During the nineteenth century a certain "Mr. Franklin" displayed at York Theatre Royal, "a new Grand Transparent Orrery". An orrery was a clever piece of apparatus fitted with revolving balls to represent the planets in orbit. About the same time York had its own planetary showmen. But astronomy, aviation and, in due course, motoring, were destined to leave the sphere of light-hearted amusement and shape the economic and social future of mankind. In these realms of progress the North had played its spectacular part.

14

Believe It or Not

ALMOST every corner of the North offers its
rewards in the realm of folklore. The various
older tales that are told afford many a glimpse
into the twilight of mankind when fairies and goblins had to be
reckoned with, dragons who devoured fair maidens, giants who tossed
boulders about as playthings, witches galore, and of course the Devil
himself in one or other of his bewildering disguises. Pandora's Box
contained not one half of the mischiefs and evils that spawned in the
minds of our ancestors.

And even today, every second person you meet, amongst the older
generation, seems to have inherited some strange fragment of folk
mystery—a kind of ancestral signature on some generic theme.

One such story has just reached me from that ardent folklorist, Frank
Weatherill of Danby-in-Cleveland. A local farmer on whom he tested
this story, responded thus, "It's a fond teeal and good for nowt!" Yet
this same strange episode concerning Fairy Cross Plain, and the lad
who was imprisoned within Round Hill nearby, has prompted a
Leeds University tutor to record it in their folk-life archives. And it
may yet appear as a children's play.

One must know, first, that the moorland parish of Danby contains
several large and distinct fairy rings. When Canon Atkinson first settled
here last century, the parish clerk assured him that "he and other

children of the hamlet used constantly to amuse themselves by running round in these rings; but they had always been religiously careful never to run quite *nine times* round any one of them . . . if we had run the full number of nine times, that would have given the fairies power over us, and they would have come and taken us away for good to go and live where they lived".

Mr Weatherill's story, here related in his own words, captures something of which Hans Anderson might have been proud.

Now there were two boys, Tom Skelderskew from Lealholm and Jim Dacrow from Danby who decided that they would go to Fairy Cross Plain and knock the bottom out of this Fairy Tale by actually running nine times withershins round one of the rings.

They selected a large fairy ring and made a mark on the edge by which to calculate the times round precisely.

It was decided that Tom would run round and Jim would count. Merrily Tom ran round and round and was laughing at the prospect of victory as he reached the mark for the ninth time when Jim shouted 'Stop', but at that moment Tom vanished from Jim's view completely.

Jim searched around shouting for Tom but got no response nor could he find him anywhere, so he ran off home and told his parents what had happened.

Jim's father thrashed him, arguing that they had both been up to something that they shouldn't and that the lad was hiding something. However a search party of friends and neighbours roamed over the area for several days and then relinquished the search.

Now we must turn to the story that Tom was able to tell on his release from the fairies in the Round Hill when he reached home *three years after his capture* and this is Tom's story:

Immediately he reached the mark on his ninth time round the fairy ring he heard Jim shout "stop", and then someone clapped a large hat over his head and some little men in green marched him off to the Round Hill where they removed some stones leading into a passage in the Hill where they took Tom and left him in the darkness. For a while Tom dare not stir and then thinking that he must attempt to do something he set off groping along the passage in constant fear that he might fall into a hole from which he could not escape, and presently, seeing a very faint light ahead he proceeded to investigate it.

On examination of this mysterious light he found it was only a solitary glow-worm hanging in a cage made of hair.

In conversation with 'glowy' he said something which gave offence and the glow-worm wouldn't talk but he had gathered sufficient information to induce him to press forward, and proceeding, came across quite a bunch of glow-worms in another cage of hair. This was veritable neon lighting to Tom after being in the intense darkness. At this point he was able to observe three notices. Straight ahead was a barrier with the notice "Royal Apartments". To the left another notice pointed to the "Kitchen", and one to the right, "Servants' Quarters". Just as Tom was deciding what to do a little green man dressed somewhat officiously shouted at him and ordered him to go to the kitchen to peel peas and it was time his majesty's dinner was well on the way.

Tom tried to raise objections and stated that he did not belong to the community, but the little man in green with a special apron waived them all and ordered him somewhat threateningly to do as he was told. At this Tom thought that it may be best for him to at least appear to be obedient, so he reluctantly went into the kitchen.

Other little green men were busy peeling peas and Tom was given a bowlful to peel and if he slacked off they pinched his funnybone and threatened further punishment would follow if he did not get on.

The little men appeared to feel superior in their demeanour towards him and only those in the lower social strata would show any real tolerance. He was fed on broad beans, dew and nettle beer and provided with a bed. Menial chores were loaded upon him and he was tired of the life meted out to him by the proud little men until one day a situation arose which afforded a considerable change in his life, bringing interest and hope.

It so happened that a young princess of the latter end of the Royal Family was sent down to the kitchen on a cooking course, as she was not an actual heiress and would probably become betrothed to someone in somewhat impecunious circumstances by Royal standards.

She contrived to get near to Tom as she was mixing and preparing cookery and he was peeling peas, so he might tell her about life in his own world. Tom recited the great fairy stories of Cinderella, Sleeping Beauty, Sir Galahad, etc. and she was very thrilled that such a learned man as he, was available for her edification, but it was sad that he should languish in drudgery under the Round Hill when he might have been out in the wide world gallantly rescuing distressed maidens and imparting his wondrous knowledge. She could see that he wished to escape and would like to assist him to do so, but in this there was grave risk to herself.

However, she decided to show him where there lay a talisman that would, when in his possession, make him immune from the power of the fairies, though she was reluctant to lose his companionship. She told the head cook that she wanted Tom to assist her to find something in a place which the cook knew was considered no place for her to be found, but though he feared it would lead to trouble he succumbed to her beguiling smile and allowed Tom to accompany her. After travelling along passages and up steps they reached a place beyond which the princess dare not proceed, so she told Tom how to remove a certain stone, where in an ambry behind he would find the dreadful object which she dare not so much as look upon for fear she would collapse like a Prince Rupert's drop, so she tearfully said her farewell and left Tom to help himself. He soon found the dreaded object which was simply a nugget of iron and then returned to the kitchen where the little men who had bullied him were now in a state of abject fear as they sensed his possession of the talisman and fell on their knees pleading for mercy. Thus Tom was now able to

The waterfront at Staithes, North Yorkshire

(*above*) York Castle Museum: early twentieth-century garage and cycle shop. (*left*) Kirkstall Abbey House Museum, Leeds: an eighteenth-century cream-ware cistern

go anywhere he pleased, so he set out to find his way out of the hill. On reaching the cross passage where he first saw the larger cage of glow-worms they dimmed down in sympathy with the community but Tom pressed on and worked his way out to freedom and home at Lealholm.

At first his parents thought that he must have run away to sea and thought to scold him for the worry he had caused, but when he unfolded his wondrous story they thought he had had enough. After his incarceration he was somewhat pale and thin but had grown taller and was little worse otherwise for doing his three years' hard labour for defying the rule of the fairy ring.

Tom in due course got married, but if ever he was tempted to eulogize his little princess of the Round Hill he saw that his wife was not within earshot.

Amongst many Irish people belief in the existence of fairies is still unshakeable. Only the other day a middle-aged Irishwoman solemnly assured me that the 'little people' were really *there*. We were travelling just then through part of the West Riding within walking distance of Almscliffe Crag and Elbolton, both traditional fairy headquarters, in Wharfedale. Perhaps she was feeling 'at home' in a strange land. In this she was by no means alone. Every time an Irish neighbour of mine in mid-Airedale ate a boiled egg, she imitated her ancestors by carefully putting the severed shell top below the egg in its cup to ensure that the fairies would never leave Ireland. To such people the fairy-lore of our northern counties is but an echo of their own past. With them I would always feel 'safe' in recounting some of our best stories. And what wonderful stories there are!

As bait for one's credulity, we have another Fairy Hill, near Middleton-in-Teesdale; fairy cupboards formed in the riverside mill-stone grit near Cotherston, and fairy steps leading through a crevice in limestone crags near Arnside. Actual tales of these 'little people'—half mortal, half spirit, sometimes friendly, sometimes peevish—range from midnight revels on some patch of greensward, to strange elfin communities who washed their silken garments by moonlight on the north-east coast near Kettleness, making such a splash and a beating with their 'bittles' that the sound reached as far as Runswick Bay.

Everybody once knew that an ordinary mortal must never speak to a fairy. Long ago, near Middridge, near Bishop Auckland, however, a farm hand was dared to mount his master's best palfrey and go to the fairy hill nearby, calling out this challenge:

> Rise, little lads,
> Wi' your iron gads,
> And set the Lord o' Middridge home.

His scepticism about the very existence of fairy people was soon shattered by hundreds of them appearing around him, led by their king who shook a large javelin as he called out:

> Sillie Willy, mount thy filly,
> And if it isn't weel carn'd and fed,
> I'll ha' thee afore thou gets hame to thy Middridge bed.

At which 'Silly Willy' fled like the wind, with all the fairies in pursuit. He managed to reach Middridge Hall first, and the door was immediately barred, after his gasping entry. Later, when the hubbub outside had died away, and the bars were carefully withdrawn, the stout oak door was seen to be deeply impaled with a javelin.

Some Cumberland fairies took a very different line of action when a servant from Eden Hall, near Penrith, surprised them at their moonlight revels and seized a goblet around which they were dancing. As the fellow fled with his prize the fairies cried out that if ever the goblet should break or fall, the luck would depart from Eden Hall.

Another version of the story declares that the beautiful goblet was filled with spring-water by the fairies and entrusted to the page-boy of Eden Hall with the assurance that the contents would cure Lady Isabel, mistress of the hall. Apparently they did!

One might have expected this rare beaker or goblet to have been fashioned in luminous crystal, conjured from the depths of some underground palace. Actually, it is of yellow glass, nearly $6\frac{1}{2}$ inches high, and enriched with coloured enamels. Somehow the fairies must have bartered with their Syrian cousins for its possession in the first place. As a thirteenth-century product of that region, the glass is now treasured by the Victoria and Albert Museum.* Though it never did 'break or fall', the luck departed from Eden Hall, as the place was demolished in 1821.

The factual history of the glass is almost as romantic as the other account. Indeed its history is regarded by the Victoria and Albert Museum authorities as being the most remarkable of any glass in existence. Experts at the museum also say that it was probably brought to Europe by a retired Crusader. Its owners, the Musgrave family, treated it with veneration and rarely allowed anybody to set eyes on it. The extreme fragility of the glass would alone account for this protective care, but there was always the legend as a further excuse. And the legend opens up another fascinating line of thought, for it states that the fairies from whom the goblet was traditionally obtained, were at the time making merry around St Cuthbert's Well. Somehow Cuthbert's aura settled upon the treasure also. A visiting antiquary, in 1785, after being allowed to see the goblet, wrote a poem concluding with the words:

* The Luck of Eden Hall is shown in Room 42, on the ground floor.

Holy Cuthbert hear my prayer,
The Luck of Eden be thy Care.

He was evidently pulled one way by the legend, and another by the fact that Eden Hall, whose church is dedicated to Cuthbert, lay on that circuitous route by which the saint's remains were taken by his faithful Congregation through the north of England, prior to settlement at Durham.

As far as I know, nobody ever claimed to have seen a river nymph or god. Yet their existence was never in doubt amongst our remote forbears. The River Wharfe was presided over by Verbeia, a goddess of healing, or so the Romans thought, for they dedicated an altar to her which can now be seen in the gardens of Myddleton Lodge, high above the river as it flows through Ilkley. By comparison Peg Powler was a vixen. She lorded it over the River Tees, claiming tribute in the form of human lives. The froth of her anger is still evidenced, so they say, by the masses of brown foam—Peg Powler's Suds—swirling down river, from High Force.

The various deities credited to Northumbrian streams and wells near Hadrian's Wall have been mentioned already; with the passing of time they had faded into amusing folklore. But at least two northern rivers had their gods restored in new guise by later generations. Peg O'Nell, deity of the River Ribble, was transmogrified into the spirit of a servant from Waddow Hall, near Waddington, who, bewitched by her mistress while fetching water, fell in the river and was drowned, near Brungerley Hipping Stones. She then took her vengeance by claiming a human life every seven years, being mollified only by votive offerings of birds or animals. The River Tweed fishermen once placated its own residing genius with gifts of salt.

The River Swale proffers a diverting variation, which owes something to ancient tradition but much more to the story that an eighteenth-century highwayman called Tom Hoggett was drowned there while trying to elude his pursuers. Ever since, his ghost has haunted these waters, luring unwary swimmers to their doom.

It would seem that up to comparatively recent times, certain country folk must have *some* 'presence' to venerate or fear in their local waters. 'Hell's Kettles', near Darlington, were one of the wonders reported by George Bickham, the 'bird's-eye-view' map maker of the eighteenth century. There could be no doubt as to who was lurking below, at the bottom of these pits, for did they not once engulf a farmer and all his equipage for dishonouring a holy day? He had presumed to carry a load of hay on St Barnabas' Day, voicing his sacrilege in these words:

"A cartload of hay, whether God will or nay."

A much pleasanter tradition was elaborated by Michael Drayton, that specialist in nymphs and satyrs, who enlivened nearly all the rivers on his maps with buxom materializations of the various female spirits. In his equally entertaining text, he has this to say about the famous Ebbing and Flowing Well at the foot of Buckhaw Brow, near Giggleswick:

> I a fountain can you show,
> That eight times in a day is said to ebb and flow,
> Who sometime was a Nymph
> . . . and since she was most fair,
> It was a Satyr's chance to see her silver hair
> Flow loosely at her back, as up a cliff she clame,
> Her beauties noting well, her features, and her frame,
> And after her he goes; which when she did espy,
> Before him like the wind, the nimble Nymph doth fly,
> They hurry down the rocks, o'er hill and dale they drive,
> To take her he doth strain, t' outstrip him she doth strive,
> Like one his kind that knew, and greatly fear'd his rape,
> And to the Topick Gods by praying to escape,
> They turned her into a Spring, which as she then did pant,
> When wearied with her course, her breath grew wondrous scant:
> Even as the fearful Nymph, then thick and short did blow,
> Now made by them a Spring, so doth she ebb and flow.

A stained-glass window in Giggleswick Church shows an angel, rather than the traditional nymph, 'troubling' the waters of this venerated well. A Christian substitution, which probably explains why, for many years, supplies from the Ebbing and Flowing Well were used here for christenings.

Today, a cool appraisal of the well's peculiarities would give due credence to the theory of a double siphon action, but folk-lore has its own claims—and I am not the one to banish them altogether. There is so much poetry in some of these hoary traditions, that to iron them all out of existence by stern modern theories and calculations, would be equal to depriving mankind of the Greek myths and legends, or the magical tales of old Ireland.

Who would wish to exorcise from our North Country annals the story of the Laidley Worm? Spindlestone Crags, near Bamburgh, and their weirdly beautiful countryside, make a fitting arena for this tale of hatred and jealousy.

Many local legends of dragons and worms, slain at last by some valiant knight, are possibly allegories of conflicts between the English and the Danes. They may even reach further back in time and point to the survival of a few giant reptiles, after Man arrived on the earthly scene.

A certain prescience is therefore advisable as one approaches the

Spindlestone region, where sea-birds wail their lament, and a sobbering wind sweeps over from the Farnes. . . .

The King of Bamburgh had a daughter, Margaret, whose great beauty so enraged her step-mother that by exercising some devilish chicanery she transferred the girl into a Laidley (loathsome) worm. From its cave nearby the worm emerged after dark to ravage the countryside for food; its appetite was insatiable:

> Word went east, and word went west,
> And word is gone over the sea,
> That a Laidley Worm in Spindleston Heughs,
> Would ruin the North Countrie.

The horrifying news at length reached the Childe of Wynde, in some overseas redoubt. Fearing that his sister Margaret might be in peril, he set sail for home, in a ship cunningly built with masts of rowan wood. When the wicked queen saw the ship approaching she bade her witch-wives go forth and sink the vessel, but against rowan wood they were powerless.

And so the ship rode into Budle Bay, where the Laidley Worm waited, thrashing the water in apparent fury. But when the Childe of Wynde stepped ashore, sword in readiness, the worm crept close and said,

> O, quit thy sword, and bend thy bow,
> And give me kisses three,
> For though I be a poisonous worm,
> No hurt I'll do to thee
>
> O, quit thy sword, and bend thy bow,
> And give me kisses three,
> If I'm not won ere set of sun,
> Won shall I never be.
>
> He sheath'd his sword and bent his bow,
> And gave her kisses three,
> She crept into her hole a worme,
> And stept out a ladye.

Bamburgh Castle has witnessed some strange things in its time, but nothing stranger—according to Duncan Frazer, the Cheviot bard of 600 years ago—than this gallant rescue of fair Margaret, and her brother's revenge on the jealous but now terrified queen. By his own magical powers he turned her into a toad, decreeing that she should stay thus until Doomsday, wandering for centuries, despised and hated, through the local lanes and fields.

We are left to suppose that no "kisses three" from any bold fellow would save *her* from this ghastly fate. So if one should ever see an outsized toad in that region, it might be wise to cross oneself and take a vow against any form of jealousy! Perhaps, after all, the moral ramifications of this story were added to supply a useful cautionary tale for the children of our remote ancestors.

I sometimes wonder how King Arthur managed to get around to so many places in a Britain whose only means of transport was the horse. It is customary to place Arthur and his knights in Cornwall. Indeed, Cornwall and other parts of the West Country may seem at first to have a monopoly of this half-mythical king, though in his *History of England*, G. M. Trevelyan muses upon the tradition that Arthur led his men against "the heathen swarming o'er the Northern Sea". Legend, at least, has given Arthur several abiding places in the northern shires.

He and his knights are supposed to sleep beneath Freeborough Hill in Cleveland. Better known is the story relating how one, Potter Thompson, discovered the same sleepers in a vault below Richmond Castle.

One day, while sauntering along the Castle Walk—that magnificent rock terrace above the River Swale—the fellow suddenly noticed a fresh cave-like opening and went in. A dim light beyond led him gingerly onwards, until he found himself in a rock chamber. Gradually, as the darkness thinned, he experienced the fulfilment of a tradition that had beguiled everybody in Richmond for centuries. Arthur and his knights lay before him, fast asleep. On a table nearby lay a sword and a horn. One of these tokens would surely convince his friends in the town that he had indeed discovered the hidden chamber. But as he started withdrawing the sword from its scabbard, one of the knights *turned over*. Terrified, Potter Thompson dropped the sword with a clatter and fled, only to hear a voice behind say, in sepulchral tones,

> Potter, Potter Thompson,
> If thou hads't either drawn
> The sword or blown the horn
> Thou'd have been the luckiest man
> That ever yet was born.

Fresh air and daylight somewhat restored the poor fellow's confidence—but he could never find the vault again. The wall that had once parted for him, had closed in the exasperating manner known only too well in the science fiction of today.

Before that long sleep, Arthur had evidently enjoyed some of the sights and sounds of Lakeland. At a spot near Pooley Bridge, still known as King Arthur's Round Table, Sir Lancelot once overthrew the Saxon giant, Tarquin, and then looked on with another privileged knight, as fifty stalwarts fought each other to win the hand of Arthur's daughter, Gyneth.

Another time, Arthur and his knights were holding their Christmas feast in Carlisle Castle when a fair damsel was shown in. Her distress was plain to see. She wrung her hands; she shed bitter tears yet managed to tell the knightly company that her husband had been carried off to a distant castle "rising darkly on a black rock over a deep lake . . ." where the dreadful master robbed his victims, held them to ransom, or flung them into the lake. And so, seizing his magic sword Excalibur, Arthur rode forth. . . .

As might be expected, the mission was fraught with peril, but we can safely leave the issue in such gallant hands, and follow Arthur on yet another excursion. This time to Sewingshields Crags on the Roman Wall.

One legend—quite out of character with the rest—is told about Arthur and Guinevere as they sat here one fair morning. The Queen dropped some remark, which so angered Arthur that he seized a rock and flung it at his consort. Fortunately she was braiding her hair just then and managed to deflect the missile with her comb. I have sat by these crags myself, but never yet have I seen that peevishly thrown rock, a boulder of some 20 tons, which is supposed to bear the teeth-marks of Guinevere's timely comb. If they exist at all, those marks are more likely to have been made by quarrymens' tools as the Wall was being built.

It is odd that here again we encounter one of those curious slumber legends. But this time Guinevere and her ladies share the dormitory, hidden away beneath the crags, where neither lowing of cattle nor raven's croak disturb their peaceful dreams.

Even as late as Tudor times, two sentinels kept regular watch on Sewingshields Crags, from sunrise to sunset, to give warning of raiders, who were liable to swoop down from lawless Liddesdale and upper Tynedale. But where innumerable raids, with the inevitable whoops, cries and the crack of gunshot failed to disturb the sleepers, a simple shepherd boy seems to have succeeded. While minding his sheep, one day, and knitting as was so often the custom, he dropped his ball of wool which rolled into a hole. Cleaving a way through the thick under-growth he followed the ball and eventually found himself in a great cavern where, in the dim light, Arthur and the rest raised up on their elbows to peer at the intruder, though one version of this fireside tale says that Arthur and Guinevere were reclining on their thrones, still drowsy from age-old sleep. . . .

There we must leave them, for all the best traditions declare that Arthur and his knights will go on sleeping—does it really matter where?—until that fated hour when England desperately needs them again, with all their chivalry and love of fair play. If only that shepherd boy had had the wit to blow the bugle that shone in that dark chamber, the long enchantment would have been broken. Arthur would have rubbed the sleep from his eyes, called up his knights, and, who knows, England might now be free of all her troubles!

This part of the Roman Wall is ripe with legendary lore. You have only to recline there, with a soft breeze teasing your face, and the tales come upon you as from some distant time when the world was young enough to believe.

It was in such a time that one of the lords of Sewingshields Castle threw a chest of gold into Broomlea Lough, placing a spell upon it so that none but an approved person should ever be able to drag it from the depths. From the Wall near Housesteads one can look down upon this eerie lake, and recall that although a gale should whip the surface into 'white horses', a certain spot always remains calm. Directly below that spot lies the treasure, awaiting recovery. But the spell was cunningly devised. The treasure could only be moved by "twa twin yauds [horses], twa twin oxen, twa twin lads, and a chain forged by a smith of kind"—that is, a blacksmith of the seventh generation of his trade.

Using the preternatural vision belonging to this lonely region, I have looked back to a certain bygone day when all those conditions were apparently fulfilled. . . .

The lake surface was sufficiently disturbed to reveal that one tranquil area quite clearly. The treasure hunter confidently made for it in his boat. The chain was lowered, the hidden chest was grappled, the youths on shore shouted their encouragement, the beasts pulled with all their strength.

I could see it all happening, there in the translucent light of a spring day. Everything was going according to plan. The kist of gold moved slowly shorewards. The very air vibrated with excitement. But alas for human hopes, the kist suddenly sank again. It had slipped the chain, which parted at a weak link. The flaw was due, it seems, to a corresponding flaw in the blacksmith's ancestry!

So there, beneath its tantalising spot of calm, the treasure still lies.

I got to my feet again and turned away, sorrowfully. What is the use of being a seventh child, as I am, if one's family tree produced not even *one* blacksmith!

The Biblical injunction that one must never suffer a witch to live, had some curious repercussions in the North. In 1639 the guild authorities of Berwick-upon-Tweed sent for "the man which tryeth the witches in Scotland" to deal with local practitioners of this evil craft. Ten years later, Newcastle also invited a Scotsman for such a purpose,

(*top*) Sir George Cayley's sketch of the ornithopter he invented. (*bottom*) Whales' teeth 'scrimshawed' by Hull whalers

Tarn Hows, near Coniston, Lakeland

(*left*) Scale-model of the 'Salamanca', made in 1812 by Matthew Murray for the Middleton Colliery Railway. (*right*) Memorial to Samuel Marsden, pioneer of the Australian wool industry, at Farsley, near Bradford

offering him "twenty shillings a piece, for all he could condemn as witches". After the bellman had gone through the town, requiring all suspects to be rounded up and tested, "thirty women were brought into the town-hall and stript, and then openly had pins thrust into their bodies, and most of them was found guilty, near twenty seven of them".

In the Riding Mill area, a few miles south of the Roman Wall, a certain Anne Armstrong gave much evidence against the black sisterhood. It was almost as though one district vied with another during the seventeenth century, for exposing witches, but Anne Armstrong had an unusually vivid imagination, for she reported covens that had been presided over by a 'being' enthroned in a gold chair, and witches' feasts at which food "came sliding down a rope when this was pulled". Anne Armstrong even claimed to have seen the Devil himself take charge of one coven at Corbridge, when everybody present repeated the Lord's Prayer backwards.

The witches of Berwick-upon-Tweed were supposed to have used their spells in favour of Oliver Cromwell at the Battle of Preston; others provoked a storm off the Yorkshire coast, causing Charles I's Queen, Henrietta, on returning from Holland, to land precipitately at Bridlington where she spent most of that night in a ditch, clothed only in her shift. Nothing was too fanciful or grotesque to lay at the door of witches, who, everybody knew, could change themselves into hares, put spells on cattle and fly about the countryside by night.

Many local traditions support this belief in flying witches. Eagle Crag and Whirlaw, above Todmorden in the Pennine country, are pointed out as the taking-off places favoured by neighbouring witches when bound for some unholy sabbat on Pendle Hill, and a few chimney stacks were actually provided with witch seats so that any of the sisterhood, while in transit, could rest there harmlessly, rather than enter the homestead below to cause mischief. One of these chimney stacks survives intact on a cottage at Feizor, near Settle. The so-called witches' seat comprises a couple of slates protruding some 8 or 9 inches on either side of the stonework.

It was often considered politic to placate the 'wise woman' in some such way, lest the evil eye be cast upon one's child or cow. Tales are still told in Littondale about Bertha, the witch who lived in a ghyll near Arncliffe. It was always best to humour her, but when she approached, villagers preferred to leap out of her way over the nearest wall. Then, in the notorious Pendle country, there was Margaret Pearson of Padiham. Normally, backsheesh in the form of provisions would be paid to her, as also to the other Pendle witches. At the famous witch trial held at Lancaster Castle in 1612, Margaret Pearson got off with a comparatively light sentence; she had to stand upon the pillory in the open market at Clitheroe, Padiham, Whalley and Lancaster displaying a label that proclaimed her offence—that of causing the death of somebody's mare. All the other women at this trial were condemned to be hanged for having bewitched to death "by devilish practices and hellish means" sixteen inhabitants of the Forest of Pendle, including Richard Assheton of Downham, Henry Mytton of Roughlee and John Hargreaves of Goldshaw Booth.

The countryside around Pendle is so delightful that only by re-reading Harrison Ainsworth's well-known novel on the subject, or some more factual account, can one visualise the horror of living here-abouts in the early seventeenth century. As we have seen, Downham is one of Lancashire's choicest villages. Pendle Hill and its satellite reef knolls loom up to the south, making a striking backcloth for the honey-coloured dwellings. One of these, Well Hall, is believed by some to have been the home of one of the witches, but the only kind of black art that brews in Downham today is on Mischief Night (4th November) when the local lads betray their Pendle ancestry by smearing all the door-knobs with black treacle!

Mistress Alice Nutter, who cleverly concealed her sorcery, some-times rode over from her home at Roughlee to plague Squire Nicholas Assheton at Downham Hall. Amid so much that is lovely, the winding moorland track between the two villages strikes the one baleful note around Pendle today. The track breasts the lower slopes of Pendle Hill, and—especially if the clouds hang low—something sinister from the past, when the witches held their covens up there, seems to cling to it. To this same evil 'hang-over' a local clergyman bore his own witness, only a few years ago.

Roughlee, however, is an attractive little place. Mistress Nutter's stone-built house has been converted into three separate homes, but some of the original, round-headed windows, and a date stone (1536) remain. Nothing could look more peaceful, yet little more than a mile away, at Newchurch village (once called Goldshaw Booth), one sees the peculiar burial-ground that supplied some of the local witches with their macabre stock-in-trade. At the Lancaster trial of 1612 James Device testified that Mother Demdike "once took eight teeth and three scalps of dead people in Newchurch".

The Washburn Valley, branching north from Wharfedale, was another hotbed of witchcraft. Edward Fairfax, scholarly uncle of the Lord General of Civil War fame, averred that his own two daughters had been put under a spell by Jennet Dibb and her tribe, of Timble and Fewston. Such is the modern interest in witchcraft that a strange book written by Fairfax, all that time ago, has been republished in our day. The book is entitled *A Discourse on Witchcraft as it was acted in the family of Mr. Edward Fairfax of Fuystone . . . in the year A.D. 1621.* It is

illustrated by a horrific picture of Yorkshire witches and imps surrounded by flying fish, a pig, an ape, a fierce dragon, a tree-lizard etc.
A witch at the centre is apparently invoking the powers lurking within
and around this ridiculous menagerie. All this, mark you, to support
Fairfax's description of the family enchantment and the eventual trial
of the witches at York Castle in 1622. Surprisingly, they were acquitted,
and Fairfax goes on to relate that a few days later "all the witches had a
feast in Timble Gill", nearby, doubtless to celebrate their acquittal.

This local activity was not confined to the superstitious seventeenth
century, as one might suppose. The late B. W. J. Kent of Tatefield
Hall, Beckwithshaw, told me that his own great uncles—a couple of
brawny farmers—would never think of approaching Bland Hill, near
Timble and Fewston, without first slipping into their pockets a bit of
rowan wood, often called witchwood. That was in mid-Victorian
times, before the site of Edward Fairfax's house and much of the
bewitched area were submerged by Swinsty Reservoir. As Tatefield
Hall stands only 4 miles away, it seems appropriate that this farmhouse
should also have a witchcraft story of its own.

It appears that a Washburn sorceress once called at Tatefield and,
very unwisely, a farm lad began to mock her. Summoning all her
powers she caused him to be levitated to the kitchen ceiling, where he
remained until rescued by one of the family. When I laughingly
suggested that the story sounded more like a seventeenth-century
fable than an account of anything that might have happened in later
times, Mr Kent—a keen antiquary and folklorist—assured me that the
whole district was long notorious for such wonder-workers, one of
whom had a secret practice within living memory.

Tangible evidence of such latter-day beliefs came to light some time
ago in a garden at Kearby, near Harewood. It was a curious yellow
bottle containing witchcraft charms—pins and needles for piercing
effigies of the doomed person, human hair and nail pairings, brimstone
and so on. A grey mug containing a mysterious powder, believed to
give immunity against the black arts, was also found. It is tempting to
connect these tokens with the times of Jinny Pullen, a local wise woman
of 150 years ago who is said to have demonstrated her rare skill by
crossing the neighbouring river Wharfe in a cinder-riddle or sieve.

In the Whitby and Cleveland areas, witch-posts were favoured to
avert evil. A good example, from East End Cottage, Egton, is preserved
in Whitby Museum, and others from Danby-in-Cleveland now give
one the creeps at Hutton-le-Hole Folk Museum. Made of mountain
ash, incised with a cross and vertical lines indicating the number of
people to be protected, such a post usually stood beside the fireplace—
a strategic spot, for to gain power over the household a witch had first
to pass threshold and hearth. Hence the witch's frequent lament:

> Oh master, oh master, we can't do no good,
> She's got a witch cross made o' mountain ash wood.

A crooked sixpence lodged in a crevice of the witch post was an added charm; if a farmer's butter would not 'come' the sixpence was taken out of its crevice by knitting needles, purposely kept in a groove above, and carefully placed in the churn. Then, of a surety, the butter began to thicken!

There was a special formula for preparing *portable* witch crosses. The rowan wood must be cut on St Helen's Day with a large household knife called a gully. Moreover, it must come from a tree never seen before by the person concerned, and brought home by a different path from the outward one. Only then would it be effective against the spells of such dangerous and elusive characters as Nanny Pearson of Goathland, Ann Grear of Guisborough and Peggy Flaunders of Marske, all nineteenth-century witches.

The credulous people of Goathland had their own way of drawing witches from their hiding places, so that they could be exposed and brought to justice. A cow's heart was pierced with pins and then roasted before some cottage fire at midnight. How this prophylactic worked is beyond comprehension. Yet it was still in vogue about 100 years ago.

But we had our *white* witches, too, in the North Country—wise women who helped rather than hindered. Last century, Hannah Green—better known as the Ling Bob Witch—dispensed love philtres and other charms to the credulous. She could locate your lost cow or settle matrimonial difficulties. Little wonder that even the local gentry came along in their smart carriages to consult the oracle of Novia House (now a farm) on Yeadon Moor. A pleasant thought for those who now use the neighbouring Leeds and Bradford Airport.

Family annals are often rich storehouses of unsuspected folklore. One such record dealing with the affairs of the Davison family of Wolsingham and Sedgefield, County Durham, was kindly loaned to me some time ago. In it there are echoes of the 1715 and 1745 rebellions; of fruitless searches by excise officers for a whisky still secreted in the Bishop's Plantation at Wolsingham; of whaling expeditions to Greenland; and of many other exciting episodes, real and fanciful. But the best story concerns a 'pickled parson'.

It seems that when one of the family first came to Sedgefield in 1791, as land agent to the rector and others, he was accommodated in the empty rectory until his own house was ready. "The story runs that the previous rector had died just before the tithes were due. To secure these his death was hushed up by the widow and the body preserved in a barrel of pickle [salt]. Later, when all the money was got in, the body was taken out and his decease announced. But a ghost then began to haunt the rectory."

One morning when John Davison, the agent's son, woke up he saw the ghost seated in a chair in his room. Later his sister claimed to have seen the same ghost outside. Whether she recognised him by some evidence of his erstwhile pickling is not made clear, but he was "running along the wall tops". That was enough. When the new rector duly arrived, he called in a Roman Catholic priest to exorcise the visitant. I imagine that as nephew to the renowned Bishop Shute Barrington of Durham Cathedral, the rector also wished to rid his house of the stigma of stolen tithes.

Northern ghost stories could fill the rest of this book, but one curious experience that occurred in York barely twenty-five years ago, must here serve as tailpiece.

The scene was the King's Manor, opposite Bootham Bar. Two men and two ladies who then lived and worked there, decided to brave whatever might happen in the basement on All Souls' Night. The manor, built on the site of the residence of the abbot of St Mary's, became the headquarters of the Council of the North; the great Earl of Strafford was one of its outstanding presidents, and thus was a frequent visitor.

Just before the clock struck twelve the would-be spectators descended to the abbot's kitchen. They had agreed that each should afterwards record independent impressions of anything seen or heard, and only then compare notes.

As midnight tolled, one of the ladies nudged her companions and pointed to an archway at the foot of a staircase in the far corner. A spectral figure was slowly coming down those steps. The top of the arch, of course, prevented a full view being obtained all at once. The feet, shod in buckled shoes, stepped leisurely down, to reveal gradually a pair of fine calves clad in gentleman's hose; then came the breeches— of pale blue silk, the doublet, then the first glimpse of a Stuart hat tucked under one arm. . . .

At that moment a door at the opposite end of the kitchen was thrown open and an enraged principal, who had just heard of the ghost-watching escapade, ordered his subordinates to their rooms. And so the watchers had to go, just when they were hoping to establish whether it was Strafford or Charles I who walked down there o' nights. The only disparity between their accounts, compared later as arranged, was concerning the colour of the visitant's breeches; one spectator thought they were pale green.

The King's Manor has since become part of York University. Perhaps the chief point reluctantly left at issue, by those watchers, will be settled by some enterprising student!

15

In Gay Mood

IN my youth when I had a reasonably thick shock of dark hair I was often asked by friends to 'let New Year in' for them. This followed a Watch Night Service at our local chapel. I would be given the key and into the friends' house I went, opening the door later to their knock. Felicitations followed, eagerly marked amongst the younger members by an exchange of kisses—happy prelude to a 'bite and sup', the first meal of the incoming year.

'First footing' is of course one of the oldest ways of welcoming the New Year, but there are many variations on this pleasant theme. The late Herbert Honeyman of Newcastle recorded how a Northumberland miner acts the part. To the chosen house he takes a log of wood or piece of coal, plus a little salt—an offering which he leaves outside as he enters. Just before midnight he is "pushed out into the cold night air to await the striking of the hour". This heralds his moment of triumph. He is the pivotal figure between one year and the next. Picking up his bundle he knocks peremptorily on the door, to be admitted by the lady of the house, who accepts his smacking kiss and the following incantation: "Here's my Sonce and here's my Sele, and here's my Happy New Year." Whereupon he solemnly spreads his offerings on the waiting fire. No priest of some ancient cult could have done better. The gods have been propitiated.

The children of Driffield, a few miles inland from Bridlington have their own way of celebrating the New Year. Early in the morning just as the shops open, a group of youngsters scatter themselves through the market town, greeting each likely tradesman with an ancient jingle beginning,

> Here we are at oor toon end,
> A shoulder of mutton an' a croon ti spend.

Knowing what is expected of them—even though the rhyme suggests a bit of normal trading—the shopkeepers respond with largesse, handling out a few small coins, together with apples, oranges and sweets.

At Hubberholme in Upper Wharfedale the year begins in a unique manner. Winter has crept down the enclosing fells, leaving a carpet of snow in the valley bottom, where the ancient church of St Michael's faces the George Inn across a swollen river. A dowly wind thrashes the bare trees, yet however bleak the weather, New Year's Eve sees much human commotion in this hamlet of half a dozen cottages. It has been going on for centuries on the same day, ever since some unknown person bequeathed a certain plot of land in the parish for the benefit of the poor and needy. It gives Hubberholme a Thomas Hardy scene of rustic simplicity, as the parson steps over the bridge from church to inn, followed at intervals by several Gabriel Oaks with sheep-dogs at heel. They are figures in some immemorial drama. They have assembled for the annual re-letting of Poor's Pasture.

The parson and his clerk settle themselves in one room of the inn, a room known for the occasion as the House of Lords. In an adjoining room the farmers group together as the House of Commons. Parliamentary business opens with the first offer for the coming year's tenancy of Poor's Pasture. This offer and succeeding ones are conveyed in turn from Commons to Lords. Echoes of the past when dales farmers counted their sheep by the ancient numerals yain, tain, eddero, peddero, pitts . . . seem to float around as each bidder estimates the grazing potentialities on offer. And of course the land is let to the highest bidder, all being duly recorded by parson and clerk in a sort of parochial Hansard. This done, convivialities become more relaxed; the sheep farmer's year has been put on its feet.

Later in the same month a very different kind of gathering brings York into the seasonal picture. On the nearest Sunday to 30th January, the anniversary of Charles I's execution, a body of Merchant Adventurers, suitably robed, moves across from their medieval hall in Fossgate to All Saints' Church, Pavement, there to hear a sermon provided for by the will of Mistress Jane Stainton, staunch Royalist and daughter of the seventeenth-century rector of this parish. York nourishes many interesting old customs, but perhaps none is quite so impressive as this one. The city seems to hold its breath for a brief moment, as the solemn procession moves its way through the populace like a voice of doom in a wilderness of bustle and self-seeking. Doom indeed, for Jane Stainton's desire that the anniversary sermon should always deal with Man's *latter end*—a flash back to the deplaced Martyr King's death—is faithfully observed.

I have beside me a collection of some fairly recent Jane Stainton sermons delivered by the Merchants' Company chaplain, the late Canon Angelo Raine. The benefactor's other bequests—her apostle spoons, her "little spoons with forks", "a piece of gold that hath the dagger in itt", her "black Japan Cabbinett" etc, were of temporal value, but this annual sermon for which the preacher receives "fifteene shillings" was to mark every succeeding year "for ever".

One can escape from that 'searching' atmosphere by fleeing to the Scottish border, there to witness another though happier religious ceremony—the blessing of the nets by the clergy of Norham. The ancient guild of Berwick-upon-Tweed laid down certain rules regarding the Tweed salmon fisheries. Scotsmen were on no account to be employed, and fishermen could only cast their nets from when "the sonne aryse unto the sonne be gone down". Rules are apt to mellow with time, but Norham honours that one old observance. The salmon net fishing season for the whole of the Tweed opens on 14th February, as signalised by the blessing of the nets.

And so we come to Shrove Tuesday, heralded at several places by the ringing of a Pancake Bell. Traditionally the bell announced a general holiday and summoned all self-respecting housewives to start preparing their pancakes. Pickering, Richmond, and Morley near Leeds, have long maintained the melodious part of the custom, pancakes or no pancakes. Although Morley may not have the outward attractions of Pickering and Richmond, the town has its compensations. At St Mary's-in-the-Wood Church the pancake signal rings forth from a bell that is said to have originated as a sanctuary bell at Kirkstall Abbey. Morley housewives have even been called to their succulent task in this time-honoured fashion, by a set of ringers that included the mayor and town clerk.

At Scarborough, Shrove Tuesday means the annual Skipping Festival along the south foreshore. The setting is sufficiently 'old world', with King Richard's House on the landward side and the harbour on the other, to suggest the many generations who have sustained this custom. Using the fisherman's 1-inch-thick ropes, the 'celebrants' first skip in their own friendly groups, and then go from pitch to pitch along the sea front, dragging in old and young. You may find yourself skipping with a bearded old sailor, a smart shopkeeper or one of the local fish-

(*left*) A Durham hand-made quilt with rose, feather and shell motifs. (*right*) Part of the Doom window at All Saints' Church, York

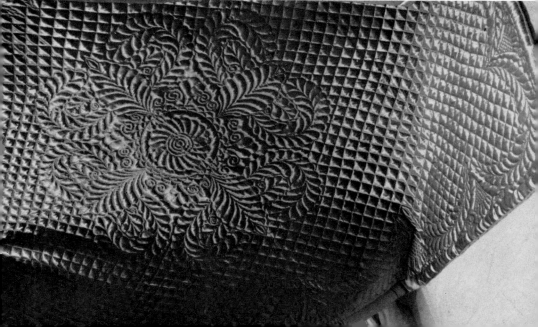

(*left*) Thomas E. Whittaker and his gnome signboard. (*below*) An oak kist made by by Mr Whittaker

wives—it matters not, as long as the fishermen's ropes are kept twirling. Could this custom have stemmed from the former shipbuilding days, when men caulking boats on this same quayside, exacted a kiss from every passing woman? Modern fun fairs nearby are tame by comparison with this free-for-all jollification. I have never been able to plumb the antiquity of this rite, but a plaster frieze above the fireplace in the King's Bedchamber at Richard III's House shows what appears to be a skipping boy. Can there be any connection? The house was built about 1350.

Another fine setting for a Shrovetide frolic is the Duke of Northumberland's pastures which slope down from Alnwick Castle to the River Aln. Normally this is a quiet desmesne, its only sounds being the burble of the river and the munching of cattle. A man could meditate here for hours absorbing its tranquility—but not on Shrove Tuesday!

A football provided by the Duke is first thrown down from the castle barbican to the waiting committee, who then march in procession, led by the duke's own piper. Over the Lion Bridge they go, one of them holding the ball aloft as if it were a royal sceptre, and the others restraining themselves until the area between the specially fixed goal posts—one-quarter of a mile apart—is reached. The posts have been decorated purposely with evergreen. The previous year's winner kicks off, and then the mêlée begins, ostensibly between the respective parishes of St Michael's and St Paul's, though anybody can join in. It is the committee's duty to pick out for later reward any particularly zealous player amongst the hundreds on the field. Ten shillings is the traditional prize for the scorer of a goal, and a pound for the winning goal. Eventually the ball is thrown into the river, and he who recovers it can keep this trophy or sell it as a much-prized treasure to some local shop.

Tea at the castle for all the players rounds off a very hilarious day.

Chester-le-Street once staged its own Shrovetide football spree, at some considerable danger to the town shop-windows, for here the field of play was the main street. At one time Alnwick's arena was similarly sited, but the youths of Chester-le-Street had no kindly duke to provide an alternative 'battle-ground' away from road traffic, and no duke's piper to lend authority to the renewed proceedings. So after many a scuffle with the prohibitious minions of the law, Chester-le-Street finally gave up the ghost of its sportive past.

Fortunately for Liverpool children, their hoary Easter custom offers no 'obstruction'. Early on Good Friday morning they blacken their faces and parade through the streets with an effigy of Judas, made from old clothes. "Judas! Judas"! they cry—an echo of all the ages since Christ's betrayal. At length, borrowing something from the later Guy

17

Fawkes event, they put the effigy on a bonfire. Their dancing figures around the pyre lend final drama to this act of denunciation.

For centuries the northern counties have had their own way of celebrating the joyous aspect of Eastertide. Most of the surviving customs are associated with the 'pace' or Pasche egg. This is usually an ordinary egg, painted in bright colours and sometimes inscribed with suitable mottoes or decorated with pictures of local scenes. For days beforehand, mothers and 'grannies' busy themselves with these homely works of art.

Easter Monday is the great day for 'pace egg' rolling. Assembling on a local hill hallowed by centuries of use for this ceremonial purpose, the villagers or townsfolk—especially the children—alternately push and roll their eggs down the hillside. When the shell breaks away from the hard-boiled centre, this is eaten, with relish.

This strange custom, which has been traced back to Druidical times, is practised with all its merriment at Arncliffe, a beautiful village in Littondale; on the slopes of Beacon Hill, Pickering; around many villages in the Whitby area; and in Avenham Park, Preston, where the event assumes the character of a tournament.

Easter Monday is the day, also, on which many children make a tour of local cottages and farmhouses, collecting the 'pace' eggs prepared in readiness for them. Some of these eggs, too, are painted, while others may be wrapped in brightly-coloured tinsel.

Early in the morning, country children can be seen setting off for the annual 'harvest' in groups of two or three, each child carrying a basket. They wear their best clothes to give the occasion a touch of dignity. It is the pomp of childhood. But how they enjoy knocking at each door and telling the owner they have called for their Easter egg!

Many villages in Northumberland are awakened on Easter Monday in this pleasant way. Drive up Coquetdale to Rothbury, then on to Thropton and beyond, and you may see the baskets of several youthful collectors gradually filling with eggs—violet eggs, red eggs, blue eggs and eggs of a dozen other different colours. The late Hastings M. Neville, rector of Ford, near the Scottish Border, once recorded how the local 'pace' eggs were prepared: ". . . broom and whin blooms were used to dye the eggs yellow. The patterns were traced on the egg with the pointed end of a rushlight. The grease preserved the pattern, while the egg was being dyed, and was afterwards rubbed off, leaving the decoration the natural colour of the shell." I wonder if that is how the 'pace' eggs were made for Wordsworth's children? These eggs add something quite charming to the interior display at Dove Cottage, Grasmere.

The most exuberant show which Easter promotes in the North is undoubtedly the "Pace Egg" play performed on Good Friday by schoolboys in the hill villages of Calderdale. This version of the play originated at Midgley and was recovered by a Halifax folklorist some forty years ago.

"Pace Egg", or to use the play's alternative name, "St George and the Dragon", is a delightful piece of mummery, spoken in local dialect, in which St George, the Bold Slasher and the Black Prince of Paradine have prominent parts, with Toss Pot as the chief villain of the show. With the exception of Toss Pot (the Devil) and his Tally Wife (a mere effigy), the boys wear coloured tunics and paste-board hats decorated with beads. In this guise they parade the village streets, brandishing wooden swords and delivering themselves of the swash-buckling lines that have echoed hereabouts for centuries. The play's connection with Easter seems remote, until one remembers the implicit triumph of good over evil.

The people who advocate a fixed date for Easter would encounter fierce opposition at Whitby. A fixed Easter would mean that the state of the tide on Ascension Day, which is governed by the Easter festival, would be variable and thus put an end to an old warmly-cherished custom, known as the planting of the Penny Hedge.

First let us see how the custom originated. Long ago, so long ago that doubting Thomases regard the event as purely legendary, a couple of huntsmen slew a hermit who had given sanctuary to the boar they sought. Before breathing his last, the hermit forgave his slayers, charging them however—for the safeguard of their souls—to plant a hedge on the river brink at Whitby at 9 a.m. on the day before Ascension Day, failing which their property was to be surrendered to the Abbot of Whitby. If ever the tide should cover the appointed place at the appointed time, they or their heirs should be absolved from the penance. The hermit evidently combined rare cunning with the wisdom of an astrologer, for well he knew that, judging by the moon phases, the tide would never be high enough on that date to interfere with the observance of his wishes.

So it is that on the eve of Ascension Day an eager group of children and adults go down to Abraham's Bosom on the East bank of the Esk to watch an agent of the Manor of Fylingdales arrange his bundle of faggots, trimmed to shape with a knife, traditionally costing no more than a penny, into a hedge, that will withstand the tides. Sober historians see in this custom a survival of the Horngarth idea, by which a number of deer were driven into an artificial enclosure in shallow water and there killed for the larder of Whitby Abbey. If one prefers the more picturesque hermit theory, the presiding bailiff's blowing of his official horn and his cry "Out on you"—as the last stake is hammered home—may bring confirmatory satisfaction.

Durham Cathedral marks the passage of time in ways that reflect episodes in its own long history. During summer months children from different parts of the diocese sometimes assemble in the Cloister Garth, where, to the strains of a music that echoes the sea-bird cries of Lindisfarne, they re-enact the life of St Cuthbert. The green of the cloister garth becomes the green of the strip of sea separating Lindisfarne from the mainland, and how well do the boys simulate the tossing of their boat over that channel as they go to and fro, dressed as monks.

The story behind those voyages is recounted for all to 'read' in the cathedral library, but down in the cloister the children give it the freshness and vigour of their own imagination. And visitors look on, quite enthralled, from the surrounding arches, which, in monastic times, framed another children's festival based on Christ's washing of the Disciples' feet.

This happened on Maundy Thursday when "the whole convent of monks . . . had every one of them a boy appointed them sytting upon the said bench [within the Cloister Walk]. When the said monks dyd wash the said childryns feete, and dryed them with a towell which being done they dyd kisse the said childrens fete . . . giving to every childe xxxd in mony and vii redde herrings and iii loves of bread, and everyone certaine wafercakes, the monks servinge every childe with drinke themselves. . . ."

The same body of monks observed the anniversary of the Battle of Neville's Cross, 17th October 1346—at which Cuthbert's banner had been held aloft—by climbing the central tower to sing their praises for victory in that battle over the Scots. They sang from the north, south and east sides, in turn, but never from the west side, presumably because that was the direction of the Scottish army's approach.

Nowadays, after evensong on the 29th May, cathedral choristers mount the 365 steps to the roof of the same tower, and sing up there as the monks did—on three sides only. To the south goes forth Richard Farrant's anthem, "Lord, for thy tender mercie's sake"; to the east, Novello's "Therefore with angels and archangels"; and to the north, Calcott's "Give peace in our time, O Lord."

North Country folk were once as renowned for their hymn-singing as the Welsh, and not only in chapel or church but at such events as football matches and public demonstrations. The 'Whitsun Sing' for which children and adults assembled in some public park after a parade through the town streets, still has its devotees here and there. Perhaps the chief continuators of communal hymn-singing today, are those who support the rush-bearing festivals. We still have such festivals at Haworth, near Keighley, at Warcop in Westmorland, and pre-eminently at Grasmere, Wordsworth's village, July and August being the favoured months.

Grasmere's festival, already mentioned in brief, is based like the others, on the one-time fairly general necessity for strewing a church floor of earth or clay, with rushes for foot warmth. Even the seats were occasionally so covered. A visitor to Grasmere in 1828 wrote, "I found the very seat floors all unpaved, unboarded, and the bare ground only strewn with rushes."

Another visitor, Benjamin Newton, recorded his own impression of the festival in his diary, under the date 24th July 1818:

Breakfast at Grasmere Inn, a little retired house behind the church. . . . As soon as breakfast was over I walked out . . . and passing by the church I peeped in at a window of the chancel and to my great surprise saw the Communion table, the rail at the altar, the seats, the windows, every part of the church crammed with all sorts of tawdry and ridiculous things stuck upon sticks, hoops and crosses, and made to stand upright. These sticks were . . . covered with coloured paper, red, green, and yellow; flowers of all sorts, roses, sweet williams, straw, etc. . . .

Meeting the Rector of Grasmere I begged him to explain the reason for his church being so fantastically ornamented, which he did by telling me the seats in the church had no flooring, but the bare earth . . . and that there was an ancient custom of strewing the seats with rushes which was annually done the day after he had gathered in his tithe wool. The old rushes were taken away and the boys and girls in the parish brought a bundle of fresh rushes to straw the seats with, and each carried a garland made after their own fancies which they deposited in the church, fixing them up as, and where, they pleased, after which they were regaled, at the expense of the parish, with cakes, and ale and gingerbread.

In essentials, the same saturnalia is gone through today, at Grasmere, every August on the Saturday nearest to St Oswald's Day. The children's "cakes and ale" are only a memory, but the gingerbread is still as great a feature of the festival as the hymn-singing. The Rushbearing March and Hymn is the traditional one accompanied in Wordsworth's day by Billy Dawson, the village fiddler. Today, a local brass band leads the singing as the clergy, choirboys and rush-sheet bearers proceed to the church, followed by village children proudly carrying their rush garlands shaped as harps, maypoles, Oswald's crown, and even baby Moses in his "ark of bulrushes". An additional hymn for the Rush-bearing, written by Canon Rawnsley in 1910, recaptures the spirit of the occasion from the opening verse:

> Today we come from farm and fell
> Wild flowers and rushes green we twine,
> We sing the hymn we love so well,
> And worship at St. Oswald's Shrine.

Until fairly recent years Ambleside maintained its own rush-bearing festival, towards the end of July. A revival would be welcomed by many. How pleasant to see, once again, some of the local children gather rushes from the banks of Windermere and shape them into traditional 'bearings' that Wordsworth and Hartley Coleridge would have recognised; and to hear them sing the Rushbearing Hymn outside the old coaching office where the hymn, "Our fathers, to the House of God", was composed in 1835 by the Reverend Owen Lloyd, friend of Hartley Coleridge and of Charles Lamb.

Other customs that have lapsed should also be restored to our North Country calendar. Rural life is the poorer for their abeyance. Downham's King and Queen festival, for example. How satisfying it must have been to scatter the witchcraft aura of this Lancashire village with the breath of Merry England! Personally I still have hopes of seeing the prettiest girl in the parish elected as queen, by a committee of young male admirers, and the handsomest youth chosen as king by the girls, and each crowned with garlands, before they proceed to Downham Hall accompanied by the traditional javelin-men and a retinue of villagers, all eager for a two-day session of dancing and games. Somebody could surely be found again to provide a Queen's Posset to round off the event!

The countryside is beginning to mellow, when Guiseley, near Leeds, stages its annual St Oswald's Pageant. After a commemorative service in the ancient church, clergy and parishoners proceed to the town cross, where some notable person delivers an address. It is noteworthy that, as in so many of our older customs, the festival centres upon the church. And, here at Guiseley, the town cross—being in effect a preaching cross—takes the church's message to those who pass by.

Later, the assembled company proceeds to the rectory garden singing verses from a ballad that extolls their patron saint, Oswald, and begins,

> Out of the North is he come as the north wind,
> Back to his home from the waves of the West.

The vivid story which the ballad unfolds is the theme of the pageant, now dramatically presented on the tree-shaded lawns spreading down from the Tudor rectory to what remains of the original moat. I seem to recall that at least once, the moat gave a semblance of reality to the scene in which Oswald arrives by boat on Iona. A later scene shows Oswald holding council with his lords at Bamburgh Castle, and crying to heaven for a man who can break down the obstinacy shown by dalesfolk towards Christian teaching. It is then that Aidan appears. Later, Aidan and Oswald arrive in this part of Airedale; their teaching gradually converts the stubborn villagers and a cross is set up as a symbol of the newly-accepted faith.

Two modern windows in Guiseley church capture the festival spirit by showing groups of boys and girls in Elizabethan costume displaying floral garlands before rectory and church. With those garlands the children seem to paraphrase the old custom of 'clipping the church' revived here about forty years ago. In *Coriolanus* Shakespeare used the word 'clip' in the sense of an embrace:

> O! let me clip you
> In arms as sound as when I woo'd.

So it is that when the children of Guiseley, a week after the annual pageant, join hands and encircle the church, singing as they move around in one uninterrupted circle, they are metaphorically *embracing* Mother Church.

Another early Church saint is resurrected at Ripon every year on the first Saturday in August. This is Wilfrid, impersonated by some likely person, and robed at the town hall in readiness for his exacting role.

I was once present at this robing. The understudy might have been the great Wilfrid himself, as he was solemnly clad in the different vestments, and handed his crozier, with a Catholic priest there to see that every detail was correct.

Then, accompanied by a 'monk' and, for good measure, the town band!—he rides his white horse through the streets of this fine old town, stopping at intervals, ostensibly to bestow his blessings and to assure the townsfolk that his recent audience with the Pope, in far off Rome, had been successful.

Today Wilfrid's appearance on his white mare marks the opening of the annual fair, held in the spacious market place. On the occasion I have just mentioned I followed in the wake of Wilfrid, past the roundabouts and swings, booths and fortune-tellers and on through the winding streets until 'Wilfrid' rested before the west doors of the cathedral, wondering as it were at the huge building that has grown from the small beginnings he knew.

Wilfrid's Fair is still a great rallying point for old Riponians. It is a red-letter day in their calendar, to be celebrated in various homely ways, not least by plentiful supplies of 'Wilfrid's Tarts', purposely made for the occasion and passed round freely, especially among wanderers who have come back for the fair; the tarts declare old allegiances and seal old friendships.

One of the chief virtues of these old customs is the sense of community they promote. They can be a focal point for concerted action flavoured with the pent-up humour of centuries. So it is at West Witton in Wensleydale, when the villagers keep St Bartholemew's Feast, towards the end of August.

The highlight of this feast is the burning of old Bartle. Nobody now can say with certainty who old Bartle was or why he should be put to the flames. Origins are for serious folklorists to argue about. The only argument in West Witton as the great day approaches, I imagine, is— who shall have the honour of preparing the effigy for his annual ride prior to the burning?

All other traffic makes way for this curious ride. Old Bartle might represent the Giant of Penhill nearby, a turn-coat monk, or even—by some odd reversal of fortune—St Bartholomew himself. No matter. He is placed in a cart and dragged up and down the village street, to the repeated ritual of this bewildering incantation:

> At Penhill crags he tore his rags,
> At Hunter's Thorn he blew his horn,
> At Capplebank Stee he brake his knee
> At Briskill Beck he brake his neck,
> At Wadham's End he couldn't fend,
> At Briskill End he made his end,
> Shout, lads, shout!

And shout they do, especially when at last poor old Bartle disintegrates on the communal bonfire.

At Goathland several miles away over the north-eastern moors, an ancient Plough Monday (January) custom is observed during August with all the old rituals from musical reels to sword dance. Plough Monday was the day when, in old times, plough lads shook the mud from their clogs and made merry, even decking themselves in a queer motley of coloured rags and ribbons. They went from door to door, begging alms, and if any villager refused he might have his garden ploughed up, for sheer devilry.

The Plough Stots at Goathland were revived nearly fifty years ago by the late F. W. Dowson. So it is that the village resounds once more to this strange litany:

> Wee'r Gooadlon' pleeaf stots cum'd ageean,
> All dek't wi' ribbons foair,
> Seea noo we'll dea the best we can,
> An' the best can dea na mair.

From one end of the village to the other they go, awakening strange echoes from the distant past as the wooden swords are twirled to the music of fiddle or concertina, and the traditional figures of Betty, Isaac and t'Owd Man move around like attendant deities. For once— as far as visitors are concerned—the sheep which regularly graze the grass verge and poke their black noses into open car doors in hopes of food—are outshone by the antics of the Stots team. And if you should see a plough being trundled in their wake, its significance should be clear. The dancers are as hungry for material recognition as the sheep!

It is never wise to say that certain old customs have become extinct. If one should embark on this generalisation, somebody is almost sure to write to the local paper with a protest, followed by details of the custom as observed, perhaps in the correspondent's own neighbourhood. Thus, in a large area like the North of England, the Mell Supper, held after the gathering of the harvest, is likely to be a continuing feature if only in a few out-of-the-way villages.

The Mell Supper is provided by the farmer and his household, and all concerned with the harvest are invited. To be soundly traditional, the feast must have a 'corn dolly' or 'kern baby' prominently displayed. According to Frazer, the 'corn dolly' made from the last sheaf of the harvest, embodies the Corn Spirit. Hastings Neville once described the Northumbrian version of the 'corn dolly' tradition: "There was much rivalry among the shearers to obtain this last 'grip', as it was termed, and to cut it. This sheaf was nicely rounded by the workers and fully dressed with a skirt, and ribbons round the neck, to represent a young girl. It was raised aloft upon a fork and carried about the field with dancing and singing to the strains of the local fiddler. . . . It was ultimately carried in procession to the farmyard, where . . . the farmers showed hospitality."

In Yorkshire, as elsewhere, the 'corn dolly' became a generic term for a variety of designs, including spirals, candlesticks and lanterns. York Castle Museum shows a fine selection in its agricultural gallery. A few are even preserved in country churches, presumably as a recognition of the beneficent Spirit behind all harvests. The skill required for making a good 'corn dolly' may now be directed along other channels, and yet, even as I write, I hear of a northern folk-lore student being supplied with a fine modern example: a magnificent chandelier made by a Scarborough man. An older type which came to her from Whitby, takes the form of a mistletoe bough enclosing a spiral supposed to protect the owner from the machinations of witchcraft!

In one of his delightfully naive essays, Robert Lynd once made a plea for the retention of certain 5th November festivities. He named a few that have fallen into oblivion, like the great procession and bonfire on Hampstead Heath, and then remarks, "It is a pity . . . to let these old celebrations fade. After all, Guy Fawkes performed a singular service to his fellow countrymen; he gave them an occasion for rejoicing. Of how few men who have dabbled in politics can as much be said? No one would ever dream of setting a day apart for letting off fireworks in memory of anything Pitt ever did. Great as were the achievements of Gladstone, no one was ever inspired by them to set up

a dummy figure with a hat on it, in his back yard, and burn Roman
Candles before it as it went up in flames."

In the North we have a great firework industry, and, despite police
restrictions, every variety of firework—from rockets, roman candles
and catherine wheels, to the latest 'space projectiles'—light up the
evening sky as crowds of children and adults gather round their
bonfires, roasting chestnuts or potatoes at intervals in the red-hot embers.
Toffee and parkin, freely handed around, are additional delights—
succulent fare with which to sustain oneself as the night gets colder and
the flames leap higher and the guy at the centre slowly crumbles into
fire-dust.

It is unthinkable that such a scintillating occasion should ever drop
from our calendar. But, as other well-loved customs have vanished, it
has seemed wise to put this one on record for future generations who
may be deprived of such joys. Already the Commemoration Service,
offering thanks for the nation's deliverance from Guy Fawkes and his
powder barrels, has disappeared from the vast majority of our churches,
and Mischief Night is hardly known, if at all, outside the northern
counties. The boyhood pranks of Mischief Night reflect the mischief
that was brewing in London on 4th November, 1605. As a boy I did
my share of tying up door-knobs, putting squibs through keyholes,
noisily removing dustbin lids, and making weird night cries. But my
wife, who comes from Suffolk, tells me that she never heard of Mischief
Night before coming to Yorkshire, the county that gave birth to Guy
Fawkes.

A search for his actual birthplace may result in some bewilderment,
for three houses in central York claim the honour. All three are within
a few yards of each other, near the Minster. One is now a hotel, another
a shop, and the third—at the corner of Minster Gate and High Petergate
—a suite of respectable offices. He was educated nearby at St Peter's
School, but unless the ban has been lifted recently, never a bonfire do
we see in the grounds here on 5th November, or an effigy to be mocked.
After all, Guy Fawkes deserves some respect as an 'old boy'!

"Here we come a'wassailing".... How many can now recall
this old Christmas custom, when East Riding children went from door
to door with their little tokens of Christ's birth? It must have been
quite touching to open the door on Christmas morning and see two or
three well muffled youngsters remove a gaily-painted lid from their
wassail box and thrust up for your delighted gaze two small figures,
Mary and the Christ Child, reclining there in soft folds of cloth or
velvet. The figures might be as naively symbolised as those in the
Nativity frescoe in Easby Church, near Richmond, or those cupped
along with the oxen and sheep in a piece of ivory, shaped to fit the

palm of the hand, now kept in Bowes Museum, Barnard Castle. But, naive or not, well worth a copper or two to speed the children's Christmas.

An occasion just as touching is the Christingle Service still held every Christmas at the Moravian School, Fulneck. It gives to this rural corner of the West Riding a dramatic exposition of life's simple yet significant things. At this service the school's Nativity players each hold an orange, for the round earth, and a lighted candle to represent Christ as the Light of the World. Fruits of the earth are also in evidence. In one version of this little tableau, held on Christmas Eve, all the candles save one are extinguished in turn as night falls. The one remaining light at the centre, represents the new light about to break upon the world, and from it the other candles are slowly, silently, re-lit. This custom has been revived in recent years.

At Dewsbury Church, also in the West Riding, the Devil's Knell rings on Christmas Eve, as many times as there have been years since the birth of Christ. The performance takes about an hour, and ends on the stroke of midnight.

For 700 years (excepting the period of the last war) Thomas de Soothill has thus been expiating his sins. In a fit of anger he murdered a servant boy and hid the body in a lake. When the crime was discovered, he expressed remorse by presenting a bell to the parish church, ordering that it should be rung every Christmas Eve as a penance, the basic idea being that when Christ was born the Devil fled—and as the bell tolls the Devil still steers clear of Dewsbury for another twelve months.

For most North Country folk Christmas mumming plays are not even a memory. Mumming belongs to an age to which motoring, the cinema and radio gave the final *coup de grace*. Or will they revive here and there, as several other customs have revived? They once had a way of renewing themselves, for to the traditional cast of St George, the Black Prince of Paradine, the Doctor who could cure every ill, and the rest, were sometimes added contemporary figures, like Lord Nelson, or even a suffragette! Even the Christmas characters might sometimes bend to winds of change.

A charming example of such adaptability was given by Dorothy Una Ratcliffe in her one-act play, *Mary of Scotland in Wensleydale*. This has been performed in Bolton Castle, as part of a local festival of dales drama. Mary Stuart while a prisoner in Bolton Castle, is greeted on Christmas Day by six village children.

First, King Holly steps forward and says his piece, then the Yew Maiden, followed by three lads who explain their different roles. "First, we're t' three Kings, then we're t' three shepherds, then we're t'oxen and t'ass." After laughing her pleasure Mary turns again to the Yew Maiden, asking what other parts she can play. The answer is shy but prompt: "I most like to pretend I'm thee!" At which King Holly chimes in, "Aye, she does, and I play Bothwell, I do, wi' a black frown an' a girt French sword, an' (pointing at the Snow Lad) he's that saft we allus mak' him play Darnley."

Surely, in our day, we have enough national or parochial figures of promise, to warrant fresh outbursts of the old mumming technique!

As if certain customs tied to particular dates or seasons were not enough to keep North Country folk amused, we have several that spread over much of the year.

Every night at nine o'clock a man wearing fawn coat and black tricorn hat steps up to the obelisk in Ripon Market Place and blows four loud blasts on a large bull horn. He then walks along to the mayor's house and blows the horn once more. This is Ripon keeping tryst with its past, for the custom originated in Saxon days. Nothing is allowed to silence the horn. Through winter and summer alike its dolorous notes shiver the air. And visitors look on in wonder.

The origin of the custom traces back to the days when Ripon was a large communal farm. The land was let off in strips to farmers who collectively owned the agricultural implements they required. A swineherd and a neatherd controlled the grazing rights, and a pinder impounded animals which had strayed on to the arable land or meadows. The head official was called the Wakeman, and it is with him and his assistants that the horn comes into our story. From the *Old Towne Book of Ripon* (bound in sheepskin and dated 1598) it is inferred that the office of Wakeman began "before the [Norman] Conquest".

The blowing of the horn announced the setting of the watch, and for a small sum paid periodically to the Wakeman, each householder had his dwelling and its contents protected from thieves during the night. It was, in effect, a form of burglary insurance.

A complete picture of the Wakeman in later days would portray him not only as custodian of the horn, but also as constable, magistrate, cleansing authority, guardian of public morals, statutory mourner at the funeral of an alderman or his wife and holder of many other offices.

He had the right to search the house of anybody he suspected of being a hedge-breaker and, if the suspected person was found guilty, to put him in the town stocks. If fire broke out during the night hours he caused the town bell to be rung as a general warning. He could order any nocturnal wanderer "to go to rest", and fine all persons who had not properly locked their doors. He rode the fairs in the company of the archbishop's steward. Anybody found slandering the Wakeman with "scornful or opprobrious words" was thrust into the stocks for twenty-four hours. The Wakeman was, in effect, the town's Poo Bah.

But, for his part, he was pledged "not to flit out of the town except God do visit the said town with pestilence".

When he retired from office he gave a farewell dinner for his aldermanic brethren at the Wakeman's House, in the market square, and then arranged for a silver badge to be made and fastened to the baldric, or shoulder sash, from which the original horn is now suspended. On this badge were inscribed his name, his term of office, and an emblem of his own trade or craft.

The baldric in question has therefore become a wonderful, indeed a unique, piece of civic regalia. Its chief feature is the charter horn presented to Ripon as long ago as A.D. 886. Now silver-mounted and covered with velvet, the horn is affixed to the velvet baldric by means of short straps which carry such hoary trade emblems of old Ripon as a woodcutter's axe, a pair of tailor's scissors, a farrier's horseshoe, a large buckle and, for a forester, a crouching stag. Spurs, hanging separately, represent the bygone spurriers' craft which produced the far-famed 'Ripon rowels'. The baldric itself is covered on both sides with badges of different Wakemen, starting with Thomas Fysher (1515), a farrier, and ending with Hugh Ripley (1603), a merchant who had the unique distinction of being last Wakeman and first mayor of Ripon. From 1604 mayors were appointed instead of Wakemen, but there was no interruption of the nightly horn-blowing.

The new baldric also has its horn. This is a splendid specimen taken from a bull of the famous Chillingham herd of wild cattle. And all the mayoral badges since 1886 keep it company, amongst the latest being one engraved with the G.P.O. crest to denote the donor's term as Ripon's assistant postmaster.

The charter horn of A.D. 886 is no longer used for the horn-blowing ceremony. There have been several successors, but the present horn—a fine Scottish bull horn—has been in use since 1865. It gives a deep, eerie sound which can sometimes be heard—like the wailing of some lost soul—at Fountains Abbey, 3 miles away. The ceremony, sole survival of the old custom of 'setting the watch', has been broadcast by the B.B.C. and a recording was made fairly recently for the citizens of the daughter town of Ripon, Wisconsin.

Thus it can be said that the nightly blowing of Ripon's horn now echoes across the Atlantic.

Ripon's motto is adapted from a verse in the Bible: "Except ye Lord Keep Ye Cittie, Ye Wakeman Waketh in Vain." In bold gilt letters the motto spreads over the façade of the Georgian town hall, which stands within a few yards of the thirteenth-century house where the Wakeman once lived. The motto was, perhaps, a neat little reminder that the Archbishop of York, who kept an eye on the town, and the Abbot of Fountains, represented an authority even higher than that of the Wakeman. However that may be, the people of Ripon, Wisconsin, have lately adopted this same motto as their own and the Wakeman's horn as their badge.

So far nobody has 'borrowed' Bainbridge's horn-blowing ceremony. Bainbridge, in Upper Wensleydale, is the sort of village people visualize when they think back, nostalgically, to the days of Merrie England. The cottages form a ring around the spacious green, making room for the village store, the old grammar school, the Rose and Crown Inn and a bridge to bring outsiders into this charmed area. My wife and I once looked on as the local schoolchildren expressed the essential spirit of the place by going through some old English country dances on the green.

Every night at 9 p.m. from Holyrood (27th September) to Shrove Tuesday, the village hornblower steps to the edge of the green and winds his horn as though there may still be wanderers on the surrounding fells needing guidance. That was the original significance of the event. Nowadays there are no wolves or other terrors awaiting wayfarers on winter nights. The old forest of Wensleydale is but a name. Customs die hard in the Yorkshire dales, however; nobody would dare suggest that Bainbridge should dispense with its ancient signature tune!

For several years Jack Metcalfe has fulfilled this historic role for Bainbridge—quite fittingly so, for his father acted the same part for forty years, and their ancestors were wardens of the Forest of Wensleydale when the horn blowing still served its original purpose.

As at Ripon, horns come and go at Bainbridge as the centuries pass. Bainbridge's early horn now enjoys well-earned silence within the walls of Bolton Castle farther down the dale, leaving a South African buffalo horn to link past and present with its own mellow blast. This horn, approximately 2 feet 6 inches long, bears the following inscription: "Presented to the village of Bainbridge by Mr. R. H. Harburn, Bishop Auckland [County Durham] who brought it home from South Africa, January 16, 1864." Three long blasts on the horn, as night falls—and the old ritual has been performed as faithfully as the continuing Floral Dance in Cornwall, or the daily Changing of the Guards at Buckingham Palace.

We in the North have, or once had, our own curious wedding customs—nothing so exacting as the Strobeck (Germany) custom which demands that before her marriage, a bride must play a game of chess with the town's chief magistrate, as evidence of her sound, native upbringing, but, in their own way ours are just as entertaining, at least for onlookers.

Native tradition at Hubberholme, in Wharfedale, Romaldkirk in

Teesdale, Bellingham in Northumberland and at Holy Island requires that as they emerge from the marriage service, a couple must have the church gates barred against them, to be released only when they have satisfied the general clamour for a ransom of money. Sometimes, indeed—as at certain East Riding villages, also on Holy Island—gun shots may be fired over the heads of the happy couple, as they leave the church, to frighten away evil spirits. That at least was the original idea.

A strange custom has been observed several times offshore at Bridlington, on the east coast. To conform with the laws and regulations of their own country, Norwegian couples living hereabouts were married in a coble 3 miles out to sea, i.e. 'in a neutral zone'. This observance recalls a variation of the old Border marriage custom.

Up till about 1856* young runaway couples could marry without fuss or bother, or parental consent, by crossing the Border into Scotland and getting some 'bogus' parson to join them in matrimony. Gretna Green, the best known of these obliging places, still gets its 'runaway' couples, although three weeks' residence in the town is now required. In 1970 eighty-five young couples from England here sought the romance of a Border marriage. In former times, Coldstream and Lamberton Toll, near Berwick-upon-Tweed, had their own flood of runaways. One couple were even married by a certain John Forster—in a boat in the middle of the River Tweed. Their great grand daughter has kindly shown me their marriage certificate. It is dated 21st March 1819, and the couple concerned—William Dickson of Ancroft, Northumberland, and Jane Burn of Berrington Law, in the same county—were evidently so proud of their romantic elaboration of the old Border custom, that the boat episode is mentioned in the brief certificate three times!

Some customs like the periodical beating of the bounds in this or that parish, ebb and flow, being observed for a time and then fall into disuse, until somebody sets the event on its feet again.

For centuries, Alnwick in Northumberland elected its 'boundary riders' in peculiar manner. Candidates for this privilege had first to robe themselves in white night-caps, carry a sword and ride horseback to the Freeman's Well, "a miry pool 4 or 5 feet deep". To the sounds of music they dismounted, scrambled through the water and having been duly 'baptised' in the accepted manner—they changed their garments, re-mounted and gaily perambulated the town boundaries.

This curious initiation is supposed to derive from King John's unfortunate experience when he visited Alnwick. Such was the condition of the roads that in one place he found himself floundering

* See the author's *Secret Britain*.

in a bog! The above custom was then inaugurated as a penance for the town's neglect.

Revival of Alnwick's penitentiary custom might be too much to hope for in these days, and yet, at Newbiggin-on-Sea, not many miles away, the riding of the bounds has long been the occasion for humour, though of the dryer sort. The custom is entrusted to the town's freemen, who add to their number by 'dunting' or bumping youthful candidates on the historic Dunting Stone that marks one point of the boundary.

At Cullercoats, near Tynemouth, the parish bounds are not ridden, but *sailed*, for the local clergy weave their way amongst the assembled boats, which they bless as they go. North Shields does something similar, though here the boundary markers sail up the Tyne. But either way one is inevitably reminded of certain birds that jealously guard their territory with challenging cries and fierce beating of wings.

Such a challenge is embodied in Richmond's Walking of the Bounds every seventh year in September.* This fine old market town in Swaledale—a town that thrives on its picturesque past—breaks out again with civic merriment. On that day a stranger might well think he had stepped back in time.

Early in the morning a strange company assembles outside the town hall: a banner bearer accompanied by halberdiers, a pinder equipped with an axe "to cut through anything or anybody" who might offer resistance to the business ahead; a bellman and town crier, a water wader and the serjeant-at-mace, all wearing traditional outfit and a suitable demeanour in support of the berobed mayor, bewigged town clerk and the entire council.

When fully assembled, like a roll-call of parochial history, the company 'crocodiles' its way through the cobbled market place and down ancient streets, to the centre of the old Green Bridge that spans the river. Now comes the bellman's great moment. With a voice that needs no microphone, he issues the immemorial challenge: "Oyez! Oyez! Oyez! I do in the name of the Mayor, Alderman and Burgesses of the borough of Richmond, Lords of the Manor and borough of Richmond, hereby proclaim and declare this to be the ancient and undoubted boundary of the said manor and borough, against the manor or lordship of Hipswell and Hudswell. God save the Queen and the Lord of the Manor—which is all of us."

Hipswell and Hudswell, on the south of the river, having been duly warned, the mayor turns fairy godfather by dipping into his bag and scattering specially minted coins for the inevitable children and anybody else agile enough to stoop and grovel for this coveted harvest.

Then, as if all that were not sufficient to impress the occasion—and the boundary—on youthful minds, the mayor pulls out his next 'plum'

* This custom will next be observed in 1976.

Rope-making at Hawes, Wensleydale

(*below left*) Chalk mould for charms against witches. (*below right*) A Yorkshire witch cross of rowan wood, to protect its owner against the 'evil eye'

St Wilfrid's understudy ready for Ripon's annual August Fair

—the marking of the boundary down the centre of the turbulent Swale. The official water wader carries the mayor pick-a-back to various parts of the river boundary, but if the mayor be a heavy weight it is usual for him to delegate these rights to the water wader, who discharges them by throwing stones mid-way into the river and repeating the same old challenge to those 'aggressive' neighbours on the south bank.

The day that has begun so well continues in much the same vein, for there are yet 15 miles of boundary to perambulate for the sake of posterity. And so the hilarious party proceeds over becks, across moors and through farms, the elderly sometimes going part way by horse or car. Others expend any spare energy in racing and games *en route*. It is a tired but happy mayor, who, at the close of day, greets everybody on the Green Bridge, once more, and completes his role as godfather by distributing prizes to the winners of those intermediary sporting events.

Let all those whose many customs have dwindled to nothing take heart again from Richmond. The town revels in ancient ceremonies. As clerk of the market, the mayor has two halberds placed outside his house or place of business every Saturday to indicate that he is 'on call'. To the first farmer who turns up with a 'respectable' sample of the new season's wheat, he presents a bottle of wine. By ancient charter the town clerk has the unique distinction of having his appointment approved by Royal warrant. When this has been duly received from the reigning monarch, a special session of the council is called, and the town clerk swears the traditional oath of faithful service, "upon the Holy Evangelists".

Add to these customs that ringing of the curfew every evening, the 'prentice' bell every morning, the 'Pancake' summons on Shrove Tuesday, the passing bell when an inhabitant dies, and the gathering peal to assemble the mourners—all at Holy Trinity, the 'town belfry'— and one begins to understand why, at the Septennial Walking of the Bounds, it is considered such an honour for anybody who can truthfully say he has covered the whole 15 miles, to sign a civic roll that records the fact, and is kept for all time in the borough archives. His name has been joined with the elect.

16

By Right of Birth

EVERY part of Britain has its own roll of honour. Names famous in history continue to thrill some people who live in the area where great men and women were born, and worked out their destiny; and rightly so. A whole series of books could be written about our North Country celebrities alone. All that can be attempted here is a brief notice of a few who made their mark in different spheres of thought and activity.

Some of them were glimpsed in earlier parts of this book, but now step forward for more detailed appraisal.

We have already seen Bede bending diligently over his books at Jarrow. "My constant pleasure", he wrote, "lay in learning or teaching or writing." Born about A.D. 673 in the country between Wear and Tyne, he never travelled far, yet, such was the scope of his mind that he could write a book still admired and quoted by historians—*The Ecclesiastical History of the English People.* G. M. Trevelyan has paid him this tribute: "The intellectual life of Bede (673-735) covered the whole of the limited range of the learning of the Dark Ages. But we moderns value him most as the 'father of English History'." Another tribute— "the teller of sweet stories"—refers to episodes like that concerning the conversion of Edwin of Northumbria (see page 92), which Bede recorded in his own engaging manner. Durham Cathedral Library treasures an Evangelarium, or book of the four Gospels, reputedly in

Bede's handwriting. This attribution has since been questioned, but the historian of the library concedes one fascinating thought: "...whoever wrote it, whether Bede or not, might have looked out from his monastery window [at Jarrow] across the salt-marshes and seen the long low line of the Roman Wall itself, standing as the Romans left it...".

Bede, the 'Venerable' as people have always liked to call him, had this much in common with later modern theologians; all knowledge and beauty were of God.

It is to Bede, also, that we owe the charming story of Caedmon, the herdsman-poet of Whitby Abbey.

At any convivial gathering, when the day's work was done, Caedmon was always the odd man out. He could neither sing, nor finger an instrument; he could give voice neither to ballad nor poesy. One night after he had left the company to find some solace amongst the oxen, he fell asleep and an angel came to him, saying, "Caedmon, sing me something."

He answered woefully, "I cannot sing, for therefore have I come hither from the feast."

The angel was importunate; "But you must sing to me!"

"What must I sing?" replied the bewildered herdsman.

"Sing," came the reply, "sing the beginning of Creation." And for the first time in his life Caedmon broke into song, a paean of praise to the Maker of All Things.

On awakening, he remembered all that had transpired and repeated it to Abbess Hilda. Recognising in this the "finger of God", Hilda elevated Caedmon from the secular order to the monastic, and there on the cliff-top his inspiration flowered, enabling him to turn the whole Scriptures into Saxon verse. The Caedmon Memorial Cross in St Mary's Churchyard, near Whitby Abbey, does ample justice to the story with a wealth of emblematic carving.

Since those distant times, the North has given birth to many outstanding figures in Christian history. Today it may seem strange that the 'Morning Star of the Reformation' should have first begun to twinkle in a remote village of which his later antagonists, even the Pope himself, had never heard. Even now there are two contestants for the honour of shooting this 'Star' into the firmament of fourteenth century religious controversy. Hipswell near Richmond may have the stronger claim, but tiny Wycliffe on the River Tees echoes John Wycliffe's very name, and certainly has family links with the great reformer. "Wycliffe village", wrote one topographer, "with nothing to sell, is content to dream, as it has done for centuries." He could have added that the dream centres chiefly around a portrait of the reformer hung in the rectory. Painted by Sir Antonio More, it was presented in 1796 by the current rector, doubtless as a kind of 'welcome'. A copy of the painting can be seen in the church.

One of our northern artists was rather outspoken about such copies. "Had I been a painter", he said, "I would never have copied the works of 'old masters', however highly they might have been esteemed. I would have gone to nature for all my patterns." This was Thomas Bewick, whose woodcuts show that he practised what he preached.

Life in and around the Tyneside village of Ovingham, where he was born in August 1753, gave him all he desired to justify truancy from school. "I spent as much time as I could filling with my pencil all the unoccupied spaces of any books with representations of such objects that took my fancy. . . . As soon as these spaces were filled I had recourse at all spare times to the gravestones and the floor of the church porch with a bit of chalk. . . . The beasts and birds, which enlivened the beautiful scenery of woods and fields surrounding my native hamlet furnished me with an endless supply of subjects."

After apprenticeship with a Newcastle engraver, Bewick developed the art of wood-engraving and began to produce his amazingly accurate work at an astonishing rate.

His *History of Quadrupeds* and *History of British Birds* were a great success. But he had his adventures too. Commissioned by a neighbour to do a 'cut' of one of the Chillingham wild bulls, he went over to the park and could only get close enough to his subject by shinning up a tree. He succeeded, where Landseer had had to flee before the fierce beasts. "The result", says the compiler of a Hancock Museum* (New-castle) brochure, *Bewick's Countryside*, "was one of the most superb wood engravings ever executed." A 'pull' of the engraving is before me as I write, along with several others, including a few rustic scenes used as tailpieces to different kinds of books. A boy climbing a roadside tree, a fisherman in his coble, an old village worthy carrying a smaller replica of himself pick-a-back. Usually the reader is left to make his own interpretations. Another tailpiece shows a blind man about to cross a stream. He ignores his own guide dog waiting there knowingly at the ford, and trusts himself instead to a boy who has chosen deeper water. The puzzled, hurt look on the dog's face is unmistakeable. Had Bewick witnessed such an incident? His own tailpiece is a commemorative bust outside his former premises in Amen Corner, overlooked by Newcastle Cathedral.

One who drew in a very different vein, was Phil May, a native of Leeds (1864-1903). Part of his apprenticeship was as a call-boy at the Leeds Grand Theatre, where he made lightning sketches of visiting actors and actresses. Another phase was at Leeds Public Library, where

* The Hancock Museum has a fine collection of T. Bewick's masterpieces.

his swift caricatures in book margins were not appreciated, so he was dismissed. He married a Leeds girl, went to Australia, returned to London, did a brilliant impression of Gladstone in sombre mood, worked for the *Graphic* and the *Sketch*, and then joined the staff of *Punch*. His initials on the famous Punch table are deftly placed between those of Thackeray and Du Maurier. The variety of his subjects can be seen by strolling through the Leeds Art Gallery. His pencil portrait of Frank Brangwyn offsets another pencil drawing, "Guttersnipe Studies", which neatly echoes a pen-and-ink sketch, "Bless you, no, I ain't got no ancestors."

On his early death at the age of 39, his lightning career was commented upon with delicate humour by a *Punch* contemporary: "One has to love Phil May. With all his faults he was too good a fellow to go anywhere but Heaven although it will be a disappointment to the other place. The first thing he would have done was to stand drinks all round". And, then, the writer might have ventured, made 'minimum line' sketches of the imps and devils.

At Browsholme Hall, near Clitheroe, there hang a couple of fine portraits—of John Parker and his son Edward, of this place, by Arthur Devis. There is significance in the fact that the same Tudor house displays several Jacobite relics, including a portrait of Bonnie Prince Charlie, on silk, which had been smuggled into England in a sympathiser's boot-heel. Arthur Devis's strong likeness to the prince, and a similar impediment of speech, caused him acute embarrassment. He is said to have been arrested in Preston during the '45 Rebellion in mistake for the Young Pretender, and narrowly escaped death on that account. In the Harris Museum and Art Gallery, at Preston, some miniatures and a self portrait of Arthur Devis (1711–87) declare that astonishing likeness.

Devis somehow wriggled out of the delicate situation and lived to paint a large number of delightful conversation pieces, now much prized by connoisseurs. He was the most distinguished of a whole family of painters, though Preston is proud of them all, and doubly proud because each of them in turn was entered on the rolls of Preston Guild, a high honour.

York has produced several artists of note. John Flaxman, whose Wedgwood designs are so well known, is of this company, also William Etty. Etty's statue overlooking Bootham Bar was executed by G. W. Milburn, my old sculptor friend, who had previously linked his own day with Saxon times by carving the Caedmon Cross, on Whitby's East Cliff.

Etty's stance opposite Bootham Bar is peculiarly apt for in life this sensitive painter of the nude and of hosts of historical and allegorical subjects was instrumental in saving that historic gateway, and other architectural features of old York, from demolition. The son of a local gingerbread maker, young Etty grew to love the lines and shapes of these symbols of the past. In later years, when they were threatened by a council blind to their continuing beauty, Etty would rush from his London studio by stage-coach to raise hue and cry against the iconoclasts. The first "stone he threw at the vandals" was on behalf of the thirteenth-century Clifford's Tower. Other 'stones' followed when the city walls and bars were scheduled for removal. On his retirement to York about 1845, with his faithful niece Betsy, as housekeeper and companion, he could look around with some satisfaction, a satisfaction shared by present-day tourists as they make their perambulation of the walls and climb the steep mound in the Castle Yard to Clifford's Tower.

Although Frederick W. Elwell, R.A., of Beverley, was a versatile artist covering subjects of many kinds, crowned by a fine portrait of George V which hangs at Holyrood Palace, his native district held him most in thrall. From the window of his own historic dwelling, North Bar House, he once painted the town's last cabby, who was at that moment bringing Elwell's neighbour home. Elwell never tired of painting his own gracious thoroughfare, with its Georgian houses and the Gothic minarets of St Mary's Church converging upon the eighteenth-century market cross, and just a hint of the Minster's gleaming towers beyond. He used to stand at his windows, often, saying to anybody within earshot, "where will you find a finer street in all England?"

At the Beverley Arms Hotel, a Georgian coaching inn a few yards from North Bar House, past and present blended to give Frederick Elwell some of his most successful canvasses. In the curious flagged kitchen, then still unaltered, he portrayed the maids plucking fowl, or snatching a hasty meal, or sipping tea while the head cook poured herself another glass of port. One of these studies now hangs in the Tate Gallery, another in Walker Art Gallery, Liverpool, while the last of the series is at Beverley Art Gallery—a fine centrepiece for about fifty of his local subjects.

During the last war I happened to be dining one day in the 'Beverley Arms', and overheard from the next table, a conversation between Elwell and some friends. He and his wife were evidently in Switzerland at the outbreak of war. After the first impact of the saddening news, Elwell walked with his wife to the foot of Mont Blanc, stood there drinking in its majesty, and then said—apropos of the war—"What do these small things matter"! There spoke the immemorial artist. Later, I often visited Elwell in his beautiful home, where he would tell me the story behind some of his local, representational pictures. One of these paintings portrays George Monkman, Beverley's mace-bearer.

"He was then about 90," said Elwell, "and so frail I had to keep him alive while the sittings were finished, with brandy. But I rather suspect he was putting it on a bit!" In the Beverley Art Gallery collection, old Monkman looks around, with his rheumy eyes, upon the varied Beverley scene as delineated by the artist of Bar House. Any Elwell enthusiast will find his own admiration greatly increased after a visit to this ancient town where Frederick Elwell tasted and communicated the very essence of its life.

Painting coaches, rather than pictures, was William Kent's early trade. He was born in the Bridlington area (1684) at a time when family coaches were beginning to flaunt their owner's monograms and armorial bearings. But Kent soon graduated to the wider field of landscape gardening and architecture. Horace Walpole once said, "Mohamet imagined an Elysium, but Kent created many."

At that time an architect was a virtuoso of many parts. Kent himself, who assisted Lord Burlington with the designs for York Mansion House, could also design cradles for his patron's offspring, or a birthday gown decorated with the five architectural orders!

When it came to landscape gardening, his skill knew no bounds. In Richmond Park, for example, he created for Queen Caroline a Merlin's Cave, complete with thatched roof! After passing through its ogee doorway you would encounter Merlin himself and other figures conjured up from the past, not least Queen Elizabeth herself. Queen Caroline might have been charmed, but it would not do for Kent's pupil, Lancelot Brown. When he came along, Merlin and all his works were banished. Brown had visualized different capabilities.

Brown also was a son of the North. He was born in Kirkharle, just across the River Wansbeck from Wallington, that fine Trevelyan estate through which he would have to pass when attending the village school (now the village hall) at Cambo. In her fine monograph on Capability Brown* Dorothy Stroud declares that "he was never to work on the Wallington estate". Yet Mrs Pauline Dower, daughter of the late Sir Charles Trevelyan, assures me of a very strong local tradition that he laid out the gardens at Wallington, the Front Park, and the general setting of Wallington with its woods and lakes". When John Ruskin came, he found Wallington "the most beautiful place possible— a large old seventeenth-century stone house in an old English terraced garden set amongst undulating country with a peculiar Northumber-landishness about it". It seems as though he was indeed admiring some of Capability Brown's handiwork. Certainly, as Sir Charles Trevelyan states in his own book on Wallington, the fishing lake at Rothley, 4 miles to the north, was created by Capability Brown for his

* *Capability Brown*, Dorothy Stroud (Country Life, 1950).

patron, Sir Walter Blackett of Wallington, out of a "barren and ugly stretch of moorland".

After an early period as landscape gardener to the Loraine family of Kirkharle Park, Brown went south, to enrich some of the nation's great landed estates, including Longleat, Stowe, Milton Abbey, Chatsworth and Sandbeck Park.

His zeal was sometimes excessive, as at Sandbeck, where—following Lord Scarbrough's commission to lay out the adjoining Roche Abbey grounds, "with poet's feeling and with painter's eye"—he proceeded to shatter the ancient monastic peace of the place by creating cascades from the leisurely stream, beside which the Cistercian brotherhood had fished, and then, ye saints!, arranging a bowling green (since abolished) in the midst.

Horace Walpole had written earlier that Roche Abbey "was hid in such a venerable chasm that you might be concealed there, even from a Squire-parson of the parish. Lord Scarbrough neglects it as much as if he was afraid of ghosts." It no longer applied. Capability Brown exorcised any lingering ghosts, here, as effectively as he did by devising a menagerie near to the Carmelite Friary on the Duke of Northumberland's vast estate. And all that was romantic in Brown's exhuberant make-up must have kindled afresh while working in the grounds of Alnwick Castle, itself. He dined frequently with the duke and duchess. Swiss porters drifted around the place, and the duchess had her retinue of pipers.

Hobnobbing with the aristocracy did not spoil Brown. In an age of moral decadence he lived a blameless life, loving his own fireside, with wife and children around him. And what tales he would be able to spin for them—tales of revitalized abbeys; of providing that mansion of many ghosts, Burton Constable Hall, near Hull, with coal-bunkers disguised as summer-houses, also a garden based on the one at Versailles; of a jester adorning his garden at Wallington; and always that flourish of bagpipes beneath the bastions and towers of his castle of dreams rising from the banks of the River Aln.

John Carr of Horbury (his birthplace) and York has already burgeoned these pages with his pleasing, if unsophisticated architecture. It is amusing to think of him working at Harewood House, in his restrained manner, while Brown exploited the picturesque capabilities of the adjacent parkland.

To recount the achievements of all our famous engineers and inventors would take us far beyond the bounds of this book. Yet their names alone cast a lustre on the North Country.

John Smeaton of Austhorpe, near Leeds, builder of the Eddystone Lighthouse, was active in many other spheres, producing anything from atmospheric engines for Northumberland collieries, to improved water-wheels for Cumberland lead mines; he also played a vital role in various harbour and canal undertakings.

In a small building at Killingworth, near Newcastle, George Stephenson, engineer and inventor of the locomotive engine, spent some of his formative years, experimenting first with miners' safety lamps, and then with locomotives, one of the earliest, *Puffing Billy*, making a certain stranger think he had seen a devil dashing its fiery way between Wylam (Stephenson's birthplace) and Newburn. Stephenson's son, Robert, branched out as a bridge-builder.

We met Samuel Cropton, inventor of the Spinning Jenny, at Hall-i'-the-Wood, Bolton. A fellow Lancastrian was Richard Arkwright, whose career began in unlikely manner as a 'subterranean barber' shaving customers for a penny, until competition forced him to cut prices by half.

Although his first experiments with his spinning machine at Preston were construed by eavesdroppers as a new form of witchcraft, he prospered to such extent that he once offered to pay the National Debt.

Foulby, a small village on the Nostell estate, near Wakefield, gave birth to John Harrison, later dubbed 'Longitude Harrison' because of his chronometer, which won him a government prize of £10,000—paid off, however in meagre instalments during the rest of his long life. Twenty years after Harrison's death in 1776, George Cayley (see Chapter 12) started his experiments in 'aerial navigation', beginning with a 'whirling arm', then a 'flying top', later still an 'ornithopter'. He was born at Scarborough, in 1773, but spent most of his life at Brompton Hall, a few miles inland. His preliminary studies of the mechanical laws of bird flight, and the spiralling fall of a sycamore seed, would seem so much nonsense to the Brompton villagers, yet for his pioneer work along these lines, he is regarded as the father of aviation, and because of this benefit to mankind, has been grouped with such contemporaries as Watt, Trevethick and George Stephenson.

While the tide of invention flowed through our northern counties, other great names were being launched. A farm-hand's son in North Yorkshire heard the call of the sea, and after apprenticeship to John Walker, a Quaker ship-owner in Whitby, discovered new continents beyond the rim of the known world. That explorer is known to fame as Captain James Cook, R.N., F.R.S., but to this day Whitby folk look upon him much in the way voiced by the old housekeeper at his former ship-master's dwelling in Grape Lane, when he returned from his first voyage. Mary Prowd had been warned that as Cook was now a distinguished officer in the King's service she must treat him with due respect. But she who had once fussed over the young apprentice, providing him with many creature comforts, could not harness her feelings. "Ah James, honey", she burst out, "How glad I am to see thee." After three years away on the *Endeavour* I expect he enjoyed her motherliness.

Whitby also resounds to the fame of Captain William Scoresby and his son, another William. The same shipyards that built Cook's stout wooden vessels also equipped the Scoresbys for their whaling expeditions to the Arctic Seas. Scoresby senior, regarded as Whitby's most successful whaler—having captured the record number of 533 whales during his career—invented amongst other nautical features, the 'crows' nest. Placed at the top gallant mast-head, it was a curious contraption of leather or canvas, fitted out with such things as speaking trumpet, telescope and signal flags.

Scoresby junior's apprenticeship to the sea began as a boy of 10, when, pretending he had left his cap aboard his dad's ship, the *Dundee*, he managed to cajole a trip to the whaling grounds. Ultimately the younger Scoresby added to his prowess as a whaler, the accomplishments of an artist and scientist, developing some of his skills while ice-bound in the Far North. These enforced 'holidays' produced his 'marine diver', designed to bring samples of deep sea-water to the surface for close investigation, and various magnetical researches. He made accurate drawings of whales, and then went to the other extreme of draughtsmanship by reproducing with the aid of his microscope, the marvellous forms of crystallised snow. Since that time, these delicate 'snow stars' have been studied and even photographed, but it was Scoresby, freezing up there in polar regions, who first revealed this rich multiplicity of symmetrical patterns including columns, pyramids, hexagons and so many others. Some curiously resemble— and by no stretch of the imagination—the pilot's wheel, with furry or zigzag 'spokes' terminating in an amazing variety of 'handles'. In his book *Arctic Regions* (1820) Scoresby reproduces ninety-six different snow-crystal designs, each considerably magnified, and credits them to the "will and pleasure of the Great First Cause".

During his subsequent years as vicar of Bradford his congregation must have felt really on the spot when he expounded those passages in Job about snow, and the leviathan of deep waters.

Scoresby's snowflake drawings are inevitably recalled by Francis Thompson's beautiful poem, "To a Snowflake" beginning:

> What heart could have thought you? –
> Past our devisal
> O filigree petal!

Thompson's career was strange almost from the very start. He was one of those who go through life as lonely as one of Wordsworth's "clouds". Against a Lancashire background—first Preston, his birth-place (1859), later Ashton-under-Lyne—the boy drifted along as in a dream, sharing his ruminations eventually with the River Ribble and the sea beyond. Even in his father's house, it was the separateness of the staircase he sought for quiet hours with Shakespeare, Shelley and Coleridge.

Rejected for the priesthood, he went to Owen's College, Manchester, to study medicine, though most of his time was spent at Old Trafford. This leisurely existence produced his well-known poem on a historic match between Lancashire and Gloucestershire in 1878:

> It is little I repair to the matches of the Southron folk,
> Though my own red roses there may blow;
> It is little I repair to the matches of the Southron folk,
> Though the red roses crest their caps, I know.
> For the field is full of shapes as I near the shadowy coast,
> And a ghostly batsman plays to the bowling of a ghost,
> And I look through my tears on a soundless-clapping host
> As the run-stealers flicker to and fro,
> To and fro,
> O my Hornby and my Barlow long ago!

Yet it is not as a cricket 'fan' that one remembers him chiefly, dearly as he loved to watch the game and memorise outstanding scores and notable teams. Ushaw College at Durham, where as usual he was a 'lone wolf', thought him unsuitable as a divinity student, but he probably did far more good with the serious poetry he gave to the world: "In No Strange Land", "Ex Ore Infantum" etc. and perhaps his greatest ode, "The Hound of Heaven".

Preston has done many fine things, but few finer, perhaps, than the assembling in its Harris Library of a splendid collection of Francis Thompson manuscripts and poems. Out of all his aloofness, came some of his best works which often show how great things are gathered into small compass:

> One grass blade in its veins
> Wisdom's whole flood contains . . .
> . . .
> God focussed to a point.

The best of William Wordsworth's poetry declares similar vision. In him, Lakeland in all its moods found a great interpreter. The main facts of his life around Grasmere are too well known to warrant any detailed mention here, but a few preliminary episodes that bring sister Dorothy into the picture again are worth recounting.

After the early death of their parents, the Cockermouth home soon became a childhood memory, William being sent to school at Hawks-head, Dorothy to relatives, the Threlkelds of Halifax. But the close bond between brother and sister, that was to continue throughout life, had already been forged, and from her Halifax home Dorothy con-stantly regaled William with stories of her new surroundings.

There was the initial journey to Halifax by chaise and the excited arrival in the yard of the old Cock Inn, followed soon after by John Wesley's appearance in the wool town to preach against the activities of the notorious coiners of Cragg Vale. If 'Dolly' shrank, as, later on, she recalled seeing the bodies of coiners hanging from chains on Beacon Hill, there were many pleasanter things to tell her ever-affectionate William. Mr Edwards displayed the most marvellous books you ever saw in the Old Market (the Edwards' bindings and fore-edge paintings became world-famous), pack-horse teams still trudged over the neighbouring hills, and Ryburn Valley—where in later years Dorothy was to stay with the Rawsons of Mill House—gave her constant delight.

It was a disillusioned William who visited her, at Mill House, in 1793. He was 23 years old and had just returned from France; his idealistic support of the Revolution had been betrayed by the atrocities of the First Terror and the rise of Napoleon. He found solace with Dorothy amid the beautiful Ryburn surroundings, and again later—after a sojourn near Keswick—at the Teesdale farm of Sockburn, near Darling-ton, where Mary Hutchinson was keeping house for her brother, Tom.

Following another visit to Sockburn, in 1799, William accompanied Dorothy to their recently acquired home, Dove Dottage, Grasmere. It was winter and they travelled for a time on horseback, crossing the Tees by moonlight and seeing Richmond Castle and the Grey Friars Tower silhouetted against a starlit sky. The rest of the journey was done on foot. One night was spent at Askrigg, in Wensleydale; the next morning they turned aside to see Hardraw Force, whose frozen waters Dorothy likened to congealed froth.

Three years later saw William and Dorothy traversing North Yorkshire again, but in the opposite direction. William was to marry Mary Hutchinson. The chaise dropped them at Leeming Lane for the night, after which they breakfasted at Thirsk—where the landlady turned rude and derisive on hearing their plan to *walk* the rest of the way. The day was hot, yet after several rests on the Hambleton Hills they pushed on to Rievaulx Abbey where Dorothy noted the thrushes trilling around the ruins, and felt she could have stayed "in this solemn, quiet spot until evening, without a thought of moving".

William, however, was eager to reach Helmsley before nightfall, and sister Dorothy records in her diary how her heart leapt for joy on beholding the charming old inn where they found lodging. Next morning they set off for Gallows Hill Farm (the Hutchinsons' new home), and on the 4th October 1802 William and Mary—"the perfect woman, nobly planned"—were married at Brompton Church. Wordsworth wrote that Mary had in her "something of angelic light"; certainly she subscribed two of the best lines to the famous daffodil poem. . . . The Grasmere menage was now fully in being.

Mary and William Wordsworth had been married ten years when another wedding took place that presaged further supreme gifts to English literature.

It is 29th December 1812 and a happy couple have come to be married at Guiseley parish church, between Leeds and Ilkley. She is a lively Cornish girl, very small, not particularly pretty, yet—standing here before the altar—the very embodiment of her groom's fond hopes. He is handsome and Irish, ardent and ambitious, a rising young clergyman whose penury at Cambridge University had been alleviated by none other than William Wilberforce. But, as they repeat their marriage vows, no thought of want overshadows Maria and Patrick. The future is to be one of "perfect and uninterrupted bliss".

This romance between Maria Branwell and the Reverend Patrick Brontë had begun only a few months before, 2 miles away, on the outer fringe of the same historic parish. Charlotte, Emily and Anne Brontë have had volumes written about them, but Guiseley, and Woodhouse Grove—where their parents first met—deserve better recognition.

Earlier in 1812 Woodhouse Grove had been converted from a private dwelling into an academy for the sons of Wesleyan ministers. John Fennell, its first governor and headmaster, was introduced by the Reverend William Morgan to Patrick Brontë, vicar of Hartshead, soon appointed examiner to the school. While conducting these duties the young clergyman met Fennell's niece Maria Branwell, who was staying here on a long holiday. By September they were already making mutual declarations of love.

After flowing past the Woodhouse Grove playing fields, the River Aire broadens towards Leeds, 7 miles distant, passing *en route* the picturesque ruins of Kirkstall Abbey. 'Aunt and Uncle Fennell', with their daughter Jane, frequently arranged picnics in the abbey grounds, and Patrick sometimes joined them. How pleasant it is to think of Patrick and Maria sauntering hand-in-hand within these Cistercian precincts! Quickened by these associations, the place evidently impressed him, for one of his own writings, *The Rural Minstrel*, includes a romantic poem about the abbey.

Amongst other features Patrick must have noticed during his courtship, were the stone-built cottages, on the hill above Woodhouse Grove, where the constant noise of handlooms once earned this area the name, Clattergate. Perhaps the clatter stirred memories of his own early occupation as a handloom weaver in County Down.

There would be nearer memories, too. In his own parish of Hartshead, near Huddersfield, Patrick Brontë had once come to grips with some Luddite rioters. Indeed, one reason for leaving Hartshead, after his marriage, may have been Maria's fear of those violent men.

In *Shirley*, Charlotte Brontë was to use some of her father's stories about the Luddites, who were opposing the introduction of mill machinery which threatened their own livelihood. When she came as governess to the White family at Upperwood House, near Woodhouse Grove, the local wool trade was still largely a cottage industry, but even here the Luddites had turned their attention to some local mills. Even so, the neighbourhood that had first brought her parents together delighted Charlotte. Despite encroachments of industry, it still has oases of natural beauty like Calverley Woods on one side of the river and Cragg Wood on the other. Upperwood House has unfortunately vanished, but on the site there is a preparatory school for Woodhouse Grove (now a public school); it is aptly named Brontë House. Whenever I pass the place I think of the unruly White children who, along with the endless sewing thrust upon her, here gave Charlotte the 'blues' and all too little leisure to enjoy the scenery.

But all that was in the unknown future. As Patrick and Maria's friendship ripened, they would enjoy other jaunts in the neighbourhood.

Esholt Springs was then a lovely spot, and perhaps that was the route they took on the day they went to discuss their wedding arrangements with the rector of Guiseley. Excepting for the first mile or so one could follow that verdant route today and re-live the occasion.

Actually it was a double wedding which graced the church on that December day long ago. First, Maria and her "dear saucy Pat" were united by the Reverend William Morgan; then Patrick performed the same ceremony for Morgan and his bride, Jane Fennell. With Maria and Jane acting as bridesmaids for each other, the double wedding must have bestowed a rare charm on the small side chapel, banishing, one hopes, any feeling of human mortality only too painfully suggested by the monuments impinging on the altar. Yet within nine years, after giving birth to six children, Maria faded from this earthly scene like a spent flower from the Haworth fields she had barely time to appreciate.

Haworth Parsonage, near Keighley, where Patrick lived out an increasingly lonely life until his death in 1861, draws a large number of visitors in these days. Its fascinating contents mark his career—covering successive incumbencies at Hartshead, Thornton near Bradford, and Haworth—as effectively as the brief triumphs and tragic deaths of his famous daughters. Yet imagination is prompt to see Charlotte, Emily and Anne along with brother Branwell, parading round the dining-room table, reciting their youthful poems and stories that foreshadowed *Jane Eyre, Wuthering Heights, The Tenant of Wildfell Hall*, and the rest of an all-too-limited output.

Of Winifred Holtby, another writer who died with her promise only partly fulfilled, Vera Brittain once said, "Death arrested her progress, but did not destroy her work or impair the golden legend that glows round her memory."

Winifred Holtby was born at Rudston House, in the East Riding, on 23rd June 1898. It is an attractive, early Victorian house, set in a spacious garden that fringes the village street. The front bedrooms look east towards the hill-top church and its close companion, the 25-foot megalith that gives the village its name. Other rooms face the apparently limitless wold country whose lineaments achieved for the budding author a kind of personality. Later, these same features—clothed with "silver barley rippling in the wind"—received their due in her first novel, *Anderby Wold*, Anderby being Rudston.

Her parents also had several associations with Beverley. She herself had a great admiration for the Minster and sometimes gave lectures on its architecture and on that of other famous North Country shrines. It is interesting that the man who elucidated the significance of the medieval woodwork in some of those churches, showing it to have been the work of the important Ripon School of Woodcarvers, was a companion of her youthful days at Rudston. He was the late Dr J. S. Purvis, F.S.A., principal of the Borthwick Institute of Historic Research at York. He and his sister once recalled for my benefit some of their joint childhood outings with Winifred, by pony and cart, to Bridlington.

This coastal resort helped to shape the Hardrascliffe of her novels. Even during her time at Somerville College, and later, she loved to spend a holiday here and "sit on the sands . . . ride donkeys, [and] listen to nigger minstrels . . .". There was always one well-loved route homewards; it starts in Bridlington High Street—a charming crescent of Georgian shops and houses—and links up, just outside the town, with Wold Gate. This ancient track clings to the chalk ridges above Boynton, Rudston and Kilham, and therefore leads to the very heart of Winifred Holtby's homeland.

Other local resorts she frequented include Withernsea and Hornsea; and there are many reasons why the River Humber should also have appealed to her. Hereabouts one has left the wold country for Holderness—that large, alluvial plain which has its own seigniory, centred upon Burton Constable Hall. One of the ancient perquisites devolving upon the Lords Paramount of this seigniory is the flotsam and jetsam of the Holderness coastline. In some of her books Winifred Holtby concerned herself with the *human* flotsam and jetsam of these parts.

This made her familiar with the quaint little creeks of Humberside and patches of reclaimed land like Sunk Island, which together form the Leame Estuary of *South Riding*.

Nobody who wishes to trace Winifred Holtby's footsteps can afford to neglect this northern shore of the Humber Estuary, with its curious villages and the two splendid medieval churches at Hedon and Patrington. It is all integral to the pattern of life that she knew and described. Naturally, Hull—the Kingsport of *South Riding*—was also part of that same, variegated pattern. She was by no means the first to rejoice in one of Hull's peculiar place-names, Land of Green Ginger, but she gave it a place in literature by borrowing it for one of her story titles. The sign greets one on passing down Whitefriargate.

Not far away there is an Elizabethan mansion that must have meant much to Winifred Holtby, especially when African problems aroused her sympathies and she began to write *Mandoa, Mandoa*, a book that vigorously champions the cause of coloured South Africa. It is Wilberforce House, in High Street, where William Wilberforce the slave emancipator, was born in 1759. A Wilberforce centenary, celebrating his great victory in the House of Commons, was marked here, two years before her tragic death in 1935. Cottingham, to which her parents had moved in 1918, is now almost a dormitory of Hull, but it was fitting that she was eventually laid to rest in Rudston churchyard, overlooking her own Anderby Wold. A marble book at the head of her grave bears this inscription:

> God give me work till my life shall end
> And life till my work is done.

Often I went long walks alone with him. I can remember a trick he had which puzzled me intensely at the time, of pausing every now and again to listen to some natural sound, such as the rustling of a tree or the singing of a bird, or the murmur of a moorland brook. He would stand quite still as if drinking something in, his expression becoming rapt and attentive. The next moment he would be walking along, laughing and talking as usual, never explaining even to me what it was that had held his attention for those trance-like moments.

These words occur early in the biography of Frederick Delius, written by his devoted sister, Clare. Incidentally, she was prompted to write this biography* by a curious psychic experience, which happened in the household of Charles L. Tweedale, then vicar of Weston, in mid-Wharfedale. I mention this experience because in our youth a friend and I often passed through this secluded village, and always felt an odd vibrancy there, derived in part from the knowledge that its vicar claimed contact with the Beyond. At his church gate he

* *Frederick Delius*, by Clare Delius (Ivor Nicholson and Watson, 1935).

F. W. Elwell's painting of 'elevenses' at the Beverley Arms Hotel

The Captain Cook Monument at Whitby

even provided pamphlets setting forth his visions and intuitions. It was these extramundane contacts which evidently made Tweedale aware that Delius, the great composer then living in France, would soon pass into that other sphere. . . .

The composer's Yorkshire background and experience provide an overture of their own. In it there was a mixture of hope and despair. A joyous hope of a musical career, countered by parental opposition and an attempt to imprison young Frederick in the family woollen business, centred at Bradford.

The parental home, Claremount, off Horton Road, was for young Frederick something of a fantasia. A passion for 'penny dreadfuls', play-acting as Bluebeard or Dick Turpin, and practical jokes resided in the same person who stood listening to heavenly sounds on the surrounding moors and suffered continually from the commercial dictums of an imperious father.

This is no place to follow Delius from those first promptings of his muse to his triumphant *Mass of Life*, but a North Countryman likes to think that the moors and dales of those youthful expeditions helped to formulate that lovely pastorale, "On hearing the first cuckoo in Spring", and other sensuous compositions.

Ilkley Moor is but a few short miles from Bradford. Delius tramped often over its bracken-covered slopes. G. K. Chesterton's Father Brown loved the same wide spaces, but for very different reasons. When Clare Delius married and settled at Stone Gappe in Lothersdale, near Skipton, her brother found there a sympathetic audience for his early pieces, including the opera *Koanga*, also fresh scope for his wanderings.

Stone Gappe had earlier become the Gateshead of *Jane Eyre*. Had not Charlotte Brontë been a despised governess there! These associations awoke in Delius a new interest in the Brontë novels. He once even thought of setting *Wuthering Heights* to music. With this in mind he sometimes strode through the moorland heather to Haworth, the very heart of Brontë-land, and by calling at the Black Bull to sit in Branwell Brontë's favourite carousing chair, probably sought to enter into the very spirit of Heathcliff, the wild man of the moors.

Another trip from Stone Gappe took him and his sister to Skipton Castle, where he was entranced by the Tudor courtyard I have already described, and the pervading 'presence' of Lady Anne Clifford as partly embodied in her spreading yew tree, and her proud monogram repeated on the square fall-pipes.

In a similar sense, the spirit of Delius, soaring into sublime regions, can be said to permeate some of the places mentioned in this book. Thoughts of Yorkshire scenery inspired him continually, even when established in that far-off French village. It was from Yorkshire, too, that solace came when blindness descended on Delius during his last

19

years at Grez-sur-Loing. Eric Fenby, a Scarborough man, became his amanuensis, a rather cool way of saying that in this young disciple from his home county, Delius found the perfect mediator. Clare Delius pays high tribute to his unique colaboration: "It was, I think, one of the most purely selfless actions of which the world has any record, and wherever the music of Delius is loved, there the name of Eric Fenby should be held in reverence."

When news of the master's death reached Bradford in June 1934, the city paid homage by sending a wreath made from the moorland heather and ling, that, along with the song of the cuckoo and curlew, had epitomised his early atunement with nature.

Unknown to Delius, in those last few years, another voice from the North was beginning to set the bells of heaven ringing. A Lancashire girl, this time, who might well have played some Delius pieces at her various piano concerts. Yet her lasting fame was not to be as an outstanding pianist. While working at the Blackburn telephone exchange at 19s. per week, this girl from Higher Walton, near Preston, discovered to her amusement that subscribers were actually ringing through to hear her own lovely voice! Kathleen Ferrier had already sung in the church choir, but was still known mainly as a gifted accompanist.

Subsequent years proved her true vocation, and her rich contralto voice began to draw astonished audiences all over the North-west, from Lytham and Blackpool to Silloth and Carlisle. Her repertoire then ranged from "Thank God for a Garden" to solo parts in *The Messiah* and *Elijah*. At her first broadcast from the Newcastle studio in 1939, she sang old favourites like "Curly Headed Babby" and "The End of a Perfect Day" with such rich tone and depth of feeling that England woke up to the new star in their midst. She was in demand everywhere. One day might see her strolling beside Solway Firth, between concerts, or on the golf links at Lytham, and another day in Suffolk for the Aldeburgh Festival.

In her biography* Winifred Ferrier tells us that during the last war no black-out conditions could keep her from venturing forth for a concert engagement. In that rather terrifying period the people needed her and her glorious renderings as never before. She gave them such songs as Vaughan William's "Silent Noon" and Quilter's "Over the Mountains" also deep draughts of Bach, Beethoven and Brahms. She was singing such songs in Durham even when I was there hastily recording the city's notable architecture in case of damage or destruction by bombs. She was a matchless interpreter of songs sacred or gay, from Elgar's "Dream of Gerontius" to "Keel Row" and "Come you not from Newcastle?" arranged by Benjamin Britten.

Kathleen Ferrier passed away in 1953, at the age of 41, before her

* *The Life of Kathleen Ferrier*, by Winifred Ferrier (Hamish Hamilton, 1955).

work was done. Or was it that newer songs were beckoning her from afar? Sometimes after a busy day I put on one of her records, to hear again that voice of unearthly beauty. But surely one has caught an echo of her mellow, resonant tones in some North Country beck, where the crags hang low and trout linger in the shadows?

Our North Country roll call could never be complete until certain other names were voiced. We should have to find a place for John Dalton, F.R.S., the self-educated Quaker chemist of Eaglesfield, Cumberland, who first propounded the atomic theory; and another place for Adam Sedgwick of Dent, the pioneer geologist. Thomas Chippendale of Otley in Wharfedale would also respond to the summons, from one of his ribbon-back chairs, while Squire Waterton of Walton Hall, near Wakefield, might usher us into his bird sanctuary, England's first. William Wilberforce of Hull and Markington, so eloquent on behalf of slave emancipation, clearly voices his "Adsum", while Chantrey and Henry Moore represent the sculptors, one from Norton near Sheffield, the other from Castleford. There would be many other notable responses, but we cannot wait for more. Others, besides Northerners now deserve a hearing.

17

Some of Our Guests

KINGS and queens were not always the easiest visitors to have in one's neighbourhood. The people of York trembled when Henry VIII rode into their city after the Pilgrimage of Grace: he was thoroughly displeased with their support of that rebellion and showed his royal displeasure by side-stepping the civic reception committee assembled at Micklegate Bar, entering, instead, by Walmgate Bar, where nobody expected him. So the obsequious speeches awaiting his arrival were still-born.

By contrast, one of our English monarchs who *did* find the North to his liking was Richard III. He always spoke of Scarborough as his "beloved town" and in 1485 granted a charter to the burgesses declaring Scarborough, Falsgrave and the Manor of Northstead to be "one Intire County of itself . . . and altogether separate from the said County of York for ever . . .". Although Richard's high-falutin grant lasted only one year (being countermanded on the accession of Henry VII) it had repercussions felt even in modern times. Northstead Manor, which Richard had bought for his own use, then stood on the fringe of Scarborough. After Richard's eclipse, this pleasant bit of property passed to the Crown. Peasholm Park and Northstead Manor Gardens occupy the site today, but since 1844 the manor, now mythical, achieved the status of the better-known Chiltern Hundreds. By applying for its stewardship as an office under the Crown, an M.P. can surrender his seat in Parliament. The last person appointed to this Scarborough sinecure, provided indirectly by Richard III, was Sir Anthony Eden, in 1957.

King Richard's House, overlooking the town's harbour, is a splendid Tudor building which traditionally became Richard's quarters when, as Duke of Gloucester, his ships were being provisioned. Richard was then Lord High Admiral for his brother, Edward IV.

Yorkshire again found favour with 'the sailor Duke' by providing him with a bride, Anne, younger daughter of Warwick the Kingmaker. This alliance gave him the freedom of Middleham Castle in Wensleydale and Sheriff Hutton Castle, near York. There is no need to follow his career further. For him, as king, the curtains soon fell. Yet, despite all the calumny heaped upon the 'crookback king', Yorkshire folk always spoke well of him. Last century a grotesque piece of sculpture portraying Richard as a devil incarnate, was fixed beside the entrance of the Scarborough house that bears his name. This has recently aroused the ire of the Fellowship of the Wild Boar, a society pledged to vindicate Richard in the eyes of posterity. If the society can prove Richard's innocence of the murder of the Princes in the Tower, nobody will be better pleased, I imagine, than the people of the shire in which he found some happiness.

On moving forward eighty years or so, we see a forlorn queen leaving Scotland to thrust herself on the "good graces" of her cousin, Elizabeth I. But the northern counties had been forewarned. Mary Stuart was to be kept under strict surveillance. So down she came through our beautiful countryside, which was perhaps a mockery to her, for she who loved the open spaces soon realised that she was as much Elizabeth's prisoner as guest. At Carlisle, even hare-hunting in the neighbouring fields was at length forbidden Mary, as it was feared that her skilled horsemanship might one day take her 'out of bounds'. Bolton Castle in Wensleydale held her captive for six months, and then they took her to Sheffield Manor—another stepping stone on the way to execution at Fotheringhay.

Somebody once spoke of Mary Stuart's "power to trouble the ages with thoughts of her". Certainly many places in the North treasure some memento or memory of the sad queen without a throne. Her aura still rests upon Lowther Castle, Workington Hall and Yanwath Hall, which marked her sorrowful progress through the Lake counties. Her demure ghost is one of the legends attaching to Walburn Hall, near Richmond, where she is supposed to have been allowed a short respite from the thick gaoler walls of Bolton Castle.

Mary's sojourn at Walburn Hall is focused in an upstairs room that bears her name. Its shallow bay window is fitted with a seat where one may visualise her bent over her embroidery frame. A characteristic sample of her work was left behind on her hasty removal from Bolton Castle, on 26th January 1569. Worked in coloured silks, it shows an Elizabethan feast with a lutanist, who may represent David Rizzio, in attendance, and many subsidiary themes—from birds and rabbits to butterflies and an outsize caterpillar—which fill corners and odd spaces.

After being shown this and other Stuart heirlooms some years ago in the home of a Harrogate lady, I cannot but wonder whether some of that curious embroidery took form and colour as Mary sat in this sunlit window. All that tradition vouchsafes, however, is that after staying at Walburn for a short time, Mary escaped by squeezing through the centre casement (she must have been slim!) and dropping to a waiting saddle below. It was one of her several brief escapes while in the North.

Charles I had a mixed reception when he came north. We have already seen him in hiding at Newcastle. He certainly had friends in York, where he stayed at the King's Manor, opposite Bootham Bar, and issued broadsheets from royal presses purposely set up nearby in St William's College. A provocative introduction to the Civil Wars! Rather than pursue that familiar story, however, I would prefer to give his queen, Henrietta Maria, some of the limelight.

In the course of time, Charles realised what a good wife and helpmate he had in this gay princess from France. True, she was far too ready to meddle in political matters. But as the Civil War drew nearer, she rallied to his cause, and when Charles was short of cash for munitions she even took some of the Crown Jewels to Holland in order to raise money on them. On returning, her ship laden with "war-like stores" from Holland, encountered a storm and was forced by Admiral Batten's guns to put in at Bridlington Quay. During that storm she had calmed her ladies by saying, "Comfort yourselves; Queens of England are never drowned." But her trials were not yet over. The house in which the Queen found refuge beside Bridlington Quay, was pounded with cannon balls during the night. She spent the rest of the nocturnal hours clad only in her négligé, in a ditch nearby, having first run back to the lodging to rescue her pet dog.

Henrietta Maria could be generous as well as brave. When the captain of the ship which had aimed his guns "at her very chamber" was later captured by the Royalists and condemned to death, she warmly protested: "But I have forgiven him all that, and as he did not kill me he shall not be put to death on my account."

Next day she went with her retinue to Boynton Hall, staying there for a whole fortnight. The house is beautifully situated at the foot of the Wolds, and the royal party will have made their way to it by Wold Gate, that ancient track running inland from Bridlington. The hall grounds are prettily watered by the Gypsey Race, the chalk stream that has the peculiarity of disappearing underground for long periods, leaving a dry watercourse above ground. Though Henrietta Maria could hardly have realised it, the ditch that 'couched' her so uncomfortably on the previous night marked the seaward end of the Gypsey Race during one of its dry spells.

There was a certain irony in the fact that she sojourned at Boynton Hall. It was the seat of the Stricklands, one of whom, in his capacity as ambassador to the States General in Holland, had been trying to thwart her money-raising plans. Fortunately for her, however, he and his brother, Sir William Strickland, were absent during the Queen's visit to Boynton Hall. Despite the family's well-known Parliamentarian allegiances, Henrietta Maria held court here, and when the Strickland ladies put out all the family plate in her honour—was she not still their Queen?—the resourceful little woman, who had learned to take storms and bombardments in her stride, delivered her own broadside. She would 'borrow' the plate, she winsomely declared, as "dear Charles" was still needing funds; a portrait of herself would be sent as bond for the loan.

The fact that I saw this very portrait, a lovely study by Cornelius Janssens, hanging in the Queen's Bedroom at Boynton a few years ago, testifies to the unduly long term of that enforced loan! Did not Bridlington people say, sometimes, that she had a witchery of her own?

On 5th March 1643 the Queen left Boynton to join her husband at York, describing herself on this occasion as "her she-majesty generalissima"—not a bad title for one who was now constantly manoeuvring on Charles' behalf and replenishing his coffers for him. And there we must leave her indomitable Highness.

Oliver Cromwell must have slept in as many beds as Elizabeth I is said to have done, all over England. But at least two places in the North Country gave him a rough night.

Prior to an engagement with Royalist forces at Preston on 17th August 1648, Cromwell halted at Stonyhurst, near Clitheroe. He could hardly have found a more delightful spot. The ancestral home of the Shireburn family had not then acquired its twin eagle towers, or the well-known rectangular ponds in the spacious grounds. Its days as a Roman Catholic college, with monks drifting through the grounds reading their breviaries, and precious things—such as the Book of Hours Mary Stuart had with her at Fotheringhay—treasured in the college museum, were far ahead. Yet Stonyhurst must have been a charming, hospitable place even before those developments. Of all its softly furnished beds, however, Cromwell would trust none, through fear of assassination. This was a Papist house, after all. He therefore chose to spend the night lying on an oak table, pulled into the middle of the room, his sword and pistols beside him as further protection. The same thing happened, apparently, the following night, after his men had routed the Royalists, and Stonyhurst was again requisitioned into service.

His experience here probably reminded him of an earlier occasion when, on the night after defeating the Royalists at Marston Moor, he met his petticoat match. This was at Ripley Castle, near Harrogate. His Ironsides were quartered elsewhere in Ripley village, and probably spent a more comfortable night than their leader, for the mistress of the castle, bristling with all her family's Royalist pride, sat through till daylight confronting Cromwell, slumped on the other side of a stout table, with a brace of cocked pistols, lest he should attempt to break the brief nocturnal truce.

The North gave Bonnie Prince Charlie and his Highlanders a reception both hot and cold. They had crossed the Esk into England on 8th November 1745, causing so much consternation in Carlisle, that a couple of local clergy were posted with a large telescope on the cathedral tower, to keep an eye on the rebels' movements. The Young Pretender was definitely not wanted. Lancaster, on the contrary, gave him a welcome on his march south, and later, during his dismal retreat. At Preston, the gay debonair figure won many female hearts, and as he left the town the people cheered him onward with the tune, "The King shall have his own again". When he returned beaten, not many days later, a band of strolling musicians echoed other sentiments by playing, "Hie thee, Charlie, home again!"

Manchester's Jacobites were jubilant when their idol arrived in the town. He lodged at "Mr Dickenson's house in Market Street Lane", won the support of important citizens like John Byrom (author of the carol, "Christians Awake") and rejoiced in the formation of a Manchester Regiment to accompany him on his march to London. After the rebels' retreat from Derby, the regiment marched back with them as far as Carlisle. The price of that Manchester welcome was grim. Officers of the regiment were sent for trial to London. The heads of two of them were later returned to Manchester to be exposed on the Exchange. They were a warning that in future Manchester folk had better be more careful to whom they opened their hearts.

At many other times, of course, royalty have enthroned themselves in the affections of northern people. A tally of their sojourns in the North would make a large volume. Here I can but choose two very dissimilar occasions.

On one notable day during the 1914-18 war, George V and Queen Mary visited the Wear shipyards to encourage the workers in their tasks, made doubly difficult by current conditions. A local record of that day's events includes a charming photograph, showing His Majesty bending down to chat with an urchin-like figure wearing cloth cap and grimy clothing evidently cut down from one of his dad's old suits. The lad was a humble rivet-heater at Laing's shipyard.

When the Princess Royal made her home in Yorkshire, first at Goldsborough Hall, later at Harewood House, the county came to know and appreciate a very gracious lady.* As a wedding present the York city fathers gave her and Lord Lascelles a replica of one of the city's finest pieces of civic plate—a gold cup made in 1672-3 by a local craftsman, Marmaduke Best. This gift was fully in accordance with our North Country manner of saying, "Cum thi ways in".

What a great variety of "off-cummed 'uns" have in some way or other enriched our northern shires! An eminent philosopher (whose name eludes me) once penned a verse beginning, "I am part of all I have met." That can apply to regions as well as persons. Let us now summon a few of those who left a lasting impression on some part of the wide region under review. Artists, authors, poets, reformers—a rich heritage indeed have they and a host of others left behind!

The mid-western reaches of our area will never be quite the same as they were before George Fox came with his shining "inward light", and, it should be added, his famous "leather britches which frightens all ye Priests and Professors". To Quakers all over the world those moorland stretches are known as the 1652 country, for that was the year in which Fox began to spread his message based on there being "something of God in every man". Is it by chance that the 1652 country, to be studded soon after with humble meeting houses for silent worship, remains one of the loveliest and unspoilt parts of England? This region spreads between the Craven Hills, Morecambe Bay, the Furness Fells and the Howgill Fells, covering altogether about 400 square miles.

Despite opposition, confiscation of property, imprisonment, torture, George Fox and the early Friends blazed a trail which it is fascinating to follow even today. The trail would take us first to Pendle Hill, where Fox had his remarkable vision, then to Firbank Fell and Preston Patrick. Sedbergh was another milestone; here, Sir John Otway of Ingmire Hall, although a Papist Justice, often refused to imprison Quaker farmers lest the hay harvest should suffer.

At Dent some of the Friends would one day be at their usual place amongst the famous 'Knitters of Dent', who worked in the evenings by rushlight, and another in prison for their simple though searching faith.

To Swarthmore Hall, near Ulverston, George Fox came while

* Only those who met the Princess Royal personally, as I once did when photographing Harewood House, could fully appreciate her womanly charm and kindness.

preaching in the neighbourhood and converted Margaret Fell. Years later, after the death of her husband, Margaret Fell married Fox. More persecution followed. In 1660 Fox was arrested at Swarthmore and taken over the Morecambe Sands to Lancaster Gaol. He was lucky to escape the treatment meted out to Miles Hubbersty, another Quaker, who was "destroyed by a wilful, wicked man, being the Carter" (or guide), wrote Fox, "who claped his hook in his [Hubbersty's] cloak and drew him from the friends near 100 yards so that he was strangled and drowned".

George Fox's journal is full of such trials. After challenging "Priest Bowles" in York Minster, he was thrown down the steps into the street. At Walney Island, near Barrow, he was attacked with "clubs and staves and fishing poles". While in gaol at Carlisle, "Great Ladies (as they were called) came haughtily to see the man that they said was to die. . . ." When he returned to Carlisle two years later and preached at the market cross against "all coxening and cheating" the magistrates' wives threatened to "pluck the hair from off my head".

John Wesley also suffered while seeking to convert the north from godless ways. It is astonishing to read that when he came to Alnmouth on the Northumberland coast in 1748 he found the place "a small sea-port town famous for all kinds of wickedness". Pretty Alnmouth must have shrunk in size and in other ways, since then! At Felton, in the Coquet Valley, he recorded that "very few seemed to understand anything of the matter" (i.e. his preaching). But Newcastle turned on him. He was preaching in the quarter that produced "The Keel Row", which begins:

> As I came through Sandgate,
> Through Sandgate, through Sandgate,
> As I came through Sandgate,
> I heard a lassie sing:
>
> O weel may the keel row,
> The keel row, the keel row,
> Weel may the keel row,
> That my laddie's in.

Echoing the song's first refrain, Wesley confided to his diary, under the date, 30th May 1742, "At seven I walked down to Sandgate, the poorest and most contemptible part of the town. . . ." His pulpit was an exterior staircase at the old guildhall. The mob would have assaulted him but for the prompt action of a local fishwife of commendable proportions. Putting her brawny arms round Wesley, she cried, "If ony yen o' ye lift up another hand to touch ma canny man, ayl floor ye direckly." Her threat saved the day for Wesley.

Henry and Mary Bell of Portington Hall, in the East Riding, were amongst Wesley's many North Country friends. When their own vicar of neighbouring Eastrington denounced Wesley and his teaching, the Bells stoutly supported the man who had frequently been their guest. After staying overnight at Portington on 29th June 1790, the Bells lent him their coach for his journey homewards, via the notorious Whitgift ferry over the Ouse, to Epworth in Lincolnshire. On that occasion Wesley also borrowed the family's travelling box, or trunk. When I visited Portington fifteen years ago, that box, and John Wesley's silver-topped cane, which he left behind as a keepsake, were still treasured by the Wilberforce-Bell family.

The Wilberforce connection reminds me of another Wesley anecdote. During student days at Pocklington School, William Wilberforce had become so enamoured of Wesley's teaching, that the future statesman's grandfather expostulated, "If Billy turns Methodist he shall not have a sixpence of mine!" It is comforting to learn that Wesley's last letter was written to Wilberforce, commending his campaign on behalf of the slaves.

York greeted Wesley with brickbats, and many a fair hearing. His diary entry for Thursday, 14th July 1757, reads: "I resolved to preach in the Square once more. One egg was thrown and some bits of dirt, but this did not hinder a large congregation from taking earnest heed to what was spoken of Christ." Most of his large gatherings met in a room overlooking the old Pump Yard, off the Shambles. They were often too large for the place, and more than once Wesley remarked that the room "felt as hot as an oven".

His reception at Whitby was such that a few years after his first visit in 1761, when he preached on the Abbey Plain, his followers could assemble peacefully in a meeting house at the bottom of the famous Church Stairs. On Christmas Eve 1787 part of the East Cliff collapsed, rendering the meeting house unsafe. A more commodious chapel was built nearby in the following year. When Wesley came to conduct the opening services, which lasted three days, the building was still incomplete; his diary states that "the unfinished galleries, having yet no fronts, were frightful to look upon. It is the most curious meeting house we have in England." He might have added, as further testimony to local Methodist zeal, that lined along those gallery fronts were several people whose legs dangled over the edge!

It was in 1797 that the son of a certain London barber made a momentous expedition into Yorkshire. That barber had sometimes sold his son's youthful paintings to shop customers for a shilling a piece, but Joseph Mallord Turner was now on the track of real fame. He liked what he saw of our fine scenery, and on a later visit he returned as guest of Squire Fawkes of Farnley Hall in mid-Wharfedale. This visit was as notable for the history of British art as for Turner himself. The association between squire and artist ripened into a warm mutual friendship, and for the next twenty years—in fact until Fawkes' death in 1825—Farnley was always 'open house' to Turner. In this neighbourhood he accomplished much important work; his great champion, John Ruskin, the first volume of whose *Modern Painters* (1843) is primarily a eulogy of Turner, regarded his Yorkshire subjects as "on the whole the chief tutors of Turner's mind".

Farnley Hall is a fine Tudor house with a sumptuous Georgian wing, It stands in wooded parkland high above the market town of Otley, and the work which Turner did for his patron—paintings of the house itself, its heirlooms, its grounds, also of the Farnley countryside—help one to visualise his sojourns there. Some of the paintings are fortunately still at Farnley.

A diary kept by Squire Fawkes's second wife describes the journeys through the neighbouring countryside when the family accompanied Turner in his quest for fresh subjects. One such expedition, in July 1816, was "miserably wet", yet despite the unfavourable conditions Turner sketched Skipton Castle, Browsholme Hall, the Trough of Bowland and Gordale Scar at Malham. Another companion on this trip was John Parker of Browsholme, one of whose descendants, Colonel Robert Parker, is the present owner of that hall.

Turner revelled in the North Country scene, as so many of his paintings testify, and it is noticeable that in these paintings he used comparatively little licence to achieve his effects. His study of The Strid, in Bolton Woods, Wharfedale, for example, captures all the grotesqueness of this famous spot without resorting to fancy. This also applies to his coastal subjects. *Scarborough Town and Castle* painted about 1809 from the approximate site of the present South Cliff bathing pool, has nothing extravagant either in form or features; the only novelty for us today is to see three-masted sailing ships riding at anchor around the harbour.

But of course Turner could and did use artistic licence if it suited his purpose. When a thunderstorm broke over Otley Chevin during one of his visits to Farnley, Hawksworth Fawkes, the squire's son, watched the storm with the artist from the terrace. Afterwards he described what happened. "All this time," said Hawksworth, "he was making notes of its form and colour on the back of a letter. I proposed some better drawing block, but he said it did very well. He was absorbed— he was entranced. There was the storm, rolling and sweeping and shafting out its lightning over the Yorkshire hills. Presently the storm passed, and he finished. 'There, Hawkey', said he. 'In two years you will see this again and call it *Hannibal Crossing the Alps*.'" Sure enough, visitors to the Royal Academy Exhibition of 1812 saw the Chevin drama metamorphosed into the Alpine epic. That picture is today on view in the Tate Gallery.

Turner's excursions into the Lake District produced many fine studies. One of his pictures shows a coach party coming ashore at Hest Bank, after having survived the treacherous sands of Morecambe Bay. The Lakeland hills provide an almost Elysian background. The wonderful sunsets over Morecambe Bay were an ever-changing study for him, while he stayed at Heysham. In his painting of Coniston Lake and the Old Man he casts a sidelong glance, as it were, at Ruskin's house, Brantwood, on the lake shore. Memorable too, is his rendering of Buttermere and Fleetwith Pike as rainbow follows storm.

Lady Anne Clifford would have been charmed to see her castle at Brougham so sympathetically treated, and to his early study of Norham Castle, that fine Border fortress mentioned in Scott's *Marmion*, Turner is said to have attributed his success in life. Yet that comment might surely include many more of his North Country subjects—Dunstanborough Castle, for example, and a fascinating study of Newcastle, looking down the Tyne, with a soldier 'on leave' in the foreground group; also some of his other paintings that illustrate Walter Scott's romantic verses. One of these shows Melrose Abbey "by the pale moonlight"; another, Rokeby in Teesdale, where, "twixt rock and river grew, a dismal grove of sable yew".

But Turner always remembered Wharfedale, where the Fawkes family had befriended him, with greatest affection. They were indeed his lodestar. After Walter Fawkes's death, Farnley Hall saw him no more. Yet, according to Ruskin, "he could never speak of the Wharfe, about whose shores the shadows of old thoughts and long-lost delights hung like morning mist, but his voice faltered".

In 1871, after establishing a fine reputation as art critic and lecturer in London and Oxford, John Ruskin bought Brantwood on the eastern shore of Coniston Water. His coming made a lasting impression on the Lake District. Octavia Hill and Canon Rawnsley, two of the three persons who helped to found the National Trust, were amongst Ruskin's close friends, and he would have rejoiced to know how much Lakeland property was to be acquired later by the now ubiquitous Trust.

Brantwood became a focal point of culture. Here, Ruskin's collection of Thomas Bewick drawings and woodcuts were offset by many Turners, supported by some of his own local paintings and various geological specimens from the neighbourhood. Apart from the Turners, these items remain at Brantwood, together with pictures by Professor W. G. Collingwood, a noted antiquary, and once Ruskin's secretary, also beautiful examples of furniture that exhibited Ruskin's love of fine craftsmanship. Here he also dreamed his dreams of a social paradise, addressed a monthly letter to the workmen of England, and equipped his dining room with seven lancet windows illustrating his own masterpiece, the *Seven Lamps of Architecture*.

Brantwood, now a centre for adult education, enables anybody sufficiently interested, to share Ruskin's enthusiasms. They can walk in his lakeside garden, which has its own little harbour; see his boat, the *Jumping Jenny*, specially built for him nearby; and follow nature trails through the 200-acre grounds which lead to the top of the fells behind the house.

And that is not all. Across the lake, in Coniston village, Ruskin Museum continues the story of his many interests. One amusing item is the rock harmonicon, or stone dulcimer, made from Skiddaw stones for this great nature lover by a Mr Till of Keswick. Given to the museum by Mrs Arthur Severn—who, with her husband, lived at Brantwood as companions for Ruskin—the musical stones ring with a peculiar cadence. One wonders how many times the bearded old sage of Brantwood struck from them a music, that, for him, echoed the very heart of his latter-day homeland.

M. H. Spielmann, biographer of Kate Greenaway, was one of Ruskin's many visitors. On Spielmann's first visit, Ruskin evidently took him into his study to see his stones, his drawings and books, keeping to the last the things he loved best of all—his Scott MSS. One would have thought the Turners were Ruskin's first choice, but the above remark is sufficient reminder that the Scottish bard frequently raided the North Country for some of his best material. He even found *personal* romance south of the Border, while surrendering himself to the magic of the Roman Wall. He stayed at Gilsland, near Carlisle in July 1797, and fell in love with Charlotte Carpenter, a dark-eyed refugee from the French terror, popping the question—so it is believed —at the traditional Popping Stone. The answer was evidently so satisfactory that the mutual pledge was sealed in local style at the riverside Kissing Bush, and the pair were married on Christmas Eve that same year in Carlisle Cathedral.

Gilsland also gave Scott a character for *Guy Mannering*. This was Tib Mumps, the landlady of an inn from which, it was rumoured, no traveller of means ever emerged! To Scott such tales were meat and drink. At Netherby, not far away, he found his Young Lochinvar, and over at Kielder in Northumberland, his Strong Man of Keelder, whose cairn-like grave of "ancient size" is now overshadowed, with the rest of the village, by the Forestry Commissions's vast plantations.

All over the North, in fact, Scott encountered people who told him their folk tales and superstitions. And what places there were to exploit in this romantic vein: the Roman Wall at Sewingshields and Thirlwall; Norham and Raby Castles, Durham Cathedral, and Heathpool deep in the Cheviots. The Hen Hole at Heathpool echoed with eerie legends that emerged later, suitably embellished, in Scott's *Minstrelsy of the Scottish Border*. He first heard these legends while "snugly settled" in a farmer's house about six miles from Wooler; and a very pleasant welcome he received thereabouts, as one of his letters makes plain: "Out of the brooks . . . we pull trouts of half a yard in length. . . . My uncle drinks the whey as I do ever since I understood it was brought to his bedside every morning at six by a very pretty dairymaid."

In the preparation of *Rokeby* and *Ivanhoe* Scott drew freely from the Yorkshire scene. Barnard Castle with its beautiful surroundings acted upon Sir Walter like a magnet. The year 1809 had seen the beginning of an affectionate intimacy between himself and John S. B. Morritt of Rokeby. And when, a few months after his first visit there, Scott found another poem necessary to help complete the purchase of his Scottish mansion, Abbotsford, he turned instinctively to friendly Rokeby.

The poem was outlined with the aid of Morritt, Rokeby and its environs were to provide the setting, and the Civil Wars of the reign of Charles I the story. Morritt spread the wealth of local lore before the master, and back at Abbotsford, while workmen were still noisily busy there, *Rokeby* began to take poetic form.

On one of his 'copy-hunting' excursions to the same district Scott said he wanted 'a good robber's cave and an old church of the right sort'. Like a magician, Morritt soon provided both. They drove to Brignall Woods, and Scott duly found the cave later associated in the poem with Guy Denzil. And a wonderful spot it is, in the grounds of Mortham Tower, once part of the Rokeby estate. They found the necessary church in the now-ruined Abbey of Egglestone; this was chosen for the culminating tragedy of the story.

Scott's footsteps are again easily followed in the "district of merry England watered by the Don"—a district which in the days of Richard Lion Heart was covered by a large forest. This was the land of Wamba the Jester, and that delightful character, the jolly clerk of Copmanhurst.

The principal scenes in *Ivanhoe* were set between Sheffield and Doncaster, though industry has since deprived the area of its former appeal. Morritt again came to the novelist's aid. Scott had written, "Do you know of a striking ancient castle . . . called Coningsburgh? I once flew past it in a small coach when its round tower and flying buttresses had a most romantic effect in the morning dawn." It was immediately identified by his Rokeby friend, so Scott drove down to this South Yorkshire village, stayed at the Sprotborough Boathouse inn, and soon found that Conisborough Castle fulfilled his artistic requirements.

In the course of *Ivanhoe* Scott mentions several other places that can be located in the same county. There is Rievaulx Abbey, where Prior Aymer plays his part, and Temple Newsam, presented as Templestowe. And the romance terminates with the wedding of Rowena and Wilfred in "the most august of temples, the noble minster of York".

On its publication, *Ivanhoe* immediately became a best-seller. It won admiration from a multitude of readers to whom some of the author's Scottish novels had not then greatly appealed. The North Country south of the Border, had again become as clay in a potter's hands.

Of very different vintage are the works of Charles Dickens, who often came north with his nose to the ground for a good story. In *Two Idle Apprentices* Dickens describes a visit to Wigton, Cumberland, where both he and Wilkie Collins prance in spirit around the town pump, and well they might, for this was once considered the 'boss' or centre of the world! By their day the pump was barren of water, but the tradition still lingered that by walking around it three times a man would gain *all knowledge*. Since then, the wise old pump has found a new home at Highmoor Hall.

In 1857 Dickens found Carlisle "congenially and delightfully idle. Something in the way of public amusement had happened last month, and something else was going to happen before Christmas; and in the meantime, there was a lecture on India for those who liked it." However, "on market morning Carlisle woke amazingly . . .". This was Dickens in his best playful mood.

His friendship with Charles Smithson brought him a harvest of good things. Smithson lived at Easthorpe Hall, near Malton, which was built as a dower house for Castle Howard by Carr of York. Smithson, a lawyer, had frequently joined Dickens's family circle in London. He was the "professional friend" mentioned in the preface to *Nicholas Nickleby*, who had assisted Dickens in a "pious fraud" by supplying the bogus letter of introduction that led, eventually, to the exposure of the Yorkshire schools and their infamous masters.

Dickens visited Easthorpe many times and in 1843 he brought his wife. One can imagine Smithson welcoming them here and congratulating Dickens on the terrific social impact made by the recently published *Nicholas Nickleby*. Within a few months of its publication the number of boys at the Bowes schools alone fell dramatically from 800 to 20. A terrace designed about 1926 for Lord Grimthorpe stretched along the south side of Easthorpe. In Dickens's time there was only a field here, but the chestnut tree under which he wrote part of *Martin Chuzzlewit* still flourishes in the garden. The house itself, unfortunately, perished by fire in 1971.

The golden sandstone of the building blended well with a fine group of trees that form an arc round the south garden and clothe the slopes that descend towards the Derwent valley. Dickens probably had

Storrs Hall Hotel, Windermere: the causeway where black boys were once smuggled ashore

Bowland, near Slaidburn, West Yorkshire

The Wishing Rocks, Brimham, Nidderdale

these trees, and others in the park at Castle Howard, in mind when, soon after this visit, he wrote to another friend: "O heaven! such green woods as I was rambling among down in Yorkshire, when I was getting that [*Martin Chuzzlewit*] done last July! For days and weeks we never saw the sky but through green boughs; and all day long I cantered over such soft moss and turf, that the horse's feet scarcely made a sound upon it. . . . We performed some madnesses there in the way of forfeits, picnics, rustic games, inspection of ancient monasteries at midnight, when the moon was shining, that would have gone to your heart, and as Mr. Weller says, 'come out on the other side'." It is delightful to think of Dickens in this hilarious mood at Kirkham Abbey and Malton Priory, two of the monasteries in question.

Because of its familiarity, that fateful trip to the Barnard Castle district, in search of evidence that later appeared in *Nicholas Nickleby* does not warrant much comment here. It was on the night of 31st January 1838 that Dickens and his companion, Hablot K. Browne, climbed stiffly from the London coach at Greta Bridge in Teesdale and thawed themselves before "a most blazing fire" at the 'George'. Next morning Boz and Phiz left the inn (now a private house) by post-chaise for Barnard Castle and the beginning of their adventure.

The Dotheboys Hall of *Nicholas Nickleby* is a two-storeyed stone house at the moorland edge of Bowes village, 4 miles from Barnard Castle. When I first visited Bowes, many years ago, sightseers were severely discouraged at this house because of the notoriety it had acquired as the original of the Boys' Academy run by Wackford Squeers. Little from the time of Dickens's visit can now be seen here, except the pump in the back yard, but a copper-kettle supposed to have been used for porridge-making at Dotheboys Hall, and some exercise books from another disreputable academy at Cotherstone nearby, are preserved at Bowes Museum, Barnard Castle's great 'temple' of art and folk-lore.

One picturesque link with that momentous trip into Teesdale disappeared about forty years ago. It was Thomas Humphrey's clock shop which had suggested the title of the author's next literary venture, *Master Humphrey's Clock*. It stood on an island site at Amen Corner in Barnard Castle and was a gossip centre such as Dickens loved. Humphrey was one of those who put him on the track of Shaw's Academy, the supposed original of Dotheboys Hall. When the shop was demolished the Bowes Museum rescued among other items a mandrel lathe used by Thomas Humphrey and a grandfather clock of his own making.

Dickens and Browne broke their homeward journey at York, which has many associations with the insatiable novelist. As Dickens was a swift worker, some of the more exciting episodes in *Nicholas Nickleby* may have already taken shape in his mind when he first stepped into the King's Manor, as the guest of Dr John Camidge, organist at the Minster.

The King's Manor is of monastic origin, but takes its name (see pages 253, 294) from Charles I's residence here just before the Civil War. From here, Dickens and Browne went over to divine service at the Minster. Then, after listening entranced to "the deep organ's bursting heart throb through the shivering air", they were joined by Camidge, who led them on an explanatory tour of the great Gothic interior, which was just recovering from the disastrous effects of Jonathan Martin's fire of 1829. Eventually, over walnuts and wine at the King's Manor, Camidge told them one of the legends concerning the Five Sisters Window. It was this story that, given new form, later appeared in *Nicholas Nickleby*. In consequence, many visitors at the Minster, even today, believe Dickens's romantic account to be true.

The late T. P. Cooper, a local antiquary, contended that Richard Chicken of York was the original Micawber. The novelist's brother, Alfred Lamert Dickens, was employed as an engineer in York during the great railway boom. As Chicken worked for a time under the younger Dickens in his Micklegate office, it seems more than likely that some account of his foibles and his continual tragi-comic appeals for money should reach the ears of the novelist. Chicken's career, distributed pathetically between the York Theatre Royal, the diocesan registry, the railway office and the workhouse, certainly creates a picture of one who was always "waiting for something to turn up".

Perhaps the Whitby district is least often associated with Dickens's trips to the North, though, judging by a few letters and local anecdotes, it made a lasting impression on his receptive mind. In the spring of 1844 he left London to attend the funeral of Charles Smithson at Malton Priory, and then gladly accepted an invitation to spend a few days with Lord Normanby at Mulgrave Castle. Mulgrave, with its woods and sea-views, must have proved a wonderful panacea for Dickens in his recent bereavement. Indeed, it is recorded that he was so delighted with the prospect from the "Quarterdeck", a landscaped 'platform' facing the sea, that he actually "danced on the green of the velvety lawn".

From the present eighteenth-century castle Dickens would look out upon Whitby and much of the rugged coastline to north and south. This view is among the finest in Yorkshire, and Lord Normanby eagerly assumed the role of guide for his exuberant guest. One of their trips was to Staithes, of Captain Cook fame. They visited Whitby Abbey, but I have little doubt that with his remarkable sense of place Dickens revelled mostly in Church Street and its architectural oddities. Threading its way through the heart of old Whitby, this street, redolent of Captain Cook and the North Sea whalers, is still very much of a vintage piece—despite recent changes.

Lord Normanby and his companion baited and lunched at the 'White Horse and Griffin' near the pocket-size town hall in Church Street. Of this ancient hostelry, Dickens wrote that it was "up a back yard and oyster-shell grottoes were the only view from the best private room". The grottoes have disappeared, along with the griffin portion of the inn's name, but an old-world air largely prevails.

Surely those neighbouring back yards still harbour a smuggler or two, or a sailor hiding from the press gang! Sometimes I like to give rein to impossible fancy and see Captain Cook and Charles Dickens (who loved ships anyway) walking arm-in-arm and chatting animatedly from their different coigns of vantage, along this venerable street of the towns' bygone jet-workers. Another who might hail them, through the alchemy of his own caprice, is that master of whimsy, the Oxford don and mathematician, who, as Lewis Carroll, could write a piece of nonsense verse about this very street, which terminates in

> . . . that awful stair
> That soars from earth to upper air,
> Where rich and poor alike must climb,
> And walk the treadmill for a time.

The "awful stair" was, of course, the flight of 199 steps leading from Church Street to St Mary's Church and the abbey. After pacing up and down this "treadmill" himself, one day, he seems to have rested on the beach and added a few more episodes to the *Alice* stories. . . .

On leaving Daresbury in Cheshire, the writer's father had settled at Croft Spa, near Darlington, as incumbent of its fine old church beside the River Tees. Though Charles Lutwidge Dodgson, then a boy of 12, had not yet assumed the mantle of Lewis Carroll, the ferment began to show in a whimsical magazine, *Under the Rectory Umbrella*, he wrote for the amusement of his brothers and sisters.

To trace the metamorphic process farther, as the years sped by, one could follow him to Hull, where he had relations, and thence to neighbouring Beverley, where a small standing rabbit wearing a satchel caught his eye in St Mary's Church and gave him the idea for the White Rabbit of Alice's Wonderland. We have already seen how Sunderland's walrus exhibit inspired his verses about the Walrus and the Carpenter. Then there were the Whitby experiences, shared in part by his first illustrator, George du Maurier.

But there is little doubt that the first seeds of genius had begun to germinate at Croft Spa. In another of his family magazines, called *Mischmasch*, episodes and verses occurred which later appeared in *Through the Looking Glass* and *Alice in Wonderland*. The child had indeed begun to reveal himself as father to the man.

Another who wove magical spells out of North Country scenes, for children of any age, was Beatrix Potter. What the real Alice was for Carroll, Noel, the sickly son of her former governess, was for the young Beatrix—a recipient of delightful stories born in an author's glowing imagination. Later, other children shared the young Kensington girl's stories, sent to them in letters illustrated with her own drawings. But Peter Rabbit, Squirrel Nutkin who danced up and down "like a sunbeam", and all the rest of this animal fraternity came to birth, not in a select quarter of London, but in the Lake District, where Beatrix spent many youthful holidays.

Some of her sketches were of Derwentwater and St Herbert's Island. Red squirrels are still to be seen hereabouts. Dick Gill, that old ferryman of Nichol End, who took passengers across the lake to Keswick or St Herbert's Island, once told me how red squirrels often frolicked into his own boat-shed; they must surely have been related to Beatrix Potter's squirrels who loaded their rafts with nuts gathered on the same lake shore, and then ferried them over to the island!

In later years, Beatrix Potter forsook London altogether and bought Hill Top, a seventeenth-century house at Sawrey, between Windermere and Hawkshead. And here the little animal people grew in number, popping in and out of her own garden and in the fields nearby. When at length her stories found a publisher, the English nursery soon began to resound to the chatter of such creations as Mrs Tiggywinkle the hedgehog, Ginger and Pickles, Samuel Whiskers, Jeremy Fisher the frog who angled from the leaves of water-lilies, Drake Puddle-Duck and Mrs Tabitha Twitchit with her brood of naughty kittens. The whole masquerade has been set to ballet by Sir Frederick Ashton, with authentic Lakeland backdrops. Beatrix Potter would surely have approved.

In 1913, when she was 47, she married William Heelis and her animal creations went virtually to earth, though her books have continued to delight succeeding generations of children. Another role had opened up for her, that of wife to a sheep farmer.

The extent of their holdings is reflected in their generous bequests to the National Trust. They range from Sawrey to Eskdale and out again to Troutbeck, where their famous sheep farm embraces the summits of Ill Bell, Froswick and Thornthwaite Crag. In Hawkshead village several cottages that Wordsworth would know, during his schooldays here, also came to the Trust from the same benefactors, along with 68 acres bordering the reeded shores of Esthwaite Water. Then of course, there is Hill Top itself, where Beatrix Potter wrote the Peter Rabbit books. Some of her furniture and original drawings are shown inside.

Thus, yet another 'visitor' who decided to stay in the North, paid 'toll' with compound interest.

18

***

Preservation and Peril

THE nature and extent of properties held in the
North Country by the National Trust would
surprise anybody unfamiliar with that now vast
organisation. In the Lake District alone the Trust owns some 73,000
acres of mountains, lake and valley, several notable houses—and about
14,000 sheep! In Northumberland, where the Trust's ownership—at
the time of writing—registers nearly 15,000 acres, the possessions
include castles, that first-rate country house, Wallington, the Farne
Islands, sections of Hadrian's Wall, and George Stephenson's birthplace
cottage at Wylam-on-Tyne.

Lancashire's contribution in mostly made up of splendid old halls,
but Silverdale, overlooking the Kent estuary and Morecambe Bay,
and 400 acres of sand dunes at Formby, near Liverpool, add their
quota of unspoilt landscape. County Durham's outstanding gift, so
far, is Washington Old Hall, near Sunderland, closely associated with
the Washington family, but various woodlands are also protected in the
lovely upper valley of the Wear.

Yorkshire's contribution is richest from the present West Riding,
with far-ranging moors, the fantastic Brimham Rocks in Nidderdale,
steep-sided Pennine valleys, country houses, together with Stainforth's
fine seventeenth-century packhorse bridge in the Ribble valley.
Malham Tarn House, perched high on a limestone plateau at the head
of Airedale, is leased by the Trust as a field centre. Other country houses

and acres of open moorland are now owned in the North Riding, while York itself is represented in the Trust's ever-expanding tally by the Treasurers' House, near the Minster.

Four magnificent areas of coast and countryside in the North have provided England with some of its finest National Parks.* The Lake District and the Pennine Dales are perhaps the best known, but the North Yorkshire moors, spreading through apparently illimitable acres of glowing autumnal heather, are sprigged with ancient pilgrim crosses reaching towards the rugged coast.

Northumberland's wild Cheviot country is bound to win fresh devotees in the coming years. Long stretches of coast in Northumberland, and alongside Solway Firth, are also being protected as areas of outstanding natural beauty, together with the Forest of Bowland.

The Lake District National Park is fortunate in having a recognised centre—the first of its kind—at Brockhole, a country house on the banks of Windermere. Its 32 acres of grounds provide several delightful amenities. A permanent exhibition traces the physical and human development of Lakeland; there are other educational facilities, too, including a lecture room; also picnic areas; and a variety of pleasant walks through a belt of woodland reaching down to the lake verge.

Authorised long-distance footpaths include the Pennine Way, the Cleveland Way through the North Yorkshire Moors, and the Lyke Wake Walk over rough moorland between Osmotherley and Ravenscar, on the north-east coast. In the next few years we may be able to enjoy a continuous walk through the best part of Wharfedale and over the Pennine watershed to Lakeland; also, by ancient tracks, through the fascinating Yorkshire Wolds.

Meanwhile, several municipalities have sponsored similar ventures of their own. Sheffield, for example, provides a round walk of 10 miles through attractive scenery that saw the beginnings of the rural cutlery trade; while Liverpool Museum authorities keep a fatherly eye on the coastal Nature Reserve of 1,216 acres between Freshfield and Ainsdale, publishing a handbook whose wild-life photographs, taken in the reserve, would amaze anybody unacquainted with this neighbourhood.

There are Nature Reserves, also, at Spurn Point—Yorkshire's farthest east; on Skipwith Common, near Selby; and at Askham Bog, which, although on the outskirts of modern York preserves flora dating back to the Ice Age.

One unique area of prehistoric flora—Cow Green, beyond High Force and Cauldron Snout in Upper Teesdale—was disastrously seized only a few years ago to provide a small reservoir for remote industrial purposes; which makes vigilance and the protective hand of

* Unfortunately, National Parks are not yet proof against exploitation for their hidden mineral wealth!

some recognised authority imperative in the event of similar future demands. The Council for the Protection of Rural England is doing considerable watch-dog service in the North, as elsewhere.

Their annual reports show what we, the people who really cherish our homeland, are constantly up against, in this matter of preservation. Fortunately, there are triumphs to report, as well as losses. Farndale, the North Yorkshire valley famous for its 7-8 mile stretches of wild, stream-side daffodils, has at last been reprieved from the long-drawn-out threat of a reservoir scheme that would have scenically ruined, not only Farndale, but much more of this quite enchanting area. The C.P.R.E. is represented at most public inquiries into any scheme that might ravish—without just cause—some well-loved piece of country-side. One triumph that must have rejoiced all who know the Kent estuary and its environs was the reversal of a decision to construct a link road (to the M6 motorway) *through* the beautifully-wooded Levens Park.

When English people fully wake up to their glorious heritage in so many spheres of natural beauty and historic interest, at least some of the would-be vandals may fold up their tents like the proverbial Arabs and silently (?) steal away, leaving what remains of our national heritage untarnished for future generations.

From what I have just written it must not be inferred that we in the North are 'agin' any kind of change. The whole of this book is a record of changes that have occurred through the centuries. In it I have attempted to present the North Country in biographical form. But, unlike any human biography, a *regional* biography is never complete, never conclusive.

We have seen how modern archaeologists are discovering more about our remote forebears, *their* changing ways of life, and *their* 'development' schemes. We have seen how different map-makers have delineated the given area in varying ways, using parody and humour as well as serious intent. But there is nothing *static* about local cartography —not for long anyhow. Even as I write, maps are having to be revised, and brought up-to-date—which is itself a purely relative term. Railways are fast disappearing from our maps. Motor-ways are scything through acres of country-side that once danced with ripening corn. Everywhere, farming is becoming increasingly mechanised. The horse-drawn ploughs of my boyhood are now an anachronism, and the fields they furrowed support housing estates or have become caravan sites.

Some of these changes are inevitable—as inevitable as the changing texture and complexion of a well-loved face. Some, like the 'anony-mous', box-like structures that too often pass, today, as civic architecture, will—I firmly believe—be regretted within a decade.

Yet despite all these developments, and others to come, the North will ever be the *North*. It is dyed and interwoven much too strongly with its own long history and its staunch traditions to countenance any large-scale merging schemes. Let other regions of Britain cherish their castles and abbeys, their ancient towns and villages, their beautiful country-side. A roving northerner will never begrudge praise to a Canterbury Cathedral or to mysterious stone circles as at Avebury or Stonehenge. But we in the North—the far-spreading, diverse, indelible North—have shrines of our own that would be quite incongruous could they be shifted, American-wise, from their native context. You cannot imagine a Durham Cathedral in the hop-fields of Kent, or a Fountains Abbey lifting up its shafts of chastely carved stone, quarried on the site, in the marshy lowlands of the West Country. They are of the very essence of the North; and its towns and villages— our 'homing places'—ring with a corresponding vitality born of local pride and inspiration.

The same sinewy strength runs through, and knits together, our northern industrial life. This supplies the 'guts' of our biography. Frown upon our coal-fields, mills and foundries if you must; yet they are but the blackened hands—the workaday toil—of some of our resident population. These same folk—as we have seen—can also laugh and indulge in sport with great zest; they can and do revel in our vast areas of natural beauty. And I believe that the same determination that built up our various industries, and fashioned our regional culture along so many different avenues, will express itself anew should any interloper—Governmental or otherwise—try to meddle unduly with our corporate personality.

Of course, within our area, there do exist a few rivalries, some of them quite intense and never more noticeable, perhaps, than at a typical Roses cricket match, i.e. a match between Lancashire and Yorkshire. An oft-told tale not only illustrates this particular brand of rivalry, but also betrays an underlying bond.

At one Roses match—it could have been at Francis Thompson's beloved Old Trafford, or at Headingley, Leeds—the game was proceeding dourly, ponderously, with very few runs being scored during a critical period. One 'foreign' spectator, completely bored by the painfully slow pace of the game, loudly expressed his disgust; whereupon two immediate neighbours set about him. "Hi," said the Red Rose supporter, "is tha fra Yorkshire?" "No!", replied the malcontent. "Well, is ta fra Lancashire?", said the other's White Rose counterpart. "No, I'm not!", came the equally fervent retort. "Well," exclaimed both Roses men, in rough unison, "thee shut up, lad; tha knaws nowt abaht it!"

Something of the old, historic rivalries between one town or village and another may be dimly reflected in that story, but how very often north-country folk had to forget their clanish differences and combine forces against that common, persistent foe from across the Scottish Border!

On a much lighter level the same holds true today. Why, down at Bath in Somerset, I hear, there is even a *joint* Lancashire and Yorkshire Society—a society founded and keenly supported by exiles from their respective jousting areas. Thus, Bolton greets Bradford, Manchester shakes hands with Sheffield, and boisterous Blackpool with sedate Harrogate. Beneath their different parochial allegiances they recognise a common, north-country 'ancestry'—an embracing togetherness.

I wonder what they talk about at those Somerset gatherings? Cricket, naturally, but I should expect many other nostalgic north-country topics too. Sooner or later some speaker will surely take his audience back—with a break in his voice—to Lindisfarne, or re-live youthful tramping excursions over Hadrian's Wall, or along the Pennine Way.

If I were there, I should recall, amongst many other experiences, one magical moment on Coniston Old Man when the heavy, clinging mist suddenly parted to reveal—as though a celestial artist had portrayed it with a rapid brush—the whole of Morecambe Bay bathed in sunshine far below. And of the many 'ghosts' from the past, who could muster anyone better for the purpose than Canon Rawnsley once skating on a frozen Derwentwater as moonlight gradually gave way to the roseate hues of dawn?

A Short Bibliography

Rediscovering England, Charlotte Simpson; Ernest Benn, 1930.
The Archaeology of Roman Britain, Collingwood and Richmond; Methuen, 1969.
North Country Profile, G. Bernard Wood; Country Life, 1961.
York, A Survey, 1959, various contributors, published for the British Association by York Herald.
Yorkshire, G. Bernard Wood, Batsford, 1967.
Yorkshire Villages, G. Bernard Wood, Hale, 1971.
Legends of the Lake Counties, Gerald Findler; Dalesman Press, 1967.
The Birth and History of Trinity House, Newcastle-upon-Tyne, David Moir; McKenzie Vincent of Glasgow, 1958.
A Mirror of Witchcraft, Christina Hole; Chatto and Windus, 1957.
English Custom and Usage, Christina Hole; Batsford, 1941.
Authors and Places, R. L. Green; Batsford, 1963.
The Brontës and Their World, Phyllis Bentley; Thames and Hudson, 1969.
A Lakeland Sketchbook, A. Wainwright; Westmorland Gazette, 1970.
English Lake District, Molly Lefebure; Batsford, about 1966.
Stories of the Border Marches, J. and J. Lang; Nelson, 1935.
Northumberland, H. L. Honeyman; Hale, Second edition 1951.
Portrait of County Durham, Peter White; Hale, Second edition 1969.
Portrait of the Pennines, Roger Redfern; Hale, 1969.
A History of Yorkshire, Tate and Singleton; Darwen Finlayson, 1960 and later editions.
Malham and Malham Moor, Arthur Raistrick; Dalesman Press, revised edition 1971.
Old Yorkshire Dales, Arthur Raistrick; David and Charles, 1967.

Index

Abraham brothers, 232
Accrington, 217–8
Adel, Leeds, 66, 100, 202
Aelred, Abbot, 83
Ainsworth, Harrison: *The Lancashire Witches,* 102, 130, 140, 174, 250
Aire, River, 55, 137, 176, 198, 202, 237, 285
Alcuin, 91, 125, 157
Aldborough, 52, 57–8, 176–7
Aldingham, 43, 78, 86, 104
Allan Bank, Grasmere, 172–3
Allen Valley, 68, 169, 170
Almscliffe Crag, 22, 234, 241
Aln, River, 75, 165, 257, 280
Alnmouth, 298
Alnwick, 65, 75, 271
Alnwick Castle, 64, 257, 280
Ambleside, 52, 261–2
Ampleforth Abbey, 84, 215
Appleby, 32, 107, 111, 112, 113, 149
Arkwright, Richard, 281
Armstrong, William (Kinmont Willie), 122
Arncliffe, 249, 258
Arnside, 41, 42, 241
Arthur, King, 246–8
Assheton family, 80, 174, 175, 250
Askrigg, 284
Aysgarth, 28

Bainbridge, 28, 29, 270
Bamburgh, 37, 97, 119, 147, 166–8, 245, 263
Barden Tower, 111
Barnard Castle, 120, 150, 189, 197, 211, 303, 305
Barrow-in-Furness, 77, 142–3
Barton Moss, 31, 55
Bassenthwaite, Lake, 172
Beamish, 191

Bede, the Venerable, 72, 74, 84, 91, 92, 100, 124, 126, 146, 274–5
Bell Scott, William, 125
Bernard of Clairvaulx, 83, 84
Berwick–upon–Tweed, 15, 37, 67, 98, 118, 122, 146, 147–8, 153, 189, 190, 248, 249, 256
Beverley, 153, 156, 214, 278–9, 287, 307
Beverley, John of, 90, 91
Beverley Minster, 90–1, 214, 215
Bewcastle Cross, 187
Bewick, Thomas, 14, 123, 125, 276, 301
Bickham, George, 64–6, 225, 243
Birley, Professor Eric, 49
Birley, Robin, 49, 50
Biscop, Benedict, 74, 98
Bishop Auckland, 270
Bishop Burton, 102
Bishopdale, 28
Bishopthorpe, 157
Blackburn, 290
Blackett family, 124, 168, 232, 280
Blackpool, 158, 290
Blackstone Edge, 24
Blanchland, 73, 168
Blencathra, 136
Blenkinsop, John, 193–5
Bogg, Edmund, quoted, 154, 155
Bolton, Lancs., 133
Bolton Castle, 112, 120, 122, 135, 267, 293, 294
Bolton, Col. John, 200, 203, 204
Bolton Priory, 25, 80, 82, 87, 111, 203
Borrowdale, 30, 32, 64, 171
Bowes, John, 196

Bowes, Teesdale, 304–5
Bowland Forest, 115, 130–1
Bowness, near Carlisle, 50
Boyd Dawkins, Professor, 53
Boynton, 287, 294–5
Bradford, 63, 138, 153, 197–8, 199, 289, 290
Brand, William, 58–9
Brandlehow Woods, 172
Brandling, Ralph, 193–5
Breamish, River, 165
Bridlington, 40, 158, 249, 271, 294, 295
Brigflatts, 87, 108
Brimham Rocks, 309
Brinkburn Priory, 72–3
Brodrick, Cuthbert, 137, 138
Brompton Hall and Village, 236, 281, 285
Brontë family, 13, 31, 32, 52, 82, 175, 184, 285–7, 289
Broomlee Lough, 47, 248
Brough, Westmorland, 112
Brougham Castle and Churches, 107–8, 111, 112, 113–4, 301
Broughton Hall, 201
Brown, Lancelot ("Capability"), 129, 130, 169, 279–80
Brownlow family, 133
Browsholme Hall, 79, 130–2, 277, 300
Bruce, Robert the, 76, 78
Budle Bay, 168, 245
Burton Constable Hall, 128–9, 188–9, 280, 287
Burnley, 184
Buttermere Lake, 31, 105, 203
Buttermere, the Round, 30, 203
Buttertubs Pass, 23, 29, 30, 210
Byland Abbey, 77, 80, 84

Byrom, John, 95, 296

Caedmon, 80, 91, 98, 275
Calder Abbey, 77
Calvert, Kit, 28, 211
Cambo, 168–9, 279
Carlisle, 15, 32, 33, 36, 67, 75, 78, 87, 122, 148, 186, 247, 290, 293, 296, 298, 302, 304
Carileph, Bishop, 86, 187
Carr, John, 128, 129, 280, 304
Carroll, Lewis (C. L. Dodgson), 143–4, 197, 307, 308
Cartmel, 41, 42, 78, 79, 87, 106, 150
Cartmel Fell Chapel, 87, 103–4, 134–5
Carvoran, 45, 46–7, 186
Castle Crag, 32, 36
Castle Howard, 128, 304
Catherine of Braganza, 63
Catterick, 44
Cayley, Sir George, 190, 236, 281
Chapman, F. Spencer, 234
Charles I, King, 60, 93, 146, 147, 227, 253, 255–6, 294, 306
Charles II, King, 63, 132, 153
Chat Moss, 31, 55, 64
Chantrey, Francis, 98, 291
Chester, 47, 51, 132–3
Chesters (Cilurnum), 46–7, 48, 134
Chester-le-Street, 85, 86, 127, 257
Chetham, Humphrey, 95, 96, 140
Cheviot Hills, 19, 37, 65, 117, 161, 310
Chillingham Castle, 123
Chillingham Wild Cattle, 123, 154, 166, 269, 276
Chipchase Castle, 123
Chippendale, Thomas, 129, 213, 291
Chollerford, 48
Chollerton, 44
Christopher, Capt. William, 100
Clayton, John, 45, 124, 134
Cleveland Hills, 134, 251, 310
Clifford, Lady Anne, 107, 109, 114, 149, 176, 289, 301
Clitheroe, 250
Cockermouth, 283
Cockersand Abbey, 79
Coifi, High Priest of Woden, 100, 101
Coleridge, S. T., 32, 106–7, 173
Collingwood, Professor, 106, 191, 301–2
Conisborough, 303

Conishead Priory, 41, 42, 78, 231
Coniston, 106, 191, 301, 302
Coniston Old Man, 191, 301, 313
Conrad, Joseph, 143
Constantine, Emperor, 51
Cook, Capt. James, 40, 99–100, 101, 159, 177, 281–2, 307
Coquet, River, 32, 72, 98, 168, 258, 298
Corbridge, 45, 115, 249
Corstopitum, 45, 49, 74
Coventina, 49, 145
Coverdale, 28
Cow Green, Teesdale, 310
Coxwold, 13
Crag Lough, 47, 124
Craster, 37
Crawley Dene, 166
Crayke, 63, 76, 86, 100
Croft Spa, 307–8
Crompton, Samuel, 133, 281
Cromwell, Oliver, 249, 295–6
Cross Fell, 22, 113, 135, 149
Crummock Water, 31
Cuerdale, near Preston, 54–5
Cullercoats, 272
Cumberland, Duke of, 149

Dacre Castle, 114, 171
Dallam Tower, 116
Dalton-in-Furness, 77, 150
Dalton, John, F. R. S., 291
Danby-in-Cleveland, 228, 251
Danes, 71, 72, 74, 76, 85, 124
Darling, Grace and William, 98, 125, 167–8
Darlington, 63, 100
Dee, Dr. John, 61–2, 140, 141
Defoe, Daniel, 24, 197
Delius, Frederick, 288–90
Dentdale, 28, 100, 200, 297
Derwent, River (East Riding), 82, 305
Derwent, River (Lakeland), 172
Derwent, River (Northumberland), 168
Derwent Island, 33, 105, 204, 308
Derwentwater, Lake, 32–3, 36–7, 107, 150, 171, 189, 204, 308, 313
Derwentwater family, 33, 150
Devil's Arrows, near Boroughbridge, 57
Devis, Arthur, 132, 277
Dewsbury, 182, 267
Dickens, Charles, 142, 214, 304–7
Dissolution of the Monasteries, 72, 73, 74, 75, 76, 79, 81, 83, 87, 90, 134, 136, 151, 202, 210

Dixon, William, 167–8
Dod Law, 58
Doncaster, 63, 237
Don Valley, 139, 206, 303
Dower, Mrs. Pauline, 126, 168
Downham, 130, 173–5, 250, 262
Drayton, Michael, 65, 244
Driffield, 255
Duddon Valley, 77, 78
Dunningley, 60, 61, 62
Dunstanborough Castle, 37, 119
Durham Cathedral, 65, 71, 84–6, 88–9, 97, 187, 231, 253, 259–60, 274–5, 312
Durham City, 63, 150–2, 153, 187, 230–1, 283, 290
Durham University, 126, 151

Eamont, River, 107, 114
Easby Abbey and Church, 80, 266
Easdale Tarn, 172
Easthorpe Hall, 304–5
Ebbing and Flowing Well, Giggleswick, 244
Eden, Sir Anthony, 293
Eden Hall, Luck of, 242–3
Eden Valley, 22, 32, 112, 113
Edinburgh, Duke of, 146–7
Edward I, King, 76, 78, 186
Edwin, King, 92, 100–1, 157, 274
Egfrith, King, 78, 98, 124
Egglestone Abbey, 80, 303
Elbolton Cave, 22, 241
Elizabeth I, Queen, 61, 109, 122, 127, 176, 293
Elizabeth II, Queen, 146–7
Elsdon, 19, 168
Elwell, Frederick, R.A., 128, 130, 214, 278–9
Elwell, James Edward, 214
Escomb Church, 98
Esholt Priory, 202
Esk Valley, near Whitby, 229, 259
Etty, William, R.A., 277–8

Fairfax family, 84, 250–1
Farndale, 311
Farne Islands, 37, 97, 98, 119, 124, 166, 167, 168, 309
Farnley Hall, 129, 300
Farsley, 198
Fawkes family, 265–6, 300–1
Feather, Tim, 184
Fell, Margaret, 121, 298
Fenby, Eric, 290
Ferrier, Kathleen, 290–1
Filey, 40, 51, 158
Finchale Priory, 86
Firbank Fell, 297
Flambard, Bishop, 86, 117

Flamborough, 40, 51
Flaxman, John, 277
Fleet Moss, 28–9
Flodden Field, 28, 65, 77, 111, 117–8, 127, 163, 164
Ford Castle, 117, 161–4, 166
Ford Village School, 161–5, 258
Formby, 309
Forster family, 97
Foulby, 281
Fountains Abbey, 25, 56, 77, 80, 81–2, 84, 269, 312
Fox, George, 108, 121, 174–5, 297–8
Freeborough Hill, 246
Friar's Crag, 36, 107, 204
Fulneck Moravian School, 166, 267
Furness, 78, 297
Furness Abbey, 41, 77, 78, 104, 142

Gainford, 178–9
George III, King, 133, 198, 199, 237
George V, King, 296–7
Gilpin family, 99, 103, 104, 114, 125, 216–7, 231
Gilsland, 302
Glanton Bird Research Station, 165–6
Glasson Dock, 142
Goathland, 252, 264–5
Goodmanham, 92, 100–1
Goole, 65
Grasmere, 106, 172–3, 203, 227, 232, 258, 260–1, 283
Grange–in–Borrowdale, 171
Gray, Thomas, 109, 176, 203
Great Gable, 32, 233, 234
Greathead, Henry, 144
Greenwell, Canon, 187–8
Greta Hall, 106
Gretna Green, 169–70, 271
Grey, Earl, 125
Guisborough Priory, 82, 188
Guiseley, 262–3, 285, 286
Gypsey streams, 65, 295

Hadrian, Emperor, 47
Hadrian's Wall, 14, 22, 37, 44, 63, 64, 65, 75, 76, 124, 125, 145, 166, 186, 187, 233, 243, 247, 248, 302, 309, 313
Halifax, 65, 67, 183, 191, 197, 237, 284
Hallamshire, 139, 206, 207
Hall–i'–th'–Wood, Bolton, 133
Hambleton Hills, 77, 284
Hardknott Pass, 30, 77
Hardraw Force, 284
Harewood, Earl of, 130
Harewood House, 129–30, 297

Harewood Village, 129
Harrison, John, 281
Harrogate, 189
Hartlepool, 72
Hartshead, 285, 286
Harvey, Harry, glass–painter, 157, 224
Hatfield, Bishop, 143
Hawes, 28, 209–10, 211
Hawkshead, 105, 150, 211, 284, 308
Haworth, 13, 31–2, 175–6, 227, 260, 286, 289
Hedon Church, 223, 288
Heelis, William, 308–9
Hell Kettles, 65, 243
Helmsley, 82, 228, 284
Helm Crag, 172, 173
Helm Wind, 22, 135, 149
Helvellyn, 105
Henhole, Heathpool, 22, 303
Henrietta Maria, Queen, 249, 294–5
Henry VI, King, 115
Henry VIII, King, 114, 127, 136, 292
Heron, Lady, 117, 164
Herschell, Sir William, 237
Hexham Priory and Town, 46, 74, 98, 124, 170
High Cup Nick, 149
High Force, 243
High Studdon, 169
Hodge Hill, 134–5
Holderness, 128, 287–8
Holme Cultram Abbey, 76, 78
Holtby, Winifred, 287–8
Holy Island, see Lindisfarne
Honister Pass, 30, 31, 171, 203
Hornyhold–Strickland, Henry, 115
Horse House Pass, 28
Horsforth, 198
Houghton–le–Spring, 231
Housesteads (Borcovicium), 46, 48, 49, 124
Howden, 228
Howgill Fells, 297
Hubberholme, 215, 255, 270
Huby, Abbot Marmaduke, 81
Huddersfield, 182
Hudson, George, 14, 157
Hulne Priory, 75
Humber Estuary, 15, 128, 139, 287, 288
Hutton–le–Hole, 189, 229
Hylton Castle, 120

Ilkley, 22, 54, 234, 289
Ingleborough, 22, 28
Ingilby family, 68
Irthing, River, 76

Jackson, George, 120
Jackson, Margery, 148

Jacobite Rebellion, 1715; 33, 97, 125, 154, 196
Jacobite Rebellion, 1745; 64, 65, 69, 148, 149, 154, 181, 277, 296
James I, King, 126, 154
James IV, King of Scotland, 117, 118, 164
James, Earl of Derwentwater, 125
Jarrow, 84, 86, 125, 126, 146, 274–5
Jervaulx Abbey, 80, 82, 210
John, King, 45, 65, 271

Kearby, 251
Kendal, 114, 149, 150, 155, 190–1, 208, 217, 218–9
Kent, B. W. J., 251
Kent, William, 128, 279
Kent Estuary, 42, 78, 79, 103, 116, 309, 311
Kents Bank, 42
Kentmere, 86, 104, 208, 217
Kenyon, George, 144
Kenyon, J. T., 217–8
Keswick, 30, 31, 33, 36, 105, 106, 150, 171, 186, 189, 202, 203, 232, 302
Kidstones Pass, 28
Kielder, 302
Killingworth, 281
Kilnsey, 112
Kilburn, 214
Kimberworth, 206
Kingsdale, 28
Kingston–upon–Hull, 56, 139, 140, 141, 188–9, 198, 288
Kirk, Dr John L., 181
Kirkby Lonsdale, 75
Kirkby Stephen, 32, 150
Kirkby Underdale, 228
Kirkdale Cave, 53
Kirkham Abbey, 80, 82, 84, 305
Kirkharle, 123, 279, 280
Kirkstall Abbey, 55–6, 80, 82, 181, 193, 256, 285
Kirkstone Pass, 171
Knaresborough, 60, 63, 65, 121, 155–6, 205
Knight, Dame Laura, 178

Lake District, 30–2, 36–7, 52–3, 105, 113, 116, 136, 142, 150, 171–3, 186, 190–1, 202–4, 232, 233, 246, 283, 301, 308–9, 310–1, 310
Lamb, Charles, 173
Lambton, Earl of, 197
Lancaster, 25, 78, 79, 121–2, 141–2, 185, 200–1, 216, 249–50, 296, 298
Lanercost Priory, 46, 76, 78
Langstrothdale, 28
Lascelles, Edwin, 129

Laughton, Charles, 160
Lawson family of Aldborough, 177
Lawson, Fred, dales' artist, 178
Lawson, Robert, merchant, 201
Lealholm, 229
Lee Gap Fair, 231, 232
Leeds, 53, 66, 68, 82, 137–8, 193–6, 197, 203, 227, 235, 276–7
Leeds Pottery, Old, 181, 194, 220–1
L'Espec, Walter, 82, 83, 229
Levens Bridge, 42
Levens Hall and Park, 116, 312
Leven Sands, 42, 78
Liddesdale, 149, 247
Lindale, 42, 190
indisfarne, 37, 40, 65, 70–2, 74, 76, 79, 85, 86, 97, 98, 118–9, 146–7, 271, 313
Littlebeck, 215–6
Little Moreton Hall, 132
Lister, Lord, 149
Littondale, 25
Liverpool, 55, 64, 96–7, 141, 185–6, 200, 219–20, 257, 310
Liverpool and Manchester Railway, 193
Lodore, 33, 36, 171
Londesborough, 92, 100
Longstone Lighthouse, 167
Lord's Island, 33, 150
Lord, Tot, 54
Long Meg and Daughters, 56
Loughrigg Fell, 203
Low Hall, Nether Yeadon, 202, 237
Lowther Castle, 114–5, 122, 293
Lowther, Richard, 122
Luddites, 182, 183, 286
Lumley Castle, 126
Lumley family, 126–8
Lune, River, 75, 79, 142, 185, 200, 201
Lutyens, Sir Edwin, 96, 119

Macaulay, Lord, 126
Malham, 25, 53, 176, 300, 309
Mallerstang, 112
Malton, 51
Malton Priory, 87, 305
McEwen, Sir John, 118
Manchester, 64, 140–1, 184, 283, 296
Manchester Cathedral, 95–6
Marsden Bay, 144
Marsden, Rev. Samuel, 181, 198–9
Marston Moor, 217, 296
Marshall family, 33, 105, 202–5, 237

Marton–in–Cleveland, 100
Maryport, 148–9, 171
Mary, Queen, 296
Mary Stuart, Queen, 112, 122, 135, 139, 267, 293–4, 295
May, Phil, 276–7
Meaux Abbey, 56
Melville, Herman: Moby Dick quoted, 188–9
Mersey, River, 15, 37, 141, 185, 219
Metcalfe family, 112
Middleham, 28, 293
Midgley, 259
Middleton Colliery Railway, near Leeds, 193–6
Middleton–in–Teesdale, 241
Mitchell, John, 236
Monk Coniston, 204
Monk Fryston, 90
Monkwearmouth, 84, 86
Moore, Henry, 291
Morden, Robert, 63
Morecambe, 158
Morecambe Bay, 40–1, 43, 78, 86, 104, 105, 134, 142, 200, 297, 298, 301, 309, 313
Morley, 256
Morrit, J. S. B., 303
Mortham Tower, 303
Moss Troopers, 48, 124, 125, 196
Mother Shipton, 155
Mount Grace Priory, 80, 82, 124, 134
Mulgrave Castle, 306
Muncaster Castle, 115
Munnings, Sir Alfred, 129
Murray, Matthew, 193–5, 204

Napes Needle, Great Gable, 233, 234
Nappa Hall, 112
National Buildings Record, 88, 94–5, 96, 139
National Trust, 36, 46, 107, 116, 119, 126, 136, 171, 172, 195, 203, 204, 301, 308–9, 310–1
Neill, Robert: Mist Over Pendle, 102, 103
Nenthead, 169
Neville, Rev. M. Hastings, 162, 164, 258, 265
Newbiggin–on–Sea, 272
Newburgh Priory, 84
Newcastle, Dukes of, 177, 234
Newcastle–upon–Tyne, 46, 63, 65, 125, 144–7, 186–7, 189, 196, 249, 276, 298
Newchurch, 174, 250
Nidd, River, 121, 155, 205, 211
Norham, 116–7, 256, 303
Normanby, Lord, 306–7

Norman Conquest, 80, 89, 90, 93
North Shields, 272
Northumberland, Dukes of, 167–8, 257, 280
Norton Conyers, 227
Norton–on–Tees, 99

Oastler, Richard, 183
Osmotherley, 310
Oswald, King and Saint, 89, 173, 262
Otley, 211, 300
Otterburn Tower, 166
Ouse, River, 87, 89, 157
Ovingham, 276
Owen, Dr David, 55
Oxenhope, 176
Oxnop Pass, 23, 29

Paine, James, 127
Parker, Col. Robert, 130–2
Parr, Katherine, Queen, 114, 150
Paslew, Abbot John, 79, 80, 131, 174
Patrington, 288
Patterdale, 105, 204
Paulinus, Bishop, 92, 101
Pearson, Constance, 176
Pendle Hill, 102, 108, 130, 131, 174–5, 217, 249, 250, 297
Pendragon Castle, 112
Pennines, 19–30, 53, 111, 112, 113, 135, 149, 170, 176, 249, 310, 313
Penrith Beacon, 114
Penyghent, 25, 28
Petilius Cerialis, Governor, 51
Pevsner, Dr N., 57, 73, 106, 116, 137–8
Pickering, 214, 256, 258
Piel Island, 77
Piercebridge, 99
Pig Yard Club, Settle, 54
Pilgrimage of Grace, 14, 79, 80, 131, 174, 292
Plompton Rocks, 129
Plough Beacon, 146
Ponden Valley, 31
Porter, River, 182
Portington Hall, 299
Portinscale, 31, 36, 171, 172
Potter, Beatrix, 308
Preston, 55, 154, 184, 249, 258, 277, 281, 283, 290, 295, 296
Preston Guild, 154
Prince Charles Edward, 25, 46, 132, 148, 149, 184, 186, 296
Princess Royal, 129, 297
Pudsay, Bishop, 117
Purvis, Canon J. S., 287

Quilting, County Durham, 211–3

Raby Castle, 120, 178, 303
Ransome, Arthur, 191
Ratcliffe, Dorothy Una, 135–6, 267–8
Ravenglass, 30, 51
Ravenscar, 51, 310
Ravenstonedale, 112
Rawdon, Airedale, 198, 199, 202, 204
Rawnsley, Canon H. D., 36–7, 106, 107, 171–2, 173, 261, 301, 313
Rawthey, River, 87, 108
Redesdale, 125, 149, 168
Ribblesdale, 25, 52, 53, 54–5, 130, 176, 243, 283
Ribchester, 52
Richard III, King, 62, 292–3
Richmond, 120, 152–3, 246, 256, 272–3, 284
Riding Mill, 249
Rievaulx Abbey, 77, 80, 82–3, 84, 229, 284, 304
Riley, E. J., 217–8
Rimmer, W. G., 202, 204
Ripley Castle, 68, 296
Ripon, 86, 153–4, 263, 268, 270, 287
Ripon Cathedral, 91–2, 215
Rising in the North, 14
Rivelin, River, 206
Robin Hood's Bay, 40, 177
Roche Abbey, 80, 82, 280
Rockingham Pottery, 220
Rokeby, 303
Rollin, Noble, 165–6
Romaldkirk, 271
Roman occupation, 22, 24, 44–53, 108, 112, 124, 134, 142, 144, 145, 157, 185, 187
Romney, George, 77–8, 150
Rosthwaite, 171
Rothay, River, 106, 173, 203, 232
Rothbury, 123, 125, 258
Rothley Castle, 232, 279
Roughlee, 250
Rudston, 58, 287, 288
Runciman, Sir Walter, 196
Runswick Bay, 40, 177, 241
Ruskin, John, 22, 36, 106, 124, 191, 300, 301–2
Ryburn Valley, 284
Rydal, 105
Rylands, John, 140

St Aidan, 37, 70, 71, 91, 97, 263
St Annes-on-Sea, 158
St Bees, 76, 77
St Bega, 76–7
St Cuthbert, 37, 40, 43, 65, 70–2, 74, 75, 76, 78, 84, 85–6, 88, 89, 91, 97, 98, 104, 124, 126, 134, 147, 168, 187, 221, 242–3, 260
St Herbert's Island, 32, 36, 171, 204, 308
St Hilda, 82, 91, 98, 275
St Mary's Abbey, York, 51, 75, 76, 80–1
St Wilfrid, 46, 74, 91, 263
St William of York, 221
Saltburn, 158, 235
Salvin, Anthony, 105, 115
Sandbeck Park, 127, 280
Sawley Abbey, 80
Sawrey, 308–9
Saxton, Christopher, 60, 61–2
Scafell, 173, 233
Scarbrough, Earls of, 127, 280
Scarborough, 40, 51, 63, 120, 153, 158, 159–60, 190, 256–7, 265, 281, 290, 292–3
Scaleby Castle, 114
Scoresby, William (senior and junior), 40, 101, 159, 282
Scorton, 227
Scots Raiders, 73, 74, 75, 76, 77, 78, 83, 112, 117, 178
Scott, Sir Giles Gilbert, 96
Scott, Sir Walter, 15, 19, 70, 71, 116, 117, 203
Scottish Border, 15, 19, 50, 67, 76, 114, 115, 117–18, 122, 123, 124–5, 146, 147, 148, 149, 150–52, 153, 162, 163, 186, 256, 271, 301, 302–3, 313
Scout Hall, near Halifax, 236
Scrope, Archbishop, 222, 223–4
Seatoller, 171
Sedbergh, 134, 234, 297
Sedgefield, 252
Sedgwick, Adam, 100, 291
Sefton Church, 103
Selby Abbey, 87, 89–90
Semerwater, 28
Settle, 25, 53, 226
Severn, Mr and Mrs Arthur, 302
Severus, Emperor, 51, 66, 74
Sewingshields, 46, 47, 48, 50, 247, 248, 303
Shap Abbey, 75
Shap Fell, 136
Sharp, Dr John, 98
Shaw, Norman, 134
Sheaf, River, 206
Sheffield, 64, 138–9, 181–2, 205–8, 293, 310
Shepherd Lord, The, 28, 111
Sheraton, Thomas, 211
Sheriff Hutton Castle, 293
Shipley, 184
Silverdale, 41, 309

Sinderhope, 169, 170
Sitwell family, 160, 190
Sizergh Castle, 115, 116
Skell, River, 81
Skiddaw, 32, 106, 122, 172
Skipton, 54, 109, 110, 111, 120, 154–5, 176, 289, 300
Skipwith Common, 310
Sladen Valley, 176
Slingsby, Cecil, 232–4
Smeaton, John, 280
Smith, Kenneth, 148
Smithson, Charles, 304, 306
Sockburn, 284
Solloway, Canon John, 90
Solway Firth, 37, 50, 76, 166, 186, 290, 310
Solway Moss, 31
Southey, Robert, 106
Southport, 158
South Shields, 144
Speke Hall, 133
Spindlestone Crags, 244, 245
Spurn Point, 37, 310
Staindrop, 178
Stainforth, 309
Stainmore Common, 111, 112
Stainton, Mistress Jane, 255–6
Staithes, 40, 176, 177–8, 306
Stake Pass, 28, 112
Stammers, Harry, glass-painter, 222, 223
Stanbury, 184
Standedge Pass, 23
Staveley, 190
Staward Pele, 169
Stephenson, George, 125, 126, 145, 190, 193, 196, 281
Stephenson, Robert, 186, 281
Sterne, Laurence, 13, 189
Stockton-and-Darlington Railway, 100, 190, 193
Stockton-on-Tees, 99, 190, 211
Stone Gappe, Lothersdale, 289
Stonyhurst College, 295–6
Storeton Quarry, Birkenhead, 185
Storrs Hall, 200, 203–4
Strafford, Earl of, 253
Strickland family, 295
Sty Head Pass, 30
Summerson, Sir John, 96, 139
Sunderland, 143–4, 196
Sunderland Point, 40, 41, 79, 142, 200–1
Swaledale, 29, 121, 152, 176, 229, 243, 246
Swarthmore Hall, 297–8

Tarn Hows, Coniston, 204
Tatefield Hall, 251
Teesdale, 98, 169, 178, 243, 275, 284, 305
Tees-side, 99

Temple Sowerby Manor, 114, 135–6
Thirlwall Castle, 46
Thirlwall, Nine Nicks of, 50, 303
Thompson, Francis, 282–3
Thompson, Robert, 214–5
Thoresby, Ralph, 68
Thwaite, 229
Tilberthwaite, 211
Till, River, 117
Timble, 250, 251
Todmorden, 249
Towler family, 210
Trevelyan family, 48, 71, 124–6, 168–9, 232–4, 246, 274
Trinity House, Newcastle-upon-Tyne, 146–7
Trollers Ghyll, 22
Trough of Bowland, 25, 300
Troutbeck, 105, 106, 171, 211, 308
Tryon–Wilson, Brigadier, 116
Tunstall Church, 52
Turner, J. M. W., 41, 73, 82, 116, 119, 129, 132, 299–301
Tweed, River, 76, 116, 117, 147, 148, 243, 256, 271
Tweedale, Rev. Charles, 288, 289
Tyne, River, 32, 45, 48, 63, 67, 74, 125, 144, 145, 187, 195, 196, 232, 247, 272, 276
Tynemouth Priory, 72, 124

Ullswater, 105, 171, 203
Ure, River, 57, 82

Vavasour family, 94
Victoria Cave, 53–4
Victoria, Queen, 53, 104, 167
Vikings, 28, 54–5, 157, 171, 172
Vindolanda, 49–50
Vine, George R., 139
Vyner family, 84

Waddow Hall, 243
Wade, General, 46
Wakefield, 183–4, 231
Walburn Hall, 293–4

Walker, George: Costume of Yorkshire, 194–5
Wallington, 123–6, 134, 168, 232, 279–80, 309
Wallsend, 186
Walney Island, 77, 143, 298
Walpole, Sir Hugh, 33, 171, 189
Wansbeck, River, 32, 279
Warburton, John, 67–8
Warcop, 260
Waring and Gillow, 142, 185, 201, 213
Wark Castle, 117
Warkworth Castle, 64
Warkworth Church, 98
Wasdale, 30, 105, 233
Washburn Valley, 250–1
Washington Old Hall, 309
Wastwater, 77
Watendlath, 171, 203, 233
Waterford, Marchioness of, 117, 161–5
Waterton, Charles, 291
Wear, River, 32, 85, 86, 88, 143, 150, 151, 169, 230, 296, 309
Wearmouth, 143
Weatherill, Frank, 228, 229, 238
Weetwood Moor, 58–9
Wensleydale, 28, 29, 32, 68, 82, 112, 155, 209–11, 270
Wesley, Rev. John, 102, 284, 298–9
West Auckland, 211
West Witton, 263–4
Whalley Abbey, 79, 80, 102–3, 131
Whalley Church, 52, 79, 80, 102, 214
Wharfedale, 25, 28, 68, 80, 82, 111, 112, 129, 155, 203, 241, 243, 288, 300
Whernside, 22, 28
Whinlatter Pass, 31
Whitaker, Dr Harold, 60–9
Whitby, 40, 101, 158, 188, 251, 258, 259, 265, 275, 281–2, 299, 306–7
Whitby Abbey, 80, 82, 87, 98, 159, 229, 307
Whitehaven, 148
Whitley Bay, 158

Whittaker, Thomas, 215–7
Whittingham, Vale of, 165, 166
Wigton, 304
Wilberforce House, Kingston-upon-Hull, 139, 189, 288
Wilberforce, William, 188, 189, 199, 200, 285, 288, 291
Wild Boar Fell, 22, 23, 112
William Rufus, King, 80
Wilkinson, John, 190
Windermere, Lake, 33, 52, 63, 106, 200, 203–4, 262, 310
Winn, Rowland, 234–6
Winster Valley, 134, 171, 190–1
Winston Church, 98
Wirral, The (Cheshire), 141
Witchcraft, 25, 57, 80, 102, 121, 171, 174, 189, 245, 248–52, 265
Wold Gate, 287, 294
Wolsingham, 252
Woodhouse Grove School, 285, 286
Wooler, 58–9
Wordsworth family, 33, 42, 56–7, 77, 105, 106, 114–5, 172–3, 190, 191, 201–5, 258, 283–5, 309
Workington Priory, 215
Worthington, Sir Hubert, 95
Wouldhave, William, 144
Wressle Castle, 193
Wrynose Pass, 30
Wycliffe, John, 80, 275
Wycollar, 175, 176
Wylam-on-Tyne, 281, 309

Yarm, 63, 64
Yeadon Moor, 252
Yealand villages, 41, 108
Yewdale, 211
York, 14, 47, 51–2, 55, 63, 65, 76, 80–1, 153, 157–8, 183, 190, 222, 237, 251, 253, 255–6, 266, 277–8, 279, 292, 294, 297, 299, 305–6, 310
York Minster, 83, 92–5, 101, 215, 221, 224, 227, 298, 304
Young, Geoffrey Winthrop, Mr and Mrs, 168–9, 232–4